STUDYING PUBLIC POLICY

POLICY CYCLES AND POLICY SUBSYSTEMS

SECOND EDITION

MICHAEL HOWLETT & M. RAMESH

OXFORD
UNIVERSITY PRESS

OXFORD
UNIVERSITY PRESS

70 Wynford Drive, Don Mills, Ontario M3C 1J9
www.oup.com/ca

Oxford University Press is a department of the University of Oxford.
It furthers the University's objective of excellence in research, scholarship,
and education by publishing worldwide in

Oxford   New York

Auckland   Cape Town   Dar es Salaam   Hong Kong   Karachi
Kuala Lumpur   Madrid   Melbourne   Mexico City   Nairobi
New Delhi   Shanghai   Taipei   Toronto

With offices in

Argentina   Austria   Brazil   Chile   Czech Republic   France   Greece
Guatemala   Hungary   Italy   Japan   Poland   Portugal   Singapore
South Korea   Switzerland   Thailand   Turkey   Ukraine   Vietnam

Oxford is a trade mark of Oxford University Press
in the UK and in certain other countries

Published in Canada by Oxford University Press

National Library of Canada Cataloguing in Publication Data

Howlett, Michael, 1955-
Studying public policy : policy cycles and policy subsystems /
Michael Howlett and M. Ramesh. — 2nd ed.

Includes bibliographical references and index.
ISBN-10: 0-19-541794-1   ISBN-13: 978-0-19-541794-4

1. Policy sciences.   I. Ramesh, M., 1960–   II. Title.

H97.H69 2003   320'.6   C2002-906139-3

Cover design: Joan Dempsey

9 – 08

This book is printed on permanent (acid-free) paper ∞.

Printed in Canada

Contents

List of Figures

Acknowledgements

Many individuals contributed to this book. In addition to the many authors and investigators whose empirical and conceptual work provides the foundation for the summaries and discussions contained herein, we are also grateful for the comments and criticisms received from the reviewers of the book's first edition and from the many students and instructors who used it.

This edition includes a considerable amount of new material, elements of which have appeared in conference papers, journal articles, and book chapters. We would like to thank all of the publication teams, reviewers, and conference participants who have constructively engaged with this material.

While the list of those to thank is far too numerous to include here, we would like to express our gratitude to some of our closest colleagues and collaborators, whose personal interventions at critical junctures very much helped to shape the direction of our thinking on the subject of 'studying public policy'. They include Jeremy Rayner, Colin Bennett, Jim Bruton, Melody Hessing, Ben Cashore, Jeremy Wilson, George Hoberg, Evert Lindquist, Ted Parson, Laurent Dobuzinskis, David Laycock, Luc Bernier, Alex Netherton, and Keith Brownsey, among others. Of course, neither edition of this book would have been possible without the continued support of our departments and universities and we would like to thank Stephen McBride, Paddy Smith, Ted Cohn, Iris Geva-May, and Maureen Covell for their help on this, and many other, related projects. At Oxford University Press, we would like to thank the many individuals who worked on and supported this volume and its predecessor. These include Brian Henderson, Rik Kitowski, Euan White, Mark Piel, and Laura Macleod, and especially Phyllis Wilson. Special thanks also go to Richard Tallman for his copy-editing skills.

Finally, we owe much to our families for their sympathy and understanding over the years. Special thanks to Bunny Raglon, Woot A. Gimp, and Anna Howlett for their steadfast refusal to take either of us too seriously. Nikisha, who is still too young to worry about books, will no doubt some day also come to share her mother Mandy's skepticism.

Part I

Introduction

Chapter 1

Policy Science and Policy Cycles

THE AMBITIONS OF THE POLICY SCIENCES

Policy science is a relatively recent discipline, emerging in North America and Europe in the post-World War II era as students of politics searched for new understandings of the relationship between governments and citizens. Before that time, studies of political life tended to focus on the normative or moral dimensions of government or on the minutiae of the operation of specific political institutions. Scholars concerned with the normative or moral dimensions of government studied the great texts of political philosophy, seeking insights into the purpose of government and the activities governments should undertake if their citizens were to attain the good life. These inquiries generated a rich discussion of the nature of society, the role of the state, and the rights and responsibilities of citizens and governments. However, the gap between prescriptive political theory and the political practices of modern states that emerged between the two world wars and during the ensuing Cold War led many to search for another method of examining politics, one that would reconcile political theory and practice through empirical analysis of existing polities.

Conversely, scholars interested in the institutions of government had been conducting detailed empirical examinations of legislatures, courts, and bureaucracies while generally ignoring the normative aspects of these institutions. These studies of the formal structure of political institutions excelled in attention to detail and procedure but for the most part remained descriptive, failing to generate the basis for evaluating the strengths, weaknesses, or purposes of such structures. In the post-war era of decolonization, the reconstruction of war-torn states, and the establishment of new institutions of international governance, students of politics sought an approach that would blend their studies with questions of justice, equity, and the pursuit of social, economic, and political development (Mead, 1985).

In this context of change and reassessment, several new approaches to the study of political phenomena appeared. Some focused on the micro level of human behaviour and the psychology of citizens, electors, leaders, and led; others concentrated on the characteristics of national societies and cultures; still others focused on the nature of national and global political systems. Most of these approaches—behaviouralism, elite studies, studies of political culture, and political cybernetics—have come and gone as scholars experimented with each before grasping its limitations and abandoning it to search for something better (Cairns, 1974).

One approach, however, is still with us. Its focus is not so much on the structure of governments or the behaviour of political actors, or on what governments should or ought to do, but on what governments actually do. This approach focuses on public policies and public policy-making, or, as its originators deemed it, *policy science*. Pioneered by Harold Lasswell and others in the United States and the United Kingdom, policy science was expected to replace traditional political studies, integrating the study of political theory and political practice without falling into the sterility of formal, legal studies (Lasswell, 1951; Torgerson, 1990).

Lasswell proposed that policy science had three distinct characteristics that would set it apart from earlier approaches: it would be multidisciplinary, problem-solving, and explicitly normative. By multidisciplinary, Lasswell meant that policy science should break away from the narrow study of political institutions and structures and embrace the work and findings of such fields as sociology and economics, law and politics. By problem-solving, he envisioned a policy science adhering strictly to the canon of relevance, orienting itself towards the solution of real-world problems and not engaging in purely academic debates that, for example, characterized interpretation of classical and sometimes obscure political texts. By explicitly normative, Lasswell meant that policy science should not be cloaked in the guise of 'scientific objectivity', but should recognize the impossibility of separating goals and means, or values and techniques, in the study of government actions (Torgerson, 1983). He expected policy analysts to say clearly which solution was better than others.

The general orientation towards the activities of governments suggested by Lasswell remains with us and forms the subject matter of this book. However, the passage of time has led to some changes in the three specific components of the policy orientation he identified (Garson, 1986; DeLeon, 1986, 1988; Hansen, 1983). First, while the emphasis on multidisciplinarity remains, a large body of literature now focuses on public policy in general. Policy science is very much a 'discipline' itself, with a unique set of concepts and concerns and a vocabulary and terminology of its own (Fishman, 1991). Although many of these concepts have been borrowed from other disciplines, they have a somewhat particular meaning when used in the context of studying public policy. Furthermore, the concept of multidisciplinarity has changed in the sense that policy scholars now take it for granted that they must borrow from other disciplines and must be experts in at least two fields: the concepts and concerns of policy science, and the history and issues present in the substantive area of policy, or the 'policy field' under examination (Anderson, 1979a).

Second, over the past 40 years the virtually exclusive concern of many policy scholars with concrete problem-solving has waned. At the outset it was hoped that the study of public policy-making and its outcomes would yield conclusions and recommendations directly applicable to existing social problems. Although laudable, this maxim foundered on the complexity of the policy process itself, in which governments often proved resistant to 'expert' advice on subjects with which they were dealing (Wildavsky, 1979; Ascher, 1986). In the real world of public policy, technical superiority of analysis was often subordinated to political necessity.

Finally, the calls for the policy sciences to remain explicitly normative also changed over time, although rather less than have the other founding principles. For the most part, policy scholars have refused to exclude values from their analyses and have insisted on evaluating both the goals and the means of policy, as well as the process of policy-making itself. However, analysts' desire to prescribe specific goals and norms declined with an increasing realization of the intractability of many public problems. Hence, many investigators now either evaluate policies in terms of simple measures such as efficiency or effectiveness, or use the record of policy efforts to establish whether governments have in practice been directing their activities towards the achievement of their stated goals, in either case without considering the desirability or rationality of these goals themselves (Greenberg et al., 1977; DeLeon, 1994).

As these changes occurred, some observers began to castigate the notion of a policy 'science' and to equate its promotion with an era of unrealized hopes and expectations for social engineering and government planning (Tribe, 1972). Although sometimes justified by the inflated claims of individual studies, this criticism should serve as a warning against premature or ill-founded prescriptions or excessive conceptual sophistry, rather than as a rejection of the need to undertake the systematic study of government actions. To the extent that the policy sciences have developed a significant body of empirical and theoretical studies of the activities of numerous governments around the globe, the early efforts and dicta of Lasswell and his followers remain valuable and continue to provide the foundation upon which the study of public policy is conducted (Wagner et al., 1991).

DEFINITION OF PUBLIC POLICY

Among the many competing definitions of 'public policy', some are very complex, while others are quite simple. Despite their variations, they all agree on certain key aspects. They agree that public policies result from decisions made by governments and that decisions by governments to retain the status quo are just as much policy as are decisions to alter it. In other respects, however, the competing definitions differ considerably (Birkland, 2001: ch. 1). Three examples of widely used definitions will suffice to convey the complex meaning of the term.

In probably the best known, and shortest, definition, Thomas Dye offers a particularly succinct formulation, describing public policy as 'Anything a government chooses to do or not to do' (Dye, 1972: 2). This formulation is perhaps too simple, for it would treat equally as public policy every aspect of governmental behaviour, from purchasing or failing to purchase paper clips to waging or failing to wage nuclear war, and provides no means of separating the trivial from the significant aspects of government activities. Nevertheless, Dye's definition is not without merits.

First, Dye specifies clearly that the agent of public policy-making is a government. This means that private business decisions, decisions by charitable organizations, interest groups, other social groups, or individuals are not in themselves public policies. When we talk about public policies we speak of the actions of governments. Although the activities of non-governmental actors may and certainly do influence what governments do, and vice versa, the decisions or activities of such groups do not in themselves constitute public policy. How the medical profession interprets the causes of lung cancer and the solutions it proposes for reducing its incidence may have a bearing on what a government eventually does about the problem. However, the profession's proposed solution to the problem is not itself a public policy; only measures that a government actually adopts or endorses constitute such a policy.

Second, Dye highlights the fact that public policies involve a fundamental choice on the part of governments to do something or to do nothing and that this decision is made by individuals staffing the state and its agencies. Public policy is, at its simplest, a choice made by government to undertake some course of action. A slightly more difficult concept is that of a 'negative' or 'non-decision': that is, a government's decision to do nothing, or simply to maintain the status quo (Crenson, 1971; R.A. Smith, 1979). Even these should be deliberate decisions, however, such as when a government decides not to increase taxes, or declines to make additional funds available for arts, health care, or some other policy area. The fact we have the freedom to paint the interiors of our homes in colours of our choice, for example, does not mean that this is a public policy, because the government never deliberately decided not to restrict our options in this area.

William Jenkins's conceptualization of public policy is a bit more precise than the one offered by Dye but illustrates many of the same themes. He defines public policy as 'a set of interrelated decisions taken by a political actor or group of actors concerning the selection of goals and the means of achieving them within a specified situation where those decisions should, in principle, be within the power of those actors to achieve' (Jenkins, 1978). This is a useful definition, not least because Jenkins explicitly views public policy-making as a process, unlike Dye's defining it as a choice, which presumes the existence of an underlying process but does not state so explicitly. Jenkins also explicitly acknowledges that public policy is usually 'a set of interrelated decisions'. In other words, rarely does a government address a problem with a single decision; most policies involve a series of decisions, some of which may be inadvertent rather than deliberate, but cumulatively these decisions constitute a policy. Thus a health policy, for example, consists of a series of decisions related to construction of health facilities, certification of personnel and medicines, and financing the provision of health care, among many other related items. Often various interrelated decisions are made by different individuals and agencies within government, such as a Department of Health as well as Finance or Welfare and by various divisions and sections within them. As Jenkins notes, to understand fully a government's health policy we need to take into account all the decisions of all the governmental actors involved in the financing and administration of its health-related activities (Tuohy, 1999).

Jenkins also improves upon Dye by suggesting that the question of a government's capacity to implement its decisions is also a significant consideration affecting the types of decisions it takes. His definition recognizes that certain limitations on governments constrain the range of options available in a policy area. These internal and external constraints on government make public policy-making, and efforts to understand it, difficult indeed. A government's choice of a policy may be limited, for instance, by lack of financial, personnel, or informational resources, by international treaty obligations, or by domestic resistance to certain options. Thus, for example, we will not understand health policy in many countries without realizing the powerful, self-serving opposition that the medical profession is able to mount against any government's effort to cut health-care costs by reducing the profession's income (Alford, 1972). Similarly, understanding the actions of domestic governments in the current era increasingly requires detailed understanding of the limits and opportunities provided by international agreements, treaties, and conventions (Milner and Keohane, 1996; Doern et al., 1996a).

Jenkins also introduces the idea of public policy-making as goal-oriented behaviour on the part of governments, an idea that provides a standard by which to evaluate public policies. In his definition, public policies are decisions taken by governments that define a goal and set out a means to achieve it. Although this says nothing about the nature of the goals or the means involved, it provides several avenues for evaluating policies that are missing from Dye's definition. These include the relevance of the goal, the congruence of goal and means, and the degree to which the means ultimately succeed or fail to achieve the initial goal.

A third, middle-range definition is provided by James Anderson, who describes a policy as 'a purposive course of action followed by an actor or a set of actors in dealing with a problem or matter of concern' (Anderson, 1984: 3). While very similar to the other two, Anderson's definition adds one additional element to those noted by Dye and Jenkins by highlighting the link between government action and the perception, real or otherwise, of the existence of a problem or concern requiring action. This problem-solving perspective is a particularly important aspect of the definition of public policy-making, which will be returned to in more detail below.

Within their limitations, any or all of these definitions serve to outline in a general sense what public policy is. All illustrate that studying public policy is a complex and difficult task. It cannot be accomplished simply by going through the official records of government decision-making found in such forms as laws, acts, regulations, and promulgations. Although these are a vital source of information, public policies extend beyond the record of concrete choices to encompass the realm of potential choices, or choices not made, and the analysis of such choices necessarily involves analysis of the complex array of state and societal actors involved in decision-making processes and their capacities for action (Howlett, 1986). Records of decisions do not reflect the unencumbered will of government decision-makers so much as the record of the interaction of that will with the constraints upon it at given historical, political, and social conjunctures (Sharkansky, 1971).

Simply describing a government's policy is nevertheless a relatively easy task compared to knowing why the state did what it did and assessing the consequences of its actions. Sometimes a government may announce the reasons for making a decision, and that may indeed be the truth. However, a government often does not give any reason for making a decision; or when it does the publicly avowed reason may not be the actual reason. In such situations it is left to analysts to determine why a particular alternative was chosen and, very often, why some other seemingly more attractive option was not selected. The tasks of understanding why a policy was not implemented as intended and evaluating the outcomes of a policy are no easier. And, to add to the complexity, how analysts explain public policy and the aspects they emphasize depend on their frames of reference (Bobrow and Dryzek, 1987; Radin, 2000; Lynn, 1999), which in turn depend on their interests, ideologies, and experiences (Danziger, 1995; Yanow, 1992; Phillips, 1996).

This latter point has significant implications for the methodologies used in policy analysis and has come to divide analysts into two camps. On the one hand, there are those who believe that reasonably objective analysis is possible with standard, 'positivist', or quantitative social science methodologies, which, by definition, focus on actual government activities. Others embrace more nuanced and subtle 'post-positivist' or interpretive techniques more common in the humanities, which are used to help discern and critique both concrete and potential government aims, intentions, and actions (Torgerson, 1996; Thompson, 2001). Although these differences should not be overstated (Howlett and Ramesh, 1998), they serve to underscore the manner in which orientations towards policy-making as a social phenomenon can affect analytical techniques and outcomes.

UNDERSTANDING PUBLIC POLICY

All of the definitions provided above posit that public policy is a complex phenomenon consisting of numerous decisions made by numerous individuals and organizations in government. These decisions are often shaped by earlier policies and frequently are linked closely with other seemingly unrelated decisions. As such, studying public policy poses analytical difficulties for which policy analysts, not surprisingly, have developed numerous solutions. The single most important of these has been to reduce the level of complexity of the analysis by emphasizing only a limited range of relevant causal or explanatory factors, even while reiterating the general need for a more holistic approach encompassing the entire range of possible variables affecting governmental decision-making.

One common approach has been to associate particular types of policies or 'policy outcomes' with the nature of the political regime—defined loosely as the organization of the political system (Wolfe, 1989; Przeworski and Limongi, 1997). It has often been argued, for example, that public policies vary according to the nature of a political system and its links with society. Much effort has gone into classifying and differentiating between regime types with the expectation that properly identifying the regime will generate important insights into the nature of the policies likely to be adopted by each type (Peters et al., 1977; Castles, 1998; Castles and McKinlay, 1997). However, classifying regime types can only be a starting point in public policy analysis because it tells us little about how the characteristics of the regime manifest themselves in individual policy decisions. It merely tells us where to look for influences on government decision-making and what general relationships we can expect to find while studying a government's activities.

Another direction that many theorists have taken is to search for causal variables in public policy-making, or for what are sometimes referred to as 'policy determinants' (Munns, 1975; Hancock, 1983). Analyses in this tradition tend to concentrate on the question of whether public policies are determined by macro-level socio-economic factors or by micro-level behavioural elements, and a great deal of competing evidence has been gathered about the relationship between public policies, the characteristics of domestic societies and the international system (Rakoff and Schaefer, 1970), and the behaviour of public policy-makers. Such studies are largely empirical, comparative, and often quantitative in orientation. While their comparative empirical focus has enhanced our understanding of public policies by dispelling common myths and assumptions about the links between policy and other social and socio-economic processes, like studies of political regimes they tend to lean towards general macro-level explanations of public policy-making and often fail to specify exactly how these structural characteristics affect the specific sectoral and temporal contexts in which policies develop (Wilensky, 1975; Wilensky et al., 1985; Wilensky and Turner, 1987).

Yet another literature focuses on 'policy content'. This approach is associated closely with the idea that the nature of a policy problem and the solutions devised to address it often determine how it will be processed by the political system. For example, whether a problem is primarily regulatory, distributive, redistributive, or constitutive in character, it has been argued, determines how it is dealt with. In a similar vein, James Q. Wilson (1974) argued that the degree of concentration of costs and benefits imposed on political actors by a particular policy shapes the type of policy processes that will accompany it. Hence, as Theodore Lowi (1972) put it, ultimately 'policy may determine politics' and not the other way around, as most analysts commonly suppose. Lester Salamon (1981), taking this insight to heart, argued that focusing on the nature of the policy tools or instruments governments have at their disposal to implement public policies is therefore the best mode of analysis for understanding public policy. However, while there is no denying that the nature of the problem has an effect on what can be done about it, it is often difficult to comprehend, or to agree upon, the precise nature of a policy problem and the patterns of costs and benefits that various solutions to it involve. Rather than being a technical exercise, the choice of policy instruments or policy content is very much affected by larger social and political constraints and contexts (Woodside, 1986; Peters and Van Nispen, 1998).

The fourth tradition concentrates on the evaluation of 'policy impacts' or outcomes. This literature has involved the assessment of the direct and indirect effects of specific policies and its analyses have tended to ignore both causal factors and the nature of the tools at the disposal of governments (Weimer and Vining, 1992). Analysts instead use techniques of statistical inference to analyze the links between specific government programs and various measures of policy 'success', such as indicators of social change and progress. Among economists, such studies have examined a wide range of topics in easily quantifiable realms such as fiscal and industrial policy-making, investigating topics such as the relations between government expenditures and corporate investment activity or labour migration. This approach focuses almost exclusively on policy outputs, however, and says very little about the policy processes that led to the creation of those outputs (Lynn, 1987).

These different literatures and analytical traditions have existed, in part, as a result of the different communities of analysts working on public policy. Governments themselves, of course, have always been involved in the study of public policies, both their own (Meltsner, 1976; Rogers et al., 1981) and those of other countries (Rose, 1991). However, much of the literature on public policy has been generated by analysts working for non-governmental organizations. Some of these analysts work directly for groups affected by public policies, such as corporations, churches, labour unions, or other non-governmental organizations. There are also analysts who work for less directly affected organizations, such as private think-tanks or research institutes, some of which can have close ties with government agencies and pressure groups. Finally, some analysts work independently, many of them in the university system (Pal, 1992).

Analysts working in these different types of organizations tend to have different interests in pursuing policy analysis (Dobuzinskis, 1996). Analysts working for governments and for groups directly affected by public policies tend to focus their research on policy outcomes. They often have a direct interest in condemning or condoning specific policies on the basis of their projected or actual impact on their client organization. Private think-tanks and research institutes usually enjoy more autonomy, though some may be influenced by the preferences of their funding organizations. Nevertheless, they remain interested in the 'practical' side of policy issues and tend to concentrate either on policy outcomes or on the instruments and techniques that generate those outcomes. Academics, on the other hand, have a great deal of independence and usually have no direct personal stake in the outcome of specific policies. They can therefore examine public policies much more abstractly than can members of the other two groups and, as such, tend to grapple with the theoretical, conceptual, and methodological issues surrounding public policy-making. Academic studies tend to look at the entire policy process and take into account a wide range of factors, including policy regimes, policy determinants, policy instruments, and policy content in their analyses (Gordon et al., 1977).

These differing degrees of neutrality and self-interest have evolved into distinctions in the literature between 'policy study' and 'policy analysis' (Brooks and Gagnon, 1990). The former term is sometimes used to refer to the study 'of' policy and the latter to study 'for' policy. Policy studies, conducted mainly by academics, relate to 'meta-policy' and generally are concerned with understanding overall public policy processes and improving theories of policy-making and methodologies of analysis. Policy analysis, in comparison, is a term often used to characterize applied research pursued by government officials or think-tanks and usually directed at systematically designing, implementing, and evaluating existing policies (Meltsner, 1976; Weimer and Vining, 1999; Pal, 1997). The former tend to be descriptive and explanatory compared to the more prescriptive orientation of the latter. Both can be contrasted with the much less systematic and self-interested critique, and with support for specific government actions that emerge from directly affected organizations and individuals. While this distinction is worth keeping in mind, it also should not be overstated as we cannot understand what a government ought to be doing (or not doing), as emphasized by the 'analysis' literature, unless we know what it can or cannot do, one of the central concerns of the 'policy studies' literature.

While understandable, the existence of very separate traditions and literatures of inquiry into public policy-making has led to a plethora of studies and sometimes conflicting conclusions about the public policy-making process. This fragmentation has burdened the policy sciences with an apparent complexity that can be bewildering to anyone approaching the discipline for the first time. In response, efforts have been made to simplify analysis by creating general models or 'frameworks of analysis' that serve to synthesize the diverse literatures on, and approaches to, the subject (Dunn, 1988).

The Policy Cycle Framework of Analysis:
An Applied Problem-Solving Model of the Policy Process

One of the most popular means for simplifying policy studies has been to simplify the public policy-making process by disaggregating it into a series of discrete stages and sub-stages. The resulting sequence of stages is referred to as the 'policy cycle'. This simplification has its origins in the earliest works on public policy analysis, but has received somewhat different treatment in the hands of different authors. The different descriptions of the policy cycle and the common logic these models possess will be presented below. Later in the chapter, we will expand the simple model of the public policy cycle to include a wider range of factors affecting the overall policy process.

The idea of simplifying the complexity of public policy-making by breaking the policy-making process down into a number of discrete stages was first broached in the early work of Harold Lasswell (1956). Lasswell divided the policy process into seven stages, which, in his view, described not only how public policies were actually made but how they should be made: (1) intelligence, (2) promotion, (3) prescription, (4) invocation, (5) application, (6) termination, (7) appraisal (Lasswell, 1971). The policy process began with intelligence-gathering, that is, the collection, processing, and dissemination of information for those who participate in the decision process. It then moved to the promotion of particular options by those involved in making the decision. In the third stage the decision-makers actually prescribed a course of action. In the fourth stage the prescribed course of action was invoked as a set of sanctions was developed to penalize those who failed to comply with the prescriptions of the decision-makers. The policy was then applied by the courts and the bureaucracy and ran its course until it was terminated or cancelled. Finally, the results of the policy were appraised or evaluated against the aims and goals of the original decision-makers.

This early analysis of the policy-making process focused on decision-making within government and had little to say about external or environmental influences on government behaviour. It simply assumed that decision-making was limited or restricted to a presumably small number of participants staffing official positions in government. Another shortcoming of this early model was its internal logic, especially with reference to placing appraisal or evaluation after termination, since policies would logically be evaluated prior to being wound down rather than afterwards. Nevertheless, this model was highly influential in the development of a policy science. Although not entirely accurate, it reduced the complexity of studying public policy by allowing each stage to be isolated and examined before putting the whole picture of the process back together.

Lasswell's formulation formed the basis for many other models (Lyden et al., 1968; Simmons et al., 1974). Typical of these was a simpler version of the policy cycle developed by Gary Brewer (1974). According to Brewer, the policy process was composed of only six stages: (1) invention/initiation, (2) estimation, (3) selection, (4) implementation, (5) evaluation, and (6) termination. In Brewer's view, invention or initiation referred to the earliest stage in the sequence when a problem would be initially sensed. This stage, he argued, would be characterized by ill-conceived definition of the problem and suggested solutions to it. The second stage of estimation concerned calculation of the risks, costs, and benefits associated with each of the various solutions raised in the earlier stage. This would involve both technical evaluation and normative choices. The object of this stage was to narrow the range of plausible choices by excluding the unfeasible ones, and to somehow range the remaining options in terms of desirability. The third stage consists of adopting one, or none, or some combination of the solutions remaining at the end of the estimation stage. The remaining three stages comprise implementing the selected option, evaluating the results of the entire process, and terminating the policy according to the conclusions reached by its evaluation.

Brewer's version of the policy process improved on Lasswell's pioneering work. It expanded the policy process beyond the confines of government in discussing the recognition of problems and clarified the terminology for describing the various stages of the process. Moreover, it introduced the notion of the policy process as an ongoing cycle. It recognized that most policies do not have a definite life cycle—moving from birth to death—but rather seem to recur, in slightly different guises, as one policy succeeds another with minor or major modification (Brewer and DeLeon, 1983). Brewer's insights inspired several other versions of the policy cycle to be developed in the 1970s and 1980s, the best known of which were set out in popular textbooks by Charles O. Jones (1984) and James Anderson (1984). Each of these contained slightly different interpretations of the names, number, and order of stages in the cycle.

If a plethora of models of policy stages and their variants is to be avoided, it is necessary to clarify the logic behind the cycle model. In the works of Brewer, Jones, and others the operative principle behind the notion of the policy cycle is the logic of applied problem-solving, even though they themselves often do not explicitly state this logic. The stages in applied problem-solving and its corresponding stages in the policy process are depicted in Figure 1.1.

Figure 1.1   Five Stages of the Policy Cycle and Their Relationship to Applied Problem-Solving

Applied Problem-Solving	Stages in Policy Cycle
1. Problem Recognition	1. Agenda-Setting
2. Proposal of Solution	2. Policy Formulation
3. Choice of Solution	3. Decision-Making
4. Putting Solution into Effect	4. Policy Implementation
5. Monitoring Results	5. Policy Evaluation

In this model, *agenda-setting* refers to the process by which problems come to the attention of governments; *policy formulation* refers to how policy options are formulated within government; *decision-making* is the process by which governments adopt a particular course of action or non-action; *policy implementation* relates to how governments put policies into effect; and *policy evaluation* refers to the processes by which the results of policies are monitored by both state and societal actors, the outcome of which may be reconceptualization of policy problems and solutions.

The most important advantage of this conception of the policy cycle model as an analytical tool is that it facilitates the understanding of public policy-making by breaking the complexity of the process into any number of stages and sub-stages, each of which can be investigated alone or in terms of its relationship to any or all the other stages of the cycle. This aids theory-building by allowing the results of numerous case studies and comparative studies of different stages to be synthesized. Second, the approach can be used at all socio-legal or spatial levels of policy-making, from that of local governments to those operating in the international sphere (Fowler and Siegel, 2002; Bogason, 2000; Billings and Hermann, 1998). Also, as discussed above, this model permits examination of the role of all actors and institutions involved in policy creation, not just those governmental agencies formally charged with the task, as was the case with earlier versions.

The principal disadvantage of this model is that it can be misinterpreted as suggesting that policy-makers go about solving public problems in a very systematic and more or less linear fashion (Jenkins-Smith and Sabatier, 1993). This, obviously, is not the case in reality, as the identification of problems and the development and implementation of solutions are often very ad hoc and idiosyncratic processes. In other words, decision-makers frequently simply react to circumstances, and do so in terms of their interests and pre-set ideological dispositions (Stone, 1988; Tribe, 1972). Similarly, while the logic of systematic problem-solving may be fine in the abstract, in practice the stages are often compressed or skipped, or followed in an order unlike that specified by the model. The cycle may not be a single iterative loop, for example, but rather a series of smaller loops in which, to cite just one case, the results of past implementation decisions may have a major impact on future policy formulation, regardless of the specifics of the agenda-setting process in the case concerned. Or, as some analysts have noted, policy formulation can sometimes precede agenda-setting as 'solutions seek problems' to which they can be applied (Kingdon, 1984; Salamon and Lund, 1989). And, in other cases, once a single iteration of the cycle has been completed, activities can continue to occur at each of the stages independently (Timmermans and Bleiklie, 1999). In short, often there is no linear progression of policy-making as implied by the model.

Second, it is unclear exactly at which level and with what unit of analysis the policy cycle model should be used. Does the model present an overall picture of all governmental activity, from the legislative to the judicial? Or is it only applicable to specific kinds of decisions taken by specific kinds of organizations such as bureaucracies? (Schlager, 1999) Third, and perhaps most importantly, the model lacks any notion of causation. It offers no pointers as to what, or who, drives a policy from one stage to another, and seems to assume that policy development must inevitably continue to move from stage to stage, rather than stall or end at a particular point in the cycle, without explaining why this should be the case (Sabatier, 1992).

The weaknesses of the framework underscore the complexity of the policy process as well as the need to develop better intellectual devices to facilitate its understanding. While the five-stage cycle helps analysis by disaggregating the policy process, it does not well illustrate the nuances and complexities of public policy-making. A better model is needed that delineates in greater detail the actors and institutions involved in the policy process, helps identify the instruments available to policy-makers, and points out the factors that lead to certain policy outcomes rather than others (Mazmanian and Sabatier, 1980). To a great extent, this is what the remaining chapters of the book seek to accomplish.

Towards an Improved Model of the Policy Cycle

Over the past five decades scholars and analysts working towards the elaboration of a policy science have addressed a series of interrelated questions about the policy process raised in numerous case studies, comparative studies, and conceptual and theoretical critiques. At a very general level, these scholars have dealt with a range of conceptual and methodological issues that have helped to clarify some of the difficulties noted above with respect to the early policy cycle frameworks. Although these studies have been undertaken from a number of theoretical viewpoints and have been oriented towards the resolution of specific questions relating to those perspectives, as will be discussed in Chapter 2, their findings have been remarkably similar and, despite their different origins, have collectively identified a common focus and set of variables that play a significant role in policy-making processes and their analysis.

Methodologically, these studies share a common focus on the processes that exist at the meso or sectoral level, involving the analysis of policy 'sectors' or 'fields' or 'domains' (Burstein, 1991; Knoke and Laumann, 1982). That is, rather than attempt to explain all government policy-making at a territorial or state level, or within a 'political system', they have focused instead at functional levels of state activity. As Benson (1982: 147–8) has put it:

> The policy sector, as conceived here, is an arena in which public policies are decided and implemented. Such arenas are conventionally bounded by substantive policy names—health care, welfare, manpower, natural resources and so on. These units are commonly held typifications that are part of the stock of knowledge held by politicians, bureaucrats, lobbyists, and others. . . . The policy sector is a cluster or complex of organizations connected to each other by resource dependencies and distinguished from other clusters or complexes by breaks in the structure of resource dependencies.

These sectors can be divided even further into specific issue subsectors, and many studies have pointed to the relationship existing between sectors and subsectors as an important one for understanding processes of policy change (Jordan et al., 1994; Cavanagh et al., 1995; Rayner et al., 2001; Hosseus and Pal, 1997).

More substantively, these studies have highlighted the critical roles played by different types of policy actors in affecting policy processes and policy outcomes. Policy-making involves a multitude of actors, who interact with each other in countless ways in pursuit of their interests. The results of their interaction are what public policy is about. But these actors are not completely independent and self-determining, since they operate within a set of existing social relations and policy ideas that serve to constrain their behaviour (Hall, 1997; Heclo, 1994).

The context of societal, state, and international institutions and the values these institutions embody condition how a problem is defined, facilitate the adoption of certain solutions to it, and prohibit or inhibit the choice of other solutions. Similarly, the set of ideas and beliefs or the 'discourse' surrounding a policy sector also serves to constrain policy actors. While there will always be conflicting interpretations of problems, almost every problem that ultimately receives government action is characterized by a surprising degree of agreement on its gravity and on the limited number of options open for resolving it. Finally, the range of instruments available to policy-makers also serves to constrain or limit their choices. Different problems permit the use of different instruments, not all of which are completely substitutable. Until we know the range of instruments available for each task, we will have difficulty knowing why a certain instrument was chosen to implement a particular policy.

Understanding the activities and interactions of policy actors is hence a key facet of understanding the policy process. Terms and concepts developed in many case studies of actor behaviour have all centred on the idea that policy actors can be usefully grouped together in conceptual units active at the sectoral and subsectoral levels of policy-making, variously termed 'subgovernments', 'advocacy coalitions', 'policy networks', and 'policy communities', among others (Jordan, 1981; Jordan and Schubert, 1992).

In addition, many studies have also identified long-term patterns in the structures or 'regimes' within which actors work, the nature of the ideas they hold, the lessons they learn from their own and others' experiences, and the types of instruments they use to implement policies (Wilson, 2000; Smith, 2000; Eisner, 1994a). The existence and longevity of these patterns suggest that despite frequent fluctuations in detail, the overall nature of the operation of policy cycles in specific sectors is quite stable, only infrequently undergoing substantial change. An improved model of the policy process, focused at the sectoral level, should deal with the manner in which *policy subsystems* affect the operation of the policy cycle. And an improved model of the policy process should provide some explanation for how and why the activities of multiple policy actors arrayed in policy subsystems tend towards an overall 'punctuated equilibrium' pattern of policy dynamics (Gersick, 1991; Gould and Eldredge, 1977; Gould, 2002).

As our text will show, an improved model of the policy-making process can be built on the foundation provided by the old policy cycle framework. The new model retains the basic elements of this framework to simplify the subject matter and to structure its analysis. But it focuses at the sectoral level in order to capture the complexities of actor behaviour and the dynamics of policy-making missed by the older framework (Hendrick and Nachmias, 1992).

As the subsequent chapters in the book will show, each of the five stages in the public policy process can be analyzed by addressing a distinct set of questions about actors, institutions, instruments, and ideas along the lines outlined above (DeLeon, 1994, 1999b; Dudley et al., 2000). In this way, an improved model of the policy process can emerge in which the analysis of each stage will contain not simply a description of the activities that occur at each point in the process, but also an outline of the sets of variables affecting activity at that stage and hypotheses about the relationships existing between each variable and the nature of actor behaviour (Skok, 1995).

By examining each stage of the policy cycle with care and elaborating on the variables affecting it, we are able to develop a taxonomy of typical *policy styles* with relevance to multiple areas of government activity (Richardson et al., 1982; Vogel, 1986). Such an analysis contributes to the development of a policy science not only by providing an improved picture of the activities at each stage of the process, but also by offering a much better understanding of why, in Dye's terms, governments choose to do what they do or not do (Feick, 1992).

Hence, the purpose of this book is to develop the elements of an analytical framework that will assist students in studying public policy. It seeks to achieve this objective first by examining the broad approaches to the subject matter and by providing inventories of the relevant policy actors, institutions, and instruments involved in public policy-making. It then breaks down the policy process into the five sub-processes or sub-stages set out above and answers the types of questions posed above concerning the nature of the variables affecting each stage. It concludes with a general commentary on the nature of policy change and stability.

The book draws on many strands in the literature and enables students to cover a broad range of material, while maintaining coherence in the analysis through the use of the policy cycle framework. It is not intended to predispose students towards particular conclusions concerning the merits and demerits of particular policy options or outcomes in particular sectors, but rather to help identify the key variables that generally affect each stage of public policy-making.

Part I provides a general introduction to the discipline. Chapter 1 has briefly charted the development of public policy as an academic discipline and explained what is generally meant by the term. It has outlined a five-stage model of the policy cycle and framed research questions relevant to the analysis of each stage and to the workings of the overall model. Chapter 2 examines in more detail several of the most commonly used approaches to studying public policy, emphasizing those employed by economists, political scientists, sociologists, and others who focus on the nature of general public policy processes. The potential and limitations of each approach are discussed along with the particular manner in which theorizing in the field has progressed over the past several decades.

Part II describes the institutional parameters within which policies are made, the nature of the actors who make them, and the instruments the actors have at their disposal for their implementation. Chapter 3 discusses the various state and societal actors and institutions that play a salient role in public policy-making. It uses the concept of a policy subsystem to capture the complex links between state and societal actors involved in public policy-making. Chapter 4 describes the characteristics of the general types of instruments available to government for implementing policies. It develops a taxonomy based on the range of possible means by which goods and services of any kind can be delivered, from the use of voluntary or community services to direct delivery by state employees. Each chapter in this part not only inventories the range of institutions, actors, and instruments that can affect policy-making, but also establishes the difficulties of assessing and predicting which institutions, actors, and instruments will actually be involved in specific policy-making instances.

Part III sets out a schema for conceptualizing the policy process in order to allow finer levels of analysis to be made. Each of Chapters 5 to 9 examines a critical component or sub-stage of the public policy process, including how and why public concerns make their way onto the government's agenda; how and why some individuals and groups enjoy special input into the formulation of governmental policy options; how and why governments typically decide on a specific course of action; why governments use the types of policy instruments they do; and how their actions and choices are typically evaluated.

Finally, Part IV sets out the conclusions of the study in the context of the general relationships found to exist between ideas, interests, and institutions. Chapter 10 presents the general pattern of the evolution of policy-making in many policy sectors, establishes a taxonomy of typical policy styles, and discusses the reasons why policies tend to develop and change through a stepped or 'punctuated equilibria' process (Gersick, 1991; Baumgartner and Jones, 1993). Chapter 11 then provides a brief commentary on the nature of contemporary policy science and the need for continued careful, systematic, empirical study if the field is to continue to develop in the way envisioned by its founders.

FURTHER READINGS

DeLeon, Peter. 1988. *Advice and Consent: The Development of the Policy Sciences*. New York: Russell Sage Foundation.

Garson, G. David. 1986. 'From Policy Science to Policy Analysis: A Quarter Century of Progress', in W.N. Dunn, ed., *Policy Analysis: Perspectives, Concepts, and Methods*. Greenwich, Conn.: JAI Press, 3–22.

Jenkins-Smith, Hank C., and Paul A. Sabatier. 1993. 'The Study of the Public Policy Processes', in Sabatier and Jenkins-Smith, eds, *Policy Change and Learning: An Advocacy Coalition Approach*. Boulder, Colo.: Westview Press, 1–9.

Lasswell, Harold D. 1951. 'The Policy Orientation', in D. Lerner and Lasswell, eds, *The Policy Sciences: Recent Developments in Scope and Method*. Stanford, Calif.: Stanford University Press, 3–15.

Sabatier, Paul A. 1999. 'The Need for Better Theories', in Sabatier, ed., *Theories of the Policy Process*. Boulder, Colo.: Westview Press, 3–17.

Torgerson, Douglas. 1986. 'Between Knowledge and Politics: Three Faces of Policy Analysis', *Policy Sciences* 19, 1: 33–59.

Tribe, Laurence H. 1972. 'Policy Science: Analysis or Ideology?', *Philosophy and Public Affairs* 2, 1: 66–110.

Wagner, Peter, et al. 1991. 'The Policy Orientation: Legacy and Promise', in Wagner, Bjorn Wittrock, and Helmut Wollman, eds, *Social Sciences and Modern States: National Experiences and Theoretical Crossroads*. Cambridge: Cambridge University Press, 2–27.

Chapter 2

Approaches to Public Policy

As Peter DeLeon has noted, policy studies have a long history and a short past. That is, the actions of government have been a focus of numerous critiques over the centuries, but their systematic analysis as a policy science dates back only several decades (DeLeon, 1994; Peters, 1999). Thus one of the difficulties encountered in studying public policy-making is the range of various approaches, originating in various schools of academic thought, that have been brought to bear on the subject (Sabatier, 1999b; Schlager, 1999). In this chapter we outline the main approaches to the study of public policy in the academic disciplines most directly concerned with state behaviour, such as economic and political science; point out their strengths and weaknesses; and suggest how policy science has profited from the insights offered by other social sciences while developing its own distinctive methodology and theories.

LEVELS, METHODS, AND UNITS OF ANALYSIS IN SOCIAL SCIENCE RESEARCH

Before beginning this survey, we should note that theories in the social sciences fall into different types or orders, depending on the type and range of social phenomena they attempt to explain and the basic method they use to derive their insights and hypotheses. That is, social scientific theories differ according to their *level of analysis*, *method of analysis*, and *unit of analysis* (see Almond and Genco, 1977). With respect to their level of analysis, some social scientific theories are 'general' or *macro*-level social theories that attempt to explain all phenomena within their purview. Others are less wide-ranging and focus only on a few very specific subsets of social life, either at a *micro* or *meso* level of analysis (Ray, 2001). Similarly, social theories also differ according to their method of analysis: some are *deductive* theories developed largely on the basis of the application of general presuppositions, concepts, or principles to specific phenomena. Others are less deductive and more *inductive*, developing generalizations only on the basis of careful observation of empirical phenomena and subsequent testing of these generalizations against other cases (Lundquist, 1987; Przeworski, 1987; Hawkesworth, 1992). And, with respect to their units of analysis, some social theories focus attention on *individuals* as the basic social actor whose behaviour and actions must be explained, while some view aggregate collections of individuals, or *groups*, as the relevant analytical unit. Still others consider larger social *structures* to have an independent impact on individual and collective actions (Hay and Wincott, 1998; Clark, 1998; Tilly, 1984).

If all the permutations within these three variations are considered, the list of social theories relevant to policy would be almost infinite. Even focusing only on examples of each of the different categories resulting from differentiating between level (macro, meso, micro), method (deductive, inductive), and unit of analysis (individual, collective, structure) would require the analysis of at least 18 representative cases. However, for our purposes, this task can be simplified somewhat by focusing only on general, or macro-level, social theories. This is acceptable because academic disciplines such as economics and political science are interested in all social behaviour and activities and tend to view public policy-making as only a subset of such behaviour, amenable to the general theories and explanations prevalent in each field. We will therefore restrict our comments to well-known general categories of social theory commonly applied in policy analysis. As such, only six representative cases will be examined, based on differences in the characteristic basic unit of analysis they employ and their method of theory construction (Dessler, 1999).

The theories examined below differ according to whether they develop their insights about policy-making in a deductive or an inductive manner and whether they focus their attention on the activities of individuals, groups, or institutions in the policy process (Oliver, 1993). Representative examples of the basic types of general theory classified according to these differences in units of analysis and method are set out in Figure 2.1.

DEDUCTIVE THEORIES

There are many adherents to deductive approaches to social science theorization and many nuanced versions of its application to specific social phenomena. In regard to understanding public policy-making, three general sub-types of this approach are discernible, depending on the unit of analysis: rational choice theory, class analysis, or actor-centred neo-institutionalism. The representative examples of each general approach to be

Figure 2.1   **General Approaches to the Study of Political
Phenomena and Illustrative Theoretical Examples**

Method of Theory Construction

	Deductive	*Inductive*
Individual	Rational Choice Theories (Public Choice)	Sociological Individualism (Welfare Economics)
Collectivity	Class Analysis (Marxism)	Group Theories (Pluralism/Corporatism)
Structure	Actor-Centred Institutionalism (Transaction Cost Analysis)	Socio-Historical Neo-Institutionalism (Statism)

Unit of Analysis

examined below are, respectively, *public choice theory*, *Marxist class analysis*, and *transaction cost analysis*.

Rational Choice Theory: Public Choice

Rational choice theory has received a great deal of attention in recent years. One variant of this approach is often referred to as public choice theory, after the Institute for the Study of Public Choice at Virginia Poly-technic (now George Mason) University, where many scholars who developed the approach worked (Dryzek, 1992; Monroe, 1991).

Rational choice theory generally applies the principles of neo-classical economics to political behaviour. Its chief assumption is that political actors, like economic ones, act 'rationally', that is, in a calculating fashion, to maximize their 'utility' or 'satisfaction'. In this model, the only political actor that counts is the individual who acts on the basis of this ascribed characteristic psychological behaviour. Public choice theory is a 'strong' version of rational choice theory and is often used in policy analyses, primarily because the deductive application of its general principles easily generates a clear and consistent set of policy prescriptions, whether or not there is any actual merit to its fundamental axioms. As James Buchanan, one of the founders of public choice theory and the first among public choice theorists to win a Nobel Prize (for Economics), put it: 'In one sense, all public choice or the economic theory of politics may be summarized as the "discovering" or "re-discovering" that people should be treated as rational utility maximizers, in all of their behavioural capacities.'

In the public choice approach it is assumed that individual political actors (whether policy-makers or voters) are guided by self-interest in choosing the course of action to their best advantage (McLean, 1987; Van Winden, 1988). This simple assumption about the basis of human behaviour leads public choice theorists to a complex series of related propositions used to explain various aspects of politics and public policy-making. This approach has been applied, for example, to studies of voting behaviour (Downs, 1957), the relationship between political and economic systems (Becker, 1958), the nature of individual and collective decision-making behaviour (Coase, 1960), and the structure and institutions of government, including bureaucracies (Downs, 1967), legislatures (Niskanen, 1971), political parties (Riker, 1962), and constitutions (Buchanan, 1975).

In these studies, each subject is analyzed in terms of individual self-interest. Thus, for example, voters are deemed to vote for parties and candidates that will best serve their interest in terms of the rewards they expect to receive from governments. Politicians are seen as constantly vying for election in order to promote their interests in the income, power, and prestige derived from being in office, and offer policies that will win them voters' support. Political parties are seen to operate in much the same way as politicians, devising policy packages that will appeal to voters. Bureaucrats' self-interest leads them to maximize their budgets because larger budgets are a source of power, prestige, perks, and higher salaries. They are largely successful in realizing their interest because, as monopoly suppliers of unpriced goods and services, they face no competition and because citizens and elected officials lack the expertise to monitor their activities. Peter Self (1985: 51) succinctly summarized the theory as follows:

> Following this approach, voters can be likened to consumers; pressure groups can be seen as political consumer associations or sometimes as co-operatives; political parties become entrepreneurs who offer competing packages of services and taxes in exchange for votes; political propaganda equates with commercial advertising; and government agencies are public firms dependent upon receiving or drumming up adequate political support to cover their costs.

With respect to public policy-making, public choice theorists view the policy process as one in which a variety of political actors engage in competitive *rent-seeking* behaviour. That is, each actor attempts to use the state to capture some portion of the social surplus ('rents') that accrues from productive social labour. Each actor would prefer, if possible, to *free ride*, that is, to obtain a share in the surplus resulting from the action of other parties at no cost to themselves (Buchanan, 1980; Kreuger, 1974). This conception of the motivations and roles of voters, parties, and politicians in the policy process leads to the conclusion that voters will constantly seek more programs from government, constrained only by their willingness to pay taxes, and that politicians, parties, and bureaucrats will be willing to supply the programs because of their own self-interest in power, prestige, and popularity. The result is a constant increase in the level of state intervention in the economy and society, often in the form of a *political business cycle*. In other words, democratic governments operate in a form of perpetual electoral campaign in which the types of decisions they take will vary according to the timing of the electoral cycle, with popular decisions dispensing benefits taken before election and unpopular ones, attributing costs, afterwards (Boddy and Crotty, 1975; Frey, 1978; Locksley, 1980; Tufte, 1978).

Public policy-making in this view is thus simply a process of the gradual extension of state provision of goods and services to the public. Public choice theorists oppose this pattern, arguing that it distorts the 'natural' operation of market-based societies and reduces overall levels of social welfare by encouraging free riders and other counterproductive forms of rent-seeking behaviour. The general conclusion of public choice theorists is that institutions must be developed to curb destructive utility-maximizing behaviour that serves the interests of particular individuals while adversely affecting the society as a whole. Hence, according to Buchanan, public choice theory does not lead to the conclusion that all collective action, all government action, is necessarily undesirable. It leads, instead, to an understanding that because people will tend to maximize their own utilities, institutions must be designed so that individual behaviour will further the interests of the group, small or large, local or national. The challenge, then, is to construct, or reconstruct, a political order that will channel the self-serving behaviour of participants towards the common good in a manner that comes as close as possible to that described for us by Adam Smith with respect to the economic order (Buchanan et al., 1978: 17).

In this view, the same mechanism of individual utility maximization that promotes the general good in the market takes a decidedly harmful form in the political arena. This leads public choice theorists to reject most of the policy analyses and prescriptions generated by other analysts, which tend to take a more sanguine view of government activity (Rowley, 1983). They argue that government intervention in the affairs of society should be limited to supplementing the market by enforcing and creating property rights where these are weak or non-existent so that market forces can operate and allocate resources in a manner beneficial to the whole society.

The simplicity and logical elegance of the theory, along with the impressive mathematical presentations that accompany studies within this framework, mask its many holes (Jones, 2001; Green and Shapiro, 1994). First of all, the theory is based on an oversimplification of human psychology and behaviour that does not accord with reality. Many political activities, for example, are undertaken for symbolic or ritualistic reasons; to treat them as goal-oriented behaviour directed at utility maximization is to underestimate the complexity of politics that surrounds public policy-making (Zey, 1992). Second, because of this oversimplification, the theory has poor predictive capacity. There is no empirical proof, for example, for its prediction that government functions will grow inexorably because of the competitive dynamics of democratic systems of representation. If anything, in most industrialized countries in recent times government expenditure has been cut back, or at least not expanded, and these fluctuations in patterns of government growth are not new: how and why this occurs is virtually inexplicable within a public choice framework of analysis (Dunleavy, 1986). Third, and again related to its faulty empirical dimension, most public choice theorization is heavily influenced by US experiences, relying, for example, on a pattern of partisan electoral competition between two parties that forces voters to choose between two clearly definable alternatives. In reality, of course, many democracies are multi-party systems in which parties have to form legislative coalitions. Such practices do not permit a neat dichotomy of choices for voters since electoral promises may be overridden by post-election legislative deal-making (Warwick, 2000). And, regardless of the public choice theorists' insistence that their analysis is 'positive' and 'value-free', the theory is explicitly normative. The notions that only social interactions in market-based exchange produce wealth and that the state exists as a kind of parasite extracting rents from the marketplace ignore the important role played by the state not only in securing the basis for the economy in property rights and defence, but also in organizing such key economic activities as education and technological innovation (Dosi et al., 1988). Thus public choice theory seeks, in effect, to promote a particular vision of orthodox liberalism (also called neo-conservatism or neo-liberalism) that would promote markets wherever possible and severely restrict the scope for government activity without any empirical justification for so doing (Hood, 1991, 1995, 1998).

Recently, even public choice theorists have realized that a gap exists between their deductive models and empirical reality. Although they are loath to drop any of their fundamental assumptions about human behaviour and psychology, they have come to realize that some modifications in their fundamental units of analysis are required. That is, it has come to be recognized that public choice theory is institutionally constrained. It has little to say, for example, about policy-making in non-democratic systems that do not rely on free elections, a central assumption of the model. Moreover, it also disregards or underestimates the effects of institutional factors in shaping actors' preferences, despite its pretensions towards institutional design (Ostrom, 1986a, 1986b). Pioneering public choice theorists tended to regard institutions themselves as changeable according to actors' preferences and were unwilling to recognize fully the durability of institutions and the pervasive impact they have on individual behaviour. The realization by many former public choice adherents of the effects of institutional structures on individual choices has moved many rational choice theorists, including many who had previously endorsed variants such as game theory (Harsanyi, 1977; Scharpf, 1990; Elster, 1986), to embrace a more subtle and supple approach to deductive social theory, a form of economistic 'neo-institutionalism' or 'actor-centred institutionalism', which will be discussed in more detail below.

Class Analysis: Marxist Social Theory

Class theories are essentially group theories, in that they accord primacy to collective entities in their analyses, but unlike inductive group theories such as pluralism or corporatism, which will be discussed in the next section of this chapter, they tend to define their units of analysis in 'objective' terms and conduct their analysis in an explicitly deductive fashion. That is, class theories ascribe group membership on the basis of certain observable characteristics of individuals, whether or not the individuals involved see themselves in those terms, and they expect behaviour that maximizes group interest to flow from this attributed orientation.

According to Stanislaw Ossowski, 'class' refers to: 'Groups differentiated in various ways within a more inclusive category, such as the category of social groups with common economic interests, or the category of groups whose members share economic conditions which are identical in a certain respect.' While there are several types of class analysis,[1] we shall concentrate on the 'Marxist' variety, which, because of its influence on the development and spread of European socialism in the nineteenth and twentieth centuries, is by far the best known and theoretically developed. In this approach class membership is determined by the presence or absence of certain characteristics, usually, but not always, related to the economy.

The various nineteenth-century writings of the German philosopher and political economist Karl Marx exhibited somewhat different notions of class. However, the one developed by Marx in his mid-nineteenth century *Manifesto of the Communist Party* is the best known. Here Marx argued that each society has two classes contesting political and economic power. In his material conception of history, human society has passed through a number of distinct stages ('modes of production'), each of which has a distinct set of technological conditions of production ('means of production') and a distinct manner in which the various actors in the production process relate with each other ('class structure' or 'relations of production') (Cohen, 1978). Each mode of production entails a particular class system, which is ultimately determined by ownership (or non-ownership) of the means of production.

In the logic of this model, in theory, each mode of production develops a dichotomous class system consisting of those who own the means of production and those who must work for the owners, and the relationship between the two groups is inherently conflictual. Slaves battled slave owners in slave societies; serfs struggled with landlords in feudal society; and workers struggle with owners in capitalist society. Continued class struggle leads to eventual collapse of modes of production and their replacement by another mode, which in turn is eventually replaced by yet another system. In practice, Marx expected that a dichotomous class system would occur only for a brief period at the tail end of a mode of production, although it would be possible to see its gradual evolution over time as a mode of production matured and developed. At other points in time, modes of production would have more complex class structures in which multiple classes would exist (Nicolaus, 1967). At its most complex, a mode of production might exhibit a class structure composed of as many as six classes: the two dominant classes from each of three modes (that which immediately preceded it, the mode itself, and the mode that would follow it). The term often used to capture the complexities of multiple class structures in mixed modes of production is a 'social formation' (Poulantzas, 1973b).

Marxist class theory interprets public policies in capitalist societies as reflecting the interests of the capitalist class. The capitalists' dominance of the base—that is, the economy—affords them control over the state and what it does. Indeed, according to Marx, the state is merely an instrument in the hands of capitalists, who use it for the purposes of maintaining the capitalist system and increasing profits ('surplus value'), necessarily at the expense of labour. Given its deductive nature, analysis of public policy from a Marxist perspective usually took the form of demonstrating how a particular policy serves the interests of capital, which is assumed as a proof that the latter used the state to further its interest. This general set of assumptions about government is often referred to as the *instrumental theory of the state*.

While a popular form of analysis in many countries and colonies around the globe in the 1930s and 1940s, by the late 1960s in Western Europe this instrumentalist line of analysis was beginning to be seen as problematic by Marxist analysts on two counts. First, even if it were true that a policy serves the interest of capital, it cannot be concluded ipso facto that the policy was enacted at the behest of capital. To show this, one would have to demonstrate that capitalists issued instructions that were faithfully carried out by state officials, proof of which is usually lacking. Second, and more importantly, this approach cannot explain policies adopted over the opposition of capitalists. In most capitalist states, for instance, the adoption of social welfare policies was vehemently opposed by many capitalists, something that cannot be explained from this perspective. The recognition of this theoretical problem forced a reappraisal of the role of the state in Marxist theory (Block, 1980; Foley, 1978; Gough, 1975; Poulantzas, 1978; Therborn, 1977, 1986).

Second, much as was the case with public choice theory, in the traditional Marxist view the means of production constituted the basic structure shaping the state, law, and ideology. As we have seen, however, this conceptualization is problematic because the state has played a crucial role in organizing the economy and shaping the mode of production (Cox, 1987). The nineteenth-century promotion of natural resource sector production and the protection of inefficient import substitution industrialization in Canada, Argentina, Australia, Brazil, and Mexico, for example, had a decisive impact on those countries' economic structures and class relations and continue to shape the various classes' interests, the policy outcomes they desire, and the policy responses they elicit (Clarke-Jones, 1987; Duquette, 1999; Hirschman, 1958). Similarly, the proliferation of Keynesian policies in the 1950s and 1960s in many countries (Hall, 1989) occurred over the opposition of entrenched business interests and cannot be understood without reference to ideological factors influencing state behaviour, just as policies promoting privatization and deregulation in many of the same countries in the 1980s (Ikenberry, 1990) cannot be traced entirely or directly to the interests of capitalists (Amariglio et al., 1988).

Like rational choice theory, which in its later phases recognized to a much greater extent the independent effects of institutions and social structures on individual behaviour, class analysis in the 1960s and 1970s placed an increased emphasis on institutional or structural factors to account for state activities and behaviour (McLennan, 1989: 117-19). To account for the state devising policies opposed by capital, for example, the notion of *relative autonomy* of the state was developed. While numerous neo-Marxists are associated with this line of reinterpretation, the view offered by Nicos Poulantzas in the early 1970s was perhaps the most prominent (Poulantzas, 1973a; Althusser and Balibar, 1977). Poulantzas argued that conflicts among the various fractions of capital, coupled with the existence of a bureaucracy staffed by individuals drawn from non-capitalist classes, permitted the state some level of autonomy from capital. This autonomy, in turn, allowed the state to adopt measures favourable to the subordinate classes if this was found to be politically unavoidable or necessary for promoting the long-term interests of capital in social stability.

While such measures may adversely affect the short-term interests of capital, and may even be vehemently opposed by capitalists, Poulantzas argued they were always in their long-term interest. This is because the structure of capitalism requires that certain essential functions be performed by the state if capitalism is to survive. Such functions include enforcing property rights, maintaining peace and order, and promoting conditions favourable to continued accumulation of profits. Hence, in this 'structural' version of neo-Marxism, policy-making was still viewed as serving the interest of capital, but not in the same instrumental sense as conceived by early Marxists (Thompson, 1978). The rise of the welfare state, for example, is explained not as a direct response to the needs of capital, but as the result of political pressures exerted by the working class on the state (Esping-Andersen, 1981, 1985; Esping-Andersen and Korpi, 1984). The structural imperatives of capitalism are not ignored, however, because they impose limits on what the state can do in response to working-class demands. Thus, it is argued, the welfare state established by capitalist governments in response to working-class demands was designed in a manner that did not undermine fundamental property rights or profits.

Actor-Centred Institutionalism: Transaction Cost Analysis

A third deductive approach explicitly recognizes the limits of similar individual and class-based theories to explain social behaviour and activity such as public policy-making. Like its inductive counterpart, 'statism', on which more information is provided below (Peters, 1999; Hall and Taylor, 1996; Kato, 1996), this approach grew directly out of expressed concerns about the ability of deductive theories based on individual and collective action to deal with the question of why political, economic, and social institutions like governments, firms, or churches existed at all, and to help assess the impact they had in fashioning constraints and providing opportunities for those actors to emerge, evolve, and interact (March and Olsen, 1984, 1989, 1995). Many variants of this approach exist, under titles such as the 'New Economics of Organization' (Moe, 1984; Yarbrough and Yarbrough, 1990; Williamson, 1996) or the 'Institutional Analysis and Development (IAD)' framework (Kiser and Ostrom, 1982; Ostrom et al., 1993). All, however, use a form of what Fritz Scharpf has termed 'actor-centred institutionalism' to understand social processes, including political and policy-oriented ones (Scharpf, 1997).

Like recent class analysis, actor-centred institutionalism emphasizes the autonomy of political institutions from the society in which they exist. And, like public choice theory, it also begins with a simple idea about calculating human behaviour. But unlike that latter approach, it takes into account the facts that rules, norms, and symbols affect political behaviour; that the organization of governmental institutions affects what the state does; and that unique patterns of historical development constrain future choices.[2] Institutions, hence, are defined to include not only formal organizations such as bureaucratic hierarchies and market-like exchange networks but also legal and cultural codes and rules that affect the calculations by individuals and groups of their optimal strategies and courses of action (Ostrom, 1999).

These assumptions focus this approach on the effects of structure on social actors and, as James March and Johan Olsen (1984: 738) put it:

They deemphasize the dependence of the polity on society in favor of an interdependence between relatively autonomous social and political institutions; they deemphasize the simple primacy of micro processes and efficient histories in favor of relatively complex processes and historical inefficiency; they deemphasize metaphors of choice and allocate outcomes in favor of other logics of action and the centrality of meaning and symbolic action.

One variant of this general approach is transaction cost analysis (North, 1990; Williamson, 1985). This approach acknowledges the crucial role played by institutions in political life, and argues that these exist in society in order to overcome impediments caused by information asymmetries and other barriers to 'perfect' exchange in society. The basic unit of analysis in this approach is related to the 'transaction' among individuals within the confines of an institutional order (Coase, 1937). Institutions of various kinds are significant to the extent that they increase or lower the costs of transactions. In this perspective institutions are 'the products of human design, the outcomes of purposive actions by instrumentally oriented individuals' (Powell and DiMaggio, 1991: 8).

In the transaction cost approach to social theory, the argument is not that institutions cause an action. It is rather that they affect actions by shaping the interpretation of problems and possible solutions and by constraining the choice of solutions and the way and extent to which they can be implemented. While individuals, groups, classes, and states have their specific interests, they pursue them in the context of existing formal organizations and rules and norms that shape expectations and affect the possibilities of their realization (Williamson, 1985).

In the political realm, in the transaction costs perspective, institutions are significant because they 'constitute and legitimize individual and collective political actors and provide them with consistent behavioural rules, conceptions of reality, standards of assessment, affective ties, and endowments, and thereby with a capacity for purposeful action' (March and Olsen, 1994: 5). In the policy realm, as with public choice theory, this analysis leads to a distinct preference for market-based forms of government action and activity, but for different reasons, avoiding the reliance of public choice theory on ascribing inherently wasteful rent-seeking behaviour to government actors.

Focusing on the nature of economic transactions, a typology of goods and services has been developed to illustrate the appropriate roles played by governments and markets in their provision. In this typology, all goods and services in society can be divided into four types according to the transactional criteria of 'exclusivity' and 'exhaustiveness', that is, whether a transaction involving a good or service is limited to a single consumer and whether it is completely consumed after an economic transaction. These criteria of exclusivity and exhaustiveness generate the four types of goods and services listed in Figure 2.2.

Figure 2.2 A General Taxonomy of Goods and Services

		Exhaustiveness	
		High	*Low*
Exclusivity	*High*	Private Good	Toll Good
	Low	Common-Pool Good	Public Good

SOURCE: Adapted from E.S. Savas, *Alternatives for Delivering Public Services: Toward Improved Performance* (Boulder, Colo.: Westview Press, 1977).

In this view, pure private goods make up the bulk of goods and services produced in society. These are goods or services, such as food, that can be divided up for sale and are no longer available to others after their consumption by consumers. At the other extreme are pure public goods or services, such as street lighting, which cannot be parcelled out and can be consumed without diminishing the sum of the good available. Between the two are toll goods and common-pool goods. The former include semi-public goods such as bridges or highways, which do not diminish in quantity after use but for the use of which it is possible to charge. Common-pool goods are those, like fish in the ocean, whose usage cannot be directly charged to individuals but whose quantity is reduced after use.

In the transaction costs perspective, the two types of social organizations considered to be the most effective in minimizing transaction costs are markets, on the one hand, and the hierarchical form of organization, or 'bureaucracy', on the other. In the market form, the costs of overcoming information and other needs are largely externalized as multiple producers and consumers share the costs of acquiring and disseminating information and other goods and services. In a hierarchy these costs are internalized, as occurs for example in large corporations in the modern era. In an optimal arrangement, it is argued, a government would seek to externalize costs onto citizens by enhancing market-based activities. Citizens would then be able to know the true price of government services and act rationally with respect to their consumption, spending, and investment decisions (Horn, 1995).

According to the principles of transaction cost analysis, governments should not interfere in transactions and activities related to private goods and services. They should simply enforce basic property rights and prevent criminal behaviours (such as theft) undermining these types of transactions. Public goods, however, should be provided by the government because markets cannot provide goods or services for which businesses cannot charge or profit. Governments should also not allow toll goods to be treated like public goods and so must charge for their usage. From this perspective, the costs of constructing and maintaining roads and bridges should not be charged to all taxpayers and then offered for 'free' to those using the facilities, which encourages the latter to treat these as public goods; rather, those using the facilities must pay for the costs. In the case of common-pool goods, the government should establish property regimes through licensing to prevent their depletion (Savas, 1977, 1987). The sale of fishing quotas through public auction, which gives the 'right' to a certain quantity of fish to those succeeding at the auction, is often cited as an example of this principle.

This analysis of appropriate institutional behaviour based on the nature of economic transactions is replicated in many other areas of social and political life by adherents of this approach to policy studies. Policy-relevant activities such as the negotiation of international treaties, the operation of multi-level systems of government, and issues of regulatory enforcement are subject to similar analyses in which the actions and decisions of policy actors are modelled as the outcomes of multiple, nested games occurring within the confines, costs, and payoffs established by institutional orders (Scharpf, 1997; Putnam, 1988; Scholz, 1984; Sproule-Jones, 1989).

This generates a useful body of insights into appropriate and inappropriate behaviour within the fixed confines of a given institutional order and makes transaction cost analysis quite compatible with, and an extension of, earlier individualist and collectivist deductive approaches to policy theorization (Dowding, 1994). However, this approach is somewhat eclectic in the sense that it directs attention to a wide range of international and domestic norms, rules, and behaviour that affect actual and perceived transaction costs and hence may be relevant to explaining policy-making (Putnam, 1988; Atkinson, 1978). This results in the tempering of its otherwise purely deductive orientation, leaving it to empirical investigations to determine the significance of specific variables on policy outcomes in specific circumstances. Its main problem, however, lies with its inability to provide a plausible coherent explanation of the origin of institutions, or their alteration, without resorting to functionalism. That is, since this approach argues that individual and collective preferences are shaped by institutions, it is unclear how institutions or rules themselves are created, and once in place, how they would change (Cammack, 1992; March et al., 2000; Peters, 1999; Gorges, 2001).

Actor-centred institutionalism hence tends to provide an excellent discussion of the constraints placed on policy actors and what is 'rational' for them to do in specific circumstances, but says very little about what causes those constraints to move in any particular direction (Bromley, 1989: ch. 1). While overcoming many of the problems associated with earlier individual and collective approaches such as public choice theory and class analysis by clearly acknowledging the need to take institutional orders into account in analyzing policy-making behaviour, transaction cost analysis is at once both limited and vague in its analysis of the history and evolution of policy-making activities.

INDUCTIVE THEORIES

Unlike the deductive theories that attempt to apply universal maxims to the study of political phenomena, inductive theories are constructed not from the 'top down' but from the 'bottom up'. They depend on the accumulation of multiple empirical studies of any phenomenon for their raw data, from which theorists attempt to extract generalizable propositions. By their very nature these theories are less elegant and parsimonious than deductive theories. They often do not have a fully integrated or unified set of theoretical propositions that can be applied to any case under consideration, since they are, by definition, always 'under construction'.

Like deductive theories, several sub-types of inductive social theories exist. These, too, can be usefully distinguished according to whether they focus on individuals, groups, or structures in their efforts to explain the political world and public policy-making.

Sociological Individualism: Welfare Economics

Many inductive social theories are also based on the individual, but usually they do not contain the simplifying psychological axioms of individual utility self-maximization characteristic of their deductive counterparts, such as public choice theory (Gerth and Mills, 1958). Welfare economics is one such theory, and is perhaps the most widely used approach to the study of public policy. Indeed, much of what is called policy analysis in the literature is often only applied welfare economics, even though this is rarely stated explicitly (Weimer and Vining, 1999).

This approach is based on the notion that individuals, through market mechanisms, should be expected to make most social decisions. Unlike their deductive counterparts, however, welfare economists recognize that markets cannot always distribute resources efficiently or, to put it another way, cannot always aggregate individual utility-maximizing behaviour so as to optimize overall social welfare. In such instances, referred to as *market failures*, welfare economists argue that political institutions can act to supplement or replace markets.

The principles of welfare economics were first worked out by the British economist Alfred Pigou (1932) during World War I. Although he only identified instances of market failures related to the tendency of some industries to generate monopolies and the inability of both consumers and investors to receive information necessary for decision-making, later analysts argued the existence of many more such market failures (Bator, 1958; Zerbe and McCurdy, 1999). At minimum, these include the following:

- *Natural monopoly* refers to the situation in certain industries with large capital requirements and disproportionate returns to scale that tends to promote a single firm over its competitors. In industries such as telecommunications, electricity, and railways, the first company to establish the necessary infrastructure, if unregulated, enjoys cost advantages that make it difficult for other firms to compete. The lack of competition, when it occurs, leads to loss of the society's economic welfare.

- *Imperfect information* occurs when consumers and investors lack adequate information to make rational decisions. Unregulated pharmaceutical firms, for instance, have no incentive to reveal adverse side effects of their products, nor do consumers have the expertise required to evaluate such products. Once again, decisions may be taken that do not serve the society as a whole.

- In the presence of *externalities*, too, the market is deemed to fail. These involve situations in which production costs are not borne by producers ('internalized') but passed on to others outside (external to) the production process. The most often cited example of an externality relates to the costs of pollution that a company in pursuit of reduced costs and increased profits imposes on the society as a whole.

- *The tragedy of the commons* is a market failure that occurs when common property resources, such as fisheries, pastures, forests, or pools of oil, are exploited without the necessary regulation to maintain the resource. In these circumstances individual users often benefit from increasing their use of the resource in the short term although all users will suffer in the long term from the increased depletion of the resource.

- *Destructive competition* is a controversial market failure resulting when aggressive competition between firms causes negative side effects on workers and society (Utton, 1986). It is argued that excessive competition can drive down profit margins and lead to the unnecessary reduction of working conditions, adversely affecting overall social welfare.

These are the core types of market failures; others have sought to broaden the concept by including other types within this schema. Thus education, industrial research and development, art and culture, and social peace and stability are argued by many as instances of activities with 'positive externalities' that the market does not supply adequately despite a social need, indicating the existence of market failure.

Sustained criticisms of the vagueness of the criteria used to define market failures have led many welfare economists to attempt to reconceptualize the original notion. Recent critics have argued that market failures are in fact only one side of an equation and that there are also innate limitations—*government failures*—to government's ability to correct market failures. They posit that in several specific instances the state cannot improve on the market, despite the latter's failings (Le Grand and

Robinson, 1984; Mayntz, 1993a; Bozeman, 2002). There are three commonly cited instances of such government failure:

- *Organizational displacement* is the situation in which an administrative agency charged with producing a particular good or service displaces public goals with its own 'private' or 'organizational' ones. These may extend to maximizing its budget or power or whatever else the organization values. In such circumstances, government action to correct market failure may simply increase inefficiency.
- *Rising costs*, the supposed disparity between government revenues and costs, are cited as another instance of government failure. Governments receive tax revenues from general sources but have specific program costs. Without a method to match costs to revenues, it is argued, governments often fail to control expenses.
- *Derived externalities* are the third type of government failure. Certain government actions, such as health-care provision, have a broad impact on society and the economy and can have the effect of excluding viable market-produced goods and services, negatively affecting overall levels of social welfare (Wolf, 1979; Le Grand, 1991; Weimer and Vining, 1999: 194).

Although the exact status and causes of government and market failures remain controversial and largely inductively derived, welfare economists have developed a theory of public policy-making based on these concepts. They argue that governments have a responsibility to correct market failures because optimal social outcomes will not result from unco-ordinated individual decision-making. In this view, governments facing a demand for action should first determine if a market failure is causing a social problem; only if one is found should government intervene to correct the problem (Stokey and Zeckhauser, 1978). However, even then, in order to avoid government failures, policy-makers must also carefully evaluate their own capacity to correct the market before attempting to do so (Vining and Weimer, 1990; Weimer and Vining, 1992).

Once it is agreed that a problem requires state intervention, the key public policy question for welfare economists is to find the most efficient way of doing so. The most efficient way, in this perspective, is the least costly one, and the technique used to determine it is cost-benefit analysis. Its objective is to find out how to achieve the same output for less input, or more output for the same input (Carley, 1980: 51). Such analysis involves evaluating all alternatives and their consequences in terms of their monetary costs and benefits and then choosing the alternative that maximizes benefits while minimizing costs. Costs and benefits in this mode of analysis are determined by:

1. Enumerating all adverse and positive consequences arising from implementation of an option in monetary terms.
2. Estimating the probability of occurrence.
3. Estimating the cost or benefit to society should it occur.
4. Calculating the expected loss or gain related to each consequence by multiplying (2) and (3).
5. Estimating the costs of such actions into the future to give a net present value (Fischoff, 1977; Bickers and Williams, 2001).

Cost-benefit analysis is essentially a technique for making the government replicate market decision-making as closely as possible for the purpose of allocating resources. It has been described as 'an attempt to use economic technique, in place of formal market bargaining or price setting, to locate a Pareto-optimal policy alternative' (Gillroy and Wade, 1992: 7; Zeckhauser and Schaefer, 1968). The criterion of *Pareto optimality* requires that an action be undertaken only if it offers the possibility of making at least one person better off without worsening the situation of any other person. However, while Pareto optimality may be achievable in a competitive market (though that is disputable as well), it is impossible to apply in the public policy arena because all government actions make some better off at the expense of others. Social security for the poor makes the rich who pay for it worse off and is therefore not Pareto optimal; nor is putting criminals in jail, because it makes them worse off.

The difficulties with the principle of Pareto optimality have resulted in its replacement in contemporary welfare economics by the so-called Kaldor criterion, which requires that policy alternatives maximizing *net* benefits over cost be chosen. Under this criterion, a policy can be chosen even if some lose as long as the total gains are higher than the sum of losses. A cost-benefit analysis is employed to find out the Kaldor-efficient allocation, and the option offering the highest benefit-to-cost ratio is selected for adoption and implementation.

While not without merits, cost-benefit analysis is often problematic. Despite numerous attempts to refine the model, there is no acceptable way of putting a dollar value on various intangible costs and consequences (Zeckhauser, 1975). There is no way, for instance, to calculate precisely the costs of social security programs in terms of their effects on the recipients' work incentive, or their benefits in terms of the social peace and tolerance they promote. Moreover, the costs and benefits of any policy are often not evenly distributed, for some pay more than others, while some benefit more. And there is often a severe problem of aggregating or summing up the various components of an option. Building a new airport involves disparate problems, such as increased noise for residents in adjoining areas, decreased travelling time for some and increased time for others, increased pollution, beneficial employment and savings effects, and so on, all of which affect different sections of the society differently and so need to be evaluated differently, yet there is no generally acceptable way of doing so (Carley, 1980: 51–5). Efforts to improve cost-benefit technique continue; however, so do criticisms.

The main problem with the conception of public policy-making offered by welfare economists, however, is not related to their methods or to the elegance of their theoretical assumptions about reciprocal market and government failures. Rather, these theorists have failed to recognize that states almost never make their policies in the essentially technical manner assumed by the theory. Even if one could identify the most efficient and effective policy, which is difficult given the limitations innate to the social sciences, the actual policy choice is a political one, bound by political institutions and made by political actors, often in response to political pressures. As such, the technical analyses generated by welfare economists are often merely another political resource used by proponents of one or another option for government action or inaction to further their claims (Weiss, 1977b). Only in very specific circumstances when welfare economists happen to be policy-makers—as happens at times in some countries in some sectors, such as taxation or fiscal management—would one expect political decisions to be based solely on welfare-maximizing criteria as defined by welfare economists (Markoff and Montecinos, 1993). The neglect of political variables by welfare economics has led its critics to describe it as 'a myth, a theoretical illusion' that promotes 'a false and naive view of the policy process' (Minogue, 1983: 76; Hogwood and Gunn, 1984: 50–1).

Group Theories: Pluralism and Corporatism

A second inductive approach to social theory that has been prominent in studies of policy-making, especially in political science, focuses on groups and not individuals. The best-known examples of this approach are 'pluralism', which originated in the United States and continues to be the dominant perspective in American political science, and 'corporatism', which is a similar group theory developed in Europe.

While evidence of pluralist thinking can be found in the works of one of the founding fathers of the United States, James Madison (Madison and Hamilton, 1961), and a French observer of early nineteenth-century America, Alexis de Tocqueville (1956), the doctrine received its first formal expression by Arthur Bentley in 1908. The theory has been considerably modified and refined over the years, but the fundamental tenets postulated by Bentley remain intact. Some prominent pluralist thinkers, responsible for a revival of Bentley's work in the US in the post-World War II era, include Robert Dahl (1956, 1961), Nelson Polsby (1963), and especially David Truman (1964).

Pluralism is based on the assumption of the primacy of interest groups in the political process. In *The Process of Government*, Bentley argued that different interests in society found their concrete manifestation in different groups consisting of individuals with similar concerns and, ultimately, that 'society itself is nothing other than the complex of the groups that compose it.' Truman modified Bentley's notion of a one-to-one correspondence between interests and groups and argued that two kinds of interests—latent and manifest—resulted in the creation of two kinds of groups—potential and organized (Truman, 1964; also see Jordan, 2000). For Truman, latent interests in the process of emerging provided the underpinnings for potential groups, which over time led to the emergence of organized groups, allowing politics to be seen as a more dynamic process than Bentley seemed to be arguing.

Groups in pluralist theory are not only many and free-forming, they are also characterized by overlapping membership and a lack of representational monopoly (Schmitter, 1977). That is, the same individual may belong to a number of groups for pursuing his or her different interests; a person, for instance, may belong at the same time to Greenpeace, the local Chamber of Commerce, and Ducks Unlimited, among others. Overlapping membership is said to be a key mechanism for reconciling conflicts and promoting co-operation among groups. In addition, the same interest may be represented by more than one group. Environmental causes, for example, are espoused by a large number of groups in every industrialized country. Politics, in the pluralist perspective, is the process by which various competing interests and groups are reconciled. Public policies are thus a result of competition and collaboration among groups working to further their members' collective interests (Self, 1985).

Contrary to the interpretation presented in many commentaries, pluralists do not believe that all groups are equally influential or that they have equal access to government (Smith, 1990: 303–4). In fact, they recognize that groups vary in terms of the financial or organizational (personnel, legitimacy, members' loyalty, or internal unity) resources they possess and the access to government they enjoy (Lindblom, 1968; Lowi, 1969; McConnell, 1966; Schattschneider, 1960). Nevertheless, as far as the policy process is concerned, as McLennan has observed, 'It is impossible to read the standard works without getting the sense that resources, information and the means of political communication are openly available to all citizens, that groups form an array of equivalent power centres in society, and that all legitimate voices can and will be heard.' As such, pluralist theories are to some extent justifiably criticized for not having a sufficiently developed notion of groups' varying capacity to affect government decision-making.

A more significant problem with the application of pluralism to public policy-making, however, is that the role of the government in making public policies is quite unclear (Smith, 1990). The early pluralists assumed that the government was a sort of 'transmission belt' registering and implementing the demands of interest groups. The government was often thought of not actually as an entity but as a place, an 'arena' where competing groups met and bargained (Dahl, 1967). The recognition that this view did not accord with the reality of what governments actually did led to its reconceptualization as a 'referee' or 'umpire' of the group struggle. In this view, the state was still ultimately a place where competing groups met to work out their differences, but this time the government was considered a kind of neutral official setting out the rules of group conflict and ensuring that groups did not violate them with impunity (Berle, 1959). As Earl Latham (1952: 390) put it:

> The legislature referees the group struggle, ratifies the victories of the successful coalitions, and records the terms of the surrenders, compromises, and conquests in the form of statutes. Every statute tends to represent compromise because the very process of accommodating conflicts of group interest is one of deliberation and consent. The legislative vote on any issue thus tends to represent the composition of strength, i.e., the balance of power among the contending groups at the moment of voting. What may be called public policy is actually the equilibrium reached in the group struggle at any given moment, and it represents a balance which the contending factions of groups constantly strive to weight in their favor.

This is an overly simplistic view of the government, as public choice critics of pluralism such as Mancur Olson (1965) were quick to point out, because it assumes that public officials do not have their own interests and ambitions, which they seek to realize through their control of the governmental machinery. It also neglects the fact that states often maintain special ties with certain groups and may even sponsor establishment of groups where there are none or if those in existence are found to be difficult to co-opt or accommodate (Pal, 1993a).

The pluralist notion of the government responding to group pressure is also misconceived because it assumes unity of purpose and action on the part of the government. As some critics have pointed out, 'bureaucratic politics' is a pervasive phenomenon that has a critical impact on public policies (Allison and Halperin, 1972). Different departments and agencies have different interests and conflicting interpretations of the same problem, and how these differences are resolved has an impact on what policies are adopted and how they are implemented.

Recognition of these problems with pluralism (Connolly, 1969) led to the emergence of what is sometimes described as 'neo-pluralism' within the American political science community. The reformulation retained the significance attributed to competition among groups, but modified the idea of approximate equality among groups and explicitly acknowledged that some groups are more powerful than others. Charles Lindblom, for example, has argued that business is more powerful than others for two reasons. First, government in a capitalist society needs a prosperous economy to serve as the basis for tax revenues to spend on programs and its own re-election. To promote economic growth, governments must maintain business confidence, which often means paying special heed to the demands of the business community. Second, in capitalist societies there is a division between public and private sectors, the former under the control of the state and the latter dominated by business. The private sector's dominance by business gives it a privileged position in comparison to other groups in that much employment and associated social and economic activity are ultimately dependent on private-sector investment behaviour (Lindblom, 1977). Unlike the classical pluralists, who seemed only to acknowledge but not incorporate the observation that some groups may be more powerful than others because of their superior organization and resources, Lindblom argued that the strength of business lay in the nature of capitalism and democracy itself. As such, business need not, though it may, exert pressure on the government to realize its interests; the government, in accordance with the imperatives of capitalism and the pursuit of its own self-interest, will ensure that business interests are not adversely affected by its actions.

Other problems with pluralist analyses of public policy-making, however, remain. One concern, which led some early critics of pluralism to adopt a more deductive, rational choice orientation, involves the motivations individuals have for joining groups. Mancur Olson, for example, argued that a fundamental flaw in pluralist theory related to the ability of individuals to gain the advantages of group membership without actually joining a group. This ability to 'free ride', Olson argued, meant that group membership could not simply be taken for granted but had to be fostered by providing 'selective incentives' to individuals to 'make it worth their while' to join (Olson, 1965; McLean, 2000).

Later studies revealed that groups form for a variety of reasons, and pointed to the role patrons played in providing start-up funding and organizational assistance to groups (Nownes and Neeley, 1996; Nownes, 1995; Nownes and Cigler, 1995). Such studies highlighted a second serious problem with pluralist theory: its excessive concentration on the role of interest groups themselves and its relative neglect of other equally important factors in the political and policy-making processes. While neo-pluralism was a significant improvement on its predecessor, it did not address all the problems innate to a concentrated focus on groups as collective social actors.

The theory also continued to overlook the role of the international system in shaping public policies and their implementation. International economic interdependence makes states' policies increasingly subject to international pressures, regardless of domestic group pressures. It is difficult to understand, for example, the industrial and trade policies of industrialized countries without reference to the international economy and the political pressures it places on policy-makers. The role of ideology was also unjustifiably neglected in the pluralist explanations of politics and public policy. The liberal tradition pre-eminent in Anglo-Saxon countries (including Canada, the US, and Australia), for example, has had a significant impact on their governments' hesitant and often contradictory intervention in the economy.

As was the case with welfare economics, these lacunae have been filled by adding an institutional dimension to pluralist analysis, in which the state is viewed as an independent actor in its own right, which can and does affect the groups that contest political life and make policy (Nordlinger, 1981). This development is discussed in the next section.

Pluralism's applicability to countries besides the United States has also been especially problematic because of differences in underlying political institutions and processes that challenge pluralist assumptions and precepts derived only from examination of the US experience (Zeigler, 1964). British parliamentary institutions found in Australia, Canada, the United Kingdom, Japan, or Sweden, for example, do not lend themselves to the kind of open access that groups enjoy in relation to legislatures in the US and other countries with similar republican systems of government (Presthus, 1973).[3] And many authoritarian countries simply lack the kinds of groups conceived by pluralists as being the basic building blocks of political analysis. Even if groups have the freedom to organize, the numbers actually formed are fewer than in the US and tend to be much more permanent and formalized. This finding led some group theorists, such as Phillipe Schmitter, to speculate that pluralism was only one form in which group systems could develop. Schmitter (1977) argued that, depending on a range of variables and historical factors, a *corporatist* form of political organization was much more likely than a pluralist one to emerge in many countries outside the US.

In Europe, theories treating groups as their primary unit of analysis have tended to take a corporatist form. The roots of corporatism extend back to the Middle Ages when there were concerns about protecting the 'intermediate strata' of autonomous associations between the state and the family (Gierke, 1958a, 1958b).[4] These included guilds and other forms of trade associations as well as, most importantly, religious organizations and churches. Corporatist theory argues that these intermediate strata have a life of their own above and beyond their constituting individuals, and that their existence is part of the 'organic' or natural order of society. Much of political life and conflict in Europe in the fifteenth and sixteenth centuries concerned efforts by emerging national states to control the operations of these 'autonomous strata' and the latter's efforts to resist state control (Cawson, 1986; Mann, 1984; Winkler, 1976).

Corporatism can be best understood, as Schmitter has observed, in contrast to pluralism. The latter proposes that multiple groups exist to represent their respective members' interests, with membership being voluntary and groups associating freely with each other without state interference in their activities. In contrast, corporatism is:

> [A] system of interest intermediation in which the constituent units are organized into a limited number of singular, compulsory, non-competitive, hierarchically ordered and functionally differentiated categories, recognized or licensed (if not created) by the state and granted a deliberate representational monopoly within their respective categories in exchange for observing certain controls on their selection of leaders and articulation of demands and supports. (Schmitter, 1977: 9)

The groups here are not thought of as free-forming, voluntary, or competitive, as in pluralism. Nor are they considered to be autonomous, for they depend on the state for recognition and support in return for a role in policy-making. Corporatism thus explicitly takes into account two problems endemic to pluralism: its neglect of the role of the state and its failure to recognize institutionalized patterns of relationships between the state and groups.

In corporatist theory, public policy is shaped by the interaction between the state and the interest group or groups recognized by the state. Interaction among groups is institutionalized within and mediated by the state (McLennan, 1989: 245). Public policy towards a declining industry, for instance, would take the form of bargaining between and among the state and relevant industry associations and trade unions as to how best to rationalize the industry and make it competitive. The making of social welfare policies similarly involves negotiations with business associations, social welfare groups, and possibly trade unions—if the proposed policies affect their members. The outcome of these negotiations depends not only on the organizational characteristics of the groups but on the closeness of their relationship with the state. The state itself is not seen as a monolith, but as an organization with internal fissures that affect its actions.

Although this conception accords fairly well with political practices in many European countries, there are still problems with corporatism as an approach to politics or the study of public policy. First, it is a descriptive category of a particular kind of political arrangement between states and societies (such as in Sweden or Austria), not a general explanation of what governments do, especially those in non-corporatist countries. Thus it has little to say about why countries such as Australia, Canada, and the United States have the particular public policies that they do, except to point out that the lack of institutionalized co-operation between the state and groups in these countries often leads to fragmented and inconsistent policies (Panitch, 1977, 1979).

Second, the theory does little to further our understanding of public policy processes, even in ostensibly corporatist countries. While it is significant to know that not all countries have open-ended competition among groups as suggested by pluralism, this in itself does not say very much about why a policy is adopted or why it is implemented in a particular manner. The close links between governments and certain groups are certainly important, but these are also only one among many factors shaping policies and policy-making (Castles and Merrill, 1989; Keman and Pennings, 1995).

Third, the theory does not contain a clear notion of even its own fundamental unit of analysis, the 'interest' group. Contemporary societies contain myriad interests, and it is not clear which are or should be represented by the state. In some cases, the relevant groups are defined in terms of ethnicity, language, or religion (Lijphart, 1969), while in others they are defined with reference to their economic activities. The bulk of corporatist literature concentrates somewhat arbitrarily on producer groups, such as industry associations and trade unions, and on their role in specific sectors, such as labour market policy and wage bargaining (Siaroff, 1999).

Fourth, the theory is vague about the relative significance of different groups in politics. Are we to treat all groups as equally influential? If not, then what determines their influence? The corporatist literature is silent on such questions. Finally, the theory has no clear conception of the nature of the state, its interests, and why it recognizes some groups and not others as representatives of corporate interests. The answers to these questions vary dramatically among scholars working in the corporatist framework. Some argue that corporatism is a manifestation of an autonomous state desiring to manage social change or ensure social stability (Cawson, 1978). Others suggest it is a system sought by the major corporate actors and thus is simply put into place by the state at their behest (Schmitter, 1985).

Despite its shortcomings, corporatist theory has played a significant role in the analysis of public policy, especially in Europe and Latin America. By highlighting the autonomous role of the state in politics, it paved the way for more sophisticated explanations of public policy-making than those provided by earlier inductive group theories such as pluralism (Smith, 1997). More significantly, by emphasizing the importance of institutionalized patterns of relationships between states and societies, it fostered the emergence of new inductive approaches such as 'statism', which offer a more comprehensive explanation of public policy-making (Blom-Hansen, 2001).

Socio-Historical Neo-Institutionalism: Statism

A third general type of inductive political theory has taken to heart the insights of critics of pluralism and corporatism and has emphasized organized social structures and political institutions it its analyses. Many analyses in this mould focus solely on the state, seeing it as the leading institution in society and the key agent in the political process. Others, however, also attribute explanatory significance to organized social actors in addition to the state.

Both interpretations have their origin in the works of late nineteenth-century German historical sociologists and legal theorists who highlighted the effects of the development of modern state institutions on the development of society. Rather than argue that the state reflected the nature of a nation's populace or social structure, theorists such as Max Weber and Otto Hintze noted how the state's monopoly on the use of force allowed it to reorder and structure social relations and institutions (Hintze, 1975; Nettl, 1968; Weber, 1978).

Sociological or historical neo-institutionalism has been summarized by Stephen Krasner (1988: 67) as follows:

> An institutionalist perspective regards enduring institutional structures as the building blocks of social and political life. The preferences, capabilities, and basic self-identities of individuals are conditioned by these institutional structures. Historical developments are path dependent; once certain choices are made, they constrain future possibilities. The range of options available to policymakers at any given time is a function of institutional capabilities that were put in place at some earlier period, possibly in response to very different environmental pressures.

This perspective explicitly acknowledges that policy preferences and capacities are usually understood in the context of the society in which the state is embedded (Nettl, 1968; Przeworski, 1990; Therborn, 1986). Like its more deductive counterpart, actor-centred institutionalism, Peter Hall described an 'institutionalist' analysis as one focused on the impact of large-scale structures on individuals and vice versa. As he put it:

> The concept of institutions . . . refer[s] to the formal rules, compliance procedures, and standard operating practices that structure the relationship between individuals in various units of the polity and economy. As such, they have a more formal status than cultural norms but one that does not necessarily derive from legal, as opposed to conventional, standing. Throughout the emphasis is on the relational character of institutions; that is to say, on the way in which they structure the interactions of individuals. In this sense it is the organizational qualities of institutions that are being emphasized. (Hall, 1986: 19)

However, historical or sociological neo-institutionalism differs from its deductive counterpart in several critical areas. First, there is no effort made in this approach to reduce institutions to less organized forms of social interaction, such as norms, rules, or conventions. Second, there is no attempt to reduce institutions to the level of individuals and individual activities, such as economic or social transactions. And, third, institutions are simply taken as 'givens', that is, as observable social entities in themselves, with little effort made to derive the reasons for their origins from a priori principles of human cognition or existence (March and Olsen, 1994).

Using such a socio-historical line of analysis yields, to use Theda Skocpol's terms, a 'state-centric' as opposed to 'society-centric' explanation of political life, including public policy-making (Skocpol, 1985). In a 'strong' version of the statist approach, as Adam Przeworski (1990: 47–8) put it in a pioneering book:

> states create, organize and regulate societies. States dominate other organizations within a particular territory, they mould the culture and shape the economy. Thus the problem of the autonomy of the state with regard to society has no sense within this perspective. It should not even appear. The concept of 'autonomy' is a useful instrument of analysis only if the domination by the state over society is a contingent situation, that is, if the state derives its efficacy from private property, societal values, or some other sources located outside it. Within a true 'state-centric' approach this concept has nothing to contribute.

In the statist version of neo-institutional analysis the state is viewed as an autonomous actor with the capacity to devise and implement its own objectives, not necessarily just to respond to pressure from dominant social groups or classes. Its autonomy and capacity are based on its staffing by officials with personal and agency interests and ambitions and the fact that it is a sovereign organization with unparalleled financial, personnel, and—in the final instance—coercive resources. The proponents of this perspective claim that this emphasis on the centrality of the state as an explanatory variable enables it to offer more plausible explanations of long-term patterns of policy development in many countries than do other types of political theory (Krasner, 1984; Skowronek, 1982; Orren and Skowronek, 1998–9).

It is difficult to accept statism in the strong form described above, however. For one, it has difficulty accounting for the existence of social liberties and freedoms or explaining why states cannot always enforce their will, such as in times of rebellion, revolution, civil war, or civil disobedience. In fact, even the most autocratic governments make some attempt to respond to what they believe to be the population's preferences. It is, of course, especially impossible for a democratic state to be entirely autonomous from a society with voting rights. And, as Lindblom and others pointed out, in addition to efforts to maintain and nurture support for the regime among the population, capitalist states, both democratic and autocratic, need to accommodate the imperatives of the marketplace in their policies. Second, the statist view suggests implicitly that all 'strong' states respond to the same problem in the same manner because of their similar organizational features. This is obviously not the case, as different states (both 'strong' and 'weak') often have different policies dealing with the same problem. To explain the differences, we need to take into account factors other than the features of the state (Przeworski, 1990).

To be fair, however, few subscribe to statism in the 'strong' form described above. Instead of replacing the pluralist notion of the societal direction of the state with the statist notion of the state's direction of society, most inductively oriented institutionalist theorists merely want to point out the need to take both sets of factors into consideration in their analyses of political phenomena (Hall and Ikenberry, 1989; McLennan, 1989). As Skocpol herself has conceded:

> In this perspective, the state certainly does not become everything. Other organizations and agents also pattern social relationships and politics, and the analyst must explore the state's structure in relation to them. But this Weberian view of the state does require us to see it as much more than a mere arena in which social groups make demands and engage in political struggles or compromises. (Skocpol, 1985: 7–8)

This milder version of statism thus concentrates on the links between the state and society in the context of the former's pre-eminence in pluralist group theory. To that extent, statism complements rather than replaces society-centredness and restores some balance to social and political theorizing, which, it can be argued, had lost its equilibrium (Orren and Skowronek, 1993; Almond, 1988; Cortell and Peterson, 2001).

CONCLUSION

The first observation to emerge from this brief discussion of the manner in which broad approaches to the study of social phenomena have been applied to public policy-making is that there are many different, often contradictory, ways to approaching the subject of public policy. An extensive literature exists both promoting and denouncing the origins, assumptions, and application of each approach to the subject. Nevertheless, a few general conclusions can be gleaned from this literature.

First, there is an overwhelming tendency in the deductive literature to apply preconceived theoretical insights to actual instances of public policy-making. This is not necessarily a problem, as using this method allows observation of divergence between actual and expected behaviour, which hopefully would lead to refinement of the initial assumptions. However, many deductive-oriented researchers often seem to forget the contingent nature of their hypotheses and the need to constantly test and refine their assumptions against empirical evidence. Consequently, instead of using the study of public policy to test the hypotheses and assess the explanatory capacity of their theories, analysts often simply read public policy-making in terms of the theoretical framework, models, or metaphors they are using (Dobuzinskis, 1992). Application of inductive theories to the study of public policy-making has also revealed that the claim of any of these approaches to the status of a complete 'general theory' is suspect. There has been a distinct evolution of thinking away from welfare economics, pluralism, and corporatism towards neo-institutional analysis, which promotes more open-ended and empirically informed inquiry.

Second, many approaches, both deductive and inductive, tend to explain the phenomena under consideration in incompatible mono-causal terms. This temptation must be resisted if we are to understand public policy. Analysts working in different theoretical frameworks study the same case differently and, not surprisingly, arrive at different conclusions. While bringing different points of view to bear on a question furthers our understanding of a phenomenon, the exercise also involves the danger of turning into a verbal dialogue among the deaf, serving no useful purpose. On the other hand, while some of the problems associated with the general theories discussed above can be overcome by layering multiple units of analysis[5] and combining inductive and deductive methodologies, there are limits to the kinds of syntheses that can be developed at a general level of analysis.

Third, the most widely used approaches in disciplines such as economics and political science, whether they are inductive or deductive in nature, tend to view human activity as part of the struggle to survive in a world in which wants are limitless and the resources available to satisfy them are limited. This view extends to all political phenomena, including public policy-making. In recent times, the policy sciences have begun to abandon this notion of all-pervasive conflict and have suggested that the lessons actors learn from their own and others' experiences are also significant determinants of their behaviour, including policy-making. That is, the objectives actors seek depend on what they believe to be desirable and achievable, which in turn depends on their previous achievements and disappointments. Discussion, arguments, and persuasion among actors are viewed as an integral part of the policy process conceived of as a process of learning by trial, error, and example.[6] The present book is strongly influenced by these emerging trends towards broadening the analytical framework of policy studies to include both conflict and learning and towards a greater emphasis on incorporating the results of empirical analyses of many policy domains into the process of theory-building in policy science.

What this overview reveals, then, is that the policy sciences cannot be furthered simply by applying existing general theoretical approaches, whether deductive or inductive. What is needed in policy analysis, as was suggested in Chapter 1, is an analytical framework that permits consideration of the entire range of factors affecting public policy, and allows hypotheses to be tested through the empirical analysis of the reality analysts are attempting to describe and understand.

Rather than seek a synthesis of general social, political, and economic theories that can explain policy-making, theoretical efforts in the policy sciences should remain firmly rooted in the middle or meso level. That is, policy theory cannot and should not claim to be more than a part of the development of general theories of social and political phenomena whose contours remain to be discerned at some point in the future. However, careful empirical studies and careful generalization can provide a useful middle-range theory and understanding of public policy-making. This theory may be inelegant, but as the discussion of the six general theories presented above reveals, precision and adequacy should be more important meta-theoretical objectives in policy analysis than parsimony and aesthetics. To begin this process of middle-range theory construction, the nature of policy actors, institutions, and instruments will be considered in more detail in Part II.

FURTHER READINGS

Hale, M.Q. 1960. 'The Cosmology of Arthur F. Bentley', *American Political Science Review* 54, 4: 955–61.

Kiser, Larry, and Elinor Ostrom. 1982. 'The Three Worlds of Action', in Ostrom, ed., *Strategies of Political Inquiry*. Beverly Hills, Calif.: Sage, 179–222.

Le Grand, Julian. 1991. 'The Theory of Government Failure', *British Journal of Political Science* 21, 4: 423–42.

McLennan, Gregor. 1989. *Marxism, Pluralism and Beyond: Classic Debates and New Departures*. Cambridge: Polity Press.

March, James G., and Johan P. Olsen. 1984. 'The New Institutionalism: Organizational Factors in Political Life', *American Political Science Review* 78: 734–49.

Nordlinger, Eric A. 1981. *On the Autonomy of the Democratic State*. Cambridge, Mass.: Harvard University Press.

Pigou, A.C. 1932. *The Economics of Welfare*. London: Macmillan.

Schmitter, Phillipe C. 1977. 'Modes of Interest Intermediation and Models of Societal Change in Western Europe', *Comparative Political Studies* 10, 1: 7–38.

Skocpol, Theda. 1985. 'Bringing the State Back In: Strategies of Analysis in Current Research', in Peter B. Evans, Dietrich Rueschemeyer, and Skocpol, eds, *Bringing the State Back In*. New York: Cambridge University Press, 3–43.

Stokey, Edith, and Richard Zeckhauser. 1978. *A Primer for Policy Analysis*. New York: W.W. Norton.

Truman, David R. 1964. *The Governmental Process: Political Interests and Public Opinion*. New York: Knopf.

Van Winden, Frans A.A.M. 1988. 'The Economic Theory of Political Decision-Making', in Julien van den Broeck, ed., *Public Choice*. Dordrecht: Kluwer, 9–57.

Winkler, J.T. 1976. 'Corporatism', *European Journal of Sociology* 17, 1: 100–36.

NOTES

1. Ossowski (1963) has argued that over the course of history there have been four different types of class analysis used to explain political phenomena: dichotomous class systems; gradation schemes; functional conceptions; and the 'Marxian' synthesis of those other models.

2. Keohane (1989: 163) described them as 'persistent and connected sets of rules (formal or informal) that prescribe behavioural roles, constrain activity, and shape expectations'.

3. However, the use of a pluralist analysis in the examination of socialist one-party states proved much more beneficial than earlier analysis based on notions of 'totalitarianism'. For example, see Hough (1972); Skilling (1966).

4. The term 'neo-corporatism' is often used simply to distance contemporary corporatist theory from the authoritarian practices of fascist governments throughout Europe and Latin America in the 1930s and 1940s, which claimed to be corporatist. Neo-corporatism is thought to be a term less likely to conjure up images of militarism, nationalism, or totalitarianism associated with fascism, but is otherwise identical to 'corporatism'. We will, however, use the terms 'corporatism' and 'neo-corporatism' interchangeably. See Malloy (1993); Schmitter (1982); von Beyme (1983).

5. See the efforts to accomplish this in the synthesis of deductive and inductive neo-institutionalisms in Aspinwall and Schneider (2000) and Hollingsworth (2000). On the limits of these efforts, see Hay and Wincott (1998).

6. While the learning theories represent a major departure for policy analysis from political, economic, or sociological theorization, only recently have they started taking the insights of actor- and institution-centred theories into account. See, for example, Stewart (1992) and Livingston (1992).

Part II

Institutions, Actors, and Instruments

Chapter 3

Policy Actors and Institutions

As the discussion in Chapter 2 has shown, there is a vibrant, though ulti-mately inconclusive, debate in the literature on the role of individuals, groups, and institutions in the public policy process. The dispute hinges on the causal significance of the actors' interests and capabilities com-pared to the institutional context or structures in which they operate. Some analysts regard individual and collective actors as the only relevant categories of analysis, while others maintain that what actors seek and do depends on the political, economic, and social structures that sur-round them.

Most of the approaches to public policy discussed in the preceding chapter treat individual and group actors as the key explanatory vari-ables. Thus the welfare economics and public choice theories regard individuals as the agents who shape policy, whereas the theories built on group and class theory, such as pluralism and Marxism, attribute pri-macy to organized groups. While some of the more nuanced of these analyses do consider the institutional context within which these actors operate, their conceptual and methodological predisposition prevents them from dealing adequately with the institutional factors affecting pub-lic policy.

Built on critiques of these early theories, the most recent outgrowths of the evolution of policy-relevant social theorization, such as statism and transaction cost analysis, attempt to take into account both actor-oriented and structural variables. Although their methodologies differ, both approaches treat state organizations as central institutional actors affecting the preferences and activities of other policy actors. Both attempt to explain public policy processes and outcomes in terms of the interacting effects of state objectives and capabilities and those of social actors.

Hence, much recent theorizing reflects the understanding that both actors and institutions play a crucial role in the policy process, even though one may be more important than the other in specific instances

(Lundquist, 1987). Individuals, groups, and classes participating in the policy process no doubt have their own interests, but how they interpret and pursue their interests and the outcomes of their efforts are shaped by institutional factors. Even more significantly, some institutional arrangements are believed to be more conducive to effective policy-making and implementation than others (Stoker, 1989; May, 1993; Siedschlag, 2000).

In this book we follow the statist tendency to define institutions narrowly as actual structures or organizations of the state, society, and the international system. Following this approach, we are less concerned, as opposed to transactions cost analysts and others, with the origins of these institutions, which are taken as empirically given. Rather we are concerned with the way institutions are organized internally and in relation to each other (March and Olsen, 1998). In addition to their formal organizational characteristics—membership, rules, and operating procedures—we do, however, recognize the insights of actor-centred institutionalists who emphasize not just the structural components of organizations but also the principles, norms, and ideas they embody. These principles, in the form of formal or informal rules and conventions, as well as ethical, ideological, and epistemic concerns, help to shape actors' behaviour by conditioning their perception of their interests and the probability of these interests being realized (March et al., 2000; Timmermans and Bleiklie, 1999). While not monolithic, omnipresent, or immutable, institutions cannot be avoided, modified, or replaced without considerable effort.[1]

INTEGRATING ACTORS AND INSTITUTIONS: THE POLICY UNIVERSE AND THE POLICY SUBSYSTEM

Since actors and institutions exist in a mutually defining relationship, it is useful to have a term that can encompass both elements of this fundamental policy relationship. For this purpose, students of the policy sciences have developed the concept of a *policy universe*, thought of as a fundamental unit containing all possible international, state, and social actors and institutions directly or indirectly affecting a specific policy area. From these potential members, a subset is drawn that comprises a sectoral *policy subsystem* (Freeman, 1955; Cater, 1964; Freeman and Stevens, 1987). The policy subsystem is a space where relevant actors discuss policy issues and persuade and bargain in pursuit of their interests. During the course of their interaction with the other actors, they often give up or modify their objectives in return for concessions from others. These interactions, however, occur in the context of various institutional arrangements surrounding the policy process, which affect how the actors pursue their interests and ideas and the extent to which their efforts succeed (Knoke, 1993; Laumann and Knoke, 1987; Sabatier and Jenkins-Smith, 1993b).

A policy subsystem includes both actors who are intimately involved in a policy process as well as others who are only marginally so. In Chapter 6 we will discuss additional terminology developed to describe the actors who participate more often and more directly in the policy process as belonging to *interest networks* and those involved to a lesser degree as belonging to *discourse communities*.[2] Ultimately, we will show how the nature of the relationship between these two components of a subsystem is a significant determinant of the nature of policy content and helps to explain much about fundamental policy dynamics (Peters, 1992a).

Figure 3.1 diagrams the basic relationship between actors and institutions that typically exists in a policy subsystem.

Figure 3.1 Institutions and Actors in a Policy Subsystem

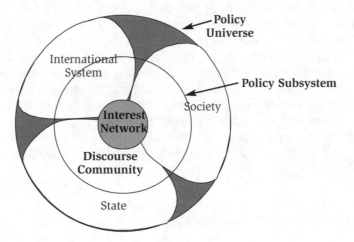

Almost an infinite variety of actors and institutions in the policy universe may actually or potentially constitute a policy subsystem. Composition varies by country, policy sector, or 'domain', and over time (Jordan and Maloney, 1997). The exact composition of a policy subsystem and the relative significance of its constituents is an empirical question that cannot be delineated a priori. All that we can say with certainty is that the policy institutions and actors come from within the machinery of the state and from the society at large. The following discussion is intended to convey a sense of the typical sources of key subsystem actors and institutions, which are drawn from the international system as well as from domestic state and social systems.

INTERNATIONAL SYSTEM

A large body of literature argues that states are increasingly constrained and shaped by global forces (Ohmae, 1995; Falk, 1997). However, for the most part, the public policy literature has tended to focus on domestic state activities and to treat the international realm as an external condition to which domestic policy actors respond rather than as an integral part of the policy process. To the extent that scholars consider international institutions and actors, they usually focus on 'global' or 'transnational' policies, such as trade, environment, and telecommunications (Gummett, 1996; Reinicke, 1998). Moreover, the international realm is often understood in monolithic terms, such that the impact of the international is considered to be constant and not variable across sectors and time. The reality, however, is that the international realm is a differentiated entity in which different international actors have different impacts on domestic policy-making and policy outputs (Hobson and Ramesh, 2002).

Recognition of the international system's influences on public policy is one of the more exciting recent developments in the discipline. The international system not only influences policy sectors that are obviously international—trade and defence, for example—but also sectors with no immediately apparent international connection, such as health care and old age pensions. The sources of influence lie in the overall structure of the international system, and a nation's place in it, and the specific 'regimes' that exist in many policy areas, about which we will say more shortly.

While the international system has probably always affected public policy to some extent, its scope and intensity have increased greatly in recent times. This is the result of what is described as *globalization* or, more precisely, *'internationalization'* (Hirst and Thompson, 1996). Although initially conceived in somewhat simplistic terms, the recent policy literature recognizes the highly complex character of internationalization, the different forms it takes across space and time, and the varying effects it has on different policy sectors and states (Bernstein and Cashore, 2000; Bennett, 1997; Brenner, 1999; Weiss, 1999). This recognition has led researchers to investigate more carefully the means, manner, and mechanisms through which domestic policy processes are linked to the international system (Coleman and Perl, 1999; Risse-Kappen, 1995; Finnemore and Sikkink, 1998; Keck and Sikkink, 1998). Such studies are still at an early stage and the challenge before scholars is to incorporate changes induced by internationalization into existing conceptions of domestic policy processes and its outcomes (Hollingsworth, 1998).

The Policy Effects of International Institutions

Assessing the effects of international institutions is a lot more difficult than assessing those in the domestic arena. For one thing, states are sovereign entities with, in theory, the legal authority to close their borders to any and all foreign influences as and when they choose. In

reality, however, it is nearly impossible for states to stop foreign influences at the border because of constraints rooted in the international system (Held and McGrew, 1993; Walsh, 1994). The extent to which a state
is able to assert its sovereignty depends on the severity of international
pressures and the nature of the issue in question, as well as features
innate to the state itself (Knill and Lehmkuhl, 2002).

To understand the disparate international factors affecting states'
behaviour, scholars have developed the concept of *'international
regimes'* to describe institutionalized arrangements in a given policy area
(Krasner, 1982; Haggard and Simmons, 1987). Regimes have been
defined by Robert Keohane and Joseph Nye (1989: 19) as 'sets of governing arrangements' or 'networks of rules, norms, and procedures that reg-
ularize behaviour and control its effects'. Regimes vary considerably in
form, scope of coverage, level of adherence, and the instruments through
which they are put into practice (Haggard and Simmons, 1987). Some
regimes are based on explicit treaties whereas others are based simply on
conventions that develop as a result of repeated international behaviour.
Some cover a variety of related issues while others are quite narrow in
coverage. Some are closely adhered to and others often are flouted. Some
are enforced through formal or informal penalties whereas others make
no such provision. Some regimes are administered by formal organizations with large budgets and staffs, while some are more akin to moral
codes (see Rittberger and Mayer, 1993).

Regimes affect public policy by promoting certain options and constraining others. More than that, they shape actors' preferences and the
ease with which they can be realized (Doern et al., 1996b). Thus a government willing to assist domestic producers by offering export subsidies, for example, may not be able to do so because of formal or informal
international constraints. Regimes of varying scope and depth can be
found in most, though not all, prominent policy areas.

Mapping all the effects of all international regimes is clearly beyond
the scope of this book. Here we will only outline the regimes prominent
in the areas of trade, finance, and production to illustrate how they affect
public policy.

The International Trade, Finance, and Production Regimes

The edifice on which the contemporary international trade regime is
based is the General Agreement on Tariffs and Trade (GATT) signed in
1947 and succeeded by the World Trade Organization (WTO) in 1995. Its
membership includes almost all states in the world and the vast majority
of world exports are governed by its provisions.

The WTO requires members to work towards lowering trade barriers
by according 'national treatment' to imports[3] and not subsidizing
exports. These requirements are intended to assist internationally competitive producers, at the expense of producers who are not competitive.

The agreement restricts governments' ability to support domestic industries, either through protection against imports or subsidy for exports, although tenacious governments do find ways of getting around the restrictions. The difficulties involved in protecting against imports create opportunities and wealth for successful exporters, and by implication the whole economy, but at the same time impose costs on uncompetitive industries and firms. These costs, again, are often borne by the whole society in the form of higher unemployment and greater public expenditure on social welfare (see Hoekman and Kostecki, 1995).

The international monetary regime has even a greater impact on public policy, especially after the adoption of a flexible exchange rate system in 1976. The fact that exchange rates of currencies are determined by financial markets according to the demand and supply of a country's currency—instead of being fixed by international agreement, as was the case under the earlier, foundational, Bretton Woods agreement of 1944—exposes governments to international financial pressures. Since the financial markets depend on dealers' interpretation of a country's present economic conditions and their expectations for the future, this system often results in unpredictable fluctuations in the value of national currencies. Governments are therefore under constant pressure not to do anything that may, rightly or wrongly, displease the foreign exchange market.

Even more important than the flexible exchange rate system are the effects of financial deregulation and technological improvements that enable the transfer of money around the globe at high speed. By the late 1990s, foreign exchange trading around the world amounted to more than $2 trillion per *day*. With such huge volumes at stake, international money markets have the ability to cause havoc for a country whose policies are viewed unfavourably by international capital. States must now be extremely careful about the effects of their policies, as these affect exchange rates, which in turn affect interest rates and export competitiveness, the repercussions of which are felt by the entire economy. A government's decision to increase expenditure on social welfare, for instance, may be viewed unfavourably by money traders, who may sell off the currency, thereby depreciating it, which may in turn necessitate an increase in interest rates by the government, the result of which will be a slow-down in the economy and higher unemployment. The net result of all these actions and reactions would be negation of the original decision to increase spending. The expected adverse market reaction to budget deficits also limits the scope for using this vital fiscal policy instrument to boost economic activity and lower unemployment (Huber and Stephens, 1998).

Similarly, the liberalization of rules restricting foreign investment, particularly since the 1980s, has led to a massive expansion of foreign direct investment and proliferation of transnational corporations (TNCs), which in turn have affected states' policy options. In 1999, there were 63,000 TNCs that owned 690,000 foreign affiliates with US$17.7 trillion in assets and annual sales exceeding US$13.6 trillion (UNCTAD, 2001). The TNCs not only control large pools of capital, but they are also major players in international trade and control much of the world's leading technology and management skills. Since their primary interest is profits, the TNCs have a motive to locate production where they see the greatest opportunity for maximizing profits.

Given their size and strength, TNCs are major players in the world economy and, by implication, in politics and public policy. They can cause serious damage to a country's economy by withholding investment or deciding to take their investment elsewhere, possibilities that policy-makers can ignore only at great economic peril. There is also now a competition among countries to attract TNCs by offering conditions the latter would find appealing. This often takes the form of a state commitment to control labour costs, maintain tax levels comparable to those in other similar nations, and set minimal restrictions on international trade and investment. All these pressures represent severe restrictions on states' policy options, not just in economic matters but in non-economic matters as well.

The Effects of Internationalization

That being said, international regimes do not affect all nations equally. The more powerful nations enjoy greater policy autonomy within the international system than their less powerful counterparts. This is not only because the powerful states have the capacity to force other nations to change their behaviour but also because others often voluntarily alter their behaviour to match the expectations of the dominant powers (Hobson and Ramesh, 2002). Thus, for example, at the present time any international trade or investment agreement opposed by a predominant trade and investment nation such as the United States is unlikely to be reached, and if it is achieved it is unlikely to be of much significance. The Chinese government is similarly able, for example, to negotiate terms with TNCs desiring access to its gigantic domestic market that are unlikely to be available to most other nations.

The internationalization of the world economy has accelerated the speed with which the effects of events elsewhere (natural calamities, wars, terrorist actions, financial crises, stock market gyrations, etc.) spread via the telecommunications media (Rosenau, 1969). This has expanded the scope for policy spillovers as previously isolated sectors converge, overlap, and collide. What were in the past seen as discrete sectors—such as telecommunications and computers, or agriculture and trade—are now increasingly viewed as elements of a single sector. Any international effort to reduce agricultural subsidies, for instance, has an effect on rural development, social welfare, and environment policies and, ultimately, overall government fiscal policy. Another example is the fear of capital flight, which haunts policy-makers when they are faced with major decisions involving large public expenditures that require tax increases or budget deficits. Traditional social policy areas such as social security and health care have thus become a part of economic policy-making as a result (Unger and van Waarden, 1995; Coleman and Grant, 1998).

Internationalization also creates new opportunities for learning from the policy experiences of others. This is the theme of much recent work on policy transfers, which especially highlights the role of transnational epistemic communities and non-governmental organizations in promoting learning activities (Haas, 1992; Evans and Davies, 1999). The lessons of privatization of telecommunications in Britain and the deregulation of airlines in the United States in the 1980s rapidly spread around the world and across policy sectors because of the active role played by the associated policy communities (Ikenberry, 1990). Moreover, internationalization promotes new patterns of policy-making (Rittberger and Mayer, 1993). When a domestic policy actor loses out in a domestic setting, it now may seek to have the policy transferred to the arena of international organizations if it expects its position to receive a more favourable reception in that venue. Powerful new international organizations and regimes such as the European Union (EU), the WTO, and the North American Free Trade Agreement (NAFTA) have opened up new action channels for domestic policy actors pursuing their interests (Howlett and Ramesh, 2002; Richardson, 1999; Cortell and Davis, 1996; Demaret, 1997).

International Actors

The role of the international actors in public policy-making is both interesting and sensitive, as only national governments and their citizens are usually expected to participate in most domestic policy processes. As the above discussion suggests, however, international actors play an increasingly significant role in many areas of domestic political life. These actors may be individuals working as advisers or consultants to national governments or members of international organizations with the authority under international agreements to regulate their members' behaviour.

International actors vary considerably in their ability to influence domestic policies, and this, to a significant extent, is the result of differences in their resource endowments. One of the strongest resources determining their influence is whether an international regime facilitates their involvement. Such actors are likely to find it easier to intervene in policy sectors in which an international regime sanctioning their intervention already exists (Risse-Kappen, 1995: 6; Coleman and Perl, 1999). The central place occupied by the International Monetary Fund (IMF) in the international monetary regime, for example, enables its officers to interfere in the intimate details of public policy-making in many nations facing serious financial or fiscal problems.

An even more significant resource is the possession of theoretical and practical expertise in a policy sector (Barnett and Finnemore, 1999). Many international organizations—for example, the UN, World Bank, IMF, OECD, World Health Organization (WHO), International Labour Organization (ILO)—are repositories of immense expertise in policy issues, and governments often rely on this expertise when making policies, thus giving such international actors significant influence in the policy process. The financial resources that international organizations can dispense to governments are another source of influence. The differences with respect to levels of expertise and finance are thus often crucial determinants of the different impact that different international actors have on domestic policies (Finnemore and Sikkink, 1998).

However, the nature of the policy subsystem that exists at the national level also affects the international actors' role in the policy process. International actors can be expected to be influential in sectors with fragmented subsystems because such fragmentation allows them greater opportunity for intervention. Conversely, international actors find it difficult to influence policies where the associated subsystem is coherent and united in opposition to external intervention (Risse-Kappen, 1995: 25; Sabatier and Jenkins-Smith, 1993b). The most conducive situation for international actors is, of course, when the subsystem is coherent and in favour of external involvement—in such instances the international actors can be expected to be an integral part of the domestic policy process (Pappi and Henning, 1999).

DOMESTIC STATE SYSTEMS

Two dimensions of the organization of domestic states have a profound effect on the ability of states to make and implement policies: *autonomy* and *capacity*. Autonomy refers to the extent of the state's independence from self-serving and conflicting social pressures. Observers of politics have long argued that the self-serving motives and actions of groups often benefit their members at the expense of the rest of the society (Olson, 1965, 1982). Consequently, policy-making institutions solely responsive to societal demands, as public choice theorists argue is supposed to be the case with democratic governments, can generate policies that benefit some groups but worsen the welfare of the society as a whole. The problem can be overcome, however, if the government is insulated from the need to respond to the societal pressures. While this may compromise some of the basic tenets of democracy, the trade-off is that it is often conducive to more effective collective welfare-enhancing policy-making (Haggard and Moon, 1990: 212). Thus it has been argued that corporatist regimes in Europe and some semi-authoritarian regimes in East Asia, for example, possess the political institutions necessary to resist group demands, and as a result have produced sound policies that, apparently paradoxically, can promote economic prosperity as well as equity (Olson, 1986; Weiss and Hobson, 1995).

But, in addition to autonomy, the state must also have the capacity to make and implement effective policies. The capacity of the state, which is a function of its organizational coherence and expertise, is also a significant determinant of its success in performing policy functions. Unity within and among various levels, branches, and agencies of the government and high levels of bureaucratic expertise are regarded as crucial to enhance state capacity. An executive bogged down in constant bargaining with the legislature or government departments in constant conflict among themselves cannot be expected to perform policy functions adequately. Similarly, the society will not be well served by a bureaucracy without the expertise necessary to tackle the complex problems it is required to address.

States with political institutions that promote autonomy and capacity are sometimes described as *strong states*; those without such institutions are *weak states* (see Atkinson and Coleman, 1989a; Katzenstein, 1977; Nordlinger, 1987). Japan is often cited as a classic example of a strong state in the industrialized world, whereas the United States is described as a weak state; other industrialized countries fall somewhere in between (Katzenstein, 1977). States such as Singapore, South Korea, and Taiwan in East Asia are often regarded as some of the strongest in the world. The executive-bureaucratic apparatus is the core of strong states; weak states have legislatures at their core and interest groups dominate policy-making. The reason why some states are strong and others are weak is usually argued to be primarily historical and related to the conditions present at their origins (Dyson, 1980).

Although describing states as strong or weak is intuitively appealing, it is not without its problems in terms of public policy analysis. First, there is no reason to believe that strong states will necessarily make policies that serve the interests of the society as a whole, rather than those of self-serving groups (Haggard and Moon, 1990: 215). It is just as possible that such states will make ill-conceived or predatory policies that will benefit state elites and lower the society's general welfare. Indeed, in such a situation, a strong state will be worse than a weak state, as far as the society is concerned, because of its higher capacity to cause damage. Military and police governments in Africa, Asia, and Latin America or many former Communist regimes in Eastern Europe are cases in point (see Migdal, 1988). Second, the overall characterization of states as strong or weak is too general to be of much analytical use in sectoral public policy analysis (Atkinson and Coleman, 1989a). No state is strong in all sectors, nor is any state weak in every sector. Thus, even the so-called strong states have shown remarkable weakness in some areas—

note the Japanese government's continued inability to 'rationalize' its agricultural policy—and the supposedly weak states may show remarkable strength in some areas, such as the US government's strong military capacity despite the fragmentation of the overall American state apparatus (Weaver and Rockman, 1993b).

Rather than characterizing states as strong or weak, we must devote efforts to examining empirically the capacity and autonomy of governmental institutions in specific sectoral and subsectoral policy processes. In this regard, whether a state has a federal or unitary form of government and whether its representative institutions are characterized by fusion or division of legislative and executive powers are two important factors affecting the sectoral role of the state.

All governments operate at multiple levels, spatially. In *unitary* systems, the existence of a clear chain of command or hierarchy linking the different levels of government together in a superordinate/subordinate relationship reduces the complexity of multi-level governance and policy-making. Thus, in France or China, for example, the national government retains, in principle, all decision-making powers. It can choose to delegate these powers to lower levels of government or dictate to them, as the case may be, but the role of the central, national government is essentially unchallenged at the top of the country's governmental hierarchy.

The salient feature of *federal* political systems with respect to public policy is the existence of at least two autonomous levels or orders of government within a country. The two levels of government found in countries like Australia, Canada, India, Brazil, Nigeria, and the US, to name only a few (Burgess and Gagnon, 1993; Duchacek, 1970), are not bound together in a superordinate/subordinate relationship but, rather, enjoy more or less complete discretion in matters under their jurisdiction and guaranteed by the constitution. This is distinct from the unitary systems found in countries such as China, Britain, Japan, and New Zealand, where there is only one level of government and the local bodies (for example, regional, county, or municipalities) owe their existence to the national government rather than to the constitution.

Federalism has been cited as a major reason for the weak policy capacity of governments in many policy sectors in Australia, Canada, and the United States. It has constrained these states' capacity to develop consistent and coherent sectoral policies. In these countries, national policies in most areas require intergovernmental agreement, which involves the federal and provincial or state governments in complex, extensive, and time-consuming negotiations with no guarantee that these negotiations will conclude in the manner envisioned by the initiating government (Banting, 1982; Schultz and Alexandroff, 1985; Atkinson and Coleman, 1989b). Similarly, both levels of government are subject to unpredictable judicial review of their measures, which further restricts the ability of governments to realize their objectives.

The existence of a federal system thus significantly affects the capacity of state officials to deal with pressing issues in a timely and consistent fashion because public policies are made and implemented by the national/central as well as state/provincial governments. It makes public policy-making a long, drawn-out, and often rancorous affair as the different governments wrangle over jurisdictional issues or are involved in extensive intergovernmental negotiations or constitutional litigation. Different governments within the same country may make contradictory decisions that may weaken or nullify the effects of a policy (see Grande, 1996; McRoberts, 1993).

Another domestic institutional variable affecting public policy concerns the links between the executive, legislature, and judiciary provided under a country's constitution. In parliamentary systems, the executive is chosen by the legislature from among its members and remains in office only as long as it enjoys majority support from legislators. In presidential systems, the executive is separate from the legislature, is usually elected directly by the voters, and need not enjoy majority support in the legislature (Stewart, 1974). The United States is the archetype of the presidential system, whereas most of the rest of the world has some version of a parliamentary system; other countries, such as France, have a hybrid of the two systems.

The separation between the executive and legislative branches of the government in presidential systems, and the fusion of the two in parliamentary ones, has important consequences for the policy process.[4] The division of powers promotes difficulties for policy-makers in presidential systems. The individual members and committees of the legislature play an active role in designing policies, including those proposed by the President. It matters only marginally if the party of the President's affiliation forms the majority in both houses of the legislature because of the local concerns that often motivate legislators. To ensure majority support for policy measures requiring legislative approval, it is common for the President to bargain with the members of the legislature, offering administrative and budgetary concessions in return for support, and thereby often changing the original intent of a policy proposal. The active involvement of the members of the legislature in drafting bills promotes multiple points of conflict with the executive; it also opens up greater opportunities for interest groups and voters to influence the policy process, the result of which may be diluted or even conflicting policies.

In parliamentary systems, in contrast, the executive can more often than not take legislative support for its measures for granted, thanks to the strict party discipline enforced on individual members of the parliament. While there may be some bargaining over a policy within a party caucus, there is little chance of changing a bill once it has been introduced in parliament. The only time when this may not be the case is when the governing party does not have an outright majority in the legislature and governs in coalition with other parties, who often demand modification to the policy in return for their support. In many countries, especially those with proportional systems of representation that allow for a proliferation of minor parties, coalition governments are routine, which complicates policy-making, though not as much as in the presidential system (Warwick, 2000). Generally speaking, however, policy-making in parliamentary systems is centralized in the executive, which usually enables the government to take decisive action if it so chooses. This is not entirely undesirable, insofar as a state's policy capability is concerned, because the adversarial politics characteristic of legislatures in presidential systems reduces the likelihood of generating coherent policies.

The structure and role of the judiciary also affect the policy process. In federal systems, there is typically an autonomous judiciary entrusted with the task of adjudicating jurisdictional disputes arising from vague constitutional language setting out the respective areas of responsibility for each order of government. The same is true for countries with entrenched bills of civil or human rights, which typically give the courts the power to strike down laws inconsistent with the individual or collective rights guaranteed under the constitution. In these countries, the judiciary acts as another potential veto point that constrains what the executive can do in policy matters (Russell, 1982). In countries without federalism or bills of rights, such as Great Britain, the courts play a more limited role, which permits policy-makers greater room for manoeuvre and latitude in their actions.

However, the role of the judiciary in the policy process varies according to the nature of the country's political institutions. British practices of judicial review, for example, developed out of efforts on the part of central officials under the monarchy to control local officials. Many of these efforts were originally resisted by the local populace, both commoners and nobles, as unwarranted interference in local affairs. When Parliament replaced the monarchy as the source of central political power, however, the same principles of central judicial review of local actions, which had been a symbol of despotism, became a symbol of democratic government. This differs substantially from judicial practices in the US, for example, where, following the American Revolution, the natural-law principles of sovereignty that had informed British legal thought were replaced by principles of natural rights and constitutional supremacy. One manifestation of this was the refusal of the American judiciary to subordinate itself to either Congress or the executive, and to insist on its own role in determining the legality of laws and regulations of all kinds. This has resulted in much more active judges in the US than in Britain, and ones who are much less likely to defer to legislative or executive desires (de Smith, 1973; Jaffe, 1965; Wade, 1965, 1966). Generally speaking, such judicial autonomy and assertiveness complicate policy-making and erode a state's policy capacity.

State Actors

Elected Officials

The elected officials participating in the policy process may be divided into two categories—members of the executive and legislators. The executive, also referred to as the cabinet in many countries, is one of the key players in any policy subsystem. Its central role derives from its constitutional authority to govern the country. While other actors also are involved in the process, the authority to make and implement policies rests ultimately with the executive. There are indeed few checks on the executive in parliamentary systems (such as Japan, Canada, Australia, and Britain) as long as the government enjoys majority support in the legislature. It is somewhat different in republican or presidential systems (as in the United States or Brazil), where the executive often has a difficult task convincing the legislature to approve its measures. But even here, the executive usually has a wide area of discretion beyond legislative control in financial and regulatory matters, as well as in defence, national security, and issues related to international treaty obligations of different kinds.

In addition to its prerogative in policy matters, the executive possesses a range of other resources that strengthen its position. Control over information is one such critical resource. The executive has unmatched information that it withholds, releases, and manipulates in a manner to bolster its preferences and weaken the cases of those opposed to it. Control over fiscal resources is another asset favouring the executive because legislative approval of the budget usually permits wide areas of discretion for the government. The executive also has unparalleled access to mass media in publicizing its positions—the 'bully pulpit' as it is termed in the US—and undermining those of its opponents. Moreover, the executive has the bureaucracy at its disposal to provide advice and to carry out its preferences. It can, and often does, use these resources to control and influence societal actors such as interest groups, mass media, and think-tanks. In many countries, as well, the government has important powers allowing it to control the timing of the introduction and passage of laws in the legislature. This confers a great deal of control over the political agenda on the executive (Bakvis and MacDonald, 1993).

Counteracting the executive's immense constitutional, informational, financial, and personnel resources are conditions that make their task difficult. The tremendous growth in the size, scope, and complexity of government functions over the years, for example, prevents generalist politicians from controlling, or often even being aware of, the many specific activities of government nominally under their control (Adie and Thomas, 1987; Kernaghan, 1979, 1985a). Moreover, in democratic governments ministers are constantly bombarded with societal demands, many of which are mutually contradictory but which they often cannot ignore because of the need to maintain voters' support (Canes-Wrone et al., 2001). Finally, and perhaps most importantly, a government may not have the organizational capacity to make coherent policies and implement them effectively.

Members of the legislature play a very different role in government. In parliamentary systems the task of the legislature is to hold governments accountable to the public rather than to make or implement policies. But the performance of this function permits opportunities for influencing policies. Legislatures are crucial forums where social problems are highlighted and policies to address them are demanded. Legislators also get to have their say during the process of approving government bills and governmental budgets to fund their implementation. In return for their consent, they are sometimes able to demand changes to the policies in question. Legislators may also raise and discuss problems of implementation and request changes. However, a legislature's policy potential often may not be realized in practice. This is because of the dominance enjoyed by the executive and its effects on the internal organization of the legislature and on the role played by legislative committees (Olson and Mezey, 1991).

Most laws are proposed by the executive and more often than not subsequently adopted by the legislature. This is especially so in parliamentary systems where the majority party forms the government and therefore is generally expected to support the passage of bills proposed by the executive. In presidential systems, on the other hand, the legislature is autonomous of the government constitutionally as well as in practice, which explains why presidents, irrespective of whether their party holds a legislative majority, must strike bargains with the legislature or risk defeat of their policy proposals.

The internal organization of the legislature is also a significant determinant of its role in the policy process. Legislatures where the membership is tightly organized along party lines, and marked by a high degree of cohesion and discipline, permit little opportunity for legislators to take an independent stand. This is particularly true in parliamentary systems where the legislators belonging to the governing party are always expected to support the government. Similarly, the role of individual legislators is lower in parliaments in which one party has a clear majority; the existence of several minor parties in coalition governments permits greater opportunity for legislators to express their opinion and force the government to compromise.

In many contemporary legislatures, most important policy functions are performed not on the floor of the legislature but in the committees established along functional or sectoral lines to review proposed legislation. Committees often build considerable expertise in the area with which they deal, and the extent to which this happens enables the legislature to exercise influence over making and implementing policies. But to build expertise, the members need to serve on the committees over a relatively long period of time. Committee members must also not necessarily vote along party lines if their autonomy and assertiveness are to be maintained.

The nature of the problem being considered also affects legislative involvement in the policy process. Technical issues are unlikely to involve legislators because they may not fully understand the problems or solutions, or they may see little political benefit in pursuing the matter. National security and foreign policy-making is also usually conducted in a shroud of secrecy and outside the legislature. Similarly, policies dealing with a problem perceived to be a crisis are unlikely to involve the legislature very much because of the time it takes to introduce, debate, and pass a bill. Policies dealing with allocation or redistribution of resources or income among components of the public generate the highest degree of passion and debate in legislatures, but usually do not have much effect on a government's overall policy orientation. However, other policies related to propagation and maintenance of certain symbolic values—such as the choice of a national flag, immigration, multiculturalism, prayers in schools, or the elimination of racism and sexism—are often so divisive that the executive may be somewhat more willing to take the legislators' views into account in forming legislation.

As a result of these limitations, legislatures generally play only a small role in the policy process in parliamentary systems. While individual legislators, on the basis of their expertise or special interest in a particular issue, can be included in a policy subsystem, legislatures as a whole are not very significant actors in the making or implementing of public policies. In congressional or republican systems, on the other hand, where the legislative agenda is less tightly controlled by the executive, individual legislators can and do play a much more significant role in policy processes and legislative committees are significant members of many policy subsystems.

Appointed Officials
The appointed officials dealing with public policy and administration are often collectively referred to as the 'bureaucracy'. Their function is to assist the executive in the performance of its tasks, as is suggested by the terms 'civil servants' and 'public servants'. However, the reality of modern government is such that their role goes well beyond what one would

expect of a 'servant'. Indeed, bureaucrats are very often the keystone in the policy process and the central figures in many policy subsystems (Kaufman, 2001).

The structure of the bureaucracy has perhaps the strongest effect on public policy processes, especially at the sectoral level. Atkinson and Coleman (1989a: 51) measure state strength in terms of the bureaucracy's strength at the sectoral level, and argue that:

> it is critical to determine, first, the degree to which ultimate decision-making power is concentrated in the hands of a relatively small number of officials and, secondly, the degree to which these officials are able to act autonomously. . . . the state is weak in a given sector when authority is dispersed and no one group of officials can take the lead in formulating policy.

Concentration of power in only a few agencies reduces occasions for conflict and permits long-term policy planning. Diffusion of power, in contrast, fosters inter-agency conflicts and lack of co-ordination; decisions may be made on the basis of their acceptability to all concerned agencies rather than intrinsic merit. The bureaucracy's autonomy from politicians and societal groups also contributes to its strength and effectiveness in policy-making. To be strong, a bureaucracy must have a clear mandate, a professional ethos, and enjoy strong support, but not interference, from politicians in its day-to-day activities. Close ties with client groups are also to be avoided if a bureaucracy is to be effective. An ability to generate and process its own information is also important if reliance on interest groups is to be avoided.

The states in countries like France, Korea, Singapore, and Japan have bureaucracies that enjoy an exalted status in government and society (Katzenstein, 1977). They are said to constitute a homogeneous elite grouping that plays the most important role in the policy process. They undergo long professional training and pursue service in the government as a lifelong career. In other societies, bureaucracies enjoy relatively low status and lack the capacity to resist pressures from legislators or social groups, which often promotes incoherence and short-sightedness in policies.

The effective mobilization of bureaucratic expertise is rarer than commonly believed (Evans, 1992). Despite the massive expansion in bureaucracies throughout the world over the last several decades, weak bureaucracies in the sense understood here are the norm rather than the exception (Evans, 1995). In many countries with corruption, low wages, and poor working conditions, bureaucracies often do not have the capability to deal with the complex problems they are asked to address. If these conditions obtain in a country, then it is quite likely that the state will have difficulty devising effective policies and implementing them in the manner intended. In many countries, even if bureaucratic expertise exists in a particular area, problems of organization and leadership prevent its effective marshalling (Desveaux et al., 1994).

Most of the policy-making and implementation functions once performed by legislatures and the political executive are now performed by the bureaucracy because the functions of modern government are too complex and numerous to be performed by the cabinet alone (see Bourgault and Dion, 1989; Cairns, 1990b; Priest and Wohl, 1980). The bureaucracy's power and influence is based on its command of a wide range of important policy resources (see Hill, 1992: 1–11). First, the law itself provides for certain crucial functions to be performed by the bureaucracy, and may confer wide discretion on individual bureaucrats to make decisions on behalf of the state. Second, bureaucracies have unmatched access to material resources for pursuing their own organizational, even personal, objectives if they so wish. The government is the largest single spender in most (if not all) countries, a situation that gives its officials a powerful voice in many policy areas. Third, the bureaucracy is a repository of a wide range of skills and expertise, resources that make it a premier organization in society. It employs large numbers of just about every kind of professional, hired for their status as experts in their areas of specialization. That they deal with similar issues on a continuing basis endows them with unique insights into many problems. Fourth, modern bureaucracies have access to vast quantities of information on the different aspects of society. At times the information is deliberately gathered, but at other times the information comes to it simply as a part of its central location in the government. Fifth, the permanence of the bureaucracy and the long tenure of its members often give it an edge over its nominal superiors, the elected executive. Finally, the fact that policy deliberations for the most part occur in secret within the bureaucracy denies other policy actors opportunities to mount opposition to its plans.

However, we must avoid exaggerating the role of the bureaucracy. The political executive is ultimately responsible for all policies, an authority it does assert at times. High-profile political issues are also more likely to involve higher levels of executive control. Executive control is also likely to be higher if the bureaucracy consistently opposes a policy option preferred by politicians. Moreover, the bureaucracy itself is not a homogeneous organization but rather a collection of organizations, each with its own interests, perspectives, and standard operating procedures, which can make arriving at a unified position difficult. Even within the same department, there are often divisions along functional, personal, political, and technical lines. Thus it is not uncommon for the executive to have to intervene to resolve intra- and inter-bureaucratic conflicts, and bureaucrats in democratic countries require the support of elected officials if they are to exercise their influence in any meaningful way (Sutherland, 1993).

Societal Structures and Actors

Political Economic Structures

The capabilities of a state are determined not just by how it is situated in the international order and how it is organized internally, but also by how it is linked to the society whose problems it is supposed to resolve through appropriate policies. To be able to make and implement policies effectively, the state needs the support of prominent social actors for its actions. The extent to which these actors are able to offer the necessary level and form of support depends, among other things, on their own internal organization. Fragmentation within and among prominent social groups weakens the state's ability to mobilize them towards the resolution of societal problems. If the societal conflicts are particularly severe, the state may find itself paralyzed in performing many policy functions.

On the other hand, unity within and among social groups makes for a stable policy environment that facilitates policy-making and promotes effective implementation. Strong organizations can bargain more effectively and need not make unreasonable demands for the sake of maintaining their members' support. And when they agree to a measure, they can enforce it upon their membership, through sanctions if necessary. Mancur Olson has argued that in societies characterized by 'encompassing' (that is, umbrella groups consisting of a variety of similar interests) rather than 'narrow' interest groups, the groups 'internalize much of the cost of inefficient policies and accordingly have an incentive to redistribute income to themselves with the least possible social cost, and to give some weight to economic growth and to the interests of society as a whole' (Olson, 1982: 92). The existence of numerous narrow interest groups, in contrast, promotes competition among groups that pressure the state to serve their members' interests only, regardless of the effects on others. The cumulative effect of such action often can be contradictory and ineffective policies that leave everyone worse off.

The problem of societal fragmentation is particularly severe when narrow sectional groups are too strong to be ignored by even a strong state, or if the state is too weak to ignore societal pressures. However, the best situation, insofar as effective making and implementing of policies is concerned, is for both state and society to be strong, with close partnership between the two. Peter Evans (1992) calls this institutional arrangement 'embedded autonomy'. In contrast, policy effectiveness is lowest when the state is weak and the society fragmented. In the former scenario, states in partnership with social groups can be expected to devise cohesive and long-term policies. In the latter, the state can be expected to produce only short-term and, usually, ineffective policies.

Business Actors

As pointed out by both neo-pluralist and corporatist theorists, the organization of business and labour is often most significant in determining a state's policy capabilities. This is because of the vital role each plays in the production process, which is, in every society, a fundamental activity that has effects far beyond the economy.

Among interest groups, business is generally the most powerful, with an unmatched capacity to affect public policy. To understand what is referred to as the 'structural power of capital', we need to comprehend the broader socio-economic context of a capitalist economy. Such an economy, by definition, entails a market form of economic organization in which ownership of the means of production is concentrated in the hands of the corporations. This fact lies at the root of business's unparalleled power (Lindblom, 1977).

The increasing globalization of production and financial activities, due to improvements in modern means of communication and transportation and the gradual removal of controls on international economic transactions, has contributed tremendously to the power of capital in recent decades. It is possible for investors and managers to respond, if they so wish, to any unwanted government action by moving capital to another location. Although this theoretical mobility is limited by a variety of factors—including the availability of suitable investment opportunities in other countries—the potential loss of employment and revenues is a threat with which the state must contend in making decisions. Because of their potential to affect state revenues negatively, capitalists—both domestic and foreign—have the ability to 'punish' the state for any action it might take of which they disapprove (Hayes, 1978).

The financial contributions that businesses make to political parties also afford them an important resource for influencing policy-makers. Elections can sometimes turn on relatively short-term issues and personalities, which necessitate large budgets to influence voters through extensive media advertising campaigns. In such situations, political parties supported by contributions from business are in a better position to run such campaigns and thus influence voting behaviour. This can lead political parties and candidates running for office to accommodate business interests more than they would those of other groups. Similarly, the financial contributions that businesses often make to public policy research institutions and individual researchers serve to further entrench their power. The organizations and individuals receiving funds tend to be sympathetic towards business interests and can provide business with the intellectual wherewithal often required to prevail in policy debates (McGann and Weaver, 1999; Abelson, 1999).

The structural strength of business has the potential to both promote and erode social welfare. The latter is likely to be the case when business lacks organizational coherence. The ability of individual firms and capitalists to pressure the government to serve their interests can lead, if the latter succumbs to the pressure, to incoherent and short-sighted policies.

Endemic conflicts among various business groups only aggravate such situations. The problem may be offset if business has a central cohesive organization—or *peak association*—able to thrash out differences and come up with coherent policy proposals. If the government does accept such proposals, they are likely to serve the interest of the broader economy (though not all sections of the society equally) rather than the interests of particular firms or economic sectors. A strong business organization is therefore a necessary, though not sufficient, condition for coherent and effective policy-making.

A strong business organization is able to adopt a bold position if necessary and convey it to the government, without incurring serious opposition from its rank and file. It usually takes the form of a peak association (a sort of federation of associations) with the authority to impose sanctions and discipline among its members, since the state must have confidence that once a commitment has been made by the association, it can expect adherence to it by individual businesses. Moreover, if the state is confident of the strength of the business association, then it can delegate some business-related responsibilities to the business association itself. Generally speaking, the US is regarded as having the weakest business organizations in the industrialized world and Japan the strongest, with countries like Britain or Canada falling closer to the US model. Other European countries, such as France, Spain, Germany, Austria, and Sweden, fall closer to the Japanese model (Katzenstein, 1977).

The strength or weakness of business and the varying patterns of government-industry relations found in a country are usually shaped by a range of historical factors (Wilson, 1990a). Although the example of Japan cited above is somewhat atypical, business is often strongly organized if it has been confronted with strong, persistent challenges from trade unions or socialist parties. The stronger the unions, the stronger will be the business influence. The threat does not necessarily have to be continuing, so long as such was the case in the past. Second, countries with strong states often have strong business organizations because, in order to pressure strong governments, business itself must be well organized. A strong state may also nurture a strong business association in order to avoid the problems arising from too many groups making conflicting demands on the same issue. The existence of strong business associations simplifies the government's job by aggregating their demands within the organization. Third, the organizational strength of business is affected by the structure of the economy. In national economies characterized by low industrial concentration or high levels of foreign ownership, it is difficult for the disparate elements to organize and devise a common position. Fourth, political culture, too, has an important bearing on the extent and nature of business involvement in politics. In countries such as the US and Canada with cultures highly supportive of business, corporations have seen few reasons to organize.

Moreover, the degree to which social norms approve of functional representation affects the strength of business. Americans, and to a lesser extent citizens of Britain, Canada, Australia, and other Anglo-American democracies, are distrustful of business representing their interests on a regular basis behind closed doors. In the corporatist countries, on the other hand, functional representation is accepted and indeed is often encouraged (Siaroff, 1999).

Labour

Labour, too, occupies a powerful position among social groups, though not so powerful as business. Unlike business, which enjoys considerable weight with policy-makers even at the individual level of the firm, labour needs a collective organization, a trade union, to have its voice heard in the policy subsystem. In addition to bargaining with employers on behalf of their members' wages and working conditions, which is their primary function, trade unions engage in political activities to shape government policies affecting them (Taylor, 1989: 1). The origin of the role of the trade unions in the public policy process is rooted in late nineteenth-century democratization, which enabled workers, who form a majority in every industrialized society, to have a say in the functioning of the government. Given the voting clout afforded them by democracy, it was sometimes easier for them to pressure the government to meet their needs than to bargain with their employers. The creation of labour or social democratic parties, which eventually formed governments in many countries, further reinforced labour's political power (Qualter, 1985).

The nature and effectiveness of the trade unions' participation in the policy process depend on a variety of institutional and contextual factors. The structure of the state itself is an important determinant of union participation in the policy process. A weak and fragmented state will not be able to secure effective participation by unions, because the latter would see little certainty that the government would be able to keep its side of any bargain. Weak businesses can also inhibit the emergence of a powerful trade union organization because the need for it is less immediate.

However, the most important determinant of labour's capacity to influence the policy process and its outcomes is its own internal organization. The level of union membership affects the extent to which states seek or even accept union participation in the policy process. The same is true for the structure of bargaining units: decentralized collective bargaining promotes a fragmented system of articulation of labour demands. Britain, Canada, and the United States, for example, have decentralized bargaining structures, whereas in Australia, Austria, and the Scandinavian countries bargaining takes place at the industry or even country-wide level (Esping-Andersen and Korpi, 1984; Hibbs, 1987). A union movement fragmented along any or all of possible regional, linguistic, ethnic, religious, or industrial versus craft, foreign versus domestic, or import-competing versus export-oriented lines will also experience difficulties in influencing the policy process. Fragmentation among labour ranks tends to promote local and sporadic industrial strife and incoherent articulation of labour's interest in the policy process (Hibbs, 1978; Lacroix, 1986).

Finally, to realize its policy potential labour needs a central organization, such as the Australian or British Trade Union Congress (TUC), the Canadian Labour Congress (CLC), and the American Federation of Labor–Congress of Industrial Organizations (AFL–CIO), even more than does business. Collective action is the only tool labour has to influence the employers' or the government's behaviour, so the more united a front it is able to put up, the more successful it is likely to be. To be effective, the trade union central needs to enjoy comprehensive membership and have the organizational capacity to deal with conflicts among its members and maintain unity. Trade unions' role in the policy process tends to be the highest in corporatist political systems, such as in the Scandinavian countries, Austria, and the Netherlands, where the state encourages the formation and maintenance of strong trade union centrals, and the lowest in pluralist political systems such as the United States and Canada, where it does not.[5]

Political Structures and Actors

The nature of a country's political economy, therefore, has an important structural impact on policy-making. In liberal capitalist, 'Western' societies, for example, this generates at least two important policy actors, business and labour, which are involved in many policy deliberations and activities. However, other important policy actors, linked to the structures and institutions of representative democracy, also exist in these societies.

The Public
Surprising as it may appear, the 'public' plays a rather small direct role in the public policy process. This is not to say that its role is inconsequential, as it provides the backdrop of norms, attitudes, and values against which the policy process is displayed. However, in most liberal democratic states policy decisions are taken by representative institutions that empower specialized actors to determine the scope and content of public policies, rather than the public per se determining policy.

One important role played by members of the public in democratic polities, of course, is voting. On the one hand, in democratic states voting is the most basic means of participating in the political and, by implication, policy processes. It not only affords citizens the opportunity to express their choice of government, but also empowers them to pressure political parties and candidates seeking their votes to offer them attractive policy packages. On the other hand, the voters' policy capacity usually cannot be actualized, at least not directly, for various reasons. In modern democracies policies are made by representatives of voters who, once elected, are not required to heed the preferences of their constituents in their day-to-day functioning. Moreover, as was discussed above, most legislators participate very little in the policy process, which tends to be dominated by experts in specific sectoral areas rather than by legislative generalists (Edwards and Sharkansky, 1978: 23). More significantly, candidates and political parties often do not run in elections on the basis of their policy platforms; and even when they do, voters usually do not vote on the basis of proposed policies alone. Having said that, it is true that politicians do heed public opinion in a general sense while devising policies, even though they do not always respond to or accommodate it.

The impact of public opinion on policy processes is more frequent and pervasive, although even less direct than voting. Despite many works over the past decades that have consistently found the relationship between public opinion and public policy-making in democratic societies to be a tenuous, complex one, there persists a tendency to view this relationship as simple, direct, and linear (see Luttbeg, 1981; Shapiro and Jacobs, 1989). That is, from at least the time of the early works on the subject by scholars such as V.O. Key (1967), E.E. Schattschneider (1960), and Bernard Berelson (1952) in the 1940s, 1950s, and 1960s, prominent political scientists and others have repeatedly found little or no direct linkage between public opinion and policy outcomes. Nevertheless, in study after study this finding has been made and remade, as investigators appear dissatisfied with it (Monroe, 1979; Page and Shapiro, 1992). As Schattschneider suggested, this is no doubt due to the sincere but sometimes simplistic notions of democracy held by many analysts, who support the notion of 'government *for* the people' and feel uneasy that that this might not be accomplished through 'government *by* the people'.[6]

But both the policy and democratic processes are much more complex than linear linkage theories suggest. Democracy means more than mob rule, and political theorists from Edmund Burke onward have noted the complex notions of popular representation that democratic governments contain (Birch, 1972). Analyzing the role of public opinion in contemporary democratic governments requires a nuanced analysis of the realities of democratic governance and policy-making processes. While a concern for popular sovereignty is laudable, as Schattschneider has suggested, theoretical speculations must be tempered by empirical facts if the nature of the relationship existing between public opinion and public policy is to be adequately described and understood.

The simplest model of the relationship between public opinion and public policy-making views government as a policy-making machine—

directly processing popular sentiments into public policy decisions and implementation strategies. As has been pointed out repeatedly over the course of studies into the subject in the past half-century in the United States and elsewhere, however, this account is problematic (Erikson et al., 1980; Erikson et al., 1989). It assumes that public opinion has a concrete, quasi-permanent character that can be easily aggregated into coherent policy positions. Innumerable studies, however, have underlined the vague, abstract, and transitory nature of public opinion, and have emphasized the difficulties encountered in aggregating the 'babble of the collective will', as Rousseau put it, into universally endorsed policy prescriptions (Rousseau, 1973; also see Lowell, 1926). Moreover, many opinion researchers and policy scholars have noted how these difficulties have multiplied as scientific and complex legal issues have come to dominate policy-making in contemporary societies, further divorcing policy discourses from public ones (see Pollock et al., 1989; Torgerson, 1996; Hibbing and Theiss-Morse, 2002).

This is only the first of several major logical and empirical problems encountered by direct linear-linkage theories of democratic representation. Even assuming that public sentiments could be delivered directly and in a consistent form to policy-makers, the model encounters several other, terminal, problems. For one, it attributes very little autonomy to governments. Exactly how governments acquire and process information is not considered to be a major issue, except insofar as these processes 'block' the transmission of popular sentiments into government action. But the processes by which government agendas are established and policy options formulated are by no means simple and unproblematic. Numerous studies have underlined the complex nature of policy construction and the multiple competing interpretations of social reality and potential policy responses to social issues that governments face in contemplating action (Holzner and Marx, 1979; Schneider, 1985; Samuels, 1991; Livingston, 1992). Many others have underlined the complex nature of decision-making processes in government, which belie the simple machine-like formulations of the linear-linkage model. Finally, the model also sees as unproblematic the various linkages that exist between the implementation or execution of policy and the enactment of policy decisions and pronouncements. Once again, an enormous literature in public administration underlines the complexity of implementation processes and belies the notion that government officials simply execute decisions in a neutral and 'objective' way (see Forester, 1984; Lindblom and Cohen, 1979; Weiss, 1977a).

Not surprisingly, these difficulties with simple models of direct public opinion effects led some students of the public opinion–public policy relationship to develop more sophisticated ones that took some of these concerns into account. However, while some proposed alternate general visions of the nature of the relationship between opinion and policy, many can be seen as attempts to rescue simple linear models by altering only secondary aspects of the general model.

Anthony Downs's well-known model of the issue-attention cycle, for instance, provides a good example of a linear-linkage model that takes into account the vague and transitory nature of public opinion on specific policy issues. As set out in his 1972 article on environmental policy-making, public policy-making in many areas of social life tends to revolve around specific issues that momentarily capture public attention and demand government action. However, he also noted that many of these problems soon fade from view as their complexity or intractability became apparent. As he put it:

> public attention rarely remains sharply focused upon any one domestic issue for very long—even if it involves a continuing problem of crucial importance to society. Instead, a systematic issue-attention cycle seems strongly to influence public attitudes and behaviour concerning most key domestic problems. Each of these problems suddenly leaps into prominence, remains there for a short time, and then—though still largely unresolved—gradually fades from the center of public attention. (Downs, 1972: 38)

The idea of a systematic issue-attention cycle in public policy-making gained a great deal of attention in subsequent years and Downs's work is often cited as an improved model for explaining the linkages between public opinion and public policy (see, e.g., Dearing and Rogers, 1996).

A reasonable conclusion to reach on the basis of the above discussion is that whatever the policy effects of public opinion, they are not direct in nature. As many students of this relationship have noted, this raises several possibilities. One is that public opinion has no effect, a possibility ruled out by the many empirical studies that have found some general correspondence between the behaviour of public policy-makers and public opinion in some issue areas (see, e.g., Weber and Shaffer, 1972; Bennett, 1980). A second is that rather than directly affecting public policy-making in specific sectors, generalized public opinion—the policy mood or policy sentiment of a population at a particular time—makes up one element of the background conditions or environment in which the policy process unfolds (Durr, 1993; Stimson, 1991; Adams, 1997; Best, 1999).

Think-Tanks and Research Organizations

Another significant set of societal actors in the policy process is composed of the researchers working at universities, research institutes, and think-tanks on particular policy issues and issue areas. University researchers often have theoretical and philosophical interests in public problems that may not lead to research results that can be translated directly into usable knowledge for policy purposes. To the extent that they do conduct research for the purpose of participating in policy debates, they often function in a manner similar to their counterparts in think-tanks. Indeed, in many instances academics undertaking directly relevant policy research are sponsored by think-tanks (Ricci, 1993; Stone et al., 1998). The following discussion will therefore concentrate on the role of these private, ideologically based organizations.

A think-tank can be defined as 'an independent organization engaged in multidisciplinary research intended to influence public policy' (James, 1993: 492). Such organizations maintain an interest in a broad range of policy problems and employ, either full-time or on a contract basis, experts on various issue areas in order to develop a comprehensive per-spective on the issues facing governments. Their research tends to be directed at proposing practical solutions to public problems or, in the case of some think-tanks, finding evidence to support the ideological or interest-driven positions they advocate. This sets them apart somewhat from academic researchers at universities, whose interests are more spe-cialized and who do not necessarily seek practical solutions to policy problems. Explicitly partisan research is also generally eschewed in academia.

However, while think-tanks are generally more partisan than their purely academic counterparts, they, too, must maintain an image of intellectual autonomy from the government or any political party if pol-icy-makers are to take them seriously. Large prominent think-tanks in the United States include the Brookings Institution, the American Enterprise Institute, and the Urban Institute. Similar organizations in Canada include the C.D. Howe Institute, the Fraser Institute, the Canadian Centre for Policy Alternatives, and the Institute for Research on Public Policy. Major think-tanks in Britain include the Policy Studies Institute and the National Institute for Economic and Social Research. Literally hundreds of such institutes are active in the Western, developed countries, some with broad policy mandates, others that are more limited in their purview, such as the Canadian Environmental Law Association (Lindquist, 1993; Abelson, 1996).

Think-tanks target their research and recommendations to those politicians who may be expected to be favourably disposed to the ideas being espoused (Abelson, 2002). They also seek originality in their ideas and, unlike the researchers working in universities or the government, spend a great deal of effort publicizing their findings (Dobuzinskis, 2000; Stone, 1996; Weaver, 1989). The need for a quick response to policy issues and problems has forced many think-tanks to develop new 'prod-uct lines'. Short pithy reports, journal articles, and policy briefs that can be quickly read and digested have replaced book-length studies as the primary output of many think-tanks. In addition, a premium has been placed on writing articles and op-ed pieces for newspapers and making appearances on radio and television programs. This new brand of research and analysis is dependent on 'the public policy food chain', which includes a range of knowledge- and policy-oriented institutions. Over the last few decades, much of the work of think-tanks has been devoted to promoting economic efficiency, since this has been an important preoccupation of the governments in the industrialized world.

A number of trends have become evident in recent years with respect to the functioning, operation, and influence of think-tanks in many countries. Some of the more prominent trends include:

- *The increasing complexity of policy debates.* The twin movements of democracy and diversity have served to involve groups that, historically, have not been represented in domestic and international affairs. Women, indigenous groups, and non-governmental organizations are now playing a central role in developing and implementing foreign affairs policies and programs. These new entrants to the policy debates have created many new specialized think-tanks and public policy research organizations.
- *The transborder nature of many contemporary problems and the networking of think-tanks and policy institutes.* At the international level, globalization/internationalization simultaneously unites and divides the countries of North/South and East/West. Transnational problems such as AIDS, hunger, and global warming require a global response. Some think-tanks have responded by becoming transnational organizations in the effort to bridge the chasm between North/South and East/West. In addition, the emergence of regional or continental economic alliances such as the EU and NAFTA has created new networks of regionally oriented policy institutions.
- *The downsizing of governments and the increasing competition among think-tanks for funding.* The proliferation of think-tanks has been accompanied by cutbacks in public funds available for research. In many countries, federal, provincial, and local governments have cut their funding for public policy research. This happened as policy units in governments were downsized or eliminated in budget-cutting exercises in the 1990s. At the same time, events occurring elsewhere, such as the end of the Cold War, had a profound impact on the funding of research organizations focused on areas such as international and security affairs since donors and governments no longer saw the need for such research. As a result, think-tanks have had to devote considerable resources to raising funds rather than conducting research and producing position papers (McGann and Weaver, 1999).

Analysts working in universities or government tend to choose to work on problems determined by the public's or the government's interest, or by their own personal curiosity about a particular subject, and have largely avoided the specific problems facing think-tanks in the contemporary environment. Through sustained analysis and critique, however, these researchers can have a notable impact on public policy, largely through what Carol Weiss has termed their 'enlightenment function' (Weiss, 1977a, 1977b; Bryman, 1988). This role can also be taken on by consultants, who can serve to carry the ideas and results of policy research directly to governments (Lapsley and Oldfield, 2001).

Political Parties

Political parties are an intermediating actor, like think-tanks, existing on the margins or border between state and societal actors. They have a significant impact on public policy, though in the modern era this usually has been only indirectly. They tend not to be represented in policy subsystems, though many of the actors in the subsystem may be influenced by the party to which they are affiliated. Political parties tend to influence public policy indirectly, primarily through their role in staffing the executive and, to a lesser degree, the legislature. Indeed, once in office, it is not uncommon for party members in government to ignore their official party platform while designing policies (Thomson, 2001).

Political parties' impact on policy outcomes has been the subject of some limited, but specific, empirical research and commentary (Blais et al., 1996; Castles, 1982; Imbeau and Lachapelle, 1993; McAllister, 1989). Findings concerning the role of parties in public policy-making, for example, have included evidence that, historically, European governments led by Christian and social democratic parties have been related positively to the development of welfare state programs (Wilensky, 1975; Korpi, 1983), and that 'left-wing' and 'right-wing' governments have had different fiscal policy orientations towards, respectively, unemployment and inflation reduction (Hibbs, 1977). Partisan differences have also been linked to different characteristic preferences for certain types of policy tools, such as public enterprises or market-based instruments (Chandler and Chandler, 1979; Chandler, 1982, 1983). However, the contemporary significance of parties has also been challenged by those who argue that government has become too complex for influence by partisan generalists, with day-to-day influence stemming more from policy specialists in government and those in the employ of interest groups and specialized policy research institutes (King and Laver, 1993; Pross, 1992). Similarly, other studies focusing on the extent of policy learning and emulation occurring between states or subnational units (Lutz, 1989; Poel, 1976; Erikson et al., 1989) and those examining the impact of international influences on domestic policy-making have argued the case for the reduced importance of parties in contemporary policy processes (Johnson and Stritch, 1997; Doern et al., 1996a).

The idea that political parties play a major role in public policy processes, of course, stems from their undeniable influence on elections and electoral outcomes in democratic states. While vote-seeking political parties and candidates attempt to offer packages of policies they hope will appeal to voters, the electoral system is not structured to allow voters a choice on specific policies. Likewise, as discussed above, the representational system also limits the public's ability to ensure that electorally salient policy issues actually move onto official government agendas (King, 1981; Butler et al., 1981). The official agenda of governments is, in fact, usually dominated by routine or institutionalized agenda-setting opportunities rather than by partisan political activity (Kingdon, 1984; Walker, 1977; Howlett, 1997a).

Even when parties do manage to raise an issue and see it move from the public to the official agenda, they cannot control its evolution past that point. As Richard Rose (1980: 153) has put it:

> A party can create movement on a given issue, but it cannot ensure the direction it will lead. Just as defenders of the status quo may find it difficult to defend their position without adapting it, so too proponents of change face the need to modify their demands. Modifications are necessary to secure the agreement of diverse interests within a party. They will also be important in securing support, or at least grudging acceptance, by affected pressure groups. Finally, a governing party will also need to make changes to meet the weaknesses spotted by civil service advisors and parliamentary draftsmen responsible for turning a statement of intent into a bill to present to Parliament.

While their direct influence may be muted, however, their indirect influence is not. The role played by political parties in staffing political executives and legislatures, of course, allows them considerable influence on the content of policy decisions taken by those individuals, including those related to the staffing of the senior public service. However, this power should not be overestimated. In modern governments, as we have seen, the degree of freedom enjoyed by each decision-maker is circumscribed by a host of factors that limit the conduct of each office and constrain the actions of each office-holder. These range from limitations imposed by the country's constitution to the specific mandate conferred on individual decision-makers by various laws and regulations (Pal, 1988; Axworthy, 1988). Various rules set out not only which decisions can be made by which government agency or official, but also the procedures they must follow in doing so.

Political parties tend to have only a diffuse, indirect effect on policy-making through their role in determining who actually staffs legislative, executive, and judicial institutions. Their role in agenda-setting is very weak, while they play a stronger, but still indirect, role in policy formulation and decision-making due to the strong role played in these two stages of the policy cycle by members of the political executive. Their role in policy implementation is virtually nil, while they can have a more direct effect on policy evaluation undertaken by legislators and legislative committees (Minkenberg, 2001).

The fact that the influence of parties on particular stages of the policy process may be muted, or that any such influence may be waning, does not necessarily lead to the conclusion that 'parties don't matter'. That is, as Richard Rose argued almost a quarter-century ago in the case of Britain:

> Parties do make a difference in the way [a country] is governed— but the differences are not as expected. The differences in office between one party and another are less likely to arise from con- trasting intentions than from the exigencies of government. Much of a party's record in office will be stamped upon it from forces out- side its control. . . . parties are not the primary forces shaping the destiny of . . . society; it is shaped by something stronger than par- ties. (Rose, 1980: 141; also see Hockin, 1977)

Mass Media

The media consist of other important intermediating actors active in the policy-making process. Some regard the role of the mass media in the policy process as pivotal (Herman and Chomsky, 1988; Parenti, 1986)[7] while others describe it as marginal (Kingdon, 1984). There is no deny- ing that the mass media are crucial links between the state and society, a position that allows for significant influence on the preferences of gov- ernment and society in regard to the identification of public problems and their solutions. Yet at the same time, like political parties, their direct role in the various stages of the policy process is often sporadic and most often quite marginal.

The role of the media in the policy process originates in the fact that in reporting problems they function both as passive reporters and as active analysts, as well as advocates of particular policy solutions. That is, news programs do not just report on a problem but often go to great lengths in locating a problem not otherwise obvious, defining its nature and scope, and suggesting or implying the availability of potential solu- tions. The media's role in agenda-setting is thus particularly significant (Spitzer, 1993; Pritchard, 1992). Media portrayal of public problems and proposed solutions often conditions how they are understood by the pub- lic and many members of government, thereby shutting out some alter- natives and making the choice of others more likely. Questions in parliamentary question periods or at presidential press conferences are often based on stories in the day's television news or newspapers.

This is particularly significant considering that news reporting is not an objective mirror of reality, undistorted by bias or inaccuracy. Reporters and editors are newsmakers, in the sense that they define what is worthy of reporting and the aspects of a situation that should be highlighted. Thus, policy issues that can be translated into an interesting story tend to be viewed by the public as more important than those that do not lend themselves so easily to narrative structures and first-person accounts and sound bites. This partially explains why, for example, crime stories receive so much prominence in television news and, as a corollary, the public puts pressure on governments to appear to act tough on crime. Similarly, groups and individuals able to present problems to the media in a packaged form are more likely than their less succinct counterparts to have their views projected (Callaghan and Schnell, 2001; Lutz and Goldenberg, 1980; Herman and Chomsky, 1988; Parenti, 1986).

We must not, however, exaggerate the mass media's role in the policy process. Other policy actors have resources enabling them to counteract media influence, and policy-makers are for the most part intelligent and resourceful individuals who understand their own interests and have their own ideas about appropriate or feasible policy options. As a rule, they are not easily swayed by media portrayals of issues and preferred policy solutions or by the mere fact of media attention. Indeed, they often use the media to their own advantage. It is not uncommon for public officials and successful interest groups to provide selective information to the media to bolster their case (Lee, 2001). Indeed, very often the media are led by state opinion rather than vice versa (Howlett, 1997a, 1997b).

Interest Groups

A fourth significant intermediating actor, as pluralist political theorists recognized, is the organized special interest group. While policy-making is a preserve of the government, and particularly of the executive and bureaucracy, the realities of modern politics enable groups formed specifically to promote the interests or positions of specialized social groups to play a significant role in the process. One of the most important resources of such interest groups is knowledge, specifically information that may be unavailable or less available to others. The members of specialized groups often know the most about their area of concern. Since policy-making is a highly information-intensive process, those with information may normally expect to play an important role in it. Politicians and bureaucrats often find the information provided by special interest groups indispensable for performing their tasks. Government and opposition politicians at times curry favour with such groups to secure the information required for effective policy-making or for attacking their opponents. Bureaucrats similarly often need these groups' help in developing and implementing many policies (Hayes, 1978; Baumgartner and Leech, 1998).

The other resources possessed by interest or pressure groups are organizational and political. Special interest groups often make financial contributions to the campaign chests of sympathetic political parties and

politicians. They also campaign for and deliver votes to sympathetic candidates who they think would support their cause in the government.
However, interest groups' political impacts on the formulation and implementation of public policies vary considerably according to their access
to differing levels of organizational resources (Pross, 1992; Baumgartner
and Leech, 2001). First, interest groups differ tremendously in terms of
size of membership. All other things being equal, larger groups can be
expected to be taken more seriously by the government.[8] Second, as discussed above in the context of business and labour associations, some
groups may form a 'peak association' consisting of representatives from
other groups with similar interests (Coleman, 1988). A coherent peak
association may be expected to be more influential than those interest
groups operating individually. Third, some groups are well funded,
which enables them to hire permanent specialized staff and influence
parties and candidates during elections. While the exact impact of interest group campaign expenditures on government policy is contentious,
there is no doubt that differences in financial resources matter (Nownes
and Neeley, 1996; Nownes, 1995, 2000; Nownes and Cigler, 1995) and
that in democratic political systems the information and power resources
of interest groups make them key members of policy subsystems. While
this does not guarantee that their interests will be accommodated, they
are unlikely to be entirely ignored except in rare circumstances when
executives make a high-level and deliberate decision to go ahead with a
policy despite opposition from concerned groups.

CONCLUSION

The chapter began by noting that policy processes draw upon actors
from a subset of members of the policy universe, increasingly at both the
domestic and international levels. Policy subsystems are constructed
from this universe, involving both state and societal actors in complex
systems of interaction. Constitutional and legal provisions are important
determinants of subsystem membership, while the power and knowledge
resources of subsystem actors critically affect the nature of their activities
and interactions. In most sectors, given their central location and access
to abundant organizational resources, the minister(s) and bureaucrats in
charge of a policy sector are usually the key governmental actors in policy processes affecting that area, with the legislators, particularly in parliamentary systems, playing a secondary role. Their societal counterparts
are drawn mainly from among special interest groups and research organizations, and business and labour, because of their key role in many
policy areas, often are major actors in many of these processes. All these
actors have their own objectives, which they seek to achieve through
subsystem membership and participation in the policy process.
     But what objectives they pursue, how they do so, and the extent to

which they succeed in their efforts depend to a large extent on the domestic and international institutional context in which they operate. At the domestic level, the structure of political institutions affects the autonomy and capacity of the executive and bureaucracy, a situation paralleled at the international level by the structure of international regimes and the role played by state resources within them. These structures have a decisive effect on actors' interest and behaviour, and on the outcomes of the policy process.

FURTHER READING

Atkinson, M., and W. Coleman. 1989. *The State, Business and Industrial Change in Canada*. Toronto: University of Toronto Press.

Cerny, Philip G. 1996. 'International Finance and the Erosion of State Policy Capacity', in P. Gummett, ed., *Globalization and Public Policy*. Cheltenham: Edward Elgar, 83–104.

Gourevitch, Peter. 1978 'The Second Image Reversed: The International Sources of Domestic Politics', *International Organization* 32: 881–912.

Haggard, Stephen, and Beth A. Simmons. 1987. 'Theories of International Regimes', *International Organization* 41, 3: 491–517.

Hayes, Michael T. 1978. 'The Semi-Sovereign Pressure Groups: A Critique of Current Theory and an Alternative Typology', *Journal of Politics* 40, 1: 134–61.

Held, David. 1991. 'Democracy, the Nation-State and the Global System', in Held, ed., *Political Theory Today*. Oxford: Polity Press, 197–235.

James, Simon. 1993. 'The Idea Brokers: The Impact of Think Tanks on British Government', *Public Administration* 71: 471–90.

Kaufman, Herbert. 2001 'Major Players; Bureaucracies in American Government', *Public Administration Review* 61, 1: 18–42.

King, Anthony. 1981.'What Do Elections Decide?', in D. Butler, H.R. Penniman, and A. Ranney, eds, *Democracy at the Polls: A Comparative Study of Competitive National Elections*. Washington: American Enterprise Institute for Public Policy Research.

Olson, David M., and Michael L. Mezey, eds. 1991. *Legislatures in the Policy Process: The Dilemmas of Economic Policy*. Cambridge: Cambridge University Press.

Rose, Richard. 1980. *Do Parties Make a Difference?* London: Macmillan.

Spitzer, Robert J., ed. 1993. *Media and Public Policy*. Westport, Conn.: Praeger.

Taylor, Andrew J. 1989. *Trade Unions and Politics: A Comparative Introduction*. Basingstoke: Macmillan.

Weaver, R. Kent, and Bert A. Rockman. 1993. 'Assessing the Effects of Institutions', in Weaver and Rockman, eds, *Do Institutions Matter? Government Capabilities in the United States and Abroad*. Washington: Brookings Institution, 1–41.

Wilson, Graham K. 1990. *Business and Politics: A Comparative Introduction*, 2nd edn. London: Macmillan.

Wilson, Graham K. 1990. *Interest Groups*. Oxford: Basil Blackwell.

NOTES

1. On the persistence of institutions and their effects, see Hoffman (1999); Keohane and Hoffman (1991); Zysman (1994); Cortell and Peterson (1999); Cammack (1992).
2. Grant Jordan has spent much effort cataloguing and categorizing the images and metaphors used to describe policy subsystems. See Jordan (1981, 1990a, 1990b); Jordan and Schubert (1992).
3. That is to say, not discriminating against imports once they have crossed the border after meeting all legal requirements, including payment of applicable tariffs.
4. For a detailed comparison of the policy consequences of parliamentary and presidential systems, see Weaver and Rockman (1993a).
5. In Australia, however, trade unions play a significant role in the policy process when the Labour Party is in office, despite the generally pluralist character of the political system.
6. The normative and ideological nature of much discussion on this subject is apparent in the titles and terms used to describe many findings. Recently, this can be seen in the otherwise excellent comparative and historical studies of Joel Brooks, who, finding very little relationship between public opinion and policy-making, terms this phenomenon 'democratic frustration', suggesting it results from a problem with the policy system failing to react properly to the democratic one. See Brooks (1985, 1987, 1990). More recently, see Petry (1999).
7. For good literature reviews on this subject, see Cook et al. (1983); Graber (1989).
8. The relative strength provided by ideological and organizational resources is a subject of some debate. See, for example, Burt (1990).

Chapter 4

Policy Instruments

In the preceding chapter we discussed the principal actors and institutions that determine and comprise the membership of policy subsystems. Before elaborating in Chapters 5 to 9 on the role played by subsystems at each stage of the policy process, we will first discuss the *policy instruments*—also called *policy tools* or *governing instruments*—that governments use to put policies into effect. These are the actual means or devices governments have at their disposal for implementing policies, and among which they must select in formulating policy. Thus, a government not only decides whether or not to do something about deteriorating water quality, for example, but also whether it should implement its decision through mass campaigns urging people to refrain from polluting activities, regulation prohibiting all activities causing the pollution, the provision of a subsidy to the polluting firms encouraging them to switch to safer production technologies, or some combination of these or other means (Gunningham et al., 1998; Gunningham and Young, 1997). The choice of which instrument to use to put a decision into effect is often no less contentious than the decision itself and is very much the subject of discussion, deliberation, and dispute among subsystem members active in the policy process.

Like much else in the policy sciences, the study of policy instruments by scholars of public policy began with Harold Lasswell and his insights into the subject in his 1936 work, *Politics: Who Gets What, When, How*. Over the decades, efforts have moved from simple description of each tool, to the development of classification schemes for categories of tools, and then to attempts to understand the reasons behind their use by governments. In this chapter we will set out one method of classification of the policy instruments available to policy-makers. We will then describe the main features of key instrument types and note the extent of their substitutability. Our intent at this stage is descriptive rather than prescriptive, because factors of context importantly determine the appropriateness of various instruments in specific circumstances (Peters and Van Nispen, 1998; Bemelmans et al., 1998). The question of why governments tend to select a particular instrument and not some other technically equal or even more appealing instrument is addressed in Chapter 8.

CLASSIFYING POLICY INSTRUMENTS

The variety of instruments available to policy-makers to address a policy problem is limited only by their imaginations. Scholars have made numerous attempts to identify such instruments and classify them into meaningful categories (see Salamon and Lund, 1989: 32–3; Lowi, 1985; Bemelmans et al., 1998). Unfortunately, many such schemes are either pitched at a high level of abstraction, making them difficult to apply in practical circumstances, or dwell on the idiosyncrasies of particular tools, thereby limiting the range of the descriptions and explanations they provide. A scheme that is sufficiently abstract to encompass the various possibilities, yet concrete enough to correspond with the way policy-makers actually interpret their choices, is required.

The origins of such a scheme stem from Lasswell's insight that governments use a variety of policy instruments to achieve a relatively limited number of political ends. Rather than face a choice among a huge number of policy tools, Lasswell (1958: 204) argued that governments had developed a limited number of 'strategies' that involved 'the management of value assets in order to influence outcomes'. Understanding these basic strategies and their component instruments, according to Lasswell, involved understanding the nature and types of governing resources that governments have at their disposal (see also French and Raven, 1959).

In the 1940s and 1950s, this insight was developed and elaborated upon by several American political scientists. In his 1941 study of federal regulatory commissions, for example, Robert Cushman developed a simple basic taxonomy of policy instruments by focusing on the insight that governments could either regulate or choose not to regulate societal activities, and that if they chose the former they could regulate either in a coercive or non-coercive manner (Cushman, 1941). In their work on governments and planning, Robert Dahl and Charles Lindblom (1953) also developed a number of spectra, or continuous scales, which highlighted the almost infinite number of possible permutations of policy tools, but also the manner in which these tools relied for their effectiveness on a limited number of criteria, such as their intrusiveness, their dependence on state agencies or markets, and a number of other variables.

In the 1960s, Theodore Lowi (1966, 1972) adopted these insights into the limited number of basic types or categories of policy tools involved in government activity. He observed that American governments had tended to favour certain types of instruments for prolonged periods, allowing analysts the opportunity to identify major transitions in government activities on this basis. He argued that a four-cell matrix based on the specificity of the target of coercion and the likelihood of its actual application would suffice to distinguish the major types and eras of government activity. The original three policy types he identified included the weakly sanctioned and individually targeted 'distributive' policies; the individually targeted and strongly sanctioned 'regulatory' policy; and the strongly sanctioned and generally targeted 'redistributive' policy. To these three, Lowi later added the weakly sanctioned and generally targeted category of 'constituent' policy.

Although widely read, Lowi's typology was difficult to operationalize and somewhat internally inconsistent, and as a result it was rarely applied. However, the notion of 'policy determining politics' proved alluring and led to other efforts to classify and comprehend policy instruments. As Charles Anderson (1971: 122) stated:

> Politics is always a matter of making choices from the possibilities offered by a given historical situation and cultural context. From this vantage point, the institutions and procedures of the state to shape the course of economy and society become the equipment provided by a society to its leaders for the solution of public problems. They are the tools of the trade of statecraft . . . the skillful policy maker, then, is he who can find appropriate possibilities in the institutional equipment of his society.

Instrument choice or 'statecraft', from this perspective, *is* public policy-making, and the role of the policy analyst is one of assisting 'in constructing an inventory of potential public capabilities and resources that might be pertinent in any problem-solving situation' (ibid.).

In the 1970s, efforts were made to better understand the nature of these instruments and tools available to governments (see Rondinelli, 1976, 1983; Goggin et al., 1990). Anderson's suggestion that public policy analysis shift from the study of policy problems and inputs to the study of policy implements and outputs was endorsed by scholars such as Bardach (1980) and Salamon (1981), both of whom suggested that policy studies had 'gone wrong' right at the start by defining policy in terms of 'areas' or 'fields' rather than in terms of tools. As Salamon (1981: 256) argued:

> The major shortcoming of current implementation research is that it focuses on the wrong unit of analysis, and the most important theoretical breakthrough would be to identify a more fruitful unit on which to focus analysis and research. In particular, rather than focusing on individual programs, as is now done, or even collections

of programs grouped according to major 'purpose,' as is frequently proposed, the suggestion here is that we should concentrate instead on the generic tools of government action, on the 'techniques' of social intervention.

Salamon also framed two important research questions to be addressed in the analysis of the tools of government action: 'What consequences does the choice of tool of government action have for the effectiveness and operation of a government program?' and 'What factors influence the choice of program tools?' (ibid., 265). Throughout the 1980s these questions were taken up by the 'policy design' literature (Bobrow and Dryzek, 1987; Dryzek and Ripley, 1988; Linder and Peters, 1984).

The first step in their answer was to inventory policy instruments (see Steinberger, 1980). One influential early attempt to develop an exhaustive catalogue of policy instruments was carried out by the Dutch economist E.S. Kirschen and his colleagues, who discovered that despite the almost infinite number of possible permutations and combinations of instruments, only a relatively small number of basic policy tools were typically used by European governments to carry out their economic policies. Kirschen nevertheless concluded that there were at least 64 general types of instruments in this sector alone, thus illustrating the dilemmas of attempting to provide a complete list of policy tools used in all policy fields (Kirschen et al., 1964).

Rather than attempt to construct such lists, most analysts looked for ways to group roughly similar types of instruments into a few general categories that could then be analyzed to determine the answers to Salamon's questions. Most authors looked to Lasswell's early work on instrument 'strategies' and tried to identify the basic 'governing resources' that different instruments relied on for their effectiveness (Balch, 1980).

Bardach (1980), for instance, argued that government had three 'technologies' at its disposal—enforcement, inducement, and benefaction—and that these required different combinations of four critical governmental resources: money, political support, administrative competency, and creative leadership. Rondinelli did much the same thing, arguing that all policy instruments depended on a limited set of 'methods of influence' that governments had at their disposal: in his case, persuasion, exchange, and authority (Rondinelli, 1983: 125).

A simple and powerful taxonomy was offered by Christopher Hood (1986a), who proposed that all policy tools used one of four broad categories of governing resources.[1] He argued that governments confront public problems through the use of the information in their possession as a central policy actor ('nodality'), their legal powers ('authority'), their money ('treasure'), or the formal organizations available to them ('organization') or 'NATO'. Governments can use these resources to manipulate policy actors, for example, by withdrawing or making available information or money, by using their coercive powers to force other actors to undertake activities they desire, or simply by undertaking the activity themselves using their own personnel and expertise.

Other schemes existed, such as Elmore's and Schneider and Ingram's, which focused on the outputs associated with instruments, rather than their inputs, but these received less attention than did Hood's.[2] This is because resource-based schemes like Hood's allowed a relatively small number of general categories of policy tools to be identified, and permitted the ready analysis of specific tools by grouping them together in very small number of general categories. Such schemes aid analysis by distinguishing clearly between policy choices involving changes in policy tools within categories and between them. In the first instance, for example, the parameters or 'settings' of a tool might be changed but not the basic category of the tool itself, as occurs, for example, when the amount or extent of a government subsidy is varied. In the second, rather than involving a change in the calibration of an instrument, changes might involve an alteration in overall tool category. An example of such a change would include one where privatization results in a government eliminating public corporations, choosing to use regulations or legal standards rather than bureaucratic forms of organization to achieve its ends.

Using Hood's idea of governing resources, a basic taxonomy of instrument categories can be set out. Figure 4.1 presents such a classification scheme with illustrative examples of the types of policy tools found in each category.

As Figure 4.1 shows, policy instruments tend to fall into two types: *substantive instruments*, such as public enterprises and user charges, designed to deliver or affect the delivery of goods and services in society; and *procedural instruments*, such as the creation of advisory committees and government reorganizations, used to alter aspects of policy deliberations. This distinction will be taken up in more detail in Chapter 8 when we examine the reasons why governments use particular types of tools or what is sometimes referred to as 'the rationale for instrument choice'.[3] Here, we will describe the general contours of the types of instruments found in each of the categories set out in Figure 4.1.

Organization-Based Instruments

Direct Provision
In our effort to understand the more exotic instruments employed by governments, we tend to forget this basic and most widely used public policy instrument. Instead of waiting for the private sector to do something it desires or regulating non-governmental performance of a task, a government can often perform the task itself, delivering goods and services

Figure 4.1 Policy Instruments, by Principal Governing Resource

(Cells provide examples of instruments in each category)

Nodality	Authority	Treasure	Organization
Information Monitoring and Release	Command and Control Regulation	Grants and Loans	Direct Provision of Goods and Services and Public Enterprises
Advice and Exhortation	Self-Regulation	User Charges	Use of Family, Community, and Voluntary Organizations
Advertising	Standard-Setting and Delegated Regulation	Taxes and Tax Expenditures	Market Creation
Commissions and Inquiries	Advisory Committees and Consultations	Interest Group Creation and Funding	Government Reorganization

SOURCE: Adapted from Christopher Hood, *The Tools of Government* (Chatham, NJ: Chatham House, 1986), 124–5.

directly by using government employees, funded from the public treasury, for a task (Leman, 1989: 54; Leman, 2002; Mayntz, 1979; Devas et al., 2001). Much of what governments do is done through this instrument, including activities such as national defence, diplomatic relations, policing, firefighting, social security, education, management of public lands, maintenance of parks and roads, and census and geological surveys.

There are several advantages of using direct provision as a policy instrument (Leman, 1989: 60). First, direct provision is easy to establish because of low information requirements, unlike other instruments, which rely heavily on non-government actors and hence require constant monitoring and supervision of their activities. Second, the large size of the agencies usually involved in direct provision enables them to build resources, skills, and information necessary for efficient performance of their task. Third, direct provision avoids many problems associated with indirect provision—discussion, negotiations, and concerns with non-compliance—that can lead governments to pay more attention to enforcing terms of grants and contracts than to results. Fourth, direct provision permits internalization within government of many types of transactions, thus minimizing the costs involved in policy implementation.

The disadvantages of direct provision, however, can be no less significant. While in theory a government can do everything that the private sector can, in practice this may not be the case. As theorists of government failures have noted, delivery of programs by the bureaucracy is often characterized by inflexibility, something that is unavoidable in liberal democratic societies, which value accountability and the rule of law and where governments must abide by formal operating procedures encoded in time-consuming legal budgeting and appointment requirements. Second, political control over the agencies and officials involved in providing goods and services may, and often does, promote political meddling to strengthen a government's re-election prospects or address other specific contemporary political needs rather than to serve the public as a whole. Political control may also lead to incoherent directives to agencies delivering goods and services because of the contradictory pressures that beset governments. Third, since bureaucratic agencies are not subject to competition, they are often not sufficiently cost-conscious, for which the taxpayers ultimately pay. Fourth, the delivery of programs may suffer because of inter- and intra-agency conflicts within the government (Bovens et al., 2001).

Public Enterprises

Also known as *state-owned enterprises* (SOEs), *Crown corporations*, or *parastatal organizations*, public enterprises are entities totally or partially owned by the state but yet enjoying some degree of autonomy from the government. There is no definitive way of identifying a public enterprise, which explains why governments quite often do not publish a definitive list of the enterprises they own. The main problem is determining how public an enterprise must be in order to be called a 'public' enterprise. At one extreme, with only a small government share of ownership, a firm may resemble a private enterprise, and at the other, with close to 100 per cent government equity ownership, an enterprise may appear to be an ordinary bureaucratic agency (Stanton and Moe, 2002).

However, three broad generalizations can be made about the basic features of public enterprises (Ahroni, 1986: 6). First, they involve a large degree of public ownership. Analysts often use an arbitrary figure of a minimum 51 per cent ownership of a firm by a government or governments to call a firm a public enterprise, since this amount ensures government control of appointments to a company's board of directors. However, in large corporations with widely held stock, a much smaller percentage would be sufficient to control board appointments. The term 'mixed enterprise' is used to describe a second category of firms owned jointly by government and the private sector. Second, public enterprises entail some degree of control or direct management by the government. Completely passive ownership of a firm operated entirely free from government control does not constitute a public enterprise. Hybrid 'special operating agencies' or 'public authorities' created in many countries in recent years to operate specific services such as airports, harbours, and water or electrical power utilities are not traditional public enterprises in that governments usually do not directly control their boards of directors (Advani and Borins, 2001; Kickert, 2001). Third, public enterprises produce goods and services that are sold, unlike public goods such as defence or street lighting for which those receiving the services are taxed. As a corollary, their sales revenues must bear some semblance to their costs, though generating profits is usually not the primary objective of these firms, as it is for their private-sector counterparts.

Public enterprises as policy instruments offer a number of advantages to governments (Mitnick, 1980: 407). First, they are an efficient economic policy instrument in situations where a socially needed good or service is not produced by the private sector because of high capital outlays or low expected returns, for example, in providing rural electrification or high-speed Internet access. Second, as with direct provision, the information threshold required to establish public enterprises is in many instances lower than when using other kinds of instruments, such as voluntary instruments or regulation. It does not require information on the target activity or the goals and preferences of the targeted firms, because the government as owner can do whatever it wishes through the enterprise itself. Third, in terms of administration, public enterprises may actually simplify management if extensive regulation is already present. Instead of building additional layers of regulation to force firms to comply with government aims, for instance, it might be desirable simply to establish a company that does so without the need for the cumbersome processes and oversight provisions attending regulation. Finally, profits from public enterprises may accrue to public funds, any surplus in which can be used to pay for public expenditures in other areas. A significant proportion of government revenue in Singapore, for example, comes from the profits of its public enterprises.

The disadvantages of public enterprises are no less significant. First, governments often find them difficult to control because managers can adopt various avoidance measures to evade government directives. Moreover, the ultimate shareholders (the voters themselves) are too diffuse, and their personal interest too distant, to exercise effective control over the company. Second, public enterprise can be inefficient in operation because continued losses do not lead to bankruptcy, as would occur in the private sector. Indeed a large number consistently lose money, which is a major reason underlying efforts to privatize them in many countries in recent years (see Howlett and Ramesh, 1993; Ikenberry, 1988). Finally, many public enterprises, such as in the area of electricity and water supply, operate in a monopolistic environment enabling them to pass the costs of their inefficiency to consumers, a strategy no different than that of a private firm enjoying a monopoly position (Musolf, 1989).

Family, Community, and Voluntary Organizations
The characteristic feature of this type of instrument is that it entails no or

little involvement by the government; the desired task is instead performed on a voluntary basis by non-governmental actors. In some cases, governments must create the conditions under which voluntary actors operate, while in others governments decide deliberately that they will do nothing ('non-decision') about a recognized public problem, because they believe a solution is already being, or will be, provided by some other actor, whether through existing private companies in the market or by family or voluntary organizations. These services are often provided by non-governmental organizations (NGOs) operating on a voluntary basis in that their members are not compelled to perform a task by the government. If they do something that serves public policy goals, it is for reasons of self-interest, ethics, or emotional gratification (Salamon, 1995).

The existence of such organizations is supported by government (in)action and they are an important tool for implementing many economic and social policies. Their usage has grown in recent decades because of increasing governmental retreat from direct provision and extensive privatization of public enterprises. NGOs are preferred in many liberal democratic societies, especially, because of their cost-efficiency, consistency with the cultural norms of individual freedom, and the support they provide for family and community ties. However, they are also found in many other types of societies.

In all societies, relatives, friends, and neighbours, or *family and community organizations*, such as churches and charities, provide numerous goods and services, and the government may take measures to expand their role in ways that serve its policy goals. It may do so either indirectly by cutting back on government services in the hope that the family or community will step in to fill the gap, or directly by promoting their involvement through preferential regulation or financial incentives such as tax deductions for charitable donations or expenses (Phillips et al., 2001).

All societies regard looking after the needs of family members and others close to them as an essential responsibility of the individual. Children, the aged, and the sick are ordinarily looked after in this manner, mainly in terms of care, but financial assistance if necessary is also common. It has been calculated that in 1978 the total cost of the transfer of cash, food, and housing within families in the United States amounted to US$86 billion (Gilbert and Gilbert, 1989: 281). Non-monetary transfers are almost impossible to estimate, however, because families provide a range of services whose value cannot be measured in monetary terms. It is estimated, for example, that about 80 per cent of home health-care services for the elderly are provided by family members (ibid., 19).

Voluntary organizations involve 'activities that are indeed voluntary in the dual sense of being free of [state] coercion and being free of the economic constraints of profitability and the distribution of profits'

(Wuthnow, 1991: 7). Voluntary organizations providing health services, education, and food to the poor and temporary shelter for battered women and runaway children are prime examples of such organizations. Voluntary groups that form to clean up beaches, riverbanks, and highways are other examples. Although these functions could well be provided by the market or the government, they may also be left wholly or partially to volunteers.

Charitable, not-for-profit groups, often church-based, used to be the primary means of fulfilling the basic needs of those who could not provide for themselves, but over the last century the expansion of the welfare state gradually diminished their importance. Even so, they are still a widely used means of addressing social problems today. In fact, in the US, often seen as the archetype of an individualist materialistic society, the non-profit voluntary sector delivers more services than the government itself (Salamon, 1987: 31). In recent years, because of the budgetary crises faced by governments, many countries have pressed to expand the role of the voluntary sector.

In theory, voluntary organizations are an efficient means of delivering most economic and social services. If it were feasible, it would obviously be cost-efficient to provide social security or health and education services or build dams and roads on the basis of voluntary efforts of individuals. Voluntary organizations also offer flexibility and speed of response and the opportunity for experimentation that would be difficult in governmental organizations (Johnson, 1987: 114). They are often quicker than the government in providing relief to victims of natural disaster, for instance. Moreover, meeting social needs in this manner decreases the need for government action, which appeals to those who believe that state intervention is inherently inimical to political freedom. Not-for-profit groups are also an equitable instrument because they are usually directed at only those in need. Another beneficial spillover is their positive contribution to promoting community spirit, social solidarity or cohesion, and political participation (Putnam, 1995a, 1995b, 1996, 2000, 2001).

However, most practical circumstances severely limit the usefulness of voluntary organizations. Their efforts are largely inapplicable to many economic problems, for example, such as the promotion of technological innovation and enhanced productivity. And even in the social sphere, their efficiency and effectiveness may be compromised by the fact that large voluntary groups can be chaotic or may become bureaucratic and in practice become little different from government organizations. If they depend on the government for funds they also may not be cost-efficient; it might be cheaper for the state to perform the task directly. In the US, for example, the government provides 40 per cent of total expenditure by voluntary organizations, a larger source of funds than private contributions (Salamon, 1987: 31). And the proportion of private funding would have been even lower without the tax deductibility allowed for such contributions.

Contemporary economic and social problems are simply too vast to be addressed adequately on the basis of voluntary efforts alone; most people have neither the time nor the resources to contribute to such activities in a substantive manner. Such organizations are therefore unlikely to work outside areas that give their active members satisfaction for religious, ethical, or political reasons. Consequently, voluntary organizations are not likely to undertake most tasks performed by modern governments.

The primary advantage of promoting the family and community as an instrument of public policy is that it does not cost the government anything unless it chooses to provide grants or subsidies for these efforts. In many circumstances, as in the case of family or community care for the long-term disabled, this is much less expensive than their care in public institutions. Moreover, the functioning of non-profit community organizations, churches, co-operatives, and families enjoys widespread political support in most societies (Quarter, 1992). But pitted against these advantages are some serious disadvantages. Family- and community-based instruments, for example, are generally weak instruments for addressing complex economic problems. Efficiency of scale may also warrant centralized provision by the government rather than decentralized provision by the family or community. Reliance on these types of instruments for solving public problems may also be inequitable because many individuals do not have anyone, or anyone with the financial resources or emotional commitment, to look after them. It is similarly inequitable for the caregivers. In most societies, for example, women tend to be the main care providers, a role increasingly difficult to perform because of increasing female participation in the labour force. As such, family and community instruments can often only be relied upon as adjuncts to other instruments needed to address the pressing social problems of our times.

Market Creation
By far the most important, and contentious, type of voluntary instrument is the *market organization*. The voluntary interaction between consumers and producers, with the former seeking to buy as much as they can with the limited amount of money at their disposal and the latter searching for highest possible profits, can usually be expected to lead to outcomes that satisfy both. In theory at least, while the primary motive on the part of both sides is self-interest, the society as a whole gains from their interaction because whatever is wanted (backed by the ability to pay) by the society is provided at the lowest price. Theoretically, then, those wanting even such critical goods as health care or education can simply buy the services from hospitals and schools operating for profit.

Markets exist when there is scarcity and a demand for particular goods or services. But government action is required both to create and to support market exchange. This is accomplished by securing the rights of buyers and sellers to receive and exchange property through the establishment and maintenance of property rights and contracts through the courts, police, and quasi-judicial systems of consumer and investor protection, such as securities and exchange commissions and competition tribunals. Even so-called 'black', 'grey', or other types of illegal or quasi-legal markets for commodities or services, such as illegal drugs or prostitution, owe their existence to governments that attempt to ban the production and sale of these goods or services, thereby creating shortages that can provide high rates of return for those willing to risk punishment and imprisonment for their provision.

Governments can use a variety of regulatory, financial, and information-based tools to affect market activities, and these will be discussed in the following sections. However, they use their organizational resources to create markets. One way this can be done is by the creation of a new set of property rights through government licensing schemes. On the basis of the assumption that the market is often the most efficient means of allocating resources, *property-rights auctions* by the government establish markets in situations where they do not exist. The market is created by setting a fixed quantity of transferable rights to consume a designated resource, which has the effect of creating an artificial scarcity and enabling the price mechanism to work. The resource can be communal radio, television, or cell-phone frequencies, oil wells, or fish stocks, anything that would not be scarce unless made so by the government (Sunnevag, 2000). Those wishing to consume the resource must bid at an auction for the limited amount available. Potential buyers will bid according to the value they attribute to the resource, with those offering the most in return for the government securing their right.

Many countries have proposed to control the use of dangerous pollutants in this manner (Bolom, 2000), and some such schemes exist in environmental agreements, such as the so-called Kyoto Protocol on greenhouse gases. In these schemes, typically, the government is expected to fix the total amount of the pollutant that can enter the market and then through periodic auctions sell the right to discharge the limited amount available. This means that firms intending to use a pollutant in their production process must buy the right to do so at an auction before they can buy the pollutant itself. Those with cheaper alternatives will avoid using the pollutant because of the extra cost of buying rights. Manufacturers for whom there is no cheap alternative continue to pay the price for the right to use the pollutant. However, even they are under constant pressure to search for alternatives because of the extra costs they must otherwise bear.

The advantage of using an auction of rights in such cases is that it restricts the use of specific types of goods while still making them available to those without alternatives. Of course, the same could be done through regulation, but then the government would have to determine who should be allowed to use the limited amount available, a difficult task because of the high information costs involved. In the case of auctions, in theory at least the decision will be made by the market according to the forces of demand and (artificially limited) supply.

Another example of the use of auctions of property rights is in controlling the number of motor vehicles on city roads. After experimenting with a number of instruments to control the rapidly increasing number of motor vehicles that were causing traffic congestion and posing an environmental hazard in the long run, the government of Singapore decided to resort to the auction of the right to vehicle ownership. The annual supply of new motor vehicles in the country is limited to about 4,000. But before one can buy a car, one must purchase a Certificate of Entitlement at an auction organized by the government. Since the annual demand for new cars is far in excess of 4,000, in recent years the successful bidders have had to pay in excess of Singapore $50,000 just to buy an entitlement (over and above the price of the car itself). This instrument has ensured that the government is able to control the number of vehicles on streets without determining which specific individuals or firms can own cars, the latter being determined by the market. Of course, the auction is also a highly lucrative source of revenue for the government.

One advantage of auctions of property rights to establish markets is that they are easy to conduct (Cantor et al., 1992). The government, based on what it considers the maximum amount of a good or service that should be permitted, fixes the ceiling and then lets the market do the rest. Second, they are a flexible instrument, which allows the government to vary the ceiling as and when it wants; the subjects must adjust their behaviour accordingly. Property-rights auctions also allow the subjects to adjust their behaviour according to other changes in their circumstances, such as with respect to development of cost-saving technology, without requiring a corresponding change in the government's policy or instrument. Third, auctions offer the certainty that only a fixed amount of undesired activity occurs, something not possible with other voluntary or mixed instruments.

One of the disadvantages of auctions is that they may encourage speculation, with speculators buying up and hoarding all rights by bidding high, thereby erecting entry barriers to small firms or consumers. Second, it is often the case that those who cannot buy the rights, because none may be available for sale, will be forced to cheat, whereas in the case of user charges or subsidies they would have an alternative, albeit often at a high price. This can result in high enforcement costs if grey or black markets are to be avoided. Third, auctions are inequitable to the extent they allocate resources according to ability to pay, rather than need, and can generate fierce opposition from those affected because of the extra costs they must bear in buying the right (Woerdman, 2000; Kagel and Levin, 2002). Thus, in Singapore the rich buy more than one car, not least because shortage has turned car ownership into a status symbol, while those who really need one, for example, to start up a business, may not be able to buy a vehicle if they do not have the additional money required to buy the certificate of entitlement.

Another way that governments can create markets is through the *privatization of public enterprises*, especially if those enterprises had previously exercised a state-sponsored monopoly on the production or distribution, or both, of a particular good or service. Privatization can be carried out in numerous ways, from issuing shares to all citizens, to the simple transfer of state shares to community organizations or their sale on public exchanges. In all cases, this amounts to the transfer of a public enterprise to the private sector and the transformation of the goal of the enterprise from public service provision to maximization of shareholder value. Moreover, though, it also usually involves the signal, either overt or covert, that new firms will be able to enter into the market formerly served by the state-owned company, allowing for the creation of a competitive market for that particular good or service.

Although some scholars see privatization as a panacea, capable at one stroke of eliminating corrupt or inefficient public-sector providers and replacing them with more efficient private-sector ones, others point out that this is not always the case. In many Eastern European post-socialist countries, for example, large-scale and largely uncontrolled privatizations resulted in many instances of massive layoffs and plant closures, with severe economic consequences for affected families, communities, and regions. In others, like Russia, where securities markets were not well developed, plants were simply transferred to their managers, who in many cases were able to reap windfall profits from their sale. It is also the case, as welfare economists have argued, that some industries have economies of scale that allow large firms to maintain their monopolistic position, regardless of whether they are owned by governments or private investors. Privatization of such firms merely transfers monopoly profits from the public sector, where they can be used to finance additional public services, to the private sector, where they are often used for personal luxury consumption (Beesley, 1992; Bos, 1991; Donahue, 1989; Le Grand and Robinson, 1984; MacAvoy et al., 1989; Starr, 1990a).

In Western countries with much smaller numbers of public enterprises, a more common form of privatization has involved *contracting out of government services*, that is, the transfer of various kinds of goods and services formerly provided 'in-house' by government employees to 'outsourced' private firms (Kelman, 2002; DeHoog and Salamon, 2002). Again, while some see any transfer of service provision from the state to the private sector as an inherent welfare gain, others note that in many cases the same employees end up being hired by the new service provider to provide the same service, but at less pay, while others have noted that the costs to administrators of establishing, monitoring, and enforcing contracts often cancels out any cost savings (see Lane, 2001; Ascher, 1987; Grimshaw et al., 2001).

A much talked about but little used form of government market creation involves the use of *vouchers*. These are papers with a monetary face value offered by the government to consumers of a particular good or service, given by consumers to their preferred supplier, who in turn presents the voucher to the government for redemption. Vouchers allow consumers to exercise relatively free choice in the marketplace, but only for specific types or quantities of goods. They are common in wartime as a means to ration supplies of materials, and have also been used in peacetime in schemes such as food stamps for the poor. This promotes competition among suppliers, which arguably improves quality and reduces costs to the government. However, vouchers can also disrupt established patterns of public service provision. Their proposed use in education, for example, may force schools to compete against each other for students, which can lead to greater inequities in service provision between wealthy and impoverished school districts (Valkama and Bailey, 2001; Steuerle and Twombly, 2002).

Establishing markets can be a highly recommended instrument in certain circumstances (Averch, 1990; OECD, 1993; Hula, 1988). It is an effective and efficient means of providing most private goods and can ensure that resources are devoted only to those goods and services valued by the society, as reflected in the individual's willingness to pay. It also ensures that if there is meaningful competition among suppliers, then valued goods and services are supplied at the lowest possible price. Since most goods and services sought by the population are of a private nature, governments in capitalist societies rely extensively on the market instrument.

In many situations, however, the market may be an inappropriate instrument to use (Kuttner, 1997). As we saw in Chapter 2, markets cannot adequately provide public goods, precisely the sort of things most public policies involve. Thus, markets cannot be used for providing defence, policing, street lights, and other similar goods and services valued by society. Markets also experience difficulties in providing various kinds of toll goods and common-pool goods (see Chapter 2 for definitions) due to difficulties involved in charging consumers for these kinds of products. The market is also a highly inequitable instrument, because it meets the needs of only those with the ability to pay. In a purely market-based system of health-care delivery, for example, a rich person with money can have a wish for cosmetic surgery fulfilled, while a poor person suffering from kidney failure will not receive treatment. It is not surprising that the use of markets in such situations faces tough political opposition in democratic societies otherwise structured along more egalitarian principles.

A 'free market' in the true sense of the term is therefore almost never used as a policy instrument in practice. When a government does choose to resort to this instrument to address a public problem, it is usually accompanied by other instruments such as regulation to protect consumers, investors, and workers; it is also accompanied frequently by subsidies intended to further promote the desired activity (Cantor et al., 1992). Thus the voluntarism of markets is relative rather than absolute.

Government Reorganizations

Unlike the instruments discussed so far, which are intended to alter the configuration of goods and services delivered in society, there are also 'procedural' instruments that rely on the use of government organizational resources. The objective of these instruments is to alter policy processes in such a way that governments can retain their legitimacy or capacity to act (Howlett, 2000). The foremost example of such an instrument is institutional reorganization whereby governments seek to achieve an objective by reorganizing the structures or processes through which they perform a function (Peters, 1992b; Carver, 2001). These activities are sometimes referred to as 'network management', in which governments use their personnel and other organizational resources to alter or restructure how policy actors interact with each other (Klijn, 1996; Klijn et al., 1995; Klijn and Koppenjan, 2000).

Reorganizations can involve the creation of new agencies or the reconfiguration of old ones. One popular technique for such purposes is *ministerial reorganization*. Some of these alterations can occur accidentally or as a by-product of organizational changes in government machinery brought about for other reasons, such as electoral or partisan ones. However, intentional organizational change to the basic structures or personnel of government departments and agencies has become an increasingly significant aspect of modern policy-making (Lindquist, 1992; Aucoin, 1997). This can involve changes in the relationships between departments and central co-ordinating agencies, or between departments, or within ministries.

In the first instance, ministries can be given greater autonomy and capacity to set their own direction, or they can be brought into tighter control by central executive agencies (Smith et al., 1993). In the second case, government departments can be divided into more specialized units, as has happened in instances where, for example, specialized departments dealing with particular industrial sectors have been created from larger units, or the reverse process of the amalgamation of specific purpose units into omnibus ministries has occurred. This has been the pattern in many countries recently, for example, where specific resource ministries such as forests and mines have been combined into departments of the environment or sustainable development (Brown, 1992). Or new units can be created to deal with new issues, as has occurred in many countries over the last two decades, for example, with the creation of new human rights agencies (Howe and Johnson, 2000). In the final instance, the same kinds of interdepartmental reforms can be made at the intradepartmental level, reducing or augmenting the autonomy of subunits or reorganizing them to expand or retract their spheres of activity. In the latter instance, this often involves the creation of specialized units within departments to enhance their planning capacity (Chenier, 1985; Prince, 1979).

Reorganizing government structures can have a very dramatic impact on existing policy processes and on the types of interactions between and among state and societal actors (Peters, 1992b). However, it is also the case that there are limits to such reorganizations. First, they can be expensive and time-consuming. Second, if they occur too frequently, their impact can be much dissipated. And third, there can be constitutional or jurisdictional limits to the kinds of activities that specific governments can take on and the fashion in which they can do so (Gilmore and Krantz, 1991).

Authority-Based Instruments

Command and Control Regulation

There are numerous definitions of regulation, but most tend to be quite restrictive in focus (Mitnick, 1978). A good general one is offered by Michael Reagan, who defines it as 'a process or activity in which government requires or proscribes certain activities or behaviour on the part of individuals and institutions, mostly private but sometimes public, and does so through a continuing administrative process, generally through specially designated regulatory agencies' (Reagan, 1987: 17). Thus, regulation is a prescription by the government that must be complied with by the intended targets; failure to do so usually involves a penalty. This type of instrument is often referred to as 'command and control' regulation.

Some regulations, such as those dealing with criminal behaviour, are laws and involve the police and judicial system in their enforcement. Most regulations, however, are administrative edicts created under the terms of enabling legislation and administered on a continuing basis by a government department or a specialized, quasi-judicial government agency (first called *independent regulatory commissions* in the US) that is more or less autonomous of government control in its day-to-day operations. Regulations take various forms and include rules, standards, permits, prohibitions, laws, and executive orders. Although we may not always be aware of their presence, among other things they govern the price and standards of a wide variety of goods and services we consume, from radio stations to energy prices, as well as the quality of water we drink and the air we breathe, among other things.

The nature of regulations varies somewhat depending on whether they are targeted towards economic or social spheres of human activity. Economic regulations control aspects of the production processes specific to particular goods and services, such as the prices and volumes of production, or return on investment, or the entry into or exit of firms from an industry. A good example of this type of regulation is that carried out by various kinds of *marketing boards*, regulatory bodies that are particularly prominent in the agricultural sector. The intent of such boards is to keep farm commodity prices high by restricting supply. Their objective is to correct perceived imbalances or inequities in economic relationships that may emerge as a result of the operation of market forces. Economic regulations have been the traditional form of regulation; their social counterparts are of more recent origin.

Social regulations refer to controls in matters of health, safety, and social practices such as civil rights and discrimination of various sorts. They have more to do with our physical and moral well-being than with our pocketbooks. Examples of social regulation include rules regarding liquor consumption and sales, gambling, consumer product safety, occupational hazards, water-related hazards, air pollution, noise pollution, discrimination on the basis of religion, race, gender, or ethnicity, and pornography (Padberg, 1992). Many areas of regulation, such as environmental protection, liquor consumption, and gambling, exist as hybrids between pure economic and pure social regulation, because the problems may have economic origins but their adverse effects are mostly social. While there is a great deal of overlap between the two, social regulations tend to be more general than economic ones and do not focus on particular industries (for example, banks or telecommunications), as do economic regulations, but on broader problems or functions, such as pollution, safety, or morality. This has important implications for their administration and enforcement because social regulation tends to cut across several sectors and come under the jurisdiction of several government agencies (see May, 2002; Salamon, 2002b).

There are several advantages of regulation as a policy instrument (see Mitnick, 1980: 401–4). First, the information needed to establish regulation is less than with many other tools because a government need not know in advance the subject's preferences, as it must in the case of voluntary instruments. It can simply establish a standard, for example, a permitted pollution level, and expect compliance. Second, where the concerned activity is deemed entirely undesirable, as is the case with films and videos depicting pedophilia, it is easier to establish regulations prohibiting the possession of such products than to devise ways of encouraging the production and distribution of other types of more benign goods or services. Third, regulations allow for better co-ordination of government efforts and planning because of the greater pre-dictability they entail. Fourth, their predictability makes them a more suitable instrument in times of crisis when an immediate response is needed. Fifth, regulations may be less costly than other instruments, such as subsidies or tax incentives. Finally, regulations may also be polit-ically appealing if the public or policy subsystem wants to see quick and definite action on the part of the government.

The disadvantages of regulation are equally telling (see Anderson, 1976). First, regulations quite often distort voluntary or private-sector activities and can promote economic inefficiencies. Price regulations and direct allocation restrict the operation of the forces of demand and sup-ply and affect the price mechanism in capitalist societies, thus causing sometimes unpredictable economic distortions in the market. Restric-tions on entry to and exit from industrial sectors, for example, can reduce competition and thus have a negative impact on prices. Second, regula-tions can, at times, inhibit innovation and technological progress because of the market security they afford existing firms and the limited opportunities for experimentation they permit. Third, regulations are often inflexible and do not permit the consideration of individual circum-stances, resulting in decisions and outcomes not intended by the regula-tion (Dyerson and Mueller, 1993). Social regulations are particularly problematic. It is almost impossible to specify in many instances exactly what is acceptable under regulation. The use of phrases such as 'safe and effective' drugs, for instance, allows for too much uncertainty. If reg-ulations specify detailed standards, however, then they can become irrel-evant in new circumstances (Bardach, 1989: 203–4). Fourth, in terms of administration, it may simply not be possible to set regulations for every undesired activity. For example, there are millions of pollutants; a special regulation would be required for each if this instrument were chosen for policy purposes. Finally, the cost of enforcement by regulatory commis-sions may be high because the costs of information, investigation, and prosecution make policy-making legalistic and adversarial (see Hahn and Hird, 1991).

Delegated or Self-Regulation

Another form of regulatory instrument is *delegated regulation*. Unlike the situation with command and control regulation, in this instance govern-ments allow non-governmental actors to regulate themselves. This is sometimes referred to as 'self-regulation' although this latter term tends to portray the resulting regulatory arrangements as more 'voluntary' than is actually the case. That is, while non-governmental entities may, in effect, regulate themselves, they typically do so with the implicit or explicit permission of governments, which consciously refrain from regu-lating activities in a more directly coercive fashion (Donahue and Nye, 2001).

These delegations can be explicit and direct, for example, when governments allow professions such as doctors, lawyers, or teachers to regulate themselves through the grant of a licensing monopoly to a bar association, a college of physicians and surgeons, or a teachers' college (see Sinclair, 1997; Tuohy and Wolfson, 1978). However, they can also be much less explicit, as occurs in situations where manufacturing companies develop standards for products or where independent certification firms or associations certify that certain standards have been met in various kinds of private practices (see Andrews, 1998; Gunningham and Rees, 1997; Iannuzzi, 2001). While many standards are invoked by government command and control regulation, others can be developed in the private sphere. As long as these are not replaced by government-enforced standards, they represent the acquiescence of a government to the private rules, a form of delegated regulation (see Haufler, 2000, 2001; Knill, 2001).

A major advantage of the use of voluntary standard-setting is cost, since governments do not have to pay for the creation, administration, and renewal of such standards, as would be the case with traditional command and control regulation. This is especially the case in areas such as professional regulation, where information asymmetries between those regulated and regulators mean public administration of standards is especially expensive and time-consuming. Such programs can also be effective in international settings, where establishment of effective governmental regimes, such as sustainable forestry practices, can be especially difficult (Elliott and Schlaepfer, 2001). However, possible savings in administrative costs once again must be balanced against additional costs to society that might result from ineffective or inefficient administration of voluntary standards, especially those related to non-compliance.[4] For example, the recent (2002) Enron scandal in the US involving the energy giant's auditing firm, Arthur Anderson, has undermined confidence in the accounting profession's ability or even willingness to police itself.

Advisory Committees and Quangos

Governments can also use their authority resources to affect policy processes. This involves alteration of the government's authority to elevate the views of some policy actors above others in formal and informal policy processes. It is based on preferential recognition extended by states to specific policy actors, enhancing their access to decision-makers and their voice in policy deliberations (Dion, 1973; Anderson, 1979b).

A standard tool in this category is the *advisory committee* (Smith, 1977; Gill, 1940). Some of these are formalized and more or less permanent, while others tend to be more ad hoc, informal, and temporary (Brown, 1955, 1972; Balla and Wright, 2001). Both involve governments selecting representatives to sit on these committees and the extension to those representatives of some special rights within the policy process. Many countries have created permanent bodies to provide advice to governments on particular ongoing issue areas, such as the economy, science and technology, and the environment (for Canada, see Phidd, 1975; Doern, 1971; Howlett, 1990). However, many other such bodies exist in almost every policy area. These range from general advisory committees and specialized clientele advisory committees to specific task-oriented committees and others (see Peters and Parker, 1993; Barker and Peters, 1993).

Permanent bodies advise governments on particular issue areas on an ongoing basis, while others are formed for shorter periods of time to look into specific issue areas. Ad hoc *task forces* or *inquiries*, including some forms of *Royal Commissions*, are created by governments largely to fashion a consensus among interested parties on the nature of a policy problem and its solution (Wilson, 1971). They are usually quite specific in their focus and conduct different types of hearings and 'stakeholder' consultations aimed at developing such a consensus. These should not be confused with the more open-ended, research-oriented bodies that are created under these same titles (Sheriff, 1983). Ad hoc task forces and similar bodies are not intended to develop new knowledge or promulgate old, but rather to provide a venue for organized and unorganized interests to present their views and analyses on pressing contemporary problems, or to frame or reframe issues in such a way that they can be dealt with by governments (Owens and Rayner, 1999).

A second tool in this category is a kind of *public–private partnership* (Linder, 1999). There are numerous different types of such partnerships, many of which are a form of contracting out used to deliver goods and services and, therefore, exist as substantive rather than procedural instruments. However, some partnerships exist primarily to enhance the capacity and permanence of private-sector actors, usually non-governmental organizations (NGOs), which are delegated minor government tasks in order to receive funding, the main purpose of which is to maintain these organizations' availability for consultations and the provision of advice to governments (Armstrong and Lenihan, 1999; Kernaghan, 1993). In some countries, such as Britain, governments have created an entire category of quasi-autonomous NGOs or QUANGOs, which fulfill an important role in policy-making processes (Hood, 1986b; Kickert, 2001).

Various issues arise with respect to the use of this tool, including who is included or excluded, how broad is the range of interests represented among committee or QUANGO members, and how specific individuals are designated as 'representative'. Design issues also involve questions of size, as larger groups may be more representative of more views but will have greater difficulty arriving at uniform recommendations. These issues have taken on more salience in recent years as efforts to increase 'stakeholder' consultations have occurred in many jurisdictions (see

Glicken, 2000; Mitchell et al., 1997). While these kinds of consultative partnerships are useful, they have some drawbacks, notably the potential to co-opt societal actors to the point where the advice they provide to governments merely reflects the aims and desires of the government itself (Phillips, 1991a; Saward, 1990, 1992). Also difficult is identifying exactly who is a 'stakeholder' and who is not, which can lead to difficulties if interested parties are missed or overlooked (Glicken, 2000; Mitchell et al., 1997). And these processes can lead to cynicism on the part of participants if they feel their positions have been ignored, or that the purpose of a task force or committee is simply to impose a predetermined view on participants rather than the other way around (Riedel, 1972; Grima, 1985).

Treasure-Based Instruments

A third general category of policy instruments relies not so much on government personnel or governmental authority for its effectiveness, but rather on government financial resources and the government's ability to raise and disburse funds. This refers to all forms of financial transfers to individuals, firms, and organizations from governments or from other individuals, firms, or organizations under government direction. These transfers can serve as incentives or disincentives for private actors to follow the wishes of government. As an incentive, the purpose of the transfer is to reward a desired activity, thereby affecting social actors' estimates of costs and benefits of the various alternatives. While the final choice is left to individuals and firms, the likelihood of the desired choice being made is enhanced because of the financial subsidy it draws (Beam and Conlan, 2002). As a disincentive, the purpose is to penalize certain types of behaviour by raising the costs that individuals and other policy actors incur in following it (Cordes, 2002).

Subsidies: Grants, Tax Incentives, and Loans
One of the most prominent forms of treasure-based instrument is *grants*, which are 'expenditures made in support of some end worthy in itself, almost as a form of recognition, reward or encouragement, but not closely calibrated to the costs of achieving that end' (Pal, 1992: 152; Haider, 1989). Grants are usually offered to producers, with the objective of making them provide more of a desired good or service than they would otherwise. The expenditure comes out of the government's general tax revenues, which requires legislative approval. Examples of grants include government funds provided to schools, universities, and public transportation.

Another prominent form of subsidy is the *tax incentive* involving 'remission of taxes in some form, such as deferrals, deductions, credits, exclusions, or preferred rates, contingent on some act (or the omission of some act)' (Mitnick, 1980: 365). Tax incentives or *tax expenditures* involve taxes or other forms of government revenues, such as royalties or licence fees, which are forgone. That is, a subsidy is provided since revenues that would normally have been collected are not.

Governments find tax incentives appealing, not least because they are hidden in complex tax codes and so escape notice, which makes their establishment and continuation relatively easy (McDaniel, 1989; Leeuw, 1998). Moreover, in most countries they do not need legislative budgetary approval, for no money is actually spent; rather, revenues are forgone (Maslove, 1994). Nor is their use constrained by availability of funds, because they involve no direct expenditure. They are also easier to administer and enforce because no special bureaucracy needs to be created to administer them, as would be the case with many other instruments. The existing taxation bureaucracy is usually entrusted with the task. The amounts 'spent' in this manner are huge. For example, Christopher Howard has estimated that US federal tax expenditures alone accounted for $744.5 billion or 42 per cent of total federal direct expenditures in the year 2000 (Howard, 2002: 417).

Loans from the government at an interest rate below the market rate are also a form of subsidy. However, the entire amount of the loan should not be treated as a subsidy, only the difference between the interest charged and the market rate (Lund, 1989).

Other policy instruments not technically considered as subsidies may involve some component of subsidy. Thus, *regulations* that restrict the quantity of a particular good or service produced or sold also involve subsidy to the producers because they can often artificially increase prices. Dairy and poultry producers in many countries are subsidized in this manner. Regulations involving marketing boards that fix prices to protect competition from driving down prices and thus hurting other existing producers, for example, also involve subsidy from consumers. *Restrictive licensing*, such as that received by the taxicab industry in most places, is another example of this kind of subsidy through regulation. *Government procurement* from local producers at a price higher than the market price is also a subsidy to these producers to the extent of the difference between the purchase price and the market price (Howard, 1997).

Subsidies offer numerous advantages as policy instruments (see Mitnick, 1980: 350–3; Howard, 1993, 1995). First, they are easy to establish if there is a coincidence of preference between what the government wants someone to do and what the latter desires. If the target population believes an action to be desirable but for some reason does not carry it out, then a subsidy may make a difference in their behaviour. For instance, firms contemplating plant modernization or labour training may be swayed to act if tax incentives for these activities are provided; similarly, people are encouraged to put away money for their retirement rather than spend it right away if they are provided with a tax exemption for so doing. Second, subsidies are a flexible instrument to administer because the individual participants decide for themselves how to respond to the subsidy in the light of changing circumstances. Likewise, they permit local and sectoral circumstances to be taken into account, as only those individuals and firms believing a subsidy to be beneficial would take it up. Third, by allowing individuals and firms to devise appropriate responses, subsidies may encourage innovation on their part. In contrast, directives, by establishing performance standards, normally discourage innovative responses from the public (it is, of course, also possible to make a subsidy contingent on innovation). Fourth, the costs of administering and enforcing subsidies may be low because it is up to potential recipients to claim benefits. Finally, subsidies are often politically more acceptable because the benefits are concentrated on a few whereas the costs are spread across the population, with the result that they tend to be supported strongly by the beneficiaries and opposed only weakly by their opponents (Wilson, 1974).

There are also disadvantages to the use of subsidies, of course. Since subsidies (except tax incentives) need financing, which must come from new or existing sources of revenues, their establishment through the formal budgetary process is often difficult. They must compete with other government programs needing funds, each backed by its own network of societal groups, politicians, and bureaucrats. Second, the cost of gathering information on how much subsidy would be required to induce a desired behaviour may also be high. Arriving at a correct amount of subsidy by trial and error can be an expensive way of implementing a policy. Third, since subsidies work indirectly, there is also often a time lag before the desired effects are discernible. This makes them an inappropriate instrument to use in a time of crisis. Fourth, subsidies may be redundant in cases where the activity would have occurred even without the subsidy, thus causing a windfall for the recipients. At the same time, they are hard to eliminate because of the opposition from existing beneficiaries who stand to lose from their removal. Fifth, subsidies may be banned by international agreements, as they are in trading industries because of the pernicious effects that subsidized imports can have on local industries and employment.

Financial Disincentives: Taxes and User Charges

A tax is a legally prescribed compulsory payment to government by a person or firm (Trebilcock et al., 1982: 53). The main purpose of a tax is normally to raise revenues for the government's financing of expenditures. However, it can also be used as a policy instrument to induce a desired behaviour or discourage an undesirable behaviour. Taxes can take a variety of forms and differ as to how they are put into effect.

Payroll taxes of various sorts are used in most countries to fund social

security programs. Under such schemes, the employer typically withholds a specified portion of the employee's salary (called the employee
contribution), matches the amount by a proportion determined by the
government (employer contribution), and then hands the amount thus
collected to the government. The purpose of payroll taxes is often to
build an *insurance* pool for designated risks such as unemployment,
sickness, industrial injury, and old age pensions. When the specified
contingency occurs, the insured is indemnified from the fund. In a sense
this is no different from private insurance one can buy for various risks,
except that some risks are regarded as crucial to the society and hence
insurance against them is made compulsory by the government. Compulsory membership in an insurance fund expands the number of insured
and thus reduces the cost of premiums by spreading the risk for specific
individual activities among the general populace (Katzman, 1988; Feldman, 2002).

Taxes can also be used to curb undesirable behaviour. In contrast to a
subsidy, which is a positive incentive and works by rewarding a desired
behaviour, taxes can be applied as a *negative incentive* (or sanction) that
penalizes an undesired behaviour. By taxing a good, service, or activity,
the government indirectly discourages its consumption or performance
by making it more expensive to purchase or produce. Many governments' policy objectives of reducing smoking, drinking, and gambling
because of their ill effects, for example, can be partially achieved through
exceptionally high taxes on cigarettes, alcohol, and gambling revenues.
Studies show that the high price of cigarettes caused by high taxes was a
key reason for reduction in cigarette consumption in Canada in the early
1990s, for example, although these taxes encouraged smuggling and
other forms of tax-avoidance behaviour (Studlar, 2002).

A particularly innovative use of a tax as a policy instrument is a *user
charge*. Instead of inducing a behaviour by rewarding it through subsidy
or requiring it through regulations, the government imposes a 'price' on
certain behaviours that those undertaking them must pay. The price may
be seen as a financial penalty intended to discourage the targeted
behaviour. User charges, similar to auctions of property rights, are a
combination of regulation and market instruments. The regulatory aspect
has to do with the government setting the charge (tax) for an activity
without prohibiting or limiting it. How much of the target activity is
undertaken is determined by market forces responding to the level of
charges. The extra cost involved leads firms and individuals to conduct
formal or informal cost-benefit analysis, and so conclude that the activity
must be ceased altogether or reduced to a level where benefits exceed
costs. Efforts to reduce costs may encourage a search for (cheaper) alternatives that will reduce the chargeable activity. A firm can reap windfalls
if it is able to implement technologies that do not involve the target
behaviour or the charge associated with it. The success of a user charge

is contingent on setting optimal charges so that only an acceptable level of undesired activity occurs.

User charges are most commonly used to control negative externalities. An example from the area of pollution control is that of user charges on pollution, known as effluent charges (Sproule-Jones, 1994; Zeckhauser, 1981). Reducing pollution has costs, the marginal rate of which tends to increase with each additional unit of reduction. If a charge is levied on effluent discharge, the polluter will keep reducing its level of pollution to the point at which it becomes more expensive to reduce pollution than simply to pay the effluent charge. In theory at least, the polluter will thus be constantly seeking to devise ways to minimize the charges it has to pay by cutting back on the level of pollution it discharges. The government would ideally set the effluent charge at the point where social benefits equal social costs, assuming that the society knows how much pollution it can live with given the costs of decreasing the level of pollution. Any other price would be inefficient; lower charges would yield excessive pollution and too high a charge would raise costs, and, ultimately, the price that consumers pay. Another innovative example of user charges is provided by Singapore's efforts to control downtown traffic congestion, discussed above. During peak hours, commuters are required to pay a set fee to enter the downtown area, which forces them to compare the costs of entering the area in their own vehicles with the cost of taking a bus or underground train, which are exempt from the charge. Research shows that the charge has had a marked impact on reducing traffic inflow into the downtown area, and other cities, like London, England, have now implemented or are considering similar schemes.

Among the advantages of taxes and user charges as policy instruments are the following. First, they are easy to establish from an administrative standpoint. Companies have few grounds to oppose such measures; they cannot claim that it is not possible to reduce the activity in question, as they can continue the existing level of activity by paying the charge. Second, taxes and user charges provide continuing financial incentives to reduce undesirable activities. Since reducing the charges firms pay would enable them to reduce prices or increase profits, it is in their self-interest to minimize the target activity. Regulations, by contrast, provide no incentive to reduce the behaviour below a specified standard. Third, user charges promote innovation by making it in a firm's interest to search for cheaper alternatives. Fourth, they are a flexible instrument, as the government can continue to adjust rates until a point is reached where the desirable amount of the target activity occurs. Moreover, unlike regulation, where the discovery of new technology would require a change in regulations, subjects respond to user charges on their own. Finally, they are desirable on administrative grounds because the responsibility for reducing the target activity is left to individuals and firms, which reduces the need for large bureaucratic enforcement machinery.

There are some disadvantages of taxes and user charges as well. First, they require precise and accurate information in order to set the correct level of taxes or charges to elicit desired behaviour. Second, during the process of experimentation to arrive at optimum charges, resources may be misallocated. The existing charges, for example, might encourage the installation of machinery that would be unviable when rates are reduced. Third, they are not effective in times of crisis when an immediate response is required. Finally, they can involve cumbersome and possibly damaging administration costs if their rates are not set properly and they encourage evasive behaviour on the part of their targets, as occurred in the smoking example cited above.

Interest Group Funding

A prominent procedural tool in this category is *interest group funding*. As public choice theorists have pointed out, interest groups do not arise automatically to press for certain policy solutions to ongoing problems, but rather require active personnel, organizational competence, and, above all, funding if they are to become a policy force. While different countries have different patterns and sources of interest group funding, governments play a large role in this activity in all democratic states (Maloney et al., 1994).

In some countries, like the US, funding for interest group creation and ongoing expenses tends to come from private-sector actors, especially philanthropic trust funds and private companies, but governments facilitate this through favourable tax treatment for estates, charitable trusts, and corporate donations (Nownes and Neeley, 1996; Nownes, 1995). In other countries, like Canada, the state plays a much greater role in providing direct financing for interest groups in specific areas where the government wishes to see such groups become, or become more, active (Pal, 1993a; Phillips, 1991a; Pross and Stewart, 1993; Finkle et al., 1994). And, of course, in corporatist countries in Europe, Latin America, and parts of Asia, states not only facilitate interest group activities through financial means, but also through the extension of special recognition and associational rights to specific groups, providing them with a monopoly or near monopoly on representation. This brings with it a greater ability to raise revenues through memberships (Jordan and Maloney, 1998; Schmitter, 1977, 1985).

Like many other procedural instruments, alteration of the interest group system through the use of financial or treasure-based instruments involves some risks. Although it may be useful for government to build social capacity in these areas in order to obtain better information on social needs and wants, this kind of 'boundary-spanning' activity[5] can also result in the co-optation or even emasculation of bona fide interests. It can also result in a significant distortion of the overall interest articulation system if only those groups favourable to the government receive funding (Saward, 1990, 1992; Cardozo, 1996).

Nodality or Information-Based Instruments

The fourth category of policy tools involves the use of information resources at the disposal of governments.

Public Information Campaigns

This is a passive instrument whereby the government puts out information with the expectation that individuals and firms will change their behaviour in a desired manner. The information is often of a general nature, intended to make the population more knowledgeable so that they can make informed choices. For instance, information on tourism, programs, and economic and social statistics is disseminated by the government through *advertising campaigns*, leaving it to the population to draw conclusions and respond accordingly (Salmon, 1989). However, the information may also be more precisely targeted to elicit a particular response, as in the case of publicizing information on the ill effects of smoking (Weiss and Tschirhart, 1994; Vedung and van der Doelen, 1998). In either case, there is no obligation on the public to respond in a particular manner (Adler and Pittle, 1984). In many countries this passive release of information may be mandated or facilitated by *freedom of information* or access to information laws. These laws allow access to specific types of government information by members of the public (Relyea, 1977; Bennett, 1990, 1992). Such legislation is usually accompanied by privacy acts and official secrets acts, which balance open access with restrictions on the release of some types of information, the exact content of which varies from country to country (Qualter, 1985).

Exhortation

Exhortation, or *suasion* as it is also called, involves only slightly more government activity than pure dissemination of information (Stanbury and Fulton, 1984). It entails a concerted effort to change the subjects' preferences and actions, rather than just informing them about a situation with the hope that they will change their behaviour in a desired manner. However, it does not include altering the attractiveness of the choice by offering rewards or imposing sanctions.

Examples of exhortation include advertisements urging people to keep fit and healthy, not to waste water or energy, and to use public transportation. *Consultations* between government officials and financial, industry, or labour representatives are also often a form of exhortation because in these meetings governments often hope to alter these parties' behaviour. This group of instruments assumes one or both of two things: (1) that the realm of private behaviour in question must remain private and government cannot legitimately apply coercive instruments; (2) that motivations are strong enough that the subjects themselves can be relied on to achieve policy goals once apprised of new information. For example, to prevent the spread of AIDS, the government can do little to force safe sexual behaviour but must instead rely on dissemination of information, hoping that people will make informed choices to avoid activities that carry risks of infection.

The use of information-based tools offers numerous advantages to governments (ibid., 297–301). It is a good starting point for a government dealing with problems to which definite solutions are unavailable. Second, it is easy to establish, and if the problem is solved through exhortation alone, then nothing more needs to be done. However, even if a better instrument is found, the policy of suasion can be changed or abandoned without much difficulty. Third, it is inexpensive in terms of both financial and personnel costs because it involves little financial commitment or enforcement by the bureaucracy. And finally, exhortation is consistent with the norms of liberal democracy, which value debate, persuasion, individual responsibility, and freedom.

However, exhortation is too weak an instrument when immediate results are required, as in times of crisis. The government may use it merely to portray itself as doing something about a problem, rather than actually doing something meaningful (Edelman, 1964: 44–72). Thus, government exhortation against violence against women, in the absence of other instruments, may be of little use. As Stanbury and Fulton conclude, 'In the absence of positive or negative inducements (or more bluntly, leverage), most efforts at suasion probably have either a low probability of success or have a relatively short shelf life.' At best, it should be used in conjunction with other instruments when they are available.

Research Inquiries, Investigative Commissions, and Freedom of Information Legislation

Information resources can also be used for procedural purposes. These instruments are quite varied and range from the selective release or withholding of government information to the creation of specialized research bodies to compile existing information into a form usable by governments. All of these tools, however, have the same end in mind: to alter the nature of the perceptions held by actors in policy subsystems so as to alter the nature of existing and future policy processes (Termeer and Koppenjan, 1997).

Governments may employ a range of temporary bodies to compile existing information into a usable form or sometimes just to procrastinate in making a decision, hoping that public pressure for action will ease over time. Foremost among these is the *ad hoc inquiry, commission, or task force.* These agencies exist in many forms in different countries and are often established to deal with new or particularly troubling policy problems. They attempt to provide a forum that combines specialized academic research and more generalized public input into the definition of and potential solution to policy problems, generating information that becomes available to all participants in the policy process and altering their knowledge, or epistemic, base as a result (Sheriff, 1983; Wraith and Lamb, 1971: 302–23; Chapman, 1973).

These commissions have some advantages in terms of removing a subject from immediate partisan debate, although this can lead to charges that they are merely delaying tactics and thereby undermine their legitimacy (Elliott and McGuinness, 2001). This often results in the use of important or respected figures to head such inquiries to ensure that their creation and deliberations remain above partisan or public reproach. This is especially the case with high-profile investigations such as Royal Commissions and presidential commissions (McDowall and Robinson, 1969; Cairns, 1990a; d'Ombrain, 1997).

In many jurisdictions, a system of *formal reviews of ongoing policy areas* is also evident. These reviews serve as 'institutionalized' task forces or investigations into ongoing issues and the efforts made by government bodies to deal with them (Bellehumeur, 1997; de la Mothe, 1996; Raboy, 1995; Banting, 1995). These reviews are usually done 'in-house' but sometimes also involve the use of outside experts (Owens and Rayner, 1999). In both cases, they generate and disseminate information on government activities, which is then used by actors in the policy process to inform themselves about government actions and, as a result, to adjust their own actions within policy subsystems accordingly.

CONCLUSION

Discussion in this chapter indicates that a parsimonious scheme for categorizing policy instruments can be generated by examining the limited number of basic 'resources' that governments can employ. While this discussion helps to outline the types of decisions policy-makers must make about exactly how they will attempt to achieve their policy goals, it tells us little about how or why those choices are made. In Chapter 8 we will discuss several causal models of instrument choice. This chapter, however, like the preceding one outlining the principal actors and institutions affecting public policy-making, has merely inventoried an important element of the public policy process. How the process actually operates is discussed in Part III.

FURTHER READINGS

Anderson, Charles W. 1977. *Statecraft: An Introduction to Political Choice and Judgement.* New York: John Wiley and Sons.

Balch, George I. 1980. 'The Stick, the Carrot, and Other Strategies: A Theoretical Analysis of Governmental Intervention', *Law and Policy Quarterly* 2, 1: 35–60.

Bemelmans-Videc, Marie-Louise, Ray C. Rist, and Evert Vedung, eds. 1998. *Carrots, Sticks and Sermons: Policy Instruments and Their Evaluation*. New Brunswick, NJ: Transaction Publishers.

Gunningham, Neil, Peter Grabosky, and Darren Sinclair. 1998. *Smart Regulation: Designing Environmental Policy*. Oxford: Clarendon Press.

Hood, Christopher. 1986. *The Tools of Government*. Chatham, NJ: Chatham House.

_____. 1986. 'The Hidden Public Sector: The 'Quangocratization' of the World?', in F.-X. Kaufman, G. Majone, and V. Ostrom, eds, *Guidance, Control, and Evaluation in the Public Sector*. Berlin: Walter de Gruyter, 183–207.

Lowi, Theodore J. 1972. 'Four Systems of Policy, Politics and Choice', *Public Administration Review* 32, 4: 298–310.

Mitnick, B.M. 1980. *The Political Economy of Regulation*. New York: Columbia University Press.

Peters, B. Guy, and F.K.M. Van Nispen, eds. 1998. *Public Policy Instruments: Evaluating the Tools of Public Administration*. New York: Edward Elgar.

Salamon, Lester M., ed. 1989. *Beyond Privatization: The Tools of Government Action*. Washington: Urban Institute, 23–50.

_____, ed. 2002. *The Tools of Government: A Guide to the New Governance*. New York: Oxford University Press.

Schneider, Anne, and Helen Ingram. 1990. 'Behavioral Assumptions of Policy Tools', *Journal of Politics* 52, 2: 510–29.

Wolf, Charles, Jr. 1988. *Markets or Governments: Choosing Between Imperfect Alternatives*. Cambridge, Mass.: MIT Press.

Woodside, K. 1986. 'Policy Instruments and the Study of Public Policy', *Canadian Journal of Political Science* 19: 775–94.

NOTES

1. On earlier, or similar, resource-based schemes, see Lundquist (1987); Anderson (1977); Baldwin (1985).
2. McDonnell and Elmore also used a fourfold classification of instruments, although they classified instruments according to the end desired rather than the resources used. For McDonnell and Elmore, instruments could be categorized as 'mandates', 'inducements', 'capacity-building', and 'system-changing'. See McDonnell and Elmore (1987); Elmore (1987). Schneider and Ingram (1990a, 1990b) proposed a similar list of categories, which they called 'incentives', 'capacity-building', 'symbolic and hortatory', and 'learning'.
3. On the distinction between procedural and substantive instruments, see, generally, Howlett (2000). On the art of political manipulation or 'heresthetics', see Riker (1983, 1986).
4. Critical assessments of the effectiveness of these instruments can be found in Gibson (1999) and Karamanos (2001).
5. On 'boundary-spanning' in interorganizational relations, see Cohen and Levinthal (1990) and Lane and Lubatkin (1998).

Part III

The Public Policy Process

Chapter 5

Agenda-Setting: Policy Determinants, Policy Ideas, and Policy Windows

Why do some issues appear on the governmental agenda for action and not others? Although often taken for granted, the means and mechanisms by which issues and concerns are recognized as candidates for government action are by no means simple. Some demands for government resolution of some public problems come from international and domestic actors, whereas others are initiated by the governments themselves. These issues originate in a variety of ways and must undergo complex processes before they are seriously considered for resolution. Agenda-setting, the first and perhaps the most critical stage of the policy cycle, is concerned with these processes.

John Kingdon, in his path-breaking inquiry on the subject in the early 1980s, provided the following concise definition of this stage:

> The *agenda*, as I conceive of it, is the list of subjects or problems to which governmental officials, and people outside of government closely associated with those officials, are paying some serious attention at any given time. . . . Out of the set of all conceivable subjects or problems to which officials could be paying attention, they do in fact seriously attend to some rather than others. So the agenda-setting process narrows this set of conceivable subjects to the set that actually becomes the focus of attention. (Kingdon, 1984: 3–4)

What happens at this early stage has a decisive impact on the entire policy process and its outcomes. The manner and form in which problems are recognized, if they are recognized at all, are important determinants of how they will ultimately be addressed by policy-makers. As Cobb and Elder (1972: 12) put it:

> Pre-political, or at least pre-decisional processes often play the most critical role in determining what issues and alternatives are to be considered by the polity and the probable choices that will be

made. What happens in the decision-making councils of the formal institutions of government may do little more than recognize, document and legalize, if not legitimize, the momentary results of a continuing struggle of forces in the larger social matrix.

At its most basic, agenda-setting is about the recognition of a problem on the part of the government. How a problem comes to be interpreted as a *public* problem requiring government action raises deeper questions about the nature of human knowledge and the social construction of that knowledge (Berger and Luckmann, 1966; Holzner and Marx, 1979), and the policy sciences literature has gone through significant changes in its understanding of what constitutes a public problem. Early works assumed that problems had an 'objective' existence waiting to be 'recognized' by governments. Later works began to acknowledge that problem recognition is very much a socially constructed process. It involves definitions of normalcy and what constitutes an undesirable deviation from that status. Hence, problem recognition is not a simple mechanical process, but a sociological one in which the 'frames' within which governments operate and think are of critical significance (Goffman, 1974; Haider-Markel and Joslyn, 2001; Schon and Rein, 1994).

In this view, the 'problems' that are the subject of agenda-setting are considered to be constructed in the realm of public and private discourse (Berger and Luckmann, 1966; Hilgartner and Bosk, 1981; Holzner and Marx, 1979; Rochefort and Cobb, 1993; Spector and Kitsuse, 1987). As Murray Edelman (1988: 12–13) has argued:

Problems come into discourse and therefore into existence as reinforcements of ideologies, not simply because they are there or because they are important for well-being. They signify who are virtuous and useful and who are dangerous and inadequate, which actions will be rewarded and which penalized. They constitute people as subjects with particular kinds of aspirations, self-concepts, and fears, and they create beliefs about the relative importance of events and objects. They are critical in determining who exercise authority and who accept it. They construct areas of immunity from concern because those areas are not seen as problems. Like leaders and enemies, they define the contours of the social world, not in the same way for everyone, but in the light of the diverse situations from which people respond to the political spectacle.

These frames, of course, are not always widely, or as strongly, held by all important policy actors, meaning that the agenda-setting process is very often one in which there is a clash of frames (Bleich, 2002). The resolution of this conflict is related more to the abilities and resources of competing actors than to the elegance or purity of the ideas they hold (Surel, 2000; Snow and Benford, 1992; Steinberg, 1998). In its original formulation by the French social philosopher Michel Foucault (1972), the notion of a political discourse was set out as a tool for understanding the historical evolution of society. The task of historical analysis, and social theory in general, was to understand the nature of the origin and evolution of discursive formations over time, and to situate current discourses into this overall conception of history. From this perspective, the idea that agenda-setting is a process in which policy-makers react to objective conditions in a rational manner is deceptive, if not completely misleading. Rather, policy-makers are involved in the same discourses as the public and in the manipulation of the signs, sets, and scenes of a political play or theatre. According to the script of these ideological discourses, different groups of policy actors are involved, and different outcomes prescribed, in the agenda-setting process (Muntigl, 2002).

In this view, then, the agenda of politics or policy-making is created out of the history, traditions, attitudes, and beliefs of a people encapsulated and codified in the terms of its political discourse (Jenson, 1991; Stark, 1992). Symbols and statistics, both real and fabricated, are used to back up one's preferred understanding of the causes of the problem. Ancient and contemporary symbols are discovered or created to make one's case. Convenient statistics are put together to bolster that case. In these statistics, as policy-makers know all too well, one finds what one looks for.

Hence, to understand agenda-setting we must comprehend how demands for a policy are made by individuals and/or groups and responded to by government, and vice versa. In addition, the conditions must be understood under which these demands emerge and are articulated in prevailing policy discourses (Spector and Kitsuse, 1987: 75–6). Towards this end, we need to understand the material interests of social and state actors as well as the institutional and ideological contexts in which they operate (Thompson, 1990).

In order to understand this complex interplay at the agenda-setting stage of the policy process, students of policy-making over the years have developed several different theoretical models of agenda-setting behaviour. These have ranged from simple one-way models in which governments are seen as responding in a quasi-automatic fashion to large-scale changes in society, to those in which the relationship between the state and social actors is seen to be much more dialectical or interrelated in nature.

EARLY UNIVARIATE MODELS OF AGENDA-SETTING

Most early works on the subject of agenda-setting began with the assumption that socio-economic conditions led to the emergence of particular sets of problems to which governments eventually responded in a lagged, causal fashion. These include models based on the idea that the issues facing all modern governments are converging towards the same set; that the interplay of economic and political cycles affect the nature of issues that attain agenda status; that these same issues are determined by swings in public mood or sentiment; and that a more specific pattern of swings in government attention is a feature of agenda-setting in modern democracies. Each of these early models will be discussed in turn.

Economic and Technological Determinism: The Convergence Theses

The idea that public policy problems and issues originate in the level of 'development' of a society, and that particular sets of problems are common to states at similar levels of development, was first broached by early observers of comparative public policy-making. By the mid-1960s Thomas Dye and others in the United States had concluded that cultural, political, and other factors were less significant for explaining the mix of public policies found in different jurisdictions than were factors related to the level of economic development of the society in question. In his study of policy development at the state level in the US, for example, Ira Sharkansky concluded that 'high levels of economic development—measured by such variables as per cent urban per capita income, median educational level and industrial employment—are generally associated with high levels of expenditure and service outputs in the fields of education, welfare and health.' This conclusion led him to argue that 'political characteristics long thought to affect policy—voter participation, the strength of each major party, the degree of inter-party competition, and the equity of legislative apportionment—have little influence which is independent of economic development' (Sharkansky, 1971).

This observation about the nature of public policy formation in the American states was soon expanded to the field of comparative public policy dealing with the different mixes of public policies found between and across nations. Authors such as Harold Wilensky (1975), Philip Cutright (1965), Henry Aaron (1967), and Frederick Pryor (1968) all developed the idea that the structure of a nation's economy determined the types of public policies its government would adopt. In its extreme form, this line of analysis led to the emergence of the *convergence thesis*.

The convergence thesis suggests that as countries industrialize, they tend to converge towards the same policy mix (Bennett, 1991; Kerr, 1983). The emergence of similar welfare states in industrialized countries, its proponents argue, is a direct result of their similar levels of economic wealth and technological development. Although early scholars indicated only a positive correlation between welfare policies and economic development, this relationship assumed causal status in the works of some later scholars. In this 'strong' view, high levels of economic development and wealth created similar problems and opportunities, which were dealt with in broadly the same manner in different countries, regardless of the differences in their social or political structures.

Wilensky, for example, noted that 'social security effort', defined as the percentage of a nation's GNP devoted to social security expenditures, varied positively with high levels of five key socio-economic and political variables. In a comparative study of 60 countries, he found that 83 per cent of the variance in levels of social security effort could be explained by examining differences in the age of the social security systems, the age of the population, the level of economic development defined in terms of GNP per capita, and whether the state was 'totalitarian' or liberal democratic (Wilensky, 1975: 658–9). He found that the strongest correlation was between social security effort and the level of GNP per capita, a correlation leading him to argue that economic criteria were more significant than political ones in understanding why those public policies had emerged. As he explained it, 'economic growth makes countries with contrasting cultural and political traditions more alike in their strategy for constructing the floor below which no one sinks' (ibid.).

In this view, agenda-setting is thus a virtually automatic process occurring as a result of the stresses and strains placed on governments by industrialization and economic modernization. It mattered little, for example, whether issues were actually generated by social actors and placed on government agendas, or whether states and state officials took the lead in policy development. What was instead significant was the fact that similar policies emerged in different countries irrespective of the differences in their social and political structures.

The convergence thesis was quickly disputed by critics who argued that it oversimplified the process of policy development and inaccurately portrayed the nature of the actual welfare policies found in different jurisdictions, policies characterized by significant divergence as well as convergence (Heidenheimer et al., 1975). It was noted, for example, that in comparative studies of policy development in the American states, economic measures explained over one-half of the interstate variations in policies in only 4 per cent of the policy sectors examined. Second, the definition of 'political factors' used by investigators was restricted to such things as voter turnout, party strength, and equity of legislative apportionment and did not include such obvious factors affecting program development as tax effort or the nature of intergovernmental grants, both significant factors in the US federal system. Third, it was intimated that the desire to make a strong economic argument had led investigators to overlook the manner in which economic factors varied in significance over time and by issue area (Sharkansky, 1971).

Similar criticisms were made against the more broadly cross-national comparisons. The measures used by Wilensky and others were criticized for failing to capture the numerous different dimensions of social welfare programs (Miller, 1976). Instead of focusing on *welfare efforts*, which is a measure of expenditure on social security as a percentage of GDP, it was argued that analysts needed to consider all the ways in which the state affects income distribution in society (Korpi, 1983). This broader approach was said to reveal a great deal of divergence in the social policies of similarly industrialized countries. It was suggested that subtle but significant differences in social welfare policies—such as whether benefits were geared to wage levels or guaranteed basic incomes—were glossed over in the analyses arguing for convergence (Esping-Andersen, 1990; Ramesh, 2000; Boychuk, 1997). Others argued that the issue was not simply social security effort, but the overall level of public expenditures in different countries, a phenomenon felt to be inextricably linked to partisan political factors and the ideological complexion of the government in power (Castles and McKinlay, 1979; Castles, 1982; Hibbs, 1977; King, 1981; von Beyme, 1984).

Interplay of Politics and Economics: Political Business Cycles

In the mid-1980s, a second explanation of agenda-setting emerged that was less deterministic and that treated political and economic factors as an integral whole. It argued that industrialization creates a need for social security (because of aging of the population and urbanization) as well as the economic resources (because of increases in productivity) to address this need. It also creates a working class with a need for social security and the political resources (because of the number of voters who belong to this class) to exert pressure on the state to meet its needs. The ideology of the government in power and the political threats it faces are also important factors in the extent to which the state meets the demand for social welfare. While some issues, such as the role of international economic forces in domestic policy formation, were still debated (Cameron, 1984; Katzenstein, 1985), this view offered a reasonable synthesis of the political-economic explanations of public policy. However, it remained at a fairly high level of abstraction and was difficult to apply to specific instances of agenda-setting (see Uusitalo, 1984).

One way that scholars sought to overcome this problem was by reintegrating political and economic variables in a new 'political economy of public policy' (Hancock, 1983). Here it was argued that both political and economic factors are important determinants of agenda-setting and should therefore be studied together, especially insofar as political-economic events can affect the *timing* of policy initiatives.

One of the most important versions of this line of argument posited the idea of a *political business cycle*. The economy, it was suggested, has its own internal dynamics, which on occasion are altered by political 'interference'. The notion of a political business cycle grew out of the literature on business cycles, which found that the economy grew in fits and starts according to periodic flurries of investment and consumption behaviour (see Schneider and Frey, 1988; Frey, 1978; Locksley, 1980). When applied to public policy-making, it was argued that in the modern era governments often intervened in markets to smooth out fluctuations in the business cycle. In democratic states, it followed that the nature of these interventions could be predicted on the basis of the political ideology of the governing party—either pro-state or pro-market—while the actual timing of interventions would depend on the proximity to elections. Policies that caused difficulties for the voting public were, according to observers, more likely to be developed when an election did not loom on the immediate horizon. As Edward Tufte (1978: 71) put it:

> Although the synchronization of economic fluctuations with the electoral cycle often preoccupies political leaders, the real force of political influence on macroeconomic performance comes in the determination of economic priorities. Here the ideology and platform of the political party in power dominate. Just as the electoral calendar helps set the timing of policy, so the ideology of political leaders shapes the substance of economic policy.

While few disagreed that partisan ideology could have an impact on the economy, this approach was criticized for its limited application to countries, such as the United States, where electoral cycles were fixed. In many other countries, the timing of elections is indeterminate and depends on events in parliaments or other branches of government, and detailed calculations of policy timing are much more difficult if not impossible for governments to make (Foot, 1979; Johnston, 1986). It was also argued that the concept of the business cycle itself was fundamentally flawed and that the model simply pointed out the interdependence of politics and economics already acknowledged by most analysts (see McCallum, 1978; Nordhaus, 1975; Schneider and Frey, 1988; Boddy and Crotty, 1975).

Ideas and Ideology: Policy Paradigms and Policy Moods

Political-economic explanations were an improvement in studies hoping to identify policy determinants and helped underscore the contingent nature of agenda-setting and issue recognition. However, they did little to identify the actual content of policy initiatives. Problems with these early 'materialist' explanations of why governments dealt with certain social problems and not others led in the 1980s to studies that focused on the effects of social and political ideas in defining the sorts of problems with which governments were preoccupied (King, 1973).

It had long been noted, of course, that the ideas individuals hold on an enduring basis have a significant effect on the decisions they make. Although efforts have been made by economists, psychologists, and others to reduce these sets of ideas to a rational calculation of self-interest, it is apparent that traditions, beliefs, and attitudes about the world and society affect how individuals interpret their interests (Flathman, 1966). These sets of ideas or ideologies, therefore, can be construed to have a significant impact on public policy-making, for it is through these ideational prisms that individuals conceive of social or other problems that inspire their demands for government action and through which they construct various proposed solutions to these problems (Chadwick, 2000; George, 1969).

However, it must be appreciated that there are different types of ideas and their effects on policy-making, and especially agenda-setting, vary quite dramatically. As Goldstein and Keohane (1993b) have noted, at least three types of ideas are relevant to policy: *world views*, *principled beliefs*, and *causal ideas* (see Braun, 1999; Campbell, 1998). These basic sets of ideas can influence policy-making by serving as 'road maps' for action, by affecting the strategic interactions that take place between policy actors, and, once institutionalized, by constraining the nature of policy options.

World views or ideologies, of course, had long been recognized as helping people make sense of complex realities by identifying, among other things, key actors in political processes and their motivations. These sets of ideas, however, tend to be very diffuse and do not necessarily translate easily into specific views on specific policy problems. While scholars recognized that the general *policy mood* or *policy sentiment* found in a jurisdiction could be an important component of its policy system, linking, for example, the election of representatives of a certain political persuasion to key offices in a democratic polity (Durr, 1993; Stimson, 1991; Stimson et al., 1995; Lewis-Beck, 1988; Suzuki, 1992; Adams, 1997), this link to agenda-setting remained quite indirect (Stevenson, 2001; Elliott and Ewoh, 2000).

Principled beliefs and causal stories, on the other hand, can exercise a much more direct influence on policy problem recognition and policy content. In the policy realm, this notion of ideas creating claims or demands on governments was taken up by Frank Fischer and John Forester (1993) and Paul Sabatier (1987, 1988), among others (see George, 1969). The concept of causal stories, in particular, has been applied to agenda-setting by Deborah Stone (1988, 1989). In Stone's view, agenda-setting usually involves constructing a 'story' of what caused the policy problem in question. As she has argued:

> Causal theories, if they are successful, do more than convincingly demonstrate the possibility of human control over bad conditions. First, they can either challenge or protect an existing social order. Second, by identifying causal agents, they can assign responsibility to particular political actors so that someone will have to stop an activity, do it differently, compensate its victims, or possibly face

punishment. Third, they can legitimate and empower particular actors as 'fixers' of the problem. And fourth, they can create new political alliances among people who are shown to stand in the same victim relationship to the causal agent. (Stone, 1989: 295)

In his work on policy change in Britain, Peter Hall referred to principled belief structures and causal ideas as constituting a *policy paradigm*, and stressed its significance at all stages of the policy process, including agenda-setting. As Hall (1990: 59) has argued, a policy paradigm establishes:

the broad goals behind policy, the related problems or puzzles that policy-makers have to solve to get there, and, in large measure, the kind of instruments that can be used to attain these goals. Like a gestalt, this framework is all the more powerful because it is largely taken for granted and rarely subject to scrutiny as a whole. It seems likely that policy-makers in all fields are guided by some such paradigm, even though the complexity and coherence of the paradigm may vary considerably across fields.

However, the influence of causal ideas and beliefs is not automatic. Although some scholars argued that some ideas simply become fashionable at specific points in time, as 'ideas whose time has come' (Kingdon, 1984; Jacobsen, 1995), others have noted that this process in fact is a complex one that requires successfully linking ideas to actors in the policy process and overcoming resistance of established actors to new ideas (Drezner, 2000; Legro, 2000). As Hansen and King (2001) have argued:

ideas are more likely to be translated into policy under three conditions: when there is a synergy between ideas and interests, when the actors possess the requisite enthusiasm and institutional position, and when timing contributes to a broad constellation of preferences that reinforce these ideas, rather than detracting from them.

That is, while ideas are an important independent variable in policy-making, the links between ideas and interests, between ideas and actors, or between ideas and circumstances are paramount in understanding their effect on agenda-setting behaviour (Blyth, 1997).

Interest Groups and the Media: The Issue-Attention Cycle

The need to characterize more accurately the sets of actors and ideas involved in agenda-setting drove other studies of this stage of the policy cycle. Many of the early works on the subject were American and were deeply imbued with the pluralist sentiments prevalent in mainstream American political science of earlier eras, and consequently focused on interest groups and the role played by those groups in creating 'pressure' on governments to consider certain policy actions. Thus, for example, in their classic work on the subject, Cobb, Ross, and Ross defined agenda-setting as 'the process by which demands of various groups in the population are translated into items vying for the serious attention of public officials' (Cobb et al., 1976: 126).

However, not all authors and studies focused on the role of interest or pressure groups, per se, in focusing government attention on certain issues. In the area of communications studies, for example, studies attributing a central role to the media in 'framing' public debate and discussion were common (McCombs, 1981). Such studies usually examined the linkages between media coverage of issues and its impact on public opinion in democratic polities, arguing that this linkage would spur governments to act on specific issues framed by the media as 'actionable', that is, as resolvable by government activity (Nelson and Oxley, 1999; Bosso, 1989).

As was discussed in Chapter 3, one very influential early model of the agenda-setting process was developed by the British scholar Anthony Downs in the 1970s, based on this kind of analysis. In Downs's view, public policy-making in many areas of social life tended to revolve around specific issues that momentarily captured public attention, resulting in demands for government action. These problems would soon fade from view as the complexity or intractability of the problem became apparent to members of the public. As he put it:

> Public attention rarely remains sharply focused upon any one domestic issue for very long—even if it involves a continuing problem of crucial importance to society. Instead, a systematic issue-attention cycle seems strongly to influence public attitudes and behaviour concerning most key domestic problems. Each of these problems suddenly leaps into prominence, remains there for a short time, and then—though still largely unresolved—gradually fades from the center of public attention. (Downs, 1972: 38)

In a democracy, where politicians ignore public demands at their peril, Downs argued, waxing and waning public attention would result in a characteristic cyclical pattern of agenda-setting and public policy-making: the *issue-attention cycle*.

This idea of a systematic pattern of agenda-setting gained a great deal of attention in subsequent years and Downs's work is one of the most often cited in the agenda-setting literature. Nevertheless, his original hypothesis was rather vague. It was not clear, for example, whether this cycle was expected to apply to 'most key domestic problems', as the above quotation suggests, or only to a subset of 'all major social problems', as was suggested elsewhere in his oft-cited 1972 article on the subject (ibid., 41).

In that article, Downs noted that not all problems would follow the same kind of cycle. The problems most likely to be affected by the issue-attention syndrome, he argued, were only those that shared three basic characteristics. First, they usually were problems that adversely affected a minority of the population. Second, these problems usually were generated as the side effects of arrangements that benefited the majority of the population. Third, the problems were capable of generating 'dramatic' moments, but not sustained periods, of media attention. Together these three characteristics would ensure that:

> most people will not be continually reminded of the problem by their own suffering from it . . . solving the problem requires sustained attention and effort, plus fundamental changes in social institutions and behaviour; . . . the media's sustained focus on this problem soon bores a majority of the public. (Ibid., 42)

This discussion, of course, suggests that other types of agenda-setting behaviour would be expected whenever a problem fails to meet any of these three conditions. That is, numerous problems exist that have, at minimum, one of the following characteristics: (1) the problem directly affects the majority of the population; (2) the problem is simple to understand and resolve; and/or (3) the problem, at some point in time, could generate continuing, sustained, 'dramatic' media coverage. Downs did not elaborate on these types of issues, however, or on the likely typical patterns of policy development and change, if any, that might characterize them (Howlett, 1997a).

Despite its frequent citation in the policy literature over the past three decades, the idea of Downsian-type issue-attention cycles has rarely been subject to empirical evaluation. In 1985, Peters and Hogwood made an effort to operationalize their own version of Downs's cycle, attempting to assess the relationship between waves of public interest as measured in Gallup polls and periodic waves of organizational change or institution-building in the US federal government. Although they found evidence of major periods of administrative consolidation and change over the course of recent US history, they noted that only seven of 12 instances of administrative reorganization met the expectations of the Downsian model. That is, they exhibited such changes during the same decade as the peak of public interest as measured by Gallup survey questions. In another four, however, changes occurred in the decade following peak public interest, while in one area—social welfare policy—change occurred prior to peak public interest. The evidence was even weaker when organizational initiations were examined. They found only four organizational initiations coincided with the same decade as peak public interest, while four occurred in the following decade and three—economic policy, housing, and social welfare—occurred prior to peak public interest (Peters and Hogwood, 1985b: 250).

On the basis of these results, Peters and Hogwood offered only partial support for Downs's hypothesis. As they argued: 'Our evidence supports

Downs' contention that problems which have been through the issue-attention cycle will receive a higher level of attention after rather than before the peak' (ibid., 251). However, they were also careful to note that there appeared to be at least two patterns or cycles at work in the issue-attention process in addition to what Downs first identified. In the first type, cycles were initiated by external or exogenous events such as war or an energy crisis and then were mediated by public attention. In this type of 'crisis' cycle, the problem would not 'fade away' as Downs hypothesized. In the second type of 'political' cycle, issue initiation originated in the political leadership and then, too, was mediated by public attention (ibid., 252; see also Hogwood, 1992).

While studies such as that by Downs were useful in adding the systematic evaluation of the role of policy actors into discussions of agenda-setting, they tended to ignore or downplay the role of the state in this process (Sharp, 1994b; Yishai, 1993). For example, they failed to note how officially scheduled political events, such as annual budgets, speeches from the throne, or presidential press conferences, could spark media attention, reversing the causal linkages originally attributed to these actors in the agenda-setting process (Cook et al., 1983; Howlett, 1997; Erbring and Goldenberg, 1980; Flemming et al., 1999). Empirical evidence gathered in many other case studies revealed that critical dimensions of interest group success and failure in gaining agenda access tended to be linked to state institutional structures and the availability of access points, or *policy venues*, from which these groups could access government officials and decision-makers (Baumgartner and Jones, 1993; Boockmann, 1998; Pross, 1992).

MULTIVARIATE MODELS OF AGENDA-SETTING

None of these early approaches generated models or theories of agenda-setting that withstood testing and examination. At best they provided some linkages between the emergence of certain general types of issues on policy agendas and certain sets of general social, political, and economic variables. The problems associated with each of the early efforts to identify a single cause or factor driving public policy agenda-setting led to the development of more complex, multivariate models, which attempted systematically to combine some of the central variables initially identified in these early studies into a more accurate theory of agenda-setting.

The Funnel of Causality

In the 1970s Anthony King (1973) in Great Britain, Richard Hofferbert (1974) in the United States, and Richard Simeon (1976a) in Canada each developed models that sought to capture the general relationships existing among interests, institutions, ideas, politics, and economic conditions in the process of agenda-setting. These models were based on the notion that the variables existed within a *funnel of causality*, in which each was 'nested' within another.

The funnel-of-causality approach reviewed and synthesized much of the existing literature on agenda-setting. Rather than viewing material, ideational, institutional, and actor-related variables as dichotomous or zero-sum, this approach argued that all these factors are involved in the creation and recognition of social or policy problems. More specifically, a series of causal variables were identified, including those related to the socio-economic and physical environment, the distribution of power in society, the prevailing ideas and ideologies, the institutional frameworks of government, and the process of decision-making within governments (King, 1973). Hofferbert and Simeon suggested that these variables were intertwined in a nested pattern of mutual interaction in which policy-making occurs within institutions, institutions exist within prevailing sets of ideas and ideologies, ideologies within relations of power in society, and relations of power within a larger social and material environment.

This synthetic model helped delineate the relations existing between the multiple material and ideational variables identified in previous studies without bogging down in attempts to specify their exact relationship or causal significance. While this is the model's greatest strength, however, it is also its greatest weakness. It is a strength because it allows some discussion between alternate viewpoints to take place, while leaving it to empirical studies to determine the exact relationship between the central variables. It is also a weakness, though, because it does little to explain the differences found in specific cases according to the actual causative agent at work. Why one issue might be influenced by ideas and another, for example, by environmental factors is not broached, let alone resolved. Similarly, the funnel-of-causality model says very little about how multiply-mediated general forces such as the environmental context, ideas, and economic interests are actually manifested by policy actors in the agenda-setting process (Mazmanian and Sabatier, 1980).

Agenda-Setting Patterns

A major breakthrough in agenda-setting studies occurred in the early 1970s when scholars such as Cobb, Ross, and Ross associated different typical agenda-setting patterns or 'styles' with different types of political regimes, and set about developing a model of agenda-setting to explain this variance. In so doing, they followed the insight of Cobb and Elder, who distinguished between the *systemic* or informal public agenda and the *institutional* or formal state agenda. The systemic agenda 'consists of all issues that are commonly perceived by members of the political community as meriting public attention and as involving matters within the legitimate jurisdiction of existing governmental authority' (Cobb and Elder, 1972: 85). This is essentially a society's agenda for discussion of *public* problems, such as crime or health care. Each society, of course, has literally thousands of issues that some citizens find to be matters of concern and would have the government do something about.

However, only a small proportion of the problems on the systemic or informal agenda are taken up by the government for serious considera-tion. Only once a government has accepted that something needs to be done about a problem can the issue be said to have entered the institu-tional agenda. These are issues to which the government has agreed to give serious attention. In other words, the public agenda is an agenda for discussion while the institutional agenda is an agenda for action, indicat-ing that the policy process dealing with the problem in question has begun.

Cobb, Ross, and Ross identified four major phases of agenda-setting that occur as issues moved between the systemic and institutional agen-das. Issues are first *initiated*, their solutions are *specified*, support for the issue is *expanded*, and if successful, the issue *enters* the institutional agenda (Cobb et al., 1976: 127).[1] In earlier studies, which were influ-enced strongly by pluralism, public problems were viewed as always moving from the systemic to the institutional agenda. However, investi-gation of actual cases of agenda-building revealed difficulties with such a conception, and Cobb and his colleagues developed several different models of agenda-setting to describe how issues actually moved from society to state or from state to the society as they proceeded onto the official agenda.

Cobb, Ross, and Ross first developed these different models after hav-ing undertaken studies of the agenda-setting process in different coun-tries. According to them, there were three basic patterns or models of agenda-setting: the outside initiation model, the mobilization model, and the inside initiation model, each associated with a particular type of political regime. They identified the *outside initiation model* with liberal pluralist societies. In this model, 'issues arise in nongovernmental groups and are then expanded sufficiently to reach, first, the public [systemic] agenda and, finally, the formal [institutional] agenda.' In this model the key role is played by social groups. Issues are initiated when a group articulates a grievance and demands its resolution by the government. Those same groups attempt to expand support for their demand, a pro-cess that may involve submerging the specific complaint within a more general one and the formation of alliances across groups. Finally, these groups lobby, contest, and join with others in attempting to get the expanded issue onto the formal agenda. If they have the requisite politi-cal resources and skills and can outmanoeuvre their opponents or advo-cates of other issues and actions, they will succeed in having their issue enter the formal agenda. Thus, as Cobb, Ross, and Ross (1976: 132) summarize it:

> The outside initiative model applies to the situation in which a group outside the government structure 1) articulates a grievance, 2) tries to expand interest in the issue to enough other groups in the population to gain a place on the public agenda, in order to 3) create sufficient pressure on decision makers to force the issue onto the formal agenda for their serious consideration.

Successful entrance onto the formal agenda does not necessarily mean a favourable government decision will ultimately result. It simply means that the item has been singled out from among a mass of others for more detailed consideration.

The *mobilization model* is quite different and was attributed by Cobb, Ross, and Ross to 'totalitarian' regimes. This model describes 'decision-makers trying to expand an issue from a formal [institutional] to a public [systemic] agenda' (ibid.). In the mobilization model, issues are simply placed on the formal agenda by the government with no necessary preliminary expansion from a publicly recognized grievance. There may be considerable debate within government over the issue, but the public may well be kept in the dark about the policy and its development until its formal announcement. The policy may be specified in some detail or it may establish only general principles whose specification will be worked out later. Expansion of support for the new policy is important, however, as successful implementation depends on a favourable public reaction to the policy. Towards this end, government leaders hold meetings and engage in public relations campaigns aimed at mobilizing public support for their decisions. As the authors put it, 'The mobilization model describes the process of agenda building in situations where political leaders initiate a policy but require the support of the mass public for its implementation . . . the crucial problem is to move the issue from the formal agenda to the public agenda.'

In the *inside initiation model*, influential groups with special access to decision-makers initiate a policy and do not necessarily want it to be expanded and contested in public. This can be due to technical as well as political reasons and is a pattern of agenda-setting one would expect to find in corporatist regimes. In this model, initiation and specification occur simultaneously as a group or government agency enunciates a grievance and specifies some potential solution to the problem. Expansion is restricted to specialized groups or agencies with some knowledge or interest in the subject. Entrance on the agenda is virtually automatic due to the privileged place of those desiring a decision. According to Cobb, Ross, and Ross:

Proposals arise within governmental units or in groups close to the government. The issue is then expanded to identification and attention groups in order to create sufficient pressure on decision makers to place the item on the formal agenda. At no point is the public greatly involved, and the initiators make no effort to get the issue on the public agenda. On the contrary, they try to keep it off. (Ibid., 136)

This line of analysis identifies several typical patterns or styles of agenda-setting. While it does so on the basis of an (unstated) notion of a relatively crude policy subsystem—one in which state and societal actors are clearly separated—the most important variable in this analysis is regime type. That is, in this model the type of agenda-setting process likely to be found in any sector is ultimately determined by the general nature of the political system; outside initiation is argued to be typical of liberal democracies, mobilization typical of one-party states, and inside initiation typical of authoritarian bureaucratic regimes.

However, it was soon recognized that these different styles of agenda-setting varied not so much by regime as by sector, as examples of each type of agenda-setting behaviour could be found within each regime type. This led to additional studies attempting to be more specific about exactly what processes were followed within political regimes, especially complex democratic polities like the United States.

Policy Windows and Policy Streams

In the 1980s, John Kingdon (1984) developed a sophisticated approach to agenda-setting based on his detailed study of agenda processes in the US federal legislative system. His model deals with the question of state and non-state influences on agenda-setting by focusing on the role played by policy entrepreneurs both inside and outside of government in taking advantage of agenda-setting opportunities—*policy windows*—to move items onto formal government agendas. It suggests that the characteristics of issues combine with the characteristics of political institutions and circumstances, and the development of policy solutions, in a fashion that can lead to the opening and closing of windows of opportunity for agenda entrance. Such opportunities can be seized upon or not, as the case may be, by policy entrepreneurs who are able to recognize and act on them.

In Kingdon's study of agenda-setting in the United States, three sets of variables—streams of problems, policies, and politics—are said to interact. The *problem stream* refers to the perceptions of problems as public problems requiring government action and past government efforts to resolve them. People come to see a condition as a 'problem' with reference to their conception of some desired state of affairs. In Kingdon's view problems typically come to the attention of policy-makers either because of sudden events, such as crises, or through feedback from the operation of existing programs (ibid., 20). The *policy stream* consists of experts and analysts examining problems and proposing solutions to them. In this stream, the various possibilities are explored and narrowed down. Finally, the *political stream* 'is composed of such factors as swings of national mood, administrative or legislative turnover, and interest group pressure campaigns' (ibid., 21). In Kingdon's view, these three streams operate on different paths and pursue courses more or less independent of one another until at specific points in time, or *policy windows*, their paths intersect.

In the right circumstances, policy windows can be seized upon by key players in the political process to gain entrance for particular issues. Policy entrepreneurs play the chief role in this process by linking or 'coupling' policy solutions and policy problems together with political opportunities (ibid., chs 7–8). As Kingdon argues, 'The separate streams of problems, policies, and politics come together at certain critical times. Solutions become joined to problems, and both of them are joined to favourable political forces.' At that point an item enters the official (or institutional) agenda and the public policy process begins.

It is important to note, however, that linking the three policy streams together is a necessary, but not sufficient, condition for issue entrance. Something else is required for these three streams to come together and secure issue entrance—the opening of a policy window. Kingdon suggested that while window openings were sometimes governed by certain fortuitous happenings—including seemingly unrelated external 'focusing events', crises, or accidents; or the presence or absence of policy entrepreneurs both within and outside of governments—at other times they were affected by institutionalized events such as periodic elections or budgetary cycles (Birkland, 1997, 1998). As he argued:

> windows are opened either by the appearance of compelling problems or by happenings in the political stream. . . . Policy entrepreneurs, people who are willing to invest their resources in pushing their pet proposals or problems, are responsible not only for prompting important people to pay attention, but also for coupling solutions to problems and for coupling both problems and solutions to politics. (Kingdon, 1984: 21)

Different types of windows were identified by Kingdon and are implicit in his work. As Kingdon stated:

> Sometimes, windows open quite predictably. Legislation comes up for renewal on schedule, for instance, creating opportunities to change, expand or abolish certain programs. At other times, windows open quite unpredictably, as when an airliner crashes or a

fluky election produces unexpected turnover in key decision-makers. Predictable or unpredictable, open windows are small and scarce. Opportunities come, but they also pass. Windows do not stay open long. If a chance is missed, another must be awaited. (Ibid., 213)

Ultimately, Kingdon suggested that two principle types of window exist: the 'problem' and 'political' windows:

Basically a window opens because of change in the political stream (e.g. a change of administration, a shift in the partisan or ideological distribution of seats . . . or a shift in national mood); or it opens because a new problem captures the attention of governmental officials and those close to them. (Ibid., 176)

To this initial distinction Kingdon added the idea that windows would also vary in terms of their predictability. While arguing that random events are occasionally significant, he stressed the manner in which institutionalized windows dominate the US agenda-setting process.[2] As he put it, 'There remains some degree of unpredictability. Yet it would be a grave mistake to conclude that the processes . . . are essentially random. Some degree of pattern is evident' (ibid., 216). In fact, he argued that many windows open on a more or less predictable, cyclical, pattern: 'Windows sometimes open with great predictability. Regular cycles of various kinds open and close windows on a schedule. That schedule varies in its precision and hence its predictability, but the cyclical nature of many windows is nonetheless evident' (ibid., 193).

Hence the general model established by Kingdon suggests the existence of at least four possible window types based on the relationship between the origin of the window—political or problem—and their degree of institutionalization or routinization. Although Kingdon did not provide a specific nomenclature to describe the four window types, the general outline of each type is discernible from an examination of his work and several of his principal sources.[3] Thus, the four principal window types are:

- *routinized political windows*, in which institutionalized procedural events dictate predictable window openings;
- *discretionary political windows*, in which the behaviour of individual political actors leads to less predictable window openings;
- *spillover problem windows*, in which related issues are drawn into an already open window; and
- *random problem windows*, in which random events or crises open unpredictable windows.

These basic types of windows and their relationship are set out in Figure 5.1. In this model, the level of institutionalization of a window type

Figure 5.1   **A Model of Policy Window Types**

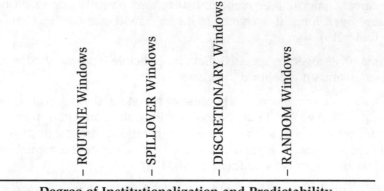

| ROUTINE Windows | SPILLOVER Windows | DISCRETIONARY Windows | RANDOM Windows |

Degree of Institutionalization and Predictability

High   Low

determines its frequency of appearance and hence its predictability (Boin and Otten, 1996; Howlett, 1997b).

Kingdon's model has been used to describe and assess the nature of US foreign policy agenda-setting (Woods and Peake, 1998); the politics of privatization in Britain, France, and Germany (Zahariadis, 1995; Zahariadis and Allen, 1995); the nature of US domestic anti-drug policy (Sharp, 1994a); the collaborative behaviour of business and environmental groups in certain anti-pollution initiatives in the US and Europe (Lober, 1997); and the overall nature of the reform process in Eastern Europe (Keeler, 1993). While a major improvement on earlier models, however, it has been criticized for presenting a view of the agenda-setting process that is too contingent on unforeseen circumstances, ignoring the fact that in most policy sectors, as Downs had noted, activities tend to occur in spurts and then congeal for lengthy periods of time. In other words, while Kingdon's model provided an excellent discussion of agenda-setting dynamics, it failed to address adequately the existence of agenda-setting stability noted by Cobb and his colleagues (see Dodge and Hood, 2002).

Policy Monopoly Models

In the 1990s, beginning from the observation that the process of agenda-setting involves both periods of stability and periods of dynamism, scholars focused on the activities of agenda-setting actors in trying to explain this pattern. Particular attention was paid to the processes of discussion, debate, and persuasion among actors interested in the policy, each actor presenting a variety of evidence and argument in support of a particular position (Majone, 1989). On this basis Baumgartner and Jones (1991,

1993, 1994) developed a model that modifies Kingdon's work and helps to explain the typical patterns of agenda-setting behaviour found in democratic polities. For Baumgartner and Jones, the 'image' of a policy problem is significant because of how it influences membership in relevant policy subsystems. Hence, they argue that:

> When they are portrayed as technical problems rather than as social questions, experts can dominate the decision-making process. When the ethical, social or political implications of such policies assume center stage, a much broader range of participants can suddenly become involved. (Baumgartner and Jones, 1991: 1047)

The key element in the process of agenda-setting, Baumgartner and Jones argue, revolves around the creation of *policy monopolies*, in which specific subsystems gain the ability to control the interpretation of a problem and thus the manner in which it is conceived and discussed. Both governments and members of the public are located in policy subsystems, and the primary relationship upon which Baumgartner and Jones focus their analysis of US agenda-setting is that between individuals and groups represented in existing subsystems and those who would like to be. In their model, subsystem members seek to alter policy images through a number of tactics related to altering the venue of policy debate, or other aspects of the prevailing policy discourse, and thereby undermine the complacency or stability of an existing policy subsystem.

The strategies adopted by groups, Baumgartner and Jones argue, generally fall into two types. In the Downsian strategy, groups can publicize a problem in order to alter its venue by encouraging the public to call upon governments to resolve it (Baumgartner and Jones, 1993: 88). In a second typical approach, which they term a 'Schattschneider' mobilization, groups involved in the policy subsystem that do not like the policies being developed or discussed by governments seek to alter the institutional arrangements within which the subsystem operates in order to expand or contract its membership (ibid., 89).

AGENDA-SETTING STYLES

This brief overview of studies into agenda-setting has shown how these have moved from simple univariate models to more sophisticated ones linking numerous variables in complex multivariate relationships. It has also shown how contemporary studies have centred on the elaboration of a basic set of agenda-setting patterns or styles, revealing much about the timing of agenda-setting activity and the overall nature of the policy dynamics that result from it.

Building on earlier univariate studies that focused on the impact on agenda-setting of such variables as the nature of the economy, the political system, policy-relevant ideas and beliefs, and the activities of central political actors, current studies have shown how these variables combine to create a relatively small number of agenda-setting styles and how fortuitous and expected political events can draw state and social attention to particular issues in fairly predictable ways.

As Cobb, Ross, and Ross first realized, the most significant variables related to the identification of typical agenda-setting styles have to do with the nature of the actors initiating policy discussions and the manner in which the government is involved in this initiation. Instead of emphasizing the nature of the political regime in determining these patterns, however, a more fruitful avenue, as Kingdon and Baumgartner and Jones suggested, is to conceptualize the agenda-setting process in terms of the interaction of the nature of the policy subsystem involved in the issue area with the nature of the problem itself. In this latter dimension, in a democratic society the level of public support for the resolution of a problem is critical (Soroka, 2002). Some problems have a wide-ranging impact on society and therefore the demands for their resolution are likely to be initiated by the public. Others are of significance only to particular groups, which, depending on the closeness of their relations with the government of the day, may be able to undertake inside initiation. Government officials may engage in either mobilization or inside initiation, depending on the level of public support for solving the problem in question: if support is forthcoming, then we are likely to see its consolidation; otherwise, the government will have to resort to mobilization.

Thus, the central question in agenda-setting is not the type of regime involved, but rather, as both Kingdon and Baumgartner and Jones recognized, (1) the nature of the policy subsystem involved with the problem, which determines whether the state or societal actors initiate the process, and (2) the level of public support for its resolution (May, 1991). That is, the mode of agenda-setting is determined by the nature of public support for the issue and by the nature of the initiating actor(s).[4]

The three typical patterns identified by Cobb, Ross, and Ross fill in three of the four possible basic agenda-setting styles generated in this way (see Figure 5.2).

Figure 5.2 Models of Agenda-Setting by Policy Type

Nature of Public Involvement

Initiator of Debate		High	Low
	Societal Actors	Outside Initiation	Inside Initiation
	State	Consolidation	Mobilization

SOURCE: Adapted from Peter J. May, 'Reconsidering Policy Design: Policies and Publics', *Journal of Public Policy* 11, 2 (1991): 187–206.

The fourth type of agenda-setting, *consolidation*, occurs when the government initiates the process of solving a public problem for which there is already extensive popular support. In such instances the issue does not have to be 'initiated', nor does public support have to be 'mobilized'. It is enough for the state to 'consolidate' the existing support and go ahead with making policy (Dye, 2001).

CONCLUSION

While the exact timing of the emergence of an issue onto the systemic or formal policy agenda depends, as Kingdon showed, on the existence of a policy window, the nature of the reception an issue receives, and, as we shall see in Chapter 6, the types of solutions put forward to it, all of these aspects of the agenda-setting process depend very much on the nature of the policy subsystem found in the area concerned. Whether or not subsystem members are capable of creating and retaining a monopoly on the interpretation and understanding of a policy issue, as Baumgartner and Jones highlighted in their work, largely determines whether the matching of problems and solutions found in the agenda-setting and subsequent policy formulation stages of the policy process will result in consideration of the issue within an existing policy paradigm or in more novel approaches to the subject (Haider-Markel and Joslyn, 2001; Jeon and Haider-Markel, 2001).

Agenda-setting is not automatic. Policy monopolies not only control how an issue is considered, but also whether or not it is given any consideration at all (David, 2000; Gent, 2000). Many studies in the 1950 and 1960s into problems of race in America, and other studies in the 1970s and 1980s into such issues as gender discrimination, attest to the fact that 'non-decisions' or decisions not to consider an issue as a social problem worthy of action are very typical results of entrenched policy actors content with the status quo (see Yanow, 1992; Bachrach and Baratz, 1962; Debnam, 1975; Frey, 1971; R.A. Smith, 1979). In addition, governments, in particular, can practise different strategies not only of agenda-setting but of *agenda denial*. That is, as the discussion in the previous chapter revealed, governments have different procedural tools at their disposal that allow them to control many aspects of policy subsystem behaviour, including its membership and the relations among those members, which can help them channel policy discourses in directions they would like them to go (Cobb and Ross, 1997b).

FURTHER READINGS

Baumgartner, Frank R., and Bryan D. Jones. 1993. *Agendas and Instability in American Politics*. Chicago: University of Chicago Press.

Bennett, Colin J. 1991. 'What is Policy Convergence and What Causes It?', *British Journal of Political Science* 21: 215–34.

Cobb, Roger W., J.K. Ross, and M.H. Ross. 1976. 'Agenda Building as a Comparative Political Process', *American Political Science Review* 70, 1: 126–38.

_____ and Marc Howard Ross, eds. 1997. *Cultural Strategies of Agenda Denial: Avoidance, Attack and Redefinition*. Lawrence: University Press of Kansas.

Downs, Anthony. 1972. 'Up and Down with Ecology—the 'Issue-Attention Cycle', *The Public Interest* 28: 38–50.

Dye, Thomas R. 1978. 'Politics Versus Economics: The Development of the Literature on Policy Determination', *Policy Studies Journal* 7: 652–62.

Kingdon, John W. 1995 [1984]. *Agendas, Alternatives and Public Policies*. Boston: HarperCollins.

May, Peter J. 1991. 'Reconsidering Policy Design: Policies and Publics', *Journal of Public Policy* 11: 187–206.

Simeon, Richard. 1976. 'Studying Public Policy', *Canadian Journal of Political Science* 9: 548–80.

Spector, Malcolm, and John I. Kitsuse. 1987. *Constructing Social Problems*. New York: Aldine de Gruyter.

Stone, Deborah A. 1988. *Policy Paradox and Political Reason*. Glenview, Ill.: Scott, Foresman.

Wilensky, H.L. 1975. *The Welfare State and Equality: Structural and Ideological Roots of Public Expenditures*. Berkeley: University of California Press.

Yanow, Dvora. 1992. 'Silences in Public Policy Discourse: Organizational and Policy Myths', *Journal of Public Administration Research and Theory* 2, 4: 399–423.

NOTES

1. Kingdon (1984: 4) further differentiates within the institutional agenda, locating the specialized agendas of government agencies, the legislative agenda of government, and the decision agenda of the executive.
2. Other authors, of course, argue that American agenda-setting is a much less random process. See Baumgartner and Jones (1993).
3. Much of Kingdon's analysis is based on earlier work undertaken by Jack Walker (1977) into the agenda-setting process followed in the US Senate. An examination of Walker's work makes it clear that Kingdon's principal hypothesis, related to the frequency of predictable and unpredictable windows, was derived from the application of Walker's observation that US Senate agenda items varied widely in terms of their level of institutionalization or 'routinization'. Kingdon also made use of Walker's distinction between 'discretionary' and 'non-discretionary' issues.
4. For empirical case studies of these effects, see Druckman (2001) and Jacoby (2000).

Chapter 6

Policy Formulation:
Policy Communities and Policy Networks

After a government has acknowledged the existence of a public problem and the need to do something about it, policy-makers need to decide on some course of action. Formulating such a course of action is the second major stage in the policy cycle: *policy formulation*. As Charles Jones (1984: 7) has observed, the distinguishing characteristic of policy formulation is simply that means are proposed to resolve somebody's perception of the needs that exist in society. Policy formulation hence involves assessing possible solutions to policy problems or, to put it another way, exploring the various options available for addressing a problem. The proposals may originate in the agenda-setting process itself, as a problem and its solution are placed simultaneously on the government agenda (Kingdon, 1984), or they may be developed after an item has moved onto the official agenda. In all cases, available options are considered and narrowed down to those that policy-makers can accept. This process of defining, considering, and accepting or rejecting options is the substance of the second stage of the policy cycle.

Lest it is misunderstood, it needs to be emphasized that choosing a solution to a public problem or fulfilling a societal need does not even remotely resemble the orderly process proposed by some analysts. We saw in the preceding chapter on agenda-setting that defining and interpreting a problem is a highly nebulous process that does not always lead to clear or agreed-upon definitions of problems. Even if policy-makers agree on the existence of a problem, they may not share the same understanding of its causes or ramifications. It is therefore to be expected that the search for a solution to a problem will be contentious and subject to a wide variety of pressures, often defeating efforts to consider policy options in a rational or systematic manner.

The essence of the search for solutions to a problem entails discovering not only which actions are considered to be technically capable of addressing or correcting a problem but also which among these is considered to be possible, or feasible, to put into place (Majone, 1975, 1989; Huitt, 1968; Meltsner, 1972; Dror, 1969; Webber, 1986). At this stage, options that are believed will not work or will for some reason be unacceptable to major actors in the policy process are eliminated. Thus, for example, those policy-makers involved in devising health policy to contain health-care costs in the industrialized countries do not usually consider a British-style nationalized health service, which is rated highly for its cost-efficiency, because of the opposition it would provoke from the medical profession fearing reduced income. Nor do they consider denying health services to the aged, who account for a disproportionately large proportion of health-care costs, because of the moral and political outrage this would cause (see Alford, 1972, 1975).

How options are excluded from consideration by policy-makers at this stage of policy formulation tells us a lot about the policy options ultimately chosen for implementation at the decision-making stage of the policy process. Among other things, certain players in the policy process can be advantaged over others if they are granted some authoritative voice in the diagnosis of a policy ill or the establishment of the feasibility of a particular proposed policy solution. This is the case, for example, with scientists or government specialists in many policy areas, but this may not be the case if there are disagreements over the ability of experts to deal with an issue in a competent or neutral manner (see Nathanson, 2000; Heikkila, 1999; Doern and Reed, 2001; Harrison, 2001; Callaghan and Schnell, 2001).

Jones (1984: 78) describes other broad characteristics of policy formulation:

1. Formulation need not be limited to one set of actors. Thus there may well be two or more formulation groups producing competing (or complementary) proposals.
2. Formulation may proceed without clear definition of the problem, or without formulators ever having much contact with the affected groups. . . .
3. There is no necessary coincidence between formulation and particular institutions, though it is a frequent activity of bureaucratic agencies.
4. Formulation and reformulation may occur over a long period of time without ever building sufficient support for any one proposal.
5. There are often several appeal points for those who lose in the formulation process at any one level.
6. The process itself never has neutral effects. Somebody wins and somebody loses even in the workings of science.

The picture of policy formulation this characterization presents is that it is a highly diffuse and complex process that varies by case. Like agenda-setting, the nuances of policy formulation in particular instances can be grasped only through empirical case studies. Nevertheless, most policy formulation processes do share some common characteristics.

First, policy formulation involves the recognition of technical and political constraints on state action. It involves recognizing limitations, which reveals what is infeasible and, by implication, what is feasible. This may seem obvious, but it is yet to be reflected in many of the voluminous writings proposing what policy-makers ought to be doing without reference to the limitations that constrain the choice of any proposed action. For instance, the public choice theorists' key assumption—that politicians choose policies that best promote their electoral appeal—presumes more room for manoeuvre than is actually the case (Majone, 1989: 76). Politicians simply cannot do everything they consider would appeal to voters.

Before we consider the limitations that policy-makers typically encounter that lead them to reject certain types of options, it is worth mentioning that the constraints need not be based on facts (Merton, 1948). If significant actors in the policy subsystem believe that something is unworkable or unacceptable, this is sufficient for its exclusion from further consideration in the policy process. As we have seen with the discussion of agenda-setting in the previous chapter, perception is just as real as reality itself in the policy process.

The constraints the members of policy subsystems encounter may be substantive or procedural. Substantive constraints are innate to the nature of the problem itself. Policy-makers wishing to eliminate poverty thus do not have the option of printing money and distributing it to the poor because inflation will offset any gains, and so they must necessarily address the problem in more indirect ways. Similarly, the goal of promoting excellence in arts or sports cannot be accomplished simply by ordering people to be the best artist or sportswoman in the world; the pursuit of these goals requires far more delicate, expensive, and time-consuming measures. The problem of global warming cannot be entirely eliminated because there is no known effective solution that can be employed without causing tremendous economic and social dislocations, which leaves policy-makers to tinker with options that barely scratch the surface of the problem. Substantive problems are thus 'objective' in the sense that redefining them does not make them go away, and their resolution or partial resolution requires the use of state resources and capacities such as money, information, and personnel, and/or the exercise of state authority.

Procedural constraints have to do with procedures involved in adopting an option or carrying it out. These constraints may be either institutional or tactical. Institutional constraints, as discussed in Chapter 3, include constitutional provisions, the organization of the state and society, and established patterns of ideas and beliefs. They inhibit the choice of some policy options and promote others (Yee, 1996). Efforts to control handguns in the United States, for example, run up against constraints imposed by the constitutional right to bear arms. Federalism imposes similar constraints on German, American, Mexican, Australian, and Canadian policy-makers, among others, in many areas of public policy where two levels of government must agree before anything can be done. How the main social groups are organized internally and are linked with the state also affects what can or cannot be done, especially the nature of political party and electoral systems, which can create 'policy horizons' or limited sets of acceptable choices for specific actors in the policy process (Warwick, 2000; Bradford, 1999). In a similar vein, the predominance of specific sets of philosophical or religious ideas in many societies can lead to difficulties with potential policy solutions that might seem routine in others (DeLeon, 1992).

TYPES OF POLICY ALTERNATIVES

A useful way to think about the nature of the policy options that are developed in the policy formulation process is in terms of the extent to which they propose solutions to problems that depart from the policy status quo. Some options call for new, substantial, or dramatic policy change, while others involve only minor tinkering with existing policies and programs (Majone, 1991).

In his work on economic policy change in Britain, Peter Hall identified three different types of change: *first-order* change in which only the settings of policy instruments varied; *second-order* change in which change occurred in the basic types or categories of instruments used to effect policy; and *third-order* change in which the goals of policy are altered (Hall, 1993).[1] While useful, some of this terminology is confusing and should be altered, while the logic of the model also suggests that there should be four basic types of change, not three.

With respect to terminology, the use of the term 'settings' to describe first-order change can be confusing, since most uses of the term would lead one to consider this to refer to the location of a policy instrument within a policy environment, when Hall means to describe the calibration or fine-tuning of an instrument's content or component parts. More significantly, Hall's model, as shown in Figure 6.1, is based on distinguishing between the means and ends of policy-making and between abstract and concrete aspects of policy outputs (see Campbell, 1998). Given these two dimensions, four distinct categories of policy change are possible, not three. These can be described as changes related to abstract *policy goals* or more concrete *program specifications*, referring to the ends of policy-making; and to basic policy *instrument type* or genus, as opposed to alterations of existing *instrument components*, when discussing changes in policy means.[2]

Figure 6.1 Types of Policy Options by Level of Generality and Policy Component Affected

Level of Generality of Policy Content

			Conceptual/Policy	Practical/Program
Affected	Policy	Element		
		Ends	Policy Goals	Program Specifications
		Means	Instrument Types	Instrument Components

SOURCE: Adapted from Peter A. Hall, 'Policy Paradigms, Social Learning and the State: The Case of Economic Policy Making in Britain', *Comparative Politics* 25, 3 (1993): 275–96.

Options that address policy goals and instrument types require the injection of some new ideas and thinking into policy deliberations. More specific options dealing with program specifications and instrument 'settings' or components, on the other hand, are much more status quo-oriented, involving relatively minor alterations in existing policies. Proposals for policy and program changes tend to arise from new actors in existing policy processes, while changes relating to instrument types and components tend to develop among existing actors as their preferences change (Krause, 1997). This general situation is set out in Figure 6.2.

Figure 6.2 A Model of the Effects of the Presence or Absence of New Actors and Ideas on Types of Policy Options Considered

	Presence of New Actors	*Continuity of Old Actors*
Presence of New Ideas	Options relating to changes in policy goals	Options relating to changes in program specifications
Continuity of Old Ideas	Options relating to changes in instrument types	Options relating to changes in instrument components

POLICY SUBSYSTEMS AND POLICY FORMULATION

The preceding discussion highlights the significance for policy formulation of the nature of the policy actors present at this stage of the policy cycle, and of the ideas and knowledge they hold about the technical and political feasibility of possible courses of action. This raises several important questions about the process of policy formulation. Among the most important are: Who is actually involved in this process? What are the qualifications for participation? (Timmermans and Bleiklie, 1999). While we will need separate empirical analysis of each specific instance of policy formulation to answer these questions, we can nevertheless set out broad parameters to assist such analyses.

As we have seen in our discussion of agenda-setting, the notion of a *policy subsystem* is a powerful concept in policy analysis. Recent studies of policy formulation especially emphasize the importance of policy subsystem structure and behaviour at the formulation stage of the policy cycle (see Howlett, 2002; Nyland, 1995; Marin and Mayntz, 1991: 297–330; Le Gales and Thatcher, 1995; Kingdon, 1984; Milward and Walmsley, 1984; Goldfinch, 2000). Unlike agenda-setting, where members of the entire policy universe theoretically can be involved in policy deliberations and actions, in policy formulation the relevant actors are usually restricted to members of policy subsystems, since a requirement of participation at this stage of the process is some minimal level of knowledge in the subject area, allowing an actor to comment, at least hypothetically, on the feasibility of options put forward to resolve policy problems.

Not surprisingly, identifying the key actors in policy subsystems, what brings them together, how they interact, and what effect their interaction has on the policy has attracted the attention of many students of policy formulation (Heclo, 1994; Hall, 1997). Over the years scholars have developed a variety of models, many of which were mutually contradictory and unnecessarily elaborate, to address these questions.[3] In the following pages, we will examine several of these models, highlight the points of agreement, and offer a model that is useful for conceptualizing the nature of policy subsystems and the role they play in the process of policy formulation.

Models of Policy Subsystems

Subgovernments, Iron Triangles, and Issue Networks

The oldest conception of a policy subsystem was developed in the United States by early critics of pluralism. They developed the notion of the 'subgovernment', understood as groupings of societal and state actors in routinized patterns of interaction (deHaven-Smith and Van Horn, 1984). This concept was based on the observation that interest groups, congressional committees, and government agencies in the US had developed a system of mutual support in the course of constant interaction over legislative and regulatory matters. These three-sided relationships in areas such as agriculture, transportation, and education were often dubbed *iron triangles* to capture the essence of their ironclad control over many aspects of the policy process (Cater, 1964). Such groupings were condemned for having 'captured' the policy process, thus subverting the principles of popular democracy by ensuring that their own self-interests prevailed over those of the general public.[4]

In the 1960s and 1970s, further research into the American case revealed that many subgovernments were not all-powerful, and that in fact their influence on policy-making varied across issues and over time (Hayes, 1978; Ripley and Franklin, 1980). Soon a more flexible and less rigid notion of a policy subsystem evolved, called by Hugh Heclo the *issue network* (Heclo, 1978).

Building on his earlier work comparing social policy-making in Britain and Sweden (Heclo, 1974: 308–10), Heclo argued that while some areas of American political life were organized in an institutionalized system of interest representation, other were not. As he put it:

> Preoccupied with trying to find the few truly powerful actors, observers tend to overlook the power and influence that arise out of the configurations through which leading policy makers move and do business with each other. Looking for the closed triangles of control, we tend to miss the fairly open networks of people that increasingly impinge upon government.

He was not denying the existence of iron triangles, of course, but merely pointing out that their membership and functioning were often not as closed or rigid as was suggested by some commentators.

Heclo conceived of policy subsystems as existing upon a spectrum, with iron triangles at one end and issue networks at the other. He explained the differences between iron triangles and issue networks in the following ways:

> The notion of iron triangles and subgovernments presumes small circles of participants who have succeeded in becoming largely autonomous. Issue networks, on the other hand, comprise a large number of participants with quite variable degrees of mutual commitment or dependence on others in their environment; in fact it is almost impossible to say where a network leaves off and its environment begins. Iron triangles and subgovernments suggest a stable set of participants coalesced to control fairly narrow public programs which are in the direct economic interest of each party to the alliance. Issue networks are almost the reverse image in each respect. (Heclo, 1978: 102)

Issue networks were thus larger, much less stable, had a constant turnover of participants, and were much less institutionalized than iron triangles.

Heclo's alternative interpretation of the nature of the policy subsystems involved in policy formulation fostered several studies in Europe and North America intended to refine the concept. These studies led to the identification of a large variety of subsystems that necessitated the development of alternate taxonomies to Heclo's simple spectrum of issue networks and iron triangles.

Policy Networks and Policy Communities

Comparative work on subsystems led to the clarification of the variables differentiating subgovernments from issue networks and to their renaming as *policy networks* and *policy communities*.

In his comparative study of foreign economic policy, Peter Katzenstein (1977) referred to policy networks as those links joining the state and societal actors together in a policy process. Although he no more than mentioned the term, other writers combined earlier discussions of policy subsystems with elements of organizational and anthropological analyses to flesh out the concept (Milward and Walmsley, 1984).[5]

One such application was made in Britain by R.A.W. Rhodes, who argued throughout the early 1980s that interactions within and among government agencies and social organizations constituted policy networks that were instrumental in formulating and developing policy. Rhodes suggested that networks varied according to their level of 'integration', which was a function of their stability of membership, restrictiveness of membership, degree of insulation from other networks and the public, and the nature of the resources they controlled (Rhodes, 1984: 14–15). In the United States similar attributes were specified by Hamm, who argued that subgovernments could be differentiated according to their 'internal complexity, functional autonomy, and (levels of internal and external) cooperation or conflict' (Hamm, 1983: 415).

In a major study of European industrial policy-making, Wilks and Wright endorsed Rhodes's typology, arguing that networks varied along five important dimensions: 'the interests of the members of the network, the membership, the extent of members' interdependence, the extent to which the network is isolated from other networks, and the variations in the distribution of resources between the members.' Refining the iron triangle–issue network spectrum developed by Heclo, they argued that this conception allowed a 'high-low' scale to be developed in which highly integrated networks would be characterized by stability of membership and inter-membership relations, interdependence within the network, and network insulation from other networks. At the other extreme, weakly integrated networks would be large and loosely structured, with multiple and often inchoate links with other groups and actors (Wilks and Wright, 1987: 301–2).

In the United States empirical efforts to clarify and reformulate the concept of policy networks also were undertaken. Salisbury, Heinz, Laumann, and Nelson, for example, argued that networks tended to have 'hollow cores' in that even the most institutionalized networks appeared to have no clear leadership (Heinz et al., 1990; Salisbury et al., 1987). Others argued that networks could be classified according to whether or not state and societal members shared the same goals and agreed on the same means to achieve those goals. Still others suggested that the number of discernible interests participating was the crucial variable defining different types of networks (McFarland, 1987).

It is important to note that all of these different conceptions construed policy networks as being essentially interest-based. That is, participants were assumed to participate in these networks to further their own ends, which were seen as essentially material and 'objectively recognizable' from outside the network. This emphasis on common material interests set studies of policy networks apart from those that focused on a second type of subsystem, the policy community.

In their early work on British policy subsystems, Richardson and Jordan had identified tight groups of policy actors, which they termed 'policy communities'. Although most observers would later term these policy 'networks' (Richardson and Jordan, 1979; Rhodes, 1984), the two terms continued to be used interchangeably for several more years (see Milward and Francisco, 1983; Sharpe, 1985). Later, Wilks and Wright (1987: 296) sought to make 'community' refer to a more inclusive category of all those involved in policy formulation and to restrict 'network' to a subset of community members who interacted with each other on a regular basis. In their view, 'Policy community identifies those actors and potential actors drawn from the policy universe who share a common policy focus. Network is the linking process within a policy community or between two or more communities.'

Although some European scholars continued to use the term 'community' to refer to tight-knit sets of policy actors (see Rhodes, 1996, 1997a; Rhodes and Marsh, 1992), the use of 'community' in a broad sense to describe policy actors who share a common idea set or outlook fit well with the earlier distinction drawn in the US by Heclo and others between small, closed 'subgovernments' and larger issue networks (Walker, 1981; Berry, 1989; Jordan and Maloney, 1997). While some scholars continued to use the two terms to refer to the two ends of a spectrum of subsystems, much as Heclo had in his initial discussion, others began to think of the two as coexisting in a 'nested' fashion in the sense that interest-driven policy networks existed as a subset of the membership of idea-driven policy communities (Chadwick, 2000; Singer, 1990; Torgerson, 1996; Rein and Schon, 1996; Dudley and Richardson, 1999).

Advocacy Coalitions

This insight, that a policy subsystem might consist of a number of sub-components, was developed at length in the 1980s in the works of Paul Sabatier and his colleagues. They developed a sophisticated scheme for studying the activities of policy actors in policy subsystems. In their work, an *advocacy coalition* refers to a subset of actors in the policy subsystem (Sabatier and Jenkins-Smith, 1993b). According to Jenkins-Smith and Sabatier:

An advocacy coalition consists of actors from a variety of public and private institutions at all levels of government who share a set of basic beliefs (policy goals plus causal and other perceptions) and who seek to manipulate the rules, budgets and personnel of governmental institutions in order to achieve these goals over time.

Jenkins-Smith and Sabatier argued that advocacy coalitions include both state and societal actors at the national, subnational, and local levels of government. Their scheme cleverly combines the role of knowledge and interest in the policy process as policy actors are seen to come together for reasons of common beliefs, often based on their shared knowledge of a public problem and their common interest in pursuing certain solutions to it. The core of their belief system, consisting of views on the nature of humankind and the ultimate desired state of affairs, is quite stable and holds the coalition together. All those in an advocacy coalition participate in the policy process in order to use the government machinery to pursue their (self-serving) goals.

While belief systems and interests determine the policies an advocacy coalition will seek to have adopted, its ability to succeed in this endeavour is affected by a host of factors. These include the coalition's resources such as 'money, expertise, number of supporters, and legal authority' (Sabatier, 1987: 664). External factors also affect what it can achieve by making some objectives easier to accomplish than others (Jenkins-Smith and Sabatier, 1993: 5). Some of these external factors—the nature of the problem, natural resource endowments, cultural values, and constitutional provisions—are relatively stable over long periods of time and are therefore fairly predictable. Others are subject to a greater degree of change, including public opinion, technology, level of inflation or unemployment, and change of political party in government. Sabatier and his colleagues advanced the discussion of policy subsystems in many ways, not least by arguing that they are not unified wholes, but usually have more than one component part. That is, in their scheme, in most cases there will be at least two advocacy coalitions in a subsystem—one supporting the status quo and one proposing changes—but there may be more.

Taxonomies of Policy Subsystems and Subsystem Components

By the end of the 1980s, it was clear from these works and others in many different countries that a variety of different types of subsystems existed, depending on the structural interrelationships existing among their component parts. Efforts then turned to developing a more consistent method of classifying these components so that the different types of subsystems could be better understood (see McCool, 1989; Ouimet and Lemieux, 2000).

In one early effort at classifying policy networks, Atkinson and Coleman developed a scheme based on the organization of state and society, and the links between the two, identifying eight basic types of subsystem. In their view, the two critical questions were whether societal interests are centrally organized and whether the state has the capacity to develop policies independent of them—in other words, the level of state autonomy from societal actors. Although initially clear, this taxonomy was muddied by the addition of a concern for the level of concentration of property owners in affected sectors, generating an eightfold system of policy subsystems. These ranged from a type of pluralism said to describe situations when all three variables were low, to the 'concertation' network, which was said to exist when the interests were centrally organized, capital was concentrated, and the state enjoyed high capacity and autonomy (Atkinson and Coleman, 1989a: 54).

Other efforts resulted in even more complex, and confusing, taxonomies. Thus, for example, Frans van Waarden (1992) attempted to combine Rhodes's analysis with that of Atkinson and Coleman, arguing that networks varied according to seven criteria: number and type of actors; function of networks; structure; institutionalization; rules of conduct; power relations; and actor strategies. Ultimately, the typology he developed included 12 types of subsystems depending on the number and type of actors and the nature of the functions they performed. Like Atkinson and Coleman's initial effort, it proved difficult to apply in practice.

Part of the problem with these classification systems had to do with the purposes for which they were developed. Some, like Atkinson and Coleman's model, were developed to understand the politics of public policy-making in a specific sector, such as industrial policy, and added a level of detail concerning a specific industrial actor (business), which is not required in the analysis of other subsystems. Others, like van Waarden, represented attempts to synthesize disparate schemes, all inductively developed from specific sectoral and issue-level case studies, without first attempting to eliminate idiosyncratic sectoral elements such as those found in Atkinson and Coleman's scheme.

Adopting a different approach to the classification of subsystems can help simplify their analysis and clarify the role they play in policy formulation. Using the analytical separation of community and network, in particular, helps to clarify the conceptualization of policy development and the various factors behind it (Atkinson and Coleman, 1992; Carlsson, 2000). This conceptual distinction helps us understand the significant difference between the two different sets of motivations guiding the actions of those involved in policy formulation: knowledge or expertise, and material interest. A *discourse community* defines its membership by reference to a specific knowledge base whereas an *interest network* is based on some common material interest. Viewed this way, two different aspects of the process of policy formulation came into sharper focus. Some members of policy subsystems are linked together by epistemic concerns—a shared knowledge base—while other members must have not only this base, but also some type of material interest allowing or encouraging regularized contact (Pappi and Henning, 1999). Although the policy subsystem itself contains elements of both ideas and interests, these can be distinguished from each other and their impacts on policy formulation can be analyzed separately (see Hoberg, 1996).

Discourse communities share some common level of understanding of a problem, its definition, and its causes,[6] although disagreements will usually be present not only over how to translate these understandings into policy solutions, but often also over aspects of these basic elements (see Hajer, 1993; Fischer, 1993). Hence, a useful distinction can be drawn between communities in which there is a dominant knowledge base and those in which there is not. A second critical dimension of policy community structure is the number of relatively distinct 'idea sets' that exist in the community (see Schulman, 1988) and if, and to what extent, a consensus exists on any particular set (see Haas, 1992; MacRae, 1993; Smith, 1993). Utilizing these two dimensions allows us to construct a simple matrix of common discourse community types (see Figure 6.3).

Figure 6.3 A Taxonomy of Discourse Communities

		Number of Idea Sets	
		Few	*Many*
Dominant Idea Set	*Yes*	Hegemonic Community	Fractious Community
	No	Contested Community	Chaotic Community

SOURCE: Adapted from Michael Howlett and M. Ramesh, 'Policy Subsystem Configurations and Policy Change: Operationalizing the Postpositivist Analysis of the Politics of the Policy Process', *Policy Studies Journal* 26, 3 (1998): 466–82.

In a situation where one idea set is dominant and unchallenged—such as is presently the case in the area of fiscal policy, where there is virtually no opposition to the balanced budget orthodoxy—a form of monopolistic or 'hegemonic' community may develop. On the other hand, where multiple sets of ideas circulate with no single idea in a dominant position, a much more chaotic community will exist. A good example of this at present concerns the situation with biogenetics policy, where ideas ranging from the 'pure science' of genome research to religious, superstitious, and conspiratorial industrial power theories coexist in the subsystem. Where several major idea sets exist and contest dominance, as Sabatier and Jenkins-Smith noted, a third type of contested community may form; for example, in many countries in areas such as environmental protection, concepts of biodiversity and sustainable development contest equally well-entrenched ones of resource exploitation and utilitarianism. Finally, where one idea set is dominant but faces challenges from less popular ideas, a fractious community is likely to be found. This is a type of community found at present in trade and development policy subsystems, for example, where a dominant free trade globalism faces a challenge from less popular but still compelling sets of ideas promoting more autarkic local or national forms of economic exchange and development.

With respect to interest networks, or more structured forms of subsystem interactions, many observers have highlighted the significance of two key variables in shaping the structure and behaviour of policy networks: the number and type of their membership and the question of whether state or societal members dominate their activities and interactions (Smith, 1993; Coleman and Perl, 1999). A reasonable classification of issue networks can be developed using these variables, as shown in Figure 6.4 (see Atkinson and Coleman, 1989a, 1989b; Coleman and Skogstad, 1990).

Figure 6.4   A Taxonomy of Interest Networks

		Number of Members	
		Few	*Many*
Dominant Actor	*State*	State Corporatist Networks	State Pluralist Networks
	Societal	Social Corporatist Networks	Social Pluralist Networks

SOURCE: Adapted from Michael Howlett and M. Ramesh, 'Policy Subsystem Configurations and Policy Change: Operationalizing the Postpositivist Analysis of the Politics of the Policy Process', *Policy Studies Journal* 26, 3 (1998): 466–82.

In this model, small networks dominated by government actors—as are commonly found in highly technical issue areas such as nuclear, chemical, or toxic substance regulation—can be distinguished from those in which many societal actors are included, as might be the case with education or other areas of state-led social policy-making. Other distinct network types exist where a few societal actors dominate a small network, as in many areas of industrial policy, or where they dominate large networks, as is the case in many countries in areas such as transportation and health-care delivery.[7]

While these types of classification schemes help to clarify the possible structure of discourse communities and interest networks in policy subsystems, and give us a general idea about the nature of the deliberative processes followed at the formulation stage of the policy cycle, they do not in themselves generate specific hypotheses or indications of the propensities of specific types of subsystems towards specific types of options. To get a better sense of that issue, it is necessary to discuss not only the separate components of subsystems, but how those components come together into specific configurations of actors and ideas, or policy subsystem types, and how those types tend to promote or inhibit consideration of certain types of policy options (Richardson, 1995).

In this regard, the insights of authors like Baumgartner and Jones with respect to agenda-setting are equally appropriate to policy formulation. That is, subsystems that are 'monopolistic', involving hegemonic policy communities, and that feature networks with fewer members will tend to promote policy options that reinforce the status quo. Those that are larger and more chaotic will be more likely to suggest alternative courses of action.

SUBSYSTEM STRUCTURE AND POLICY FORMULATION STYLE

That subsystems play a significant role in the process of policy formulation has been hinted at by several authors (Zijlstra, 1978–9; Rhodes and Marsh, 1992). Sabatier, for example, has argued that the nature of the policy subsystem responsible for policy formulation is an important element in the analysis of policy change as coalition members mediate the exchange of interests and ideas in public policy-making. Although they focused their analysis on the role of 'external perturbations' such as elections, wars, accidents, or crises that can disrupt established subsystems, they also recognized that internal subsystem behaviour must be such that the opportunities presented by external 'shocks' actually lead to internal change.[8]

More specifically, authors such as Marsh and Rhodes (1992b), Bressers and O'Toole (1998), and Zahariadis and Allen (1995) have suggested that the 'cohesiveness' or 'closedness' of policy subsystems is an important factor affecting the propensity for new or innovative policy solutions to emerge from the policy formulation process.[9] Hence, one of the most significant aspects of subsystem structure involves the nature of the relationship, or the configuration, that exists between the two component parts of the subsystem: the discourse community and interest network (see Bulkley, 2000; Schaap and van Twist, 1997). This is because subsystems featuring closely integrated communities and networks will be more cohesive and better able to resist the entrance of new ideas and actors into policy processes than will those with sizable intellectual and psychological distances between the two subsets of actors.

This suggests that the principal factor that can be used to identify the propensity of a policy subsystem to promote innovative policy options involving substantial changes to existing policy arrangements is a subsystem structure that allows new actors and new ideas to enter into policy deliberations (Schmidt, 2001). Conversely, the predominance of status quo policy options can be explained by reference to the fact that the same sets of actors and ideas are involved in the policy process over a long period of time.[10]

Observers have often noted how policy-makers, in the course of interaction among themselves and in their day-to-day dealings with a public problem, tend to develop a common way of looking at and dealing with a problem (Kenis, 1991; Haas, 1992; Sabatier, 1988). Slight adaptation and adjustment of views on the basis of experience and new information is endemic to the policy process, but most studies have found that understandings of the nature of public problems and the acceptable or feasible solutions to them are often remarkably durable and, once in place, difficult to change (Pierson, 2000; Sabatier, 1988). This common understanding within a policy subsystem, however, can at times break down, setting the stage for the emergence of new and different policy actors and discourses, consideration of new policy options, and, ultimately, innovative policy outcomes.[11]

This suggests that the relevant general types of policy subsystems that determine the outcomes of the policy formulation process are as set out in Figure 6.5.

Figure 6.5 Basic Policy Subsystem Configurations

		Receptive to New Actors	
		No	*Yes*
Receptive to New Ideas	*No*	Closed Subsystem (Integrated Policy Community and Network)	Resistant Subsystem (Closed Policy Community and Open Network)
	Yes	Contested Subsystem (Open Policy Community and Closed Network)	Open Subsystem (Unintegrated Policy Community and Network)

SOURCE: Adapted from Michael Howlett and M. Ramesh, 'Policy Subsystem Configurations and Policy Change: Operationalizing the Postpositivist Analysis of the Politics of the Policy Process', *Policy Studies Journal* 26, 3 (1998): 466–82.

CONCLUSION: POLICY FORMULATION STYLES

As Hanspeter Kriesi and Maya Jegen (2001: 251) put it, 'to know the actor constellation is to know the parameters determining the choices among the substantive policy options.' In other words, the structure of the subsystem greatly affects its propensity to develop certain types of policy options. As was suggested above, this is because the options developed—whether they affect policy goals, program specifications, instrument types, or instrument components—are affected by the presence or absence of new actors and new ideas at the policy formulation stage (see Menahem, 2001; Montpetit, 2002; Bulkley, 2000).

The existence of subsystems open to new ideas and new actors is required if options pertaining to policy goals are to emerge from the policy formulation stage. If a subsystem is open only to either ideas or actors, but not both, options that emerge are likely to relate only to alterations in program specifications or instrument types. In the case of closed subsystems, a fairly typical type, as Baumgartner and Jones suggested, options will tend to be restricted to the calibration of existing policy instruments. The relationship of subsystem structure to policy options and the resulting policy formulation styles are set out in Figure 6.6.

Figure 6.6 A Model of Policy Formulation Styles

		Entrance of New Actors	
		Yes	No
Entrance of New Ideas	Yes	Policy Renewal (Open Subsystems)	Program Reform (Contested Subsystem)
	No	Policy Experimentation (Resistant Subsystems)	Instrument Tinkering (Closed Subsystem)

Although the development of these concepts is relatively recent, they have been put to good use in dealing with a number of policy sectors (Atkinson and Coleman, 1989a; Pross, 1992). Studies based on the notion of policy communities and policy networks have revealed a great deal about policy formulation in such areas as fisheries policy (Pross and McCorquodale, 1990), women's issues (Phillips, 1991b), environmental policy (Bruton and Howlett, 1992: 25), pharmaceuticals (Atkinson and Coleman, 1989b), information policy (Bennett, 1992), and many others (Coleman and Skogstad, 1990). The development of the concept of complex policy subsystems composed of knowledge-based discourse communities and interest-based networks has had a significant impact on recent studies of public policy formulation.

These studies have also pointed to the need to understand the process of changes in subsystems if the general process of policy change and development is to be understood (see Jenkins-Smith et al., 1991; Baumgartner and Jones, 1991). What type of subsystem exists in a given sector or issue area is of major significance in understanding the dynamics of policy formulation within that area. Which policy options on the institutional agenda will be considered seriously for adoption, and the types of solutions or options considered to be feasible for resolving policy problems, is largely a function of the nature and motivation of key actors arrayed in policy subsystems (Howlett, 2002).

FURTHER READINGS

Atkinson, Michael, and William Coleman. 1992. 'Policy Networks, Policy Communities and the Problems of Governance', *Governance* 5, 2: 154–80.

Daugbjerg, Carsten, and David Marsh. 1998. 'Explaining Policy Outcomes: Integrating the Policy Network Approach with Macro-Level and Micro-Level Analysis', in Marsh, ed., *Comparing Policy Networks*. Buckingham: Open University Press, 52–71.

DeLeon, Peter. 1992. 'Policy Formulation: Where Ignorant Armies Clash By Night', *Policy Studies Review* 11, 3/4: 389–405.

Hall, Peter A. 1993. 'Policy Paradigms, Social Learning and the State: The Case of Economic Policy Making in Britain', *Comparative Politics* 25, 3: 275–96.

Heclo, Hugh. 1978. 'Issue Networks and the Executive Establishment', in A. King, ed., *The New American Political System*. Washington: American Enterprise Institute for Public Policy Research, 87–124.

Heinz, John P., et al. 1993. *The Hollow Core: Private Interests in National Policy Making*. Cambridge, Mass.: Harvard University Press.

Jordan, A. Grant. 1981. 'Iron Triangles, Woolly Corporatism and Elastic Nets: Images of the Policy Process', *Journal of Public Policy* 1, 1: 95–123.

Knoke, David. 1993. 'Networks as Political Glue: Explaining Public Policy-Making', in W.J. Wilson, ed., *Sociology and the Public Agenda*. London: Sage, 164–84.

Lindquist, Evert A. 1992. 'Public Managers and Policy Communities: Learning to Meet New Challenges', *Canadian Public Administration* 35, 2: 127–59.

Majone, Giandomenico. 1975. 'On the Notion of Political Feasibility', *European Journal of Political Research* 3: 259–74.

Marin, Bernd, and Renate Mayntz, eds. 1991. *Policy Networks: Empirical Evidence and Theoretical Considerations*. Boulder, Colo.: Westview Press.

Milward, H. Brinton, and Gary L. Walmsley. 1984. 'Policy Subsystems, Networks and the Tools of Public Management', in Robert Eyestone, ed., *Public Policy Formation*. Greenwich, Conn.: JAI Press, 3–25.

Rhodes, R.A.W. 1997. *Understanding Governance: Policy Networks, Governance, Reflexivity, and Accountability*. Buckingham: Open University Press.

Sabatier, Paul. 1988. 'An Advocacy Coalition Framework of Policy Change and the Role of Policy-Oriented Learning Therein', *Policy Sciences* 21, 2/3: 129–68.

NOTES

1. Examples of first-order changes in a health sector, for example, would

include altering staffing levels in hospitals or altering physician fee schedules. Second-order changes would involve changing the type of instrument used to deliver health care, such as moving from user fees to mandatory insurance arrangements. Third-order change would involve a shift in policy goals, such as moving away from a biomedical focus on the individual to a more holistic goal of collective, social, or community well-being.

2. For similar models based on a similar critique of Hall, see Daugbjerg (1997); Smith (2000).

3. Grant Jordan has spent much effort cataloguing and categorizing the images and metaphors used to describe policy subsystems involved in policy formulation. See Jordan (1981, 1990a, 1990b); Jordan and Schubert (1992). More recently, see Borzel (1998); Thatcher (1998).

4. For early studies in this vein, see Bernstein (1955); Huntington (1952); Lowi (1969).

5. Aldrich and Whetton (1980), for example, talked about 'action sets' and 'networks', the former referring to a group of organizations created for a specific purpose and the latter to the more general forms of interorganizational co-ordination in which organizations were bound together by common relationship. See also Benson (1982).

6. At this point, it is worth noting that a similar conception of a policy community has emerged in the international relations literature in which loose groupings of knowledge actors are said to underlie international institutions and regimes. These *epistemic communities* are defined, in the words of Peter Haas (1992: 3), as 'a network of professionals with recognized expertise and competence in a particular domain and an authoritative claim to policy-relevant knowledge within that domain or issue-area'. He elaborates: 'Although an epistemic community may consist of professionals from a variety of disciplines and backgrounds, they have (1) a shared set of normative and principled beliefs, which provide a value-based rationale for the social action of community members; (2) shared causal beliefs, which are derived from their analysis of practices leading or contributing to a central set of problems in their domain and which then serve as the basis for elucidating the multiple linkages between possible policy actions and desired outcomes; (3) shared notions of validity—that is, intersubjective, internally defined criteria for weighing and validating knowledge in the domain of their expertise; and (4) a common policy enterprise—that is, a set of common practices associated with a set of problems to which their professional competence is directed, presumably out of the conviction that human welfare will be enhanced as a consequence.' This is a clear elucidation of the knowledge base that binds communities of actors together and how it affects their behaviour. The emphasis on 'professionalism', however, means the concept refers to only a specific subset of policy communities. To avoid confusion, we use the term 'discourse community' in this book to refer to both 'epistemic' and other types of policy communities. See also E. Haas (1975); Keohane (1990).

7. On the links between these types and traditional corporatist and pluralist conceptions of interest intermediation, see Sciarini (1986).

8. See also the modifications to this position contained in Sabatier (1993b). External changes affect the resources—money, expertise, number of supporters, and legal authority—available to subsystem members and thereby lead to alterations in their behaviour and in policy outcomes. Sabatier (1987: 664). See also Jenkins-Smith et al. (1991).

9. Although this insight is similar to that used to generate a simple spectrum or continuum of subsystem types—ranging from integrated to unintegrated and usually related to a single variable such as subsystem size—this does not fully capture the complexity of subsystem structure. See Marsh and Rhodes (1992b). While it is common to associate small subsystems with integration and large ones with incohesiveness, many studies have shown that small subsystems can exhibit unintegrated communities and networks, while being large, similarly, does not prevent subsystems from being unified and cohesive. See, for example, Giuliani (1999); Kriesi and Jegen (2001).

10. The analysis of incremental decision-making, for example, attributes a propensity for policy change to occur as a result of analysis of the marginal differences between existing and proposed policy options to the fact that the same sets of policy-makers must bargain among themselves to arrive at a decision, and therefore are unlikely to overturn agreements based on past negotiations and compromises. See Hayes (1992).

11. Much as was argued by Thomas Kuhn and others in the case of the advance of scientific knowledge. See Kuhn (1962, 1974). In his early works Kuhn was unclear about what exactly constituted a 'scientific paradigm'. However, in his later works he was more specific, arguing that a paradigm was synonymous with the notion of a 'disciplinary matrix'. It was 'what the members of a scientific community, and they alone, share'. See Kuhn (1974: 463); Masterman (1970).

Chapter 7

Public Policy Decision-Making: Beyond Rationalism and Incrementalism

The decision-making stage of the policy process is the one from which emerges some formal or informal statement of intent on the part of authorized public actors to undertake, or refrain from undertaking, some action (O'Sullivan and Down, 2001). Actually undertaking that course of action remains the subject of the next stage of the policy cycle, policy implementation, discussed in Chapter 8.

Gary Brewer and Peter DeLeon (1983: 179) characterize the decision-making stage of the public policy process as:

> the choice among policy alternatives that have been generated and their likely effects on the problem estimated . . . . It is the most overtly political stage in so far as the many potential solutions to a given problem must somehow be winnowed down and but one or a select few picked and readied for use. Obviously most possible choices will not be realized and deciding not to take particular courses of action is as much a part of selection as finally settling on the best course.

This definition makes several important points about the decision-making stage of the policy cycle. First, decision-making is not a self-contained stage, nor is it synonymous with the entire public policy-making process. Rather, it is a specific stage rooted firmly in the previous stages of the policy cycle. It involves choosing from among a relatively small number of alternative policy options, as identified in the process of policy formulation, to resolve a public problem. Second, this definition highlights the fact that different kinds of decisions can result from a decision-making process. That is, decisions can be 'positive' in the sense that they alter the status quo in some way, or they can be 'negative' in the sense that they fail to do so. Third, this definition underlines the point that public policy decision-making is not a technical exercise but an inherently political process. It recognizes that public policy decisions create 'winners' and 'losers', even if the decision is to do nothing and to retain the status quo.

Brewer and DeLeon's definition, of course, says nothing about the actors involved in this process, or the desirability, likely direction, or scope of public decision-making. To deal with these issues, different theories have been developed to describe how decisions are made in government as well as to prescribe how decisions ought to be made. The nature of public policy decision-makers, the different types of decisions that they make, and the development and evolution of decision-making models designed to help understand the relationship between the two are described below.

AUTHORITATIVE AND NON-AUTHORITATIVE ACTORS IN THE DECISION-MAKING PROCESS

With the exception of usually infrequent exercises in direct democracy such as referenda (Wagschal, 1997; Butler and Ranney, 1994), the number of relevant policy actors decreases substantially with the progress of the public policy process to the decision-making stage. Thus, agenda-setting involves a wide variety of state and societal actors; theoretically at least, virtually any member of the policy universe could become active and involved in the agenda-setting process. At the stage of policy formulation, the number of actors remains potentially large, but in practice tends to include only those state and societal actors who are members of a specific policy subsystem.

When it comes time to decide on a particular option, however, the relevant group of policy actors is almost invariably restricted to those with the capacity and authority to make binding public decisions. In other words, the public policy decision-making stage normally involves only those who occupy formal offices in government. Excluded are virtually all non-state actors, including those from other levels of governments, both domestically and internationally. Only those politicians, judges, and government officials actually empowered to make authoritative decisions in the area in question can participate with both 'voice' and 'vote' at this stage of the policy cycle (Aberbach et al., 1981).[1] This is not to say that other actors, including non-state ones as well as those belonging to other governments, are not active at this stage of the policy process. These actors can and do, of course, engage in various kinds of 'lobbying' activities aimed at persuading, encouraging, and sometimes even coercing authoritative office-holders to adopt options of which they approve. However, unlike office-holders, those other actors have, at best, a 'voice' in the decision-making process, but they do not have a 'vote' per se (see Pal, 1993b; Richardson et al., 1978; Sarpkaya, 1988).

This is also not to say that decision-makers, given their occupancy of

strategic offices, can adopt whatever policy they wish. As has been discussed in earlier chapters, the degree of freedom enjoyed by each decision-maker is in fact circumscribed by a host of rules governing political
and administrative offices and constraining the actions of each office-
holder. As we have seen, these rules range from the country's constitution to the specific mandates conferred on individual decision-makers
such as judges and civil servants by various laws and regulations
(Markoff, 1975; Page, 1985a).

As was discussed in Chapter 3, at the macro level, different countries
have different constitutional arrangements and different sets of rules governing the structure of governmental agencies and the conduct of officials. Some political systems concentrate decision-making authority in
the elected executive and the bureaucracy, while others permit the legislature and judiciary to play a greater role. Parliamentary systems tend to
fall in the former category and presidential systems in the latter. Thus, in
Australia, Britain, and Canada and other parliamentary democracies, the
cabinet and bureaucracy are often solely responsible for making many
policy decisions. They may at times have decisions imposed on them by
the legislature in situations when the government does not enjoy a parliamentary majority, or by the judiciary in its role as the interpreter of the
constitution, but these are not routine occurrences. In the United States
and other presidential systems, although the authority to make most policy decisions rests with the executive (and the cabinet and bureaucracy
acting on the President's or Governor's behalf), those requiring legislative approval often involve intensive negotiation with the members of the
legislature, while some are modified or overturned on a regular basis by
the judiciary on constitutional or other grounds (Weaver and Rockman,
1993b).

At the micro level, various rules usually set out not only which decisions can be made by which government agency or official, but also the
procedures that must be followed in each case. As Allison and Halperin
have noted, over time such rules and operating procedures often provide
decision-makers with 'action channels'—a regularized set of standard
operating procedures for producing certain types of decisions (Allison
and Halperin, 1972). These rules and standard operating procedures help
explain why so much of the decision-making in government is of a routine and repetitive nature.[2] Nevertheless, while they circumscribe the
freedom available to decision-makers, especially those in administrative
or judicial positions, considerable discretion always remains with individual decision-makers to arrive at their own judgement of the 'best'
course of action to follow in specific circumstances. Since decision-makers themselves vary greatly in terms of background, knowledge, and
predilections that affect how they interpret a problem and the solutions
to it (Huitt, 1968), different decision-makers operating in similar institutional environments can respond differently when dealing with the same

or similar problems. Hence, even with standard operating procedures in place, exactly what process is followed and which decision is considered 'best' varies.

TYPES OF CHOICES: NEGATIVE, POSITIVE, AND NON-DECISIONS

Regardless of who is making a decision, whether a relatively large group of legislators in a partisan political setting or a single civil servant in a more insulated bureaucratic one, only a relatively few general types of decisions can emerge from this process. That is, although the actual substance of individual decisions can be infinitely varied, these decisions can either perpetuate the policy status quo or alter it.

Traditional 'positive' decisions that alter the status quo are the subject of most of the decision-making literature and of most of the discussion in this chapter. However, it is important to note at the outset that other kinds of decisions uphold the status quo. Here we can distinguish between 'negative' decisions, in which a conscious decision is taken to preserve the status quo, and what are sometimes termed 'non-decisions', discussed in Chapter 5, in which options to deviate from the status quo are systematically excluded from consideration (see Zelditch et al., 1983; R.A. Smith, 1979).

Non-decisions have been the subject of many inquiries and studies (see Bachrach and Baratz, 1962, 1970: ch. 3; Debnam, 1975; Bachrach and Baratz, 1975; Zelditch and Ford, 1994; Spranca et al., 1991). Very little research into negative decisions, however, exists. This is partly due to the difficulties associated with identifying instances in which policy options to alter the status quo are explicitly rejected in favour of its maintenance (see Howlett, 1986). Nevertheless, the elements of these decisions can be discerned from an examination of how they affect the operation of the policy cycle. That is, negative decisions are instances of arrested policy cycles. Unlike the situation with non-decisions, in which certain options are filtered out at the agenda-setting or policy formulation stages and may never even enter into policy deliberations, with negative decision-making, agenda-setting and policy formulation do occur and alternative courses of action to those presently in place are put forward to authoritative decision-makers. However, unlike the situation with positive decisions, the policy process does not move onto the policy implementation stage. With a negative decision, the policy cycle begins, moves through agenda-setting and policy formulation, but does not move past the decision-making stage, where a decision to retain the status quo is made (van der Eijk and Kok, 1975).

MODELS OF PUBLIC POLICY DECISION-MAKING

Whether a public policy decision is negative or positive, it involves the development and expression of a statement of intent on the part of authoritative decision-makers to undertake some course of action or inaction. The processes through which these decisions emerge are, of course, of great interest to students of government, as well as to those of private-sector management, psychology, and many other fields of study. In what follows, we turn to an overview of the models developed in these fields to help describe, conceptualize, and analyze decision-making processes in both simple and complex situations. We will set out the elements of these models and discuss their success and failure in dealing with decision-making processes in governments. Although numerous different models exist in the large literatures on the subject in these diverse fields, we shall see that they all suggest that a variety of different decision-making styles exist, and that the likelihood of one being followed can be ascertained with some certainty by examining the nature of the actors involved in the decision-making process and the constraints under which they operate.

Early Models: Rationalism and Incrementalism

The decision-making stage of the policy cycle received a great deal of attention in the early years of the development of the policy sciences, when analysts borrowed heavily from models and studies of decision-making in complex organizations developed by students of public administration and business organization.

By the mid-1960s, discussions about public policy decision-making had ossified into two purportedly incompatible models, one of which— *the rational model*—asserted that public policy decision-making was very much a search for maximizing solutions to complex problems in which policy-relevant information was gathered and then focused in a scientific fashion on the assessment of policy options. The other model—often termed *the incremental model*—described public policy decision-making as a less technical and more political activity, in which analysis played a much smaller role in determining outcomes than did bargaining and other forms of interaction and negotiation between key decision-makers (see Mossberger, 2000: ch. 2). The mainstream position throughout much of this period was that while the 'rational' model was more preferable for showing how decisions ought to be taken, the 'incremental' model best described the actual practice of decision-making in governments (Dror, 1968; Etzioni, 1967; Howard, 1971).

However, by the mid-1970s it was apparent to many observers that neither model accurately represented all instances of decision-making and that different decision-making opportunities featured different methods and styles of decision-making; and that the range of decision-making styles varied beyond the two 'ideal types' represented by the rational and incremental models (Smith and May, 1980; Allison, 1969, 1971). This led to efforts to develop alternative models of decision-making in complex organizations. Some attempted to synthesize the rational and incremental models. Others—including the so-called 'garbage can' model of decision-making—focused on the irrational elements of organizational behaviour in order to arrive at a third path beyond rationalism and incrementalism (Cohen et al., 1972; March and Olsen, 1979a). Only recently have efforts been made to move beyond these debates between rationalists, irrationalists, and incrementalists and develop a more nuanced understanding of the complex processes associated with public policy decision-making.

The Rational Model and Its Critics

First developed in the area of economic analysis, and especially in the analysis of producer and consumer choices, the 'rational' theory of decision-making postulated that in developing and expressing a preference for one course of action over another, decision-makers would attempt to approximate in practice a strategy that, in theory, would maximize the expected outcomes of the choices they could make (Edwards, 1954). Decision-making in the public policy arena was seen as akin to the process in the marketplace where buyers and sellers seek to maximize 'utility' from their limited resources.

The idealized model of rational decision-making, which decision-makers were expected to follow as closely as possible in all circumstances, was one in which they would undertake the following series of sequential activities:

1. A goal for solving a problem is established.
2. All alternative strategies of achieving the goal are explored and listed.
3. All significant consequences of each alternative strategy are predicted and the probability of those consequences occurring is estimated.
4. Finally, the strategy that most nearly solves the problem or solves it at least cost is selected. (Carley, 1980: 11)

The rational model is 'rational' in the sense that it prescribes procedures for decision-making that, in theory, will lead to the choice of the most efficient possible means of achieving policy goals. Rooted in Enlightenment rationalism and positivism, schools of thought that sought to develop detached, scientific knowledge to improve human conditions (Jennings, 1987; Torgerson, 1986), this model assumes that maximal outcomes can be achieved through the ordered gathering of relevant information allowing the 'best' alternative to be identified and selected (Weiss, 1977b). Decision-makers are assumed to operate as technicians or business managers, who collect and analyze information that allows them to adopt the most effective or efficient way of solving any problem they confront. It is for its 'neutral', technical approach to problem-solving that this approach is also known as 'scientific', 'engineering', or 'managerialist' in nature (Elster, 1991: 115).

Early attempts to establish a science of organizational behaviour and business and public administration all featured efforts to promote the increased application and use of the rational model of decision-making. Elements of the model can be found in the work of early students of public administration such as Henri Fayol in France and Luther Gulick and Lyndal Urwick in Britain and the United States. Drawing on the insights gleaned by Fayol (1949) from his studies of the turn-of-the-century French coal industry, in the 1930s Gulick and Urwick, for example, promoted what they termed the 'POSDCORB' model of management in which they urged organizations to maximize their performance by systematically planning, organizing, staffing, directing, co-ordinating, reporting, and budgeting their activities (Gulick, 1937). 'Directing' a particular course of action, for Gulick and Urwick and the management theorists who followed in their footsteps, amounted to weighing the benefits of any decision against its expected costs and arriving at a 'steady stream' of decisions required for the organization to function (see, e.g., Kepner and Tregoe, 1965).[3]

Ideally, the process would involve attributing costs and benefits to each option, comparing these across widely divergent options, and estimating the probability of failure and success for each option (Edwards, 1954; March, 1994). It was recognized from very early on, however, that it would not always be possible to achieve 'full' rationality in practice. This was because even if a decision-maker wished to adopt maximizing decisions, it might not be possible to do so due to limitations of information and time. However, for many analysts these were not considered to be terminal or insurmountable problems. Rather, they simply recognized the difficulties that could be found in translating decision-making theory into decision-making practice, which meant that the resulting decisions might not be perfectly rational or error-proof, but would normally be close enough to approximate 'perfect' rationality.

Some analysts, however, claimed that these limitations on rationality had much more serious implications for decision-making theory and practice. Perhaps the most noted critic of the rational model was the late American behavioural scientist Herbert Simon, the only student of public administration ever to win a Nobel Prize. Simon and others argued that the limitations on rationality previously noted were not simply 'deviations' that might be overcome by more careful analysis, or that would crop up only in exceptional circumstances. Rather, these shortcomings were impossible to avoid and serious enough to undermine completely any notion of 'pure' rationality and outcome maximization contained in the early rational model.

Simon, in particular, argued in a series of books and articles in the 1950s that several specific hurdles prevented decision-makers from ever attaining 'pure' rationality in their decisions (Simon, 1955, 1957b). First, he noted that this form of decision-making would generate maximal results only if *all* possible alternatives and the costs of each alternative were assessed before a decision was made. However, he noted there were cognitive limits to decision-makers' ability to consider an almost infinite number of possible options, forcing them to consider selectively only a limited number of alternatives that they deemed were likely, or probable, or feasible. Simon noted that such pre-decisional choices were likely to be made on ideological, professional, cultural, or other similar grounds, if not randomly, without reference to their implications for efficiency, thereby severely undermining the claim to rationality of the subsequent selection of a course of action from among the remaining options (see Fernandes and Simon, 1999).

Second, Simon noted that the rational model also assumed that it is possible for decision-makers to know the consequences of each decision in advance, which is rarely the case in reality. Again, without being able to predict the future, it would be impossible to assess objectively the costs and benefits of different options as required by the rational model. Third, Simon noted that each policy option entails a bundle of favourable and adverse consequences and the 'costing' of each 'bundle' was not a simple matter, as it would involve a preliminary ranking of potential partial gains that, again, could not itself be taken on 'rational' grounds. Fourth, Simon also noted that very often the same option can be efficient or inefficient depending on other, and changing, circumstances. Hence, it is often not possible for decision-makers to arrive at unambiguous and long-lasting conclusions about which alternative is superior, as the rational model requires (see Einhorn and Hogarth, 1986).

Numerous efforts to modify the rational model followed on the heels of criticisms such as these, all in the effort to preserve the idea of 'maximization' in decision-making (Kruse et al., 1991: ch. 1). Theories of 'fuzzy' decision-making, for example, argued that even if costs and benefits associated with specific policy options could not be clearly stated or specified with great precision, probabilistic techniques could be used to illuminate the *range* of 'maximized' outcomes, allowing at least an approximately rational choice to be made (Bellman and Zadeh, 1970; Whalen, 1987; Mendoza and Sprouse, 1989). Other studies, mainly in the field of psychology, attempted to specify, on the basis of field experiments, exactly what sorts of common biases decision-makers exhibited in dealing with the uncertainties described by Simon (see Slovic et al., 1977, 1985). This is the case, for example, with *prospect theory* (see Kahneman and Tversky, 1979; Tversky and Kahneman, 1981, 1982, 1986; Haas, 2001), which postulated that humans 'overweight losses relative to comparable gains, engage in risk-averse behaviour in choices but risk-

acceptant behaviour in choices among losses, and respond to probabili-
ties in a nonlinear manner' (Levy, 1997: 33). This was done in the hope
of allowing some specification of the cognitive limits of decision-making,
thus allowing the development of 'second-best' maximizing rational
models that would take into account limitations of human behaviour in
the face of uncertainty (see Yates and Zukowski, 1976; Suedfeld and Tetlock, 1992; Einhorn, 1982).

Simon, however, concluded that public decisions ostensibly taken in
accordance with the precepts and methods outlined by the rational
model would never *maximize* benefits over costs, but would merely tend
to *satisfy* whatever criteria decision-makers set for themselves in the
instance in question. This 'satisficing' criterion, as he put it, was a real-
istic one given the 'bounded rationality' with which human beings are
endowed and with which they must work when taking decisions (see
March, 1978, 1994). Although he did not himself develop an alternative
model of decision-making built on the notion of satisficing (see Jones,
2001: ch. 3), his insights would be later taken up by Charles Lindblom,
who would incorporate them into the best-known alternative to the rational model, the *incremental* model of decision-making.

The Incremental Model and Its Critics

Doubts about the practicality or even usefulness of the rational model led
to efforts to develop a theory of public policy decision-making more
closely approximating the actual behaviour of decision-makers in real-life
situations. This fostered the emergence of the incremental model, which
portrayed public policy decision-making as a political process characterized by bargaining and compromise among self-interested decision-makers (Braybrooke and Lindblom, 1963; Dahl and Lindblom, 1953;
Lindblom, 1959). In this model, the decisions eventually made represent
what is politically feasible rather than desirable, and what is possible
rather than 'maximal' in the sense of the term used by adherents of the
rational model.

The credit for developing the incremental model of public decision-
making is attributed to Yale University political scientist Charles Lindblom and his colleagues at other North American universities (Dahl and
Lindblom, 1953; Lindblom, 1955, 1958, 1959). He took to heart the ideas
of bounded rationality and satisficing behaviour among decision-makers
developed by Simon and, on the basis of his observations of actual decision-making processes in governments, outlined what he suggested were
the common elements of the 'strategies of decision' actually followed by
decision-makers. The model he put forward arranged these strategies
into a 'mutually supporting set of simplifying and focusing stratagems'
and included the following elements:

    a. Limitation of analysis to a few somewhat familiar policy alterna-
       tives . . . differing only marginally from the status quo;

b. An intertwining of analysis of policy goals and other values with the empirical aspects of the problem (that is, no requirement that values be specified first with means subsequently found to promote them);

c. A greater analytical preoccupation with ills to be remedied than positive goals to be sought;

d. A sequence of trials, errors, and revised trials;

e. Analysis that explores only some, not all, of the important possible consequences of a considered alternative;

f. Fragmentation of analytical work to many (partisan) participants in policy making (each attending to their piece of the overall problem domain). (Lindblom, 1979: 517)

In Lindblom's view, decision-makers both did and should develop policies through a process of making 'successive limited comparisons' with earlier decisions, those with which they are familiar. As he put it in his oft-cited article on 'The Science of Muddling Through', decision-makers work through a process of 'continually building out from the current situation, step-by-step and by small degrees' (Lindblom, 1959: 81). Decisions thus arrived at are usually only marginally different from those that exist. In other words, the changes from the status quo in decision-making are *incremental*.

According to Lindblom, there are two reasons why decisions do not usually vary substantially from the status quo. First, since bargaining requires distribution of limited resources among various participants, it is easier to continue the existing pattern of distribution rather than try to impute values to radically new proposals. The benefits and costs of the present arrangements are known to the policy actors, unlike the uncertainties surrounding new arrangements, which make agreement on changes difficult to reach. The result is either continuation of the status quo or small changes from it. Second, the standard operating procedures that are the hallmark of bureaucracy tend to promote the continuation of existing practices. The methods by which bureaucrats identify options and the methods and criteria for choice are often laid out in advance, inhibiting innovation and perpetuating existing arrangements (Gortner et al., 1987: 257).

Lindblom also argued that the rational model's requirement of separation between ends and means was unworkable in practice not only due to the time, information, and cognitive constraints identified by Simon and others, but also because it assumed policy-makers could clearly separate means from ends in assessing policies and could then agree upon both. Lindblom argued that in most policy areas, ends are inseparable from means, and which goals are pursued often depends on whether or not viable means are available to accomplish them. The essence of incrementalism, Lindblom argued, was to try to systematize decision-making processes by stressing the need for political agreement and learning by trial and error, rather than simply bumbling into random decisions (Lindblom and Cohen, 1979).

While the incremental model may be an accurate description of how public policy decisions are often made, and that, too, is debatable (see Berry, 1990; Jones et al., 1997), critics found several faults with the implications of the line of thinking it suggests (see Weiss and Woodhouse, 1992). First, it was criticized severely for its lack of any kind of goal orientation. As John Forester (1984: 23) put it, incrementalism 'would have us cross and recross intersections without knowing where we are going'. Second, the model was criticized for being inherently conservative, given its suspicion of large-scale change and innovation. Third, it was criticized for being undemocratic, to the extent it confined decision-making to bargaining within a select group of senior policy-makers (Gawthrop, 1971). Fourth, by discouraging systematic analysis and planning and undermining the need to search for promising new alternatives, it was said to promote short-sighted decisions that can have adverse consequences for society in the long run (Lustick, 1980). In addition to criticisms of the desirability of decisions made incrementally, the model was also criticized for its narrow analytic usefulness. Yehezkel Dror (1964), for example, noted that incrementalism can only work when there is a great deal of continuity in the nature of problems that policies are intended to address and in the means available to address them, a continuity that does not always exist. Incrementalism is more characteristic of decision-making in a relatively stable environment, rather than in situations that are unusual, such as a crisis (Nice, 1987; Lustick, 1980).

Lindblom countered many of these criticisms in his own writings, stating that incrementalism was neither inherently conservative nor short-sighted, since the relative *size* and *direction* of increments were not predetermined but would emerge from the deliberative bargaining process that characterized incremental policy-making (Lindblom, 1979: 517). And he also suggested that the incremental method was neither inherently democratic nor undemocratic, but would simply follow the structure of representation present in different political systems and situations (Lindblom, 1968).

However, in responding to one major criticism—that incrementalism was better suited for or more likely to occur in some policy-making contexts than others—adherents of the incremental model had to accept that the nature of the decision-making process would vary according to factors such as the number of decision-makers involved and whether or not they shared a consensus on the goals and objectives of policy-making (Bendor, 1995). This meant that the model was neither the ideal method of decision-making, as had been suggested by some adherents, nor, as Lindblom himself had alleged in some of his writings, the *only* possible method. Rather, it was only one of several possible types or styles of decision-making.

Early Efforts To Move Beyond Rationalism and Incrementalism

By the early 1980s, it had become apparent to many observers that the continuing debate between the advocates of rationalism and those of incrementalism was interfering with empirical work and the theoretical development of the subject. As Smith and May (1980: 156) argued:

> A debate about the relative merits of rationalistic as opposed to incrementalist models of decision-making has featured for some years now and although the terms of this debate are relatively well known it has had comparatively little impact upon empirical research in the areas of either policy or administrative studies.

Rather than continue with this debate, the authors suggested that:

> we require more than one account to describe the several facets of organizational life. The problem is not to reconcile the differences between contrasting rational and incremental models, nor to construct some third alternative which combines the strongest features of each. The problem is to relate the two in the sense of spelling out the relationship between the social realities with which each is concerned.

An awareness of the limitations of both the rational and incremental models of decision-making led policy scholars to look for alternatives. These came in many forms. Despite Smith and May's admonition, some analysts attempted to synthesize the two models, an initially unlikely objective but one that is not impossible to achieve. Others embraced the elements of unpredictability and capriciousness opened by the fall of incrementalism as the main alternative to the rational model. While neither of these theoretical directions proved particularly fruitful, a third effort to clarify the exact nature of alternative decision-making styles, and the likely conditions under which they would be employed, proved to be of more lasting value and continues to inform present-day work on the subject.

Attempts at Syntheses: Two-Stage 'Mixed Scanning' Models
The initial response of many scholars to criticisms of incrementalism as an alternative to the rational model was to attempt to 'rescue' both models by combining them in a kind of constructive synthesis. As early as 1967, for example, Amitai Etzioni developed his *mixed scanning* model to bridge the shortcomings of both rational and incremental models by combining elements from both.

Accepting the criticisms of the rational model as largely unworkable in practice and of the incremental model as only appropriate to certain types of policy environments, Etzioni suggested that combining the two models allowed both criticisms to be overcome, while providing decision-makers with a guide to 'optimal' decision-making. Adopting a similar position to that of Simon, Etzioni and, later, many others suggested that the decision-making process in fact consisted of two stages, a 'pre-decisional' or 'representative' stage of assessing a problem and 'framing' it—which would utilize incremental analysis—and a second analytical phase in which specific solutions would be assessed—which would be more rational in nature (see Voss, 1998; Svenson, 1979; Alexander, 1979, 1982).

In Etzioni's 'mixed scanning' model, optimal decisions would result from a cursory search ('scanning') for alternatives, followed by a detailed probe of the most promising alternatives. This would allow for more innovation than permitted by the incremental model, without imposing the unrealistic demands prescribed by the rational model. Etzioni argued that indeed this was how decisions were made in reality, where it is not uncommon to find a series of incremental decisions followed by a substantially different decision when decision-makers are faced with a problem significantly different from those dealt with before. Thus, he presented his model as both a prescriptive and descriptive approach to decision-making that would overcome the conceptual limitations of earlier models while conforming to the actual practice of decision-makers on the ground.

In more recent work, students of US foreign policy decision-making developed a similar two-stage model of decision-making processes, sometimes referred to as the 'poliheuristic' model (see Mintz and Geva, 1997; Mintz et al., 1997). In this view, decision-makers use a variety of cognitive shortcuts ('heuristics') to compensate for limitations in knowledge and initially winnow alternatives to a set of 'feasible' or 'acceptable' ones (Fernandes and Simon, 1999; Voss and Post, 1988). These heuristics include the use of historical analogies, a preference for incremental policies, the desire for consensus among competing policy actors, and the desire to claim credit or avoid blame for potential policy outcomes (see George, 1980; Weaver, 1986; Hood, 2002; Vertzberger, 1998). In the second stage, a limited number of alternatives are subjected to a more rational, 'maximizing' analysis.

As Mintzberg found in his 1976 study of 'strategic' or non-routine decision-making with uncertain outcomes:

> When faced with a complex, unprogrammed situation, the decision makers seek to reduce the decision into subdecisions to which he applies general purpose, interchangeable sets of procedures or routines. In other words, the decision makers deal with unstructured situations by factoring them into familiar, structural elements. Furthermore, the individual decision maker uses a number of problem-solving shortcuts—satisficing instead of maximizing, not looking too far ahead, reducing a complex environment to a series of sim-

plified conceptual 'models'. (Mintzberg et al., 1976: 247; see also Weiss, 1982)

It is not clear, however, exactly how these models differ from the incremental and rational ones they were ostensibly designed to replace. That is, the techniques of marginal analysis put forward by Lindblom and others already envisioned a limited search for, and selection of, alternatives, which would then be singled out for more detailed analysis. And it is also not clear how mixed scanning would overcome the problems associated with the rational model, since without the systematic comparison of all possible alternatives it is impossible to assure that a final decision was a maximizing one. Nevertheless, Etzioni's call for a less overtly political type of incrementalism than that based on Lindblom's 'partisan mutual adjustment' was well received by many public policy practitioners. Among policy scholars, however, it was quickly bypassed in favour of other models—such as the so-called 'garbage-can' theory discussed below—that purported to come more directly to terms with the reality of uncertainty and ambiguity facing policy-makers in day-to-day decision-making situations.

Embracing Irrationalism: The Garbage-Can Model

In the late 1970s, a very different model asserted and, in fact, embraced the inherent lack of rationality in the decision-making process identified by Simon and others. Developed in part by one of Simon's co-authors, James March, and March's Norwegian colleague, Johan Olsen, the so-called *garbage-can model* of decision-making denied to the decision-making process even the limited rationality attributed to it by incrementalism (March and Olsen, 1979b). March and Olsen, along with another colleague, Michael Cohen, began with the assumption that both the rational and incremental models presumed a level of intentionality, comprehension of problems, and predictability of relations among actors that simply did not obtain in reality. In their view, decision-making was a highly ambiguous and unpredictable process only distantly related to searching for means to achieve goals. Rejecting the instrumentalism that characterized most other models, Cohen, March, and Olsen (1979: 26) argued that decision opportunities were:

> a garbage can into which various problems and solutions are dumped by participants. The mix of garbage in a single can depends partly on the labels attached to the alternative cans; but it also depends on what garbage is being produced at the moment, on the mix of cans available, and on the speed with which garbage is collected and removed from the scene.

Cohen, March, and Olsen deliberately used the garbage-can metaphor to strip away the aura of scientific authority attributed to decision-making by earlier theorists. They sought to drive home the point that goals are often unknown to policy-makers, as are causal relationships. In their view, actors simply define goals and choose means as they go along in a policy process that is necessarily contingent and unpredictable. As Gary Mucciaroni (1992: 461) phrased it, in this model:

> There is plenty of room for chance, human creativity, and choice to influence outcomes. What gets on the agenda at given points in time is the result of a fortuitous conjunction—whatever the combination of salient problems, available solutions, and political circumstances that exist. Events, such as the opening of a window of opportunity, are often unpredictable, and participants often are unable to control events once they are set in motion. Yet, individual actors are not completely without an ability to affect outcomes. Entrepreneurs decide which problems to dramatize, choose which solutions to push, and formulate political strategies to bring their issues onto the agenda. Actors in the process develop problem definitions and solutions that are plausible and compelling, link them together, and make them congruent with existing political conditions.

March and Olsen (1979a) provided evidence from several case studies of decision-making processes in European universities to substantiate their proposition that public decisions are often made in too ad-hoc and haphazard a fashion to be called incremental, much less rational. Others, such as Paul Anderson (1983), for example, also provided evidence that even decisions with respect to the important international events such as those surrounding the 1962 Cuban Missile Crisis, one of the most critical issues of the Cold War period, were made in terms of simplistic yes/no binary choices on proposals that would emerge in the course of discussion.

Be that as it may, while its key tenets may well be a fairly accurate description of how at times organizations make decisions, in other instances it would be reasonable to expect more order. As critics such as Mucciaroni argued, rather than present a general model of decision-making, the garbage-can idea represents only a type or style of decision-making characteristic of a particular political or organizational environment:

> Perhaps the mode of policy-making depicted by the garbage can model is itself embedded in a particular institutional structure. Put another way, the model may be better at depicting decision-making in the United States, where the institutional structure is fragmented and permeable, participation is pluralistic and fluid, and coalitions are often temporary and ad hoc. By contrast, policy-making in other countries takes place among institutions that are more centralized and integrated, where the number of participants is limited

and their participation is highly structured and predictable. (Mucciaroni, 1992: 466)

Challenging and controversial, the main strength of the garbage-can model was in helping to break the logjam of what had become a rather sterile debate between rationalists and incrementalists over the merits of their models, thereby allowing for more nuanced studies of decision-making within institutional contexts to be undertaken.

Embracing Complexity: Decision Accretion, Multiple Arenas, and the 'Rounds' Model of Decision-Making

By the 1980s many studies pointed to the significance of decision-making structures and contexts for understanding how decisions are actually taken in complex organizations. In her work on knowledge utilization in the policy process, for example, Harvard University researcher Carol Weiss noted that in many instances policy decisions are not decided in a 'brisk and clear-cut style' in a single institution or setting at a single point in time. Rather, many decisions, from the momentous to the inane, are actually taken piecemeal, without any overall plan of attack or conscious deliberation, but rather appear more like a pearl in an oyster, having been accreted in multiple layers over a relatively lengthy period of time through the actions of multiple decision-makers (Weiss, 1980).

Unlike incrementalism, which also paints a similar portrait of policy-making as the buildup of previous decisions, or the garbage-can model, which also describes policy emergence as largely fortuitous, notions of decision accretion do not rely on intra-organizational bargaining processes or fluid sets of participants to explain this pattern. Instead, it is said to emerge due to the nature of the decision to be made and the structure of the organizations that make them. As Weiss argued:

> In large organizations, decisions on complex issues are almost never the province of one individual or one office. Many people in many offices have a say, and when the outcomes of a course of action are uncertain, many participants have opportunities to propose, plan, confer, deliberate, advise, argue, forward policy statements, reject, revise, veto, and re-write. (Ibid., 399)

In such situations, Weiss suggested, individuals often do not even realize when a decision has been made. Each person takes only some small step in a large process with seemingly small consequences. But over the course of time, 'these many small steps foreclose alternative courses of action and limit the range of the possible. Almost imperceptibly, a decision has been made, (sometimes) without anyone's awareness that he or she was deciding' (ibid., 401).

This analysis highlights the significance of *multiple arenas* and *multiple rounds* of decision-making for many modern-day public policy decisions. That is, as Weiss and others have suggested, decision-making often tends to occur in multiple locations or venues, each with a distinct set of actors, rules of procedure, and ability to influence the outcome of a decision process in a preferred direction (see Klijn, 2001; Mintzberg et al., 1976).[4] In addition, each venue or arena can be involved in one or more simultaneous decision-making processes, increasing the likelihood that couplings and uncouplings of issues can occur in a highly contingent fashion (see Roe, 1990; Perrow, 1984; van Bueren et al., 2001).

As Teisman (2000) has suggested, in this process decision-making tends to take place in a number of 'rounds' in which different sets of actors participate and propose different sets of solutions to problems. In each arena, different actors can 'score points' in terms of having their definition of a problem or solution adopted. These decisions are collected in a 'round' in which the results of each round are fed back into other arenas for continued discussion and debate, in a process in which new actors can be activated, new arenas become involved, and new or modified decisions emerge (see Hammond, 1986).

Focusing on the nature of the interactions between actors both within and between arenas, and on the tactics and strategies used to influence arena outcomes, it is argued, allows some predictions to be made about the likely kinds of decisions that can emerge from these lengthy and complex processes (see Allison and Halperin, 1972; Sager, 2001; Stokman and Berveling, 1998). Moreover, it also allows for the conscious design of decision-making processes in order to clarify the roles of different actors and stages in the process and to ensure that outcomes are less 'irrational' and contingent than might otherwise be the case with instances of pure 'decision creep' (de Bruijn and ten Heuvelhof, 2000). Much work on decision tools and strategies, such as environmental impact statements, risk analysis, and intergovernmental diplomacy, has involved the study of these formal decision processes so that governments seeking particular policy outcomes might better design their form and structure (see Kennett, 2000; Bregha et al., 1990; Koppenjan, 2001; Gregory et al., 2001).

CLASSIFYING DECISION-MAKING STYLES

As we have seen, the early rational and incremental models suggested that diverse decision-making styles can be found in the public policy process. Later models, such as the mixed scanning, garbage-can, and decision round models, provide some indication of which variables are responsible for the use of a particular style in a particular circumstance: the nature of a policy problem; the number and type of actors involved; the nature of the informational, temporal, and institutional constraints within which they operate; and the pre-existing sets of ideas or 'frames' and decision-making routines with and through which decision-makers approach their tasks.

The idea that there is a range of possible decision-making styles is not a new one (see Wildavsky, 1962; Scharpf, 1991). In some of his earlier writings, for example, Charles Lindblom and several of his co-authors held out the possibility that incremental decision-making could coexist with efforts to achieve more 'rational' decisions. Thus Braybrooke and Lindblom (1963), for example, argued that four different types of decision-making could be discerned, depending on the amount of knowledge at the disposal of decision-makers and the amount of change the selection involved from earlier decisions. This generated the model shown in Figure 7.1.

Figure 7.1 An Early Model of Four Types of Decision-Making

		Level of Available Knowledge	
		High	*Low*
Level of Change	*High*	Revolutionary	Analytic
	Low	Rational	Disjointed Incremental

SOURCE: Adapted from David Braybrooke and Charles Lindblom, *A Strategy of Decision: Policy Evaluation as a Social Process* (New York: Free Press of Glencoe, 1963).

In Braybrooke and Lindblom's view, the overwhelming majority of decisions were likely to be taken in an incremental fashion, involving minimal change in situations of low available knowledge. However, three other possibilities also existed, the rational model emerging as one possibility and two other poorly defined styles—'revolutionary' and 'analytic'—also existing as infrequently utilized alternatives given specific change and knowledge configurations.

Later in his career, Lindblom revisited this idea, arguing that a spectrum of decision-making styles existed according to how systematic the associated decision-making analysis was. These ranged from 'synoptic' decision-making, which is similar to the rational ideal, to 'blundering', that is, simply following hunches or guesses without any real effort at systematic analysis of alternative strategies, which is similar to the garbage-can model. The spectrum is illustrated in Figure 7.2.

Figure 7.2 An Early Spectrum Model of Decision-Making Styles

Synoptic – Strategic - Disjointed Incremental - Simple Incremental – Blundering

$$\longleftarrow\qquad\qquad\qquad\qquad\longrightarrow$$

Level of Rationality

SOURCE: Adapted from Charles E. Lindblom and D.K. Cohen, *Usable Knowledge: Social Science and Social Problem Solving* (New Haven: Yale University Press, 1979).

Neither of these early taxonomies took into account the principal variables identified as significant in the selection process by more recent decision-making models. A more promising start in this direction was made by John Forester in his work on decision-making styles. Forester (1984, 1989) argued that there were at least five distinct decision-making styles associated with six key sets of conditions. According to him, 'what is rational for administrators to do depends on the situations in which they work.' That is, the decision-making style and the type of decision made by decision-makers would be expected to vary according to issue and institutional contexts. As he put it:

> Depending upon the conditions at hand, a strategy may be practical or ridiculous. With time, expertise, data, and a well-defined problem, technical calculations may be in order; without time, data, definition, and expertise, attempting those calculations could well be a waste of time. In a complex organizational environment, intelligence networks will be as, or more, important than documents when information is needed. In an environment of inter-organizational conflict, bargaining and compromise may be called for. Administrative strategies are sensible only in a political and organizational context. (Forester, 1984: 25)

Forester suggests that for decision-making along the lines suggested by the rational model to take place, the following conditions must be met. First, the number of *agents* (decision-makers) will need to be limited, possibly to as few as one person. Second, the organizational *setting* for the decision will have to be simple, and will be closed off from the influences of other policy actors. Third, the *problem* must be well-defined; in other words, its scope, time horizon, value dimensions, and chains of consequences must be well understood. Fourth, *information* must be as close to perfect as possible; in other words, it must be complete, accessible, and comprehensible. Finally, there must be no urgency for the decision, that is, *time* must be infinitely available to the decision-makers to consider all possible contingencies and their present and anticipated consequences. When these conditions are met completely, rational decision-making can be expected to prevail.

To the extent that these five conditions are not met, as is almost always the case, Forester argues that we will find other styles of decision-making. Thus the number of agents (decision-makers) can expand and multiply almost to infinity; the setting can include many different organizations and can be more or less open to external influences; the problem can be ambiguous or susceptible to multiple competing interpretations; information can be incomplete, misleading, or purposefully withheld or manipulated; and time can be limited or artificially constrained and manipulated.[5] These variables and parameters are set out in Figure 7.3.

Figure 7.3 Basic Parameters of Decision-Making

Variables	*Dimensions*
1. Agent	Single—Multiple
2. Setting	Single, Closed—Multiple, Open
3. Problem	Well-Defined—Multiple, Vague
4. Information	Perfect—Contested
5. Time	Infinite—Manipulated

SOURCE: Adapted from John Forester, 'Bounded Rationality and the Politics of Muddling Through', *Public Administration Review* 44, 1 (1984): 26.

From this perspective, Forester suggests that there are five possible styles of decision-making: optimization, satisfycing, search, bargaining, and organizational. *Optimization* is the strategy that obtains when the conditions (mentioned above) of the rational-comprehensive model are met. The prevalence of other styles depends on the degree to which the conditions are not met. When the limitations are cognitive, for reasons mentioned earlier, we are likely to find the *satisfycing* style of decision-making. The other styles mentioned by Forester are overlapping and therefore difficult to distinguish clearly. A *search* strategy is one he argued was likely to occur when the problem is vague. A *bargaining* strategy is likely to be found when multiple actors deal with a problem in the absence of information and time. The *organizational* strategy involves multiple settings and actors with both time and informational resources but also multiple problems. Suffice it to say that these types involve greater number of actors, more complex settings, more intractable problems, incomplete or distorted information, and limited availability of time for making a decision.[6]

While a major improvement over earlier classifications and taxonomies, and certainly an improvement over the rational and incremental models and their 'garbage-can' opponents, Forester's was only a first step in establishing an improved model of decision-making styles. A major problem with his particular taxonomy, for example, is that it does not actually follow from his arguments. A close examination of his discussion of the factors shaping decision-making (Forester, 1984: 26) reveals that one would expect to find many more possible styles than five flowing from the possible combinations and permutations of the variables he cites. Although many of these categories are indistinguishable in practice and, in any event, would serve little analytical purpose, it remains unclear why one should expect only the five styles he cites to emerge.

An improvement on Forester's model of decision-making styles can be made by recasting his variables to relate more clearly and consistently the decision-making styles to the types of variables found to be significant in earlier investigations into public decision-making. Combining Forester's concepts of 'agent' and 'setting', for example, highlights the role played by different kinds of policy subsystems—that is, different numbers and types of actors situated in different numbers and types of institutional settings[7]—in the decision-making process (March, 1994). The complexity of the policy subsystem affects the number of venues, the nature of dominant policy ideas and interests, and the level of agreement or opposition to an option within the subsystem and among decision-makers (see Bendor and Hammond, 1992). Some options accord with the core values of the subsystem members while other do not, thereby structuring decisions into hard and soft choices (Pollock et al., 1989). Similarly, it is possible to combine Forester's notions of 'problem', 'information', and 'time' resources, which can all be seen as relating to the types of constraints identified by Simon and Lindblom and others as placed on decision-makers in their activities (see Payne, 1982; Simon, 1973). That is, the making of decisions is clearly constrained to varying degrees by information and time limitations (Rochefort and Cobb, 1993; Webber, 1992; Pappi and Henning, 1998), as well as by the intractability or 'wickedness' of the problem (Rittel and Webber, 1973; Sharkansky, 1997: ch. 2). But it is often the case that these constraints run together because part of the issue of problem tractability is related to lack of information on the subject and a lack of time required to gather or develop it (Radford, 1977).

Thus, two significant variables that can be used to construct a simple taxonomy of decision-making styles are (1) the complexity of the policy subsystem involved in the decision and (2) the severity of the constraints decision-makers face in making their choices (see Lindquist, 1988; Martin, 1998: ch. 2). Figure 7.4 outlines the four basic decision-making styles that emerge on the basis of these two dimensions.

In this model, decisions involving complex policy subsystems—for example, with multiple actors in multiple settings—are more likely to be involved in adjustment strategies than in searches, a point made by both incrementalists and proponents of decision round theory. As incrementalists also suggest, situations of high constraint are likely to result in a bargaining approach to decision-making while low constraint situations are more likely to generate rational or optimizing activity (t'Hart and Kleiboer, 1995; de Bruijn and ten Heuvelhof, 2000).

Four basic decision-making styles emerge from this analysis. Lindblom-style *incremental adjustments* are likely to occur where policy subsystems are complex and constraints on decision-makers are high. In such situations one would expect the adoption of large-scale, high-risk options to be rare. In the opposite scenario, where the policy subsystem is simple and constraints are low, more traditional *rational searches* may result in the adoption of new options and major changes. When a complex subsystem exists and constraints are low, an adjustment strategy is

Figure 7.4 **An Improved Model of Basic Decision-Making Styles**

Complexity of the Policy Subsystem

		High	*Low*
Severity of Constraints	*High*	Incremental Adjustment	Satisfycing Search
	Low	Optimizing Adjustment	Rational Search

SOURCE: Modelled after Martin J. Smith, 'Policy Networks and State Autonomy', in S. Brooks and A.-G. Gagnon, eds, *The Political Influence of Ideas: Policy Communities and the Social Sciences* (New York: Praeger, 1994).

likely, but one that may tend towards *optimization*, as proponents of two-stage, mixed scanning models suggest. Finally, where constraints are high but subsystems simple, satisfycing decisions are likely, as Simon suggested, since more maximizing strategies are likely to be ineffective in such situations.

CONCLUSION

This discussion demonstrates that the essential character of the public decision-making process is very much the same as that of the other stages we have examined. That is, like the earlier stages of agenda-setting and policy formulation, the decision-making stage is affected by the nature of the policy subsystem involved and by the constraints under which key policy actors, in this case authoritative decision-makers, operate. This results in a situation where, as John Forester (1984: 23) put it, what is rational for administrators and politicians to do:

> depends on the situations in which they work. Pressed for quick recommendations, they cannot begin long studies. Faced with organizational rivalries, competition and turf struggles, they may justifiably be less than candid about their plans. What is reasonable to do depends on the context one is in, in ordinary life no less than in public administration.

FURTHER READINGS

Allison, Graham T., and Morton H. Halperin. 1972. 'Bureaucratic Politics: A Paradigm and Some Policy Implications', *World Politics* 24 (Supplement): 40–79.

Bachrach, Peter, and Morton S. Baratz. 1962. 'Decisions and Nondecisions: An Analytical Framework', *American Political Science Review* 56, 2: 632–42.

Cahill, Anthony, and E. Sam Overman. 1990. 'The Evolution of Rationality in Policy Analysis', in Stuart S. Nagel, ed., *Policy Theory and Policy Evaluation*. New York: Greenwood, 11–27.

Cohen, M., J. March, and J. Olsen. 1972. 'A Garbage Can Model of Organizational Choice', *Administrative Science Quarterly* 17, 1: 1–25.

Etzioni, Amitai. 1967. 'Mixed-Scanning: A "Third" Approach to Decision-Making', *Public Administration Review* 27: 385–92.

Forester, John. 1984. 'Bounded Rationality and the Politics of Muddling Through', *Public Administration Review* 44: 23–30.

Lindblom, Charles. 1959. 'The Science of Muddling Through', *Public Administration Review* 19: 79–88.

March, James G. 1994. *A Primer on Decision-Making: How Decisions Happen*. New York: Free Press.

Mucciaroni, Gary. 1992. 'The Garbage Can Model and the Study of Policy Making: A Critique', *Polity* 24, 3: 460–82.

Simon, Herbert. 1955. 'A Behavioral Model of Rational Choice', *Quarterly Journal of Economics* 69, 1: 99–118.

Smith, Gilbert, and David May. 1980. 'The Artificial Debate between Rationalist and Incrementalist Models of Decision-Making', *Policy and Politics* 8: 147–61.

Teisman, Geert R. 2000. 'Models for Research into Decision-Making Processes: On Phases, Streams and Decision-Making Rounds', *Public Administration* 78, 4: 937–56.

Weiss, Carol H. 1980. 'Knowledge Creep and Decision Accretion,' *Knowledge: Creation, Diffusion, Utilization* 1, 3: 381–404.

NOTES

1. On the origins of legitimate authority in government, see Weber (1978).
2. For an excellent review of the literature, see Lindquist (1988).
3. For a critique of this position from within the ranks of management theorists, see Wagner (1991).
4. On the application of this model to the US and EU cases, see Jones (1994) and Peterson (1995).
5. Others, of course, also discussed these elements. On the significance of problem constraints, see Weick (1976) and Hisschemoller and Hoppe (1995). On time constraints and their effects on decision-making behaviour, see Maule and Svenson (1993) and Payne et al. (1988).
6. On these different strategies, see March (1981).
7. On the significance of the organizational context and the ideational frames constructed by decision-makers within these contexts for decision-making, see Black (1997); Hammond and Knott (1999); Metcalfe (1978); Mintz (1993).

Chapter 8

Policy Implementation:
Policy Design and Implementation Styles

After a public problem has made its way to the policy agenda, various options have been proposed to resolve it, and a government has made some choice among those options, what remains is putting the decision into practice. This is the policy implementation stage of the policy cycle, where policy decisions are translated into action. It is defined as the process whereby programs or policies are carried out, the translation of plans into practice. While some decisions have been made on the general shape of a policy, still others are required for it to be set into motion. Funding must be allocated, personnel assigned, and rules of procedure developed, among other matters.

Until the early 1970s, implementation was often regarded as unproblematic in a policy sense. Although a large, century-old literature existed in fields such as public administration, organizational behaviour, and management concerned with effective execution of government decisions (Wilson, 1887; Goodnow, 1900; Gaus, 1931), many public policy scholars ignored or downplayed the problematic aspects of this stage of the policy cycle, assuming that once a policy decision was made, the administrative arm of government would simply carry it out (Hargrove, 1975). Within the policy sciences, this view began to change with the publication of Pressman and Wildavsky's 1973 work on program implementation. Their study of federal programs for unemployed inner-city residents of Oakland, California, showed that job creation programs were not actually being carried out in the manner anticipated by policy-makers. Other studies confirmed that the Great Society programs instituted by the Johnson administration (1963–8) in the US were not achieving their intended objectives and argued that the problem was rooted in the manner in which they were being implemented (see van Meter and van Horn, 1975; Bardach, 1977). Research in other countries arrived at similar conclusions (Hjern, 1982; Mayntz, 1979). The upshot of all these studies was a more systematic effort in the 1980s to understand the factors that facilitated or constrained implementation of public policies (Sabatier and Mazmanian, 1981).

This 'second generation' of implementation research in the policy sciences was quickly embroiled in a dispute over the analytical focus required to describe and analyze its subject matter: the so-called 'top-down' versus 'bottom-up' debate.[1] Some studies generated analyses and prescriptions that perceived effective policy implementation to be a 'top-down' process concerned with designing mechanisms to ensure that the implementing officials could be made to do their job more effectively. This approach was opposed by those who subscribed to a 'bottom-up' approach, which focused on studying more carefully the actions of those affected by and involved in the implementation of a policy (Sabatier, 1986). While both of these approaches generated valuable insights, like many other similar dichotomous debates in the field, they tended to ossify into hardened positions that stifled conceptual development and research, leading to calls in the late 1980s and 1990s for new approaches that would represent a 'third generation' of more 'scientific' implementation research (see Lester et al., 1987; Goggin et al., 1990; DeLeon, 1999a).

Scholars in many countries answered this call and the 1990s proved to be a very fertile decade for implementation research (Lester and Goggin, 1998; O'Toole, 2000b). In addition to studies using the insights of game theory and principal-agent models of behaviour (e.g., Scholz, 1984, 1991; Hawkins and Thomas, 1989a)—which focused on questions such as the nature of enforcement involved in the use of traditional administrative techniques—a third approach emerged. Rather than studying the purely administrative concerns of putting a program into practice, this approach looked at the implementation process as one in which the various tools of government described in Chapter 4 were applied to concrete cases through a process of policy design (see Salamon, 1981; Mayntz, 1983).[2] Since, as we have seen in Chapter 4, the general contours of available policy instruments are reasonably well known, studies in this mould tended to concentrate on the reasons or rationales for the choice of particular tools by the government and the potential for their use in future circumstances (see Hood, 1986a; Linder and Peters, 1989). Recent work in this area has moved beyond the question of individual instrument choices and has delved into the description of instrument 'mixes' and 'implementation styles', that is, relatively long-lasting, quasi-permanent preferences exhibited at the issue, sectoral, and sometimes the national and international levels for specific types or combinations of instruments (see Lowi, 1985; May et al., 1997: ch. 5; Knill, 1998; Kagan and Axelrad, 1997).

In this chapter we set out the factors that make the practice and analysis of policy implementation a difficult task, and discuss the evolution of thinking on the subject from 'first' to 'third' generation. In particular, the chapter will expand on the description of policy instruments contained in Chapter 4 and assess the factors identified in the literature as affecting the choice of instruments for implementing policy. Finally, the manner in which the procedural and substantive instruments outlined in Chapter 4 combine to create distinctive implementation styles will be discussed.

ACTORS AND ACTIVITIES IN POLICY IMPLEMENTATION

Bureaucracy, and the intra- and inter-organizational conflicts endemic to it, is a significant actor in and determinant of policy implementation. Different bureaucratic agencies at different levels of government (national, state or provincial, and local) are involved in implementing policy, each with its own interests, ambitions, and traditions that affect the implementation process and shape its outcomes (see Bardach, 1977; Elmore, 1978). Implementation by public agencies is often an expensive, multi-year effort, meaning that continued funding for programs and projects is usually neither permanent nor guaranteed but rather requires continual negotiation and discussions between the political and administrative arms of the state. This creates opportunities for politicians, agencies, and other members of policy subsystems to use the implementation process as simply another opportunity for continuing struggles they may have lost at earlier stages of the policy process, such as policy formulation or, more often, decision-making, if their preferred solution to a problem was not selected.

While politicians are significant actors in decisions affecting the implementation process, most of the day-to-day activities of routine administration typically fall within the purview of salaried public servants. In most countries there is a set of traditional or *civil or common laws*, which form a 'default' or basic set of principles governing how individuals will interact with each other and with the state in their day-to-day lives. These laws are often codified in writing—as is the case in many continental European countries—but they may also be found in less systematic form in the overall record of precedents set by judicial bodies, as is the case in Britain and its former colonies. Even in common-law countries, *statutory laws* are passed by parliaments to replace or supplement the civil or common law (Gall, 1983; Bogart, 2002).

These 'statutes' take the form of Acts which, among other things, usually designate a specific administrative agency as empowered to make whatever 'regulations' are required to ensure the successful implementation of the principles and aims of the enabling legislation. Acts usually also create a series of rules to be followed in the implementation process, as well as a range of permissible offences and penalties for non-compliance with the law. Regulations to give effect to these general principles in specific circumstances are then prepared by civil servants employed by administrative agencies, often in conjunction with target groups (Kagan, 1994). Regulations cover such items as the standards of behaviour or performance that must be met by target groups and the criteria to be used to administer policy. These serve as the basis for licensing or approval and, although unlegislated, provide the de facto source of direction and background to the implementation process in modern states. As was discussed in Chapter 4, this general form of implementation is sometimes referred to as '*command and control*' regulation whereby a command is given by an authorized body and the administration is charged with controlling the target group to ensure compliance (Sinclair, 1997; Kerwin, 1994, 1999).

In the modern era, such legal processes form the basis for implementation in all but the worst instances of dictatorship or personal rule. This is because legal processes are a necessary part of adapting general statements of intent, which usually result from the decision-making stage, to the specific circumstances and situations that administrators face on the ground. The actual practice of administering policy in this situation is performed overwhelmingly by civil servants operating in various kinds of administrative agencies, such as ministries, departments, branches, and agencies, and by members of appointed boards and tribunals created specifically for regulatory purposes.

The usual form of such administrative venues, the *ministry* or *department*, has been discussed in Chapter 4. *Tribunals* are created by statute and perform many quasi-judicial functions, including appeals concerning licensing, certification of personnel or programs, and issue of permits. Appointed by government, they usually represent, or purport to represent, some diversity of interests and expertise. *Administrative hearings* are conducted by tribunals in a quasi-judicial fashion in order to aid them in their activities. Hearings are bound by rules of natural justice, and their procedures may also be dictated by statutory provisions (which may be general and discretionary). Hearings are designed to lead to binding decisions on the agency in question but may be subject to various kinds of political, administrative, and judicial appeals. *Public hearings* may be statutorily defined as a component of the administrative process and directed towards securing regulatory compliance. In most cases, however, hearings are held at the discretion of a decision-making authority and are often 'after the fact' public information sessions rather than true consultative devices (Talbert et al., 1995; Grima, 1985).

While authoritative decision-makers, both political and administrative, remain a significant force in the implementation stage of the policy process, they are joined at this stage by additional members of the relevant policy subsystems, as the number and type of policy actors comes more and more to resemble that found at the formulation stage (Bennett and McPhail, 1992). *Target groups*, that is, groups whose behaviour is intended or expected to be altered by government action, play a major direct and indirect role in the implementation process. The political and economic resources of target groups, especially, have a major effect on the implementation of policies (Montgomery, 2000). Powerful groups affected by a policy can condition the character of implementation by supporting or opposing it. It is therefore quite common for regulators to strike compromises with groups, or attempt to use the groups' own resources in some cases, to make the task of implementation simpler or less expensive. Although this is typically done informally, in some jurisdictions like the US, more formal efforts have been made in many sectors to incorporate regulator-regulatee negotiations in the development of administrative standards and other aspects of the regulatory process (Coglianese, 1997). Changing levels of public support for a policy can also affect implementation. Many policies witness a decline in support after a policy decision has been made, giving greater opportunity to administrators to vary the original intent of a decision (see Hood, 1983, 1986a).

EARLY MODELS OF PUBLIC POLICY IMPLEMENTATION

Scientific Administration and Street-Level Bureaucrats: The Top-Down vs Bottom-Up Debate

Most early studies on policy implementation focused on questions of management and institutional design, which in the 1970s came to be known as the *top-down* approach to the subject (Nye, 2002). This approach 'assumes that we can usefully view the policy process as a series of chains of command where political leaders articulate a clear policy preference which is then carried out at increasing levels of specificity as it goes through the administrative machinery that serves the government' (Clarke, 1992: 222). This approach was quite useful in setting out a variety of managerial and organizational design principles, or maxims of administration, which were expected to generate an optimal or maximizing match between political intent and administrative action. Under the guise of scientific administration, these principles—which, for example, included entreaties for managers to limit the span of control found in organizations and reduce the number of levels in administrative hierarchies—were expected to allow them to find and execute the one-best-way for administrators to implement policies.[3]

In the 1950s and 1960s, however, the scientific nature of these principles came under attack as critics like Herbert Simon (1946) pointed out their often contradictory and proverbial—rather than scientific—nature. It was also noted that this approach assumes that decision-makers provide implementers with clear goals and direction when, as we have seen in Chapter 7, in reality government intentions can emerge from bargaining processes and thus result in often vague, unclear, or even contradictory goals and direction. The most serious shortcoming of this approach, however, was its focus on senior politicians and officials, who often play only a marginal role in day-to-day implementation compared to lower-level officials and members of the public.

This criticism of the top-down approach's neglect of lower-level officials led in the 1980s to the development of the so-called *bottom-up* or 'street-level' approach to the study of public policy implementation (see Hjern and Porter, 1993; Hjern, 1982; Barrett and Fudge, 1981). This more empirical approach to the subject urged analysts to begin with all the public and private actors involved in implementing programs and systematically examine through interviews and survey research their personal and organizational goals, their implementation strategies, and the network of contacts they build. Studies conducted in bottom-up fashion have shown that the success or failure of many programs often depends on the commitment and skills of the actors directly involved in implementing programs (Lipsky, 1980).

The key advantage of the bottom-up perspective is that it directs attention to the formal and informal relationships constituting the policy subsystems involved in making and implementing policies. As we have seen, policy subsystems consisting of key private and public actors in a policy sector play a crucial role at all stages of the policy process. This is just as true of policy implementation as it is of agenda-setting, policy formulation, decision-making, and other stages of the policy cycle (Hall and O'Toole, 2000; Kiviniemi, 1986).

Despite some rhetoric to the contrary, however, it was obvious to most observers that these two approaches were not contradictory but complementary (Sabatier, 1993a). That is, the top-down approach starts with the decisions of the government, examines the extent to which administrators carry out or fail to carry out these decisions, and seeks to find the reasons underlying the extent of the implementation. The bottom-up approach merely begins at the other end of the implementation chain of command and urges that the activities of so-called street-level implementers be fully taken into account. Moreover, much of the debate between these approaches is methodological, over the best way to analyze implementation activities, over the best means to develop testable hypotheses about the nature of the implementation process and the factors that influence success and failure. Taken together, the top-down and bottom-up approaches provide better insights into policy implementation than either does on its own (Fox, 1990; Sabatier, 1986).

Hence, to further the study of implementation processes in a fashion that would shed light on its operation in specific circumstances and aid in the overall conceptualization of the policy process, many students of public policy turned away from the top-down versus bottom-up debate to examine policy implementation as a question of compliance and control. They began to focus on the reasons why both high-level and street-level implementers often took the course of action they did, rather than what was expected of them by decision-makers.

Principal-Agent Theory

In both top-down and bottom-up case studies, gaps between legislative or political intent and administrative practice were frequently held up as a major reason for policy failure (see Kerr, 1976; Ingram and Mann, 1980b; Mulford, 1978). In the *principal-agent* theory that was subsequently developed to explain this phenomenon, these gaps were viewed as the inevitable results of the structure of politico-administrative institutions in modern states, in which decision-makers must delegate responsibility for implementation to officials they only indirectly control. The existence of structural discretion on the part of the administrative 'agents' of political 'principals' introduced the potential for inefficient or ineffective translation of government intent into reality.[4]

The principal-agent problem in policy implementation, in this view, is seen to arise from the common practice in most countries, set out above, whereby general laws passed by the political branches of government are put into effect through detailed regulations created by administrative agencies charged with implementing the law. This legal framework establishes a particular kind of principal-agent relationship between politicians and administrators in which there is an inherent problem of securing the latter's compliance (see Cook and Wood, 1989; Gormley, 1989). The administrators have their own understanding, ambitions, and fiscal and knowledge resources that may come in the way of policies being implemented as originally conceived by decision-makers.

This structural problem is compounded by several other difficulties built into such systems. First, it is often the case that implementation involves not one but a number of government agencies. This means that implementation increasingly takes place in complex 'inter-organizational' contexts in which issues of co-ordinating implementation efforts are not trivial but require the creation of another layer of specialized administrative agencies designed specifically for that purpose, such as interdepartmental or intergovernmental committees, or so-called 'staff' or 'central agencies', exacerbating principal-agent dilemmas (see Smith et al., 1993; Campbell and Szablowski, 1979; Mayntz, 1993b; Rogers and Whetton, 1982). Other frequently encountered difficulties relate to the nature of implementation problems, the circumstances surrounding them, or the organization of the administrative machinery in charge of the program. For principal-agent theorists, these are the realities of implementation, as distinct from the stated objectives of decision-makers and the formal procedures prescribed for achieving those objectives.[5]

The nature of the problems themselves affects the implementation of programs designed to address them in several ways. First, policy decisions involve varying degrees of technical difficulties during implementation, some of which are more intractable than others. Implementing some programs can be expected to be unproblematic, as in the case of closing down an illegal casino or opening a new school in a new neighbourhood, because these are specific single decisions whose translation into practice is usually rather routine. The same is not true for programs designed to address long-term, chronic, or ill-defined problems such as eliminating compulsive gambling or improving pupils' educational standards. Public problems such as domestic violence or educational under-achievement are rooted in so many causes that programs designed to address single or even multiple causes can normally be expected to fall short of their objectives. The problem of speeding on city streets has more simple origins and can therefore be addressed more easily, even though it is unlikely to be eradicated entirely. Similarly, programs designed to eliminate pollution or tax and welfare frauds must face the reality that no available technology will allow complete achievement of these objectives. Even if the technology is available, it may be more expensive than the society is willing to pay. As was discussed in Chapter 7, 'wicked' problems are simply more difficult to tackle because of their complex, novel, or interdependent nature and because they involve not a single decision but a series of decisions on how to carry out the government's policy (Churchman, 1967; Rittel and Webber, 1973). Dealing with such problems enhances administrative discretion inasmuch as the more complex and difficult the problem, the greater the range of discretion administrators will have in dealing with it.

The nature of the affected target group is also an issue. The size of the target group, for example, is a factor affecting administrative discretion insofar as the larger and more diverse the group, the more difficult it is to affect its behaviour in a desired fashion. Thus, because of the small number of manufacturers involved, for example, policy designed to improve the safety features of automobiles is easier to implement than a policy designed to make thousands of careless drivers observe traffic safety rules (Hood, 1986a). The extent of the behavioural change the policy requires of the target group hence is a key determinant of the level of difficulty faced in its implementation. A policy of eradicating sexism, racism, or religious intolerance is more difficult to implement, because of the deep roots of these attitudes in societies' cultural belief systems. By contrast, increasing the electricity supply requires almost no change in behaviour on the part of consumers (Schneider and Ingram, 1990, 1993a).

In addition to the nature of the problem being addressed by the policy, administrative discretion in the implementation process is also affected by its social, economic, technological, and political contexts (Hutter and Manning, 1990). Changes in social conditions may affect the interpretation of the problem and thus the manner in which ongoing programs are implemented. Thus, many of the problems currently being faced by social security programs in industrialized countries arise from the fact that they were not designed to cope with the ever-increasing proportion of the aged or continuous high rates of unemployment that impose a very heavy burden on public finance. Changes in economic conditions can have a similar impact on policy implementation. A program targeting the poor and unemployed, for instance, can be expected to undergo changes after an economic upturn or downturn. Economic conditions also vary by region, necessitating greater flexibility and discretion in implementation. Third, the availability of new technology can also be expected to cause changes in policy implementation. Policies towards pollution control, for example, often change in the course of implementation after a more effective or cheaper technology has been discovered. Fourth, variations in political circumstances are also important. A change of government may lead to changes in the way policies are implemented. Many conservative governments, for example, have been known to tighten the availability of social security programs established by labour or socialist governments without necessarily changing the policy itself (Mazmanian and Sabatier, 1983: 31).

Because of these aspects of the implementation process and environment, a great deal of discretion is often placed in the hands of civil servants who quickly become more expert in an administrative area than the generalists who tend to staff political offices. Civil servants can decide how and to whom the laws will be applied (Calvert et al., 1989; McCubbins et al., 1987, 1989), placing politicians and administrators in a particular kind of principal-agent relationship, such as those commonly found in relationships between lawyer and client, physician and patient, or buyer-broker-seller, in which the principal is dependent on the good-will of the agent to further his or her interests when it may not be in the interests of the agent to do so (Ellig and Lavoie, 1995; Francis, 1993; Banks, 1995). The particular dynamics of this relationship affects the tenor and quality of their interactions and limits the ability of political 'principals' to circumscribe effectively the behaviour of their erstwhile 'agents' (Bozeman, 1993; Milward and Provan, 1998).

Principal-agent theorists argue that many noble efforts on the part of governments and citizens to create better and safer worlds have foundered on these 'realities' of implementation and its built-in principal-agent problem. This has led not only to a greater appreciation of the difficulties encountered in policy implementation, but also to attempts to design policies in a manner offering a reasonable chance of success in implementation. While many government decisions continue to be taken without adequate attention to the difficulties of implementation, there is a broad recognition now of the need to take these concerns into account at earlier stages of the policy process, such as policy formulation (Spence, 1999). It is easier and more effective for policy-makers to take these limitations into account and devise an appropriate response *ex ante* rather than *ex post* (Linder and Peters, 1984, 1988, 1990).

IMPLEMENTATION AS POLICY DESIGN:
THEORIES OF POLICY INSTRUMENT CHOICE

Principal-agent theory pointed to the implications of the design of administrative structures for effective implementation and underlined the importance of mechanisms to ensure continuing oversight of administrative actors by their political 'masters'. This focus extended the insight of 'bottom-up' implementation studies of the need for structures allowing senior officials to control street-level ones while granting those on the ground enough autonomy to perform their work effectively (McCubbins and McCubbins, 1994; McCubbins and Schwartz, 1984). This renewed emphasis on the significance of institutional design for effective policy implementation dovetailed in the 1990s with other efforts to study the characteristics of policy instruments and the reasons for their selection by governments, undertaken with the aim of improving the implementation process through the selection of appropriate tools for the job to be done.

The instrument-choice approach to policy implementation began from the observation that, to a great extent, policy implementation involves applying one or more of the basic techniques of government discussed in Chapter 4—variously known as *policy tools*, *policy instruments*, or *governing instruments*—to the resolution of policy problems (see Bressers and Klok, 1988; Schneider and Ingram, 1990a: 513–14; McDonnell and Elmore, 1987; Elmore, 1978, 1987). This approach begins from the premise that regardless of whether we study the implementation process in a top-down or bottom-up fashion, the process of giving form or substance to a government decision or statement of intent always involves choosing one or several tools from those available in the government tool box (Hood, 1986a; Linder and Peters, 1991). After having developed basic inventories of these tools, as described in Chapter 4, the instrument choice perspective then addressed the question of why implementers should choose a particular instrument from among the many available. Later, these studies turned to the question of whether these choices resulted in any distinct implementation patterns or styles that could be discerned in the policy processes found in different jurisdictions (Rothmayr et al., 1997).

Answering these questions moved implementation analysis away from its roots in the study of public administration and helped to integrate implementation research with the general inquiries and concerns of the policy sciences. Specifically, these studies highlighted the close links between policy formulation, decision-making, and implementation.

Systematic analyses of instrument choices usually begin with the attempt to identify a single or limited number of dimensions along which categories of policy instruments are said to vary. For this purpose, as we noted in Chapter 4, a useful distinction can be drawn between 'substantive' and 'procedural' instruments, that is, between those affecting the substance of policy outputs and those directed instead towards the manipulation of policy processes. In the case of substantive instruments, or those expected to somehow alter the nature or configuration of goods and services in society, taxonomies were elevated from pure description and classification to a more theoretical or conceptual level through the construction of models that focused on such elements as 'the extent of legitimate coercion' inherent in the use of different policy tools. This aspect of policy tools could be used as a basic criterion for explaining the relationship existing between general categories of instruments and the reasons why one would be used rather than another.[6]

More recent studies expanded this analysis, focusing on other aspects such as the level of direct state involvement in the provision of goods and services as the chief criterion for distinguishing between categories of 'effector' instruments (see Baxter-Moore, 1987). In other words, different substantive policy instruments could be seen as affecting different numbers and types of actors involved in productive activities in society. In such schemes, 'voluntary' instruments requiring minimal state involvement are placed at one end of a continuum, with 'compulsory' instruments involving virtually exclusive state activity at the opposite end. Between the two poles, as shown in Figure 8.1, lie a wide range of 'mixed' instruments involving varying levels of state and private involvement in the operation of mixed markets (Hula, 1988).

Figure 8.1 A Spectrum of Substantive Policy Instruments

Family & community	Voluntary organizations	Private market	Information & exhortation	Subsidy	Tax & user charges	Regulation	Public enterprise	Direct provision

Voluntary	Mixed	Compulsory

Low		High

Level of State Activity Involved in Goods and Service Production and Delivery

SOURCE: Adapted from Michael Howlett, 'Managing the "Hollow State": Procedural Policy Instruments and Modern Governance', *Canadian Public Administration* 43, 4 (2000): 412–31.

With respect to procedural instruments, whose fundamental purpose is to alter or manipulate aspects of policy subsystem or network behaviour in a policy process, these similarly could be seen as affecting the nature, number, and activities of different sets of actors in a policy process. These tools manipulate the links and nodes of the networks of actors involved in policy-making (see Klijn, 1996; de Bruijn and ten Heuvelhof, 1995, 1997),[7] just as substantive instruments manipulate market relations. A wide range of network or subsystem manipulations are possible, ranging from limited voluntary 'network management' to more fundamental and coercive 'subsystem restructuring' (de Bruijn and ten Heuvelhof, 1991, 1995; O'Toole, 2000a; Klijn and Teisman, 1991; Klijn and Koppenjan, 2000). Incorporating this insight also allows procedural policy instruments to be arrayed in a single spectrum according to the level of state manipulation of subsystem membership and activities they typically involve (see Figure 8.2).

Figure 8.2 A Spectrum of Procedural Policy Instruments

Network self-creation and operation	Information management and distribution	Research and interest group funding	Standing/access and advisory committee creation	Institutional reform and government reorganization
Management		*Mixed*		**Restructuring**
Low				*High*

Level of State Manipulation of Subsystem Membership and Structure

SOURCE: Adapted from Michael Howlett, 'Managing the "Hollow State": Procedural Policy Instruments and Modern Governance', *Canadian Public Administration* 43, 4 (2000): 412–31.

In this spectrum, procedural policy instruments can be seen to range from limited information suppression or release designed to mildly affect subsystem behaviour through 'voluntaristic' responses from targeted actors, to institutional reforms designed to restructure existing subsystems by more or less compulsory means.[8]

The Rationale for Instrument Choice:
Early 'Technical' vs 'Political' Models

To say anything meaningful about policy implementation, however, the instrument choice perspective requires a model linking specific choices of instruments to specific rationales. Two different groups of scholars have worked on this question of the 'rationale of instrument choice', and the solutions they have put forward to answer this question have varied dramatically. Economists have for the most part tended to interpret the choice of policy instrument as, at least in theory, a technical exercise of matching the attributes of specific tools to the job at hand. Political scientists, on the other hand, have tended to argue that instruments are more or less substitutable on a purely technical basis, and have instead focused on the political forces they believe govern instrument selection (see Peters and Van Nispen, 1998).

Studies by economists have been shaped by the theoretical debates, discussed in Chapter 2, between neo-classical and welfare economists on the proper role of the state in the economy. While all prefer voluntary instruments, some economists permit greater scope for the use of compulsory and mixed instruments to correct market failures (Bator, 1958; Economic Council of Canada, 1979; Utton, 1986). In contrast, others approve the use of such instruments only for providing pure public goods; their use for any other reason is viewed as distorting the market process and leading to suboptimal aggregate social outcomes (Breyer, 1979, 1982; Posner, 1974; Stigler, 1975; Wolf, 1987). Welfare economists' greater theoretical acceptance of state intervention leads them to more systematic analyses of instrument choice. However, they still tend to treat the choice of instrument as a strictly technical exercise that consists of evaluating the features of various instruments, matching them to different types of market failures, estimating their relative costs, and choosing the instrument that most efficiently overcomes the market failure in question (Mitnick, 1980; Stokey and Zeckhauser, 1978; Weimer and Vining, 1992).

Other economists generally rely on public choice theory to explain patterns of instrument use. As we saw in Chapter 2, they argue that in a democracy the dynamics of self-serving behaviour by voters, politicians, and bureaucrats promotes an increasing tendency to tax and spend, and to regulate and nationalize private activity. It is argued that democratic politics leads states to choose instruments that provide concentrated benefits to marginal voters while spreading the costs to the entire population (see Buchanan, 1980; Trebilcock and Hartle, 1982). For electoral reasons, governments make efforts to choose instruments that do not reveal their true costs to the voters who ultimately pay for them.

While the incorporation of some political factors into the analysis is an improvement on earlier purely economic approaches, such analyses do little to further the explanation of systematic patterns of instrument choices. It is very difficult, for example, to match types of instruments with patterns of the distribution of costs and benefits (Wilson, 1974) since one must first know whether governments want to claim credit or avoid blame for the action to be undertaken (Weaver, 1986; Hood, 2002). Most instruments can be used for both purposes, and which purpose is chosen depends on highly idiosyncratic and contextual factors. Similarly, the economic theories of instrument choice lack a solid empirical base in studies of actual instrument choices by governments. The rationales for policy instrument choice they provide are based on theoretical assumptions concerning what governments do or ought to do, rather than on empirical investigations into what they actually do (Howard, 1995; Bohm and Russell, 1985; Peters, 2002).

Studies by political scientists, as the following discussion will show, tend to display a wider variety and are generally more empirical in nature. To those looking for theoretical parsimony, they may not appear as elegant as the studies generated by economists, but they help to grapple with the complexity of policy instruments and inductively develop a plausible theory of instrument choice (see Howlett, 1991) and policy implementation.

One oft-cited political science approach to theorizing the question of policy instrument choice was developed in the 1970s by Bruce Doern and several of his Canadian associates (Doern, 1981; Phidd and Doern, 1983; Tupper and Doern, 1981). Assuming that all instruments are *technically substitutable*—that is, that at least in theory any instrument could be bent, shaped, and twisted to perform any task—they argued that in a liberal democratic society governments would simply *prefer* to use the least coercive instruments available and would 'move up the scale' of coercion as necessary to overcome any societal resistance they encountered to the achievement of their aims. In other words, any instrument can theoretically accomplish any chosen aim, but governments choose the least coercive instruments possible for the task at hand, given the state of societal resistance they encounter to their actions. Overall, this conception led Doern and his colleagues to suggest that a typical pattern of instrument use in many states was for governments to begin with minimal activities such as exhortation and move slowly, as necessary, towards direct provision.

There are serious problems with this understanding of substitutability among instruments and with this model of the rationale for instrument choice. First, no government has the complete range of instruments available to it: social and political constraints favour the choice of some instruments and inhibit the choice of others (Woodside, 1986). Second, the conception of changes in instrument choice consisting of a slow movement up the coercion scale does not conform to the empirical evi-

dence gathered by many scholars working in this field. Many governments, for example, have begun towards the top of the scale in creating
public enterprises to deal with elements of emerging technologies without ever having experimented with less coercive tools (see Tupper, 1979;
Laux and Molot, 1988). Third, the idea of social resistance provoking
governments to move towards more coercive instruments is also problematic. While in some policy areas—notably the economy—it may be
true that there is often societal resistance to further government action,
in many other fields this is not the case. In the area of social policy, for
example, social pressure often runs the other way, urging greater regulation and expenditures than governments, for fiscal, ideological, and other
reasons, may be willing to provide.

A second widely cited political science model of instrument choice
was developed by Christopher Hood in the 1980s. Like Doern et al., he
began with the observation that instrument choice was not a technical
exercise but 'a matter of faith and politics' (Hood, 1986a: 9). He posited
that the choice is shaped by resource constraints, political pressures,
legal constraints, and the lessons learned from past instrument failures
(ibid., 118–20, 141–3). Although he did not spell out the exact nature of
these forces, Hood did discuss a number of 'normal' patterns of government 'retooling' over time. These include: '1. A shift from information-
based instruments to those based on other resources; and 2. A shift from
reliance on coercion alone to the use of financial and organizational
resources.' Furthermore, he argued that technological change may erode
the usefulness of old instruments and lead to the application of new
ones, often on the basis of analogies between historical and present circumstances drawn by policy-makers.

While Hood admitted the essentially contingent nature of the process
of instrument choice, he argued that the process was driven by identifi-
able forces based on the government's implementation experience with
various instruments and their effects on social actors. According to him,
different instruments vary in effectiveness according to the nature of the
social groups they are intended to influence; for example, if large and
well-organized social groups exist, governments will use persuasion and
expenditure instruments. The size of the target group is significant since
the larger the group to be affected, the more likely it is that governments
will use passive (voluntary) rather than active (compulsory) instruments
because of concerns about cost and effectiveness. However, he also
argued that, regardless of the size of the social group affected, governments will not employ coercive instruments if they want voluntary compliance from a social group. On the other hand, if a government wants to
redistribute resources among those groups, it will use them (ibid.,
138–9).

Thus, for Hood, instrument choice is a function of the nature of the
state's goals and resources and the organization and capacity of targeted

societal actors. Overall, he argued, these led liberal democratic govern-ments to practise the ethos of 'using bureaucracy sparingly': that is, towards a distinct preference for use of information and authority instru-ments since those instruments are 'non-depletable' (Hood, 1983). In fact, he argued, the most preferred resource is nodality or information-based influence, since only instruments based on this resource both are non-depletable and place minimum constraints on citizens. When coercion is required, it is primarily due to the desire to target more closely particular societal groups for action. Even then, authority is preferred to organiza-tion because the former is less resource-intensive.

Hood's model improved on some elements of Doern's formulations but also has its own problems. Why should governments inherently desire to use bureaucracy sparingly? Why should resources like treasure and organization be considered less replenishable than resources such as information or authority, when it is apparent to most observers that the extended use of either propaganda or force has diminishing returns? These questions remained unanswered in Hood's analysis.

The Rationale for Instrument Choice: Subsystem Models

In one of the most sophisticated early works on the subject of instrument choice, Linder and Peters developed a third model integrating many of the various conceptions put forward in both the economics and political science literatures (Linder and Peters, 1989). Synthesizing many of the insights and observations made by Doern, Hood, and others, they listed the following factors as playing a critical role in shaping such choices.

First, like many economists, they agreed that the *features of the policy instruments* are important for selection purposes, because some instru-ments are more suited for a task at hand than are others. They argued that instruments vary according to four general categories of features, each ranging on a scale from low to high:

1. *resource intensiveness,* including administrative cost and opera-tional simplicity;
2. *targeting,* including precision and selectivity;
3. *political risk,* including nature of support and opposition, public visibility, and chances of failure; and
4. *constraints on state activity,* including difficulties with coercive-ness and ideological principles limiting government activity. (Ibid., 47)

Second, like many political scientists, they argued that a nation's *policy style and political culture*, and the depth of its social cleavages, have a critical bearing on the choice of an instrument. Each nation has a pecu-liar style, culture, and pattern of social conflicts that predispose its deci-sion-makers to choose particular instruments. Third, they argued that the choice of an instrument is circumscribed by the *organizational culture* of the concerned implementing agencies and the nature of their links with clients and other agencies. Fourth, they argued that the *context of the problem situation*, its timing and the scope of actors it includes, will also affect the choice of instrument. Ultimately, however, for Linder and Peters instrument choice is a matter of the administrative *decision-makers' subjective preferences*, based on their professional background, institutional affiliation, and cognitive makeup. They are the ones who define the situational context constraining choice and, in the process, implant their professional and personal preferences on instrument choice.

This analysis suggests that the choice of policy instruments is shaped by the characteristics of the instruments, the nature of the problem at hand, governments' past experiences in dealing with the same or similar problems, the subjective preference of the decision-makers, and the likely reaction to the choice by affected social groups. It highlights the significance of two interlinked general variables that can help explain instrument choices. These are, first, *the extent of state planning capacity*, or the organizational ability of states to affect societal actors; and second, *subsystem complexity*, especially the number and type of actors governments must face in implementing their programs and policies (ibid.; Bressers and O'Toole, 1998; Schneider and Ingram, 1990a: 513–14; Grabosky, 1995; Grantham, 2001). Thus, in the case of substantive instruments, the type of instrument chosen by governments to implement policy decisions affecting economic and social activity will depend on the intersection of state capacity for intervention and the complexity of the actors that states wish to influence (see Kriesi and Jegen, 2000; Cantor et al., 1992: ch. 2; Varone, 2000).

In this view, organizational instruments that create or restructure markets should only be used, or can only be used effectively, when high levels of state capacity coexist with complex subsystems, as is the case, for example, with promoting technological innovation. Only a state with a high level of organizational capacity working within a complex implementation subsystem can effectively implement, for example, an extensive industrial policy targeting the creation of 'sunrise' industries. If a state faces a complex set of implementation actors but has only limited capacity, on the other hand, it is more likely to employ treasure-based instruments to manipulate existing production relationships. This occurs in many situations in which governments may not have access to the information or expertise required to have a more direct impact on goods and services delivery by market actors, as is the case, for example, with regulation of the oil and gas industry.

When a state has high capacity but faces a relatively simple social or policy environment characterized by few actors and a small number of significant inter-organizational relationships, it can use authority-based instruments to regulate markets. This is a fairly common situation found in mature industries and activities, such as telephone or electricity production and distribution systems dominated by only a few actors. Finally, when state capacity is low and the policy environment not very complex, reliance on existing markets or the use of voluntary instruments is common, as was the case prior to the twentieth century in many areas of social security and health care. In the present era, examples of such implementation activities are information-based government campaigns directed at preventing auto theft or discouraging drinking and driving.[9]

These factors also affect the choice of procedural instruments (Saward, 1992; Rhodes, 1997b; Howse et al., 1990; Bennett, 1992a). Governments with a high capacity facing complex policy environments are able to use 'directive' procedural instruments such as government reorganization to create new or restructure existing policy subsystems (see Suchman, 1995; Heritier, 1997, 1999). Lower-capacity governments facing policy environments of lower complexity use instruments such as information manipulation, for example, by releasing or withholding documents to affect the behaviour of policy actors (McGuire, 2002).

Where low-capacity governments face complex implementation environments they are not able to rely on information provision to alter actor behaviour but can use selective funding to support specific interest groups or create new ones to meet their needs (see King and Walker, 1991; Browne, 1991; Pal, 1993a). In low-complexity situations, high-capacity governments can more directly alter subsystem structures by recognizing new actors or privileging old ones through authoritative means, for example, by establishing specialized quasi-independent advisory committees and/or QUANGOs (see Hood, 1986b, 1988; Brown, 1972; Smith, 1977; Dion, 1973).

Effective use of procedural instruments, like that involving substantive instruments, hence requires that a government has the capacity to effect changes while the actual extent of resource use required will vary with the size and complexity of the policy actors it is attempting to influence (see Saward, 1990; Bryson and Crosby, 1993; Maloney, 2001).

This model does not delve into the detail of fine gradations of instrument use within each general category, of course, nor does it deal with the specific contexts of individual decisions, which can result in errors being made in instrument choices (see Varone and Landry, 1997), nor does it address the question about optimal and suboptimal instrument mixes in particular policy areas or sectors.[10] However, it suggests that although instrument choices for policy implementation are complex, general patterns of such choices can nevertheless be discerned and explained, and basic advice rendered to public managers about which types of instruments are appropriate in specific circumstances (see Bressers, 1998; Bressers and O'Toole, 1998; Mandell, 2000).

CONCLUSION: MODELS OF IMPLEMENTATION STYLES

Implementation studies over the past 30 years have generated insights into implementation activities and instrument use, which shed light on the possibilities and constraints affecting this stage of the policy process and the ability of practitioners to design and improve policy implementation. While some studies undertaken in this vein have been, and continue to be, influenced by the idea that implementation is purely technical in nature, and hence open to rapid change and reconfiguration, most studies have linked implementation activities to larger-scale and more permanent arrangements of policy instruments, or *implementation styles*. Despite somewhat different methodologies and frameworks, these approaches share the view that implementation involves much more than simply executing previous decisions or matching goals with means. They endorse the notion that policy implementation can only be meaningfully understood and evaluated in terms of the existing range of actors and institutions within which implementers make their decisions (Linder and Peters, 1991: 131).

The central precept of these approaches is that the implementation process and its outcomes are shaped by political factors related to state capacity and subsystem complexity (Atkinson and Nigol, 1989: 114). Since these variables tend to change only very slowly, thus it follows that implementation activities tend to exhibit a surprising amount of similarity across policy sectors and over time. What British policy-makers might accomplish through public enterprises, for example, might tend to be implemented in the US through regulations. This is something economists, for example, repeatedly find, to their displeasure, when their proposals for utilizing new types of economic instruments to control social ills such as pollution are rejected in favour of the continuing use of regulation, as has become almost habitual in many countries dealing with this type of problem (Doern, 1998; Doern and Wilks, 1998).

Although numerous permutations and combinations are possible, the model of basic implementation styles found in Figure 8.3 sets out the typical mixes of procedural and substantive policy instruments found in many jurisdictions. Governments facing a variety of limitations and dealing with broad policy targets will tend to use low-cost instruments such as exhortation while restructuring or reforming basic policy institutions to alter the fundamental network structure of specific sectors and issue areas. This results in an implementation style of *institutionalized voluntarism*. An example of this style is when the Canadian government established new structures to deal with official language policy and bilingualism while devoting substantial sums to advertising during the extended national unity crisis of the 1970–90 period (see Rose, 1993; Ryan, 1995).

Figure 8.3   A Model of Basic Implementation Styles

Nature of the Policy Target

		Broad	Narrow
Severity of Constraints on State	High	Institutionalized Voluntarism (*Information-based substantive tools and institutional reorganization*)	Representative Legalism (*Regulation-based substantive tools and financial manipulation*)
	Low	Directed Subsidization (*Treasure-based substantive tools and recognition manipulation*)	Directed Provision (*Organization-based substantive tools and information manipulation*)

Faced with lower constraints but similarly broad targets, governments tend to develop implementation styles based on the use of treasure-based tools, while extending recognition to specific interest groups in the form of consultations and advisory committees. In many countries, the use of this implementation style of *directed subsidization* is very common and examples can be found in many policy areas, including many economic and industrial ones (see Atkinson and Coleman, 1989b).

In situations where governments face precise targets under situations of high constraint, they tend to use forms of compulsory substantive instruments—including such tools as regulation—along with procedural tools such as the extension of financial incentives for the formation and organization of specific policy actors. This results in an implementation style of *representative legalism*, which has been used in many countries recently in areas such as human rights and women's issues as governments have created new regulations to deal with specific issues in these areas while extending funding to multicultural, human rights, and women's groups (see Burt, 1990; Pal, 1993a; Finkle et al., 1994).

Finally, in situations where they face low constraints and narrow targets, governments tend to use substantive organizational tools such as government corporations, public enterprises, and directly administered pubic service delivery, combined with procedural tools such as public hearings, reviews, and evaluations. Examples of this fourth implementation style of *directed provision* are also found in many countries and in many areas, such as radio and television broadcasting and, in the past, railway and airline transportation in Canada and elsewhere (see Dwivedi, 1982; Hodgetts, 1973; de la Mothe, 1996).

FURTHER READINGS

Bardach, Eugene. 1977. *The Implementation Game: What Happens After a Bill Becomes a Law*. Cambridge, Mass.: MIT Press.

Bressers, Hans Th.A. 1998. 'The Choice of Policy Instruments in Policy Networks', in B.G. Peters and F.K.M.V. Nispen, eds, *Public Policy Instruments: Evaluating the Tools of Public Administration*. New York: Edward Elgar, 85–105.

Doern, G. Bruce, and Richard W. Phidd. 1992. *Canadian Public Policy: Ideas, Structure, Process*, 2nd edn. Toronto: Nelson.

Ellig, Jerry, and Don Lavoie. 1995. 'The Principle-Agent Relationship in Organizations', in P. Foss, ed., *Economic Approaches to Organizations and Institutions: An Introduction*. Aldershot: Dartmouth.

Goggin, Malcolm L., et al. 1990. *Implementation Theory and Practice: Toward a Third Generation*. Glenview, Ill.: Scott, Foresman/Little, Brown.

Gunningham, Neil, and Darren Sinclair. 1999. 'Regulatory Pluralism: Designing Policy Mixes for Environmental Protection', *Law and Policy* 21, 1: 49–76.

Hjern, Benny. 1982. 'Implementation Research—The Link Gone Missing', *Journal of Public Policy* 2, 3: 301–8.

Hood, Christopher. *The Tools of Government*. Chatham, NJ: Chatham House.

Howlett, Michael. 2000. 'Managing the "Hollow State": Procedural Policy Instruments and Modern Governance', *Canadian Public Administration* 43, 4: 412–31.

Kagan, Robert A. 1991. 'Adversarial Legalism and American Government', *Journal of Policy Analysis and Management* 10, 3: 369–406.

Klijn, Erik-Hans, Joop Koppenjan, and Katrien Termeer. 1995. 'Managing Networks in the Public Sector: A Theoretical Study of Management Strategies in Policy Networks', *Public Administration* 73: 437–54.

Linder, Stephen H., and B. Guy Peters. 1989. 'Instruments of Government: Perceptions and Contexts', *Journal of Public Policy* 9, 1: 35–58.

O'Toole, Laurence J. 2000. 'Research on Policy Implementation: Assessment and Prospects', *Journal of Public Administration Research and Theory* 10, 2: 263–88.

Pressman, Jeffrey L., and Aaron B. Wildavsky. 1984. *Implementation: How Great Expectations in Washington are Dashed in Oakland*, 3rd edn. Berkeley: University of California Press.

Sabatier, Paul A. 1993. 'Top-down and Bottom-up Approaches to Implementation Research', in Michael Hill, ed., *The Public Policy Process: A Reader*. London: Harvester Wheatsheaf, 266–93. First published in 1986 in *Journal of Public Policy*.

Schneider, Anne, and Helen Ingram. 1993. 'Social Construction of Target Populations: Implications for Politics and Policy', *American Political Science Review* 87, 2: 334–47.

Simon, H.A. 1946. 'The Proverbs of Administration', *Public Administration Review* 6: 53–67.

Woodside, K. 1986. 'Policy Instruments and the Study of Public Policy', *Canadian Journal of Political Science* 19, 4: 775–93.

NOTES

1. On the 'generations' of implementation research, see Goggin et al. (1990).
2. For a review of a similar literature in the foreign policy field, see Hermann (1982).
3. The POSDCORB principles set out by Gulick and Urwick in their 1947 study, discussed in Chapter 7 above, serve as the 'high point' of this movement.
4. On 'agency loss' as a 'governing failure', see Weimer and Vining (1999).
5. The following discussion draws heavily on Mazmanian and Sabatier (1983: 21–5).
6. A path-breaking effort in this process was found in the work of Doern and his collaborators in the 1970s and 1980s. See Doern and Aucoin (1971); Doern and Wilson (1974a, 1974b); Tupper and Doern (1981).
7. On the manipulation of networks, see Leik (1992).
8. On this latter point and the role played by government agencies in this process, see Smith et al. (1993); Savoie (1999).
9. For examples of each type of instrument choice, see Vogel (1996); Eisner (1994b); Tupper (1979); Laux and Molot (1988); Hall and Banting (2000).
10. Early studies of instrument choice tended to look at instances of single instrument selection and, on the basis of such cases, attempted to discern the reasons why governments would choose one general category of instrument over another. It became quickly evident to investigators, however, that most programs tended to involve 'bundles' of instruments rather than single tools (see Gunningham and Sinclair, 1999; Gunningham and Young, 1997; Rhodes, 1997b). Sophisticated students of policy implementation turned their attention to describing these packages of implementation techniques, with the aim of discerning what combinations of instruments were self-reinforcing, which were redundant, and which were actually counterproductive (see Gunningham et al., 1998; Gunningham and Sinclair, 1999; Gunningham and Young, 1997; Sinclair, 1997).

Chapter 9

Policy Evaluation:
Policy Analysis and Policy Learning

Once the need to address a public problem has been acknowledged, various possible solutions have been considered, and some among them have been selected and put into practice, a government often assesses how the policy is working. At the same time, various interested members of policy subsystems and of the public are engaged in their own assessment of the workings and effects of the policy in order to express support for or opposition to the policy, or to demand changes to it. The concept of *policy evaluation* thus refers broadly to the stage of the policy process at which it is determined how a public policy has actually fared in action. It involves the evaluation of the means being employed and the objectives being served. As Larry Gerston (1997: 120) has defined it, 'policy evaluation assesses the effectiveness of a public policy in terms of its perceived intentions and results.' How deep or thorough the evaluation is depends on those ordering its initiation and/or those undertaking it, and what they intend to do with the findings.

After a policy has been evaluated, the problem and solutions it involves may be rethought completely, in which case the cycle may swing back to agenda-setting or some other stage of the cycle, or the status quo may be maintained. Reconceptualization may consist of minor changes or fundamental reformulation of the problem, including terminating the policy altogether (DeLeon, 1983). How evaluation is conducted, the problems the exercise entails, and the range of results to which it typically leads are the concerns of this chapter. It then outlines the patterns of policy change to which different types of policy evaluation typically lead.

ASSESSING POLICY SUCCESS OR FAILURE

As Bovens and t'Hart (1996: 4) have argued, 'the absence of fixed criteria for success and failure, which apply regardless of time and place, is a serious problem' for anyone who wants to understand policy evaluation. Policies can succeed or fail in numerous ways. Sometimes an entire policy regime can fail, while more often specific programs within a policy field may be designated as successful or unsuccessful (Mucciaroni, 1990). And both policies and programs can succeed or fail either in substantive terms—that is, as objectively or perceived to be delivering or failing to deliver the goods—or in procedural terms—as being legitimate or illegitimate, fair or unfair, just or unjust (Bovens and tHart, 1995; Weaver, 1986; McGraw, 1990; Hood, 2002).

'Success' is always difficult to define. In some fairly simple instances, especially those dealing with spectacular failures such as airline crashes or nuclear reactor meltdowns, analyses can pinpoint such well-known factors as technical failures, managerial incompetence, and corruption (Bovens and t'Hart, 1996; Gray and t'Hart, 1998) or lesser-known ones such as 'practical drift' as being responsible for a calamity.[1] Although some of the lessons of these individual accidents—such as the significance for the potential for failure of the loosely or tightly coupled nature of the complex organizational systems that produced a problem (Perrow, 1984)—can be carried over into policy studies, in many circumstances the operation of a policy system is too idiosyncratic, the number of actors too numerous, and the number of outcomes too small to permit clear and unambiguous post-mortems. Nevertheless, such efforts are made and the results of these investigations, whether accurate or not, are fed back into the policy process, influencing the direction and content of further iterations of the policy cycle.

Judgements about policy success and failure often depend in part on the imputation of notions of intentionality to government actors—so that the results of policy-making can be assessed against expectations. However, this is not a simple task (see Sieber, 1981: ch. 2). First, as we have seen, government intentions may be vague and ambiguous, or even potentially contradictory or mutually exclusive. Second, labels such as 'success' and 'failure' are inherently relative and will be interpreted differently by different policy actors. Moreover, such designations are also semantic tools themselves used in public debate and policy contestation in order to seek political advantage. That is, policy evaluations affect considerations and consequences related to assessing blame and taking credit for government activities at all stages of the policy process, all of which can have electoral, administrative, and other consequences for policy actors (Bovens and t'Hart, 1996: 9). As Bovens and t'Hart (ibid., 21) note, 'judgements about the failure or success of public policies or programs are highly malleable. Failure is not inherent in policy events themselves. "Failure" is a judgement about events.' Such judgements, by nature, are at least partially linked to factors such as the nature of the causal theories used to frame policy problems at the agenda-setting stage and the conceptual solutions developed at the formulation stage, as well as the expectations decision-makers have about likely program or policy results and the extent of time allowed, and considered reasonable, to elapse before evaluators make their assessments (ibid., 37). Policy evaluation processes, recognizing these built-in biases, often simply aim to provide policy 'judges' with enough information to be able to make reasonably intelligent, defensible, and replicable assessments.

ACTORS IN THE POLICY EVALUATION PROCESS

Policy evaluation almost always involves bureaucrats and politicians within government dealing with the policy in question, and it usually also involves organized non-governmental members of policy subsystems as well. In addition, it may also involve members of the public, who often will have the ultimate say on a government's policy record when they vote at elections (Brewer and DeLeon, 1983: 319–26). Thus the sites of policy evaluation are broader than often presented in the literature, which tends to concentrate overwhelmingly on evaluation by bureaucrats and 'outside' private consultants and think-tanks. Policy evaluation is not an exclusive preserve of the government. In fact, policy evaluation involves most of the key actors arrayed in policy subsystems in a variety of formal and informal venues for assessing and critiquing policy outcomes and processes.

At one extreme, policy analysts working in departments or specialized units in the administration routinely apply formal techniques such as cost-benefit analysis or various kinds of performance measures in order to try to quantify program outputs and accurately assess program results (see Meltsner, 1976; Friedman, 2002). These analysts can have a substantial impact on subsequent rounds of policy-making because of several different roles they can play in the evaluation process. They can affect the 'framing' and assessment of policy success and failure by how they develop and apply various measures, indicators, and benchmarks to program outputs, sometimes serving as critics or 'advocates' of particular approaches to problems (see Davies, 1999; de la Porte et al., 2001; Levy, 2001). They can also serve as 'brokers' linking policy-makers to implementers, or to those outside the formal institutions of government who are generating new knowledge on social problems and the techniques for resolving or attempting to resolve these problems (see Meltsner, 1976; Guess and Farnham, 2000).

At the other extreme, public protests by affected interest groups also represent an evaluation of existing policy, although this kind of evaluation is post hoc, informal, and external to the policy 'loop'. Such evaluation may involve critiques of both the substance and process of policy, and can lead to changes in administrative organizations and procedures, such as an increase or decrease in access to information by the public (see Snow and Benford, 1992). In between these two poles lie a variety of other venues and means of policy evaluation that involve institutional-ized links between formal and informal policy evaluators in government and civil society. These include the judiciary, which is able to review leg-islative and administrative actions to determine the extent to which poli-cies match up to larger, often constitutionally established principles of social justice and conduct (see de Smith, 1973; Edley, 1990; Humphries and Songer, 1999; Jaffe, 1965). It also includes more recent efforts on the part of administrators to bring public views into the evaluative process through the use of such procedural instruments as focus groups, surveys, inquiries, and task forces (see Hastak et al., 2001; Peters and Parker, 1993; Schwartz, 1997; Wraith and Lamb, 1971).

Evaluation thus includes both informal and spontaneous responses to policy measures and, as such, involves not only authoritative decision-makers and members of policy subsystems active at the formulation and implementation stages of the policy process, but, like the agenda-setting stage, can also potentially involve members from the entire policy uni-verse.

TYPES OF POLICY EVALUATION

The presence of distinct types of policy evaluators results in several dis-tinct types of policy analysis and evaluation. At a general level, policy evaluations can be classified into three broad categories—*administrative evaluation*, *judicial evaluation*, and *political evaluation*—which differ in the way they are conducted, the actors they involve, and their effects. In what follows, the key venues for these kinds of policy evaluation are set out, along with a description of the actors involved in these processes and their activities.

Administrative Evaluation:
Managerial Performance and Budgeting Systems

Administrative evaluation is the focus of many published academic stud-ies on policy evaluation. It is usually undertaken within the government, occasionally by specialist agencies whose only task is evaluation of poli-cies, but more often by financial, legal, and political overseers attached to existing government departments, specialized executive agencies, leg-islatures, and judiciaries. Private consultants may also be hired by the various branches and agencies of the government to conduct evaluation for a fee.

Administrative evaluation is usually, though not always, restricted to examining the efficient delivery of government services and attempting to determine whether or not 'value for money' is being achieved while still respecting principles of justice and democracy. It is intended to ensure that policies are accomplishing their expected goals at the least possible cost and with the least possible burden on individual citizens. This concern for efficiency lies behind numerous formal evaluative systems, such as managerial performance and personnel reviews, as well as the conduct of annual audits and the creation of budgeting systems that attempt to match goals and expenditures. Administrative evaluation requires collection of precise information on program delivery and its compilation in a standardized fashion to allow comparisons of costs and outcomes over time and across policy sectors. As such, these efforts are quite technical and increasingly sophisticated, although the increase in complexity is not necessarily matched by a similar increase in usefulness (Friedman, 2002).

Administrative policy evaluations come in a variety of forms and differ widely in levels of sophistication and formality. Those undertaken by government agencies in the effort to minimize costs are generally of five different types: (1) effort evaluation; (2) performance evaluation; (3) adequacy of performance evaluation; (4) efficiency evaluation; and (5) process evaluation (Suchman, 1967).

Effort evaluation attempts to measure the quantity of program inputs, that is, the amount of effort governments put into accomplishing their goals. The input may be personnel, office space, communication, transportation, and so on—all of which are calculated in terms of the monetary costs they involve. The purpose of the evaluation is to establish a baseline of data that can be used for further evaluations of efficiency or quality of service delivery.

Performance evaluation examines program outputs rather than inputs. Examples of the outputs may be hospital beds or places in schools, numbers of patients seen or children taught. The main aim of performance evaluation is simply to determine what the policy is producing, often regardless of the stated objectives. This type of evaluation produces data that are used as inputs into the more comprehensive and intensive evaluations mentioned below.

Adequacy of performance evaluation (also known as *effectiveness evaluation*) involves more complexity than simply adding up program inputs or outputs; it is intended to find out if the program is doing what it is supposed to be doing. In this type of evaluation, the performance of a given program is compared to its intended goals to determine whether the program is meeting its goals and/or whether the goals need to be adjusted in the light of the program's accomplishments. On the basis of the findings, recommendations for altering or changing programs or policies may be made. While this type of evaluation is most useful to policymakers, it is also the most difficult to undertake. The information needs are immense and the level of sophistication required to carry out the process is higher than is generally available in government.

Efficiency evaluation attempts to assess the costs of a program and judge if the same amount and quality of outputs could be achieved more efficiently, that is, at a lower cost. Input and output evaluations are the building blocks of this form of evaluation, which is of great significance in climates of budgetary restraint. The difficulties involved in the more comprehensive effectiveness evaluations mean that policy-makers must often content themselves with efficiency evaluations as a 'second-best' alternative.

Finally, *process evaluations* examine the organizational methods, including rules and operating procedures, used to deliver programs. The objective is usually to see if a process can be streamlined and made more efficient. Towards this objective, implementation of a policy is usually broken down into discrete tasks, such as strategic planning, financial management, and client relations, and then one or more of these tasks are evaluated for efficiency, effectiveness, and/or accountability.

These different types of administrative evaluation of public policy have generated a variety of formal evaluative systems or techniques (Nachmias, 1979; Suchman, 1967, 1979). In the 1970s and 1980s these included such systems as the Program Planning and Budgeting System (PPBS) first developed at the Ford Motor Company and then adopted by the US Department of Defense and ultimately the entire US federal government; Zero-Based Budgeting (ZBB), a variant of PPBS developed at the Xerox Corporation and adopted by the Carter administration in the US and, later, in many other countries; and Management by Objectives (MBO), a self-reporting managerial performance system implemented in the US (Reid, 1979; Rogers, 1978; Wildavsky, 1969).

These techniques have been employed to varying degrees by different governments around the world. In addition, different countries and governments developed their own evaluative systems. Thus in Canada, for example, in the 1980s a new Policy and Expenditure Management System (PEMS) was established at the federal level, along with a new Office of the Controller General (OCG) mandated specifically to carry out evaluation research, while the federal Treasury Board tried to introduce a new government-wide Operational Performance Measurement System (OPMS) (Canada, Treasury Board, 1976, 1981; Rogers et al., 1981). More recently, such techniques include efforts to establish performance indicators or benchmarks that can allow public-sector efforts and outcomes to be compared across agencies or with private-sector counterparts (Swiss, 1991; Kernaghan et al., 2000). Such efforts have been popularized in North America in the efforts to 'reinvent' government, and have become a predominant tool of the so-called 'New Public Management', which has affected administrative reform in Europe, Australasia, and Latin America as well as North America.[2]

While much effort has been put into developing these techniques of policy evaluation, they have largely failed to overcome the limitations innate to rationalist policy analysis (Dobell and Zussman, 1981; Jordan and Sutherland, 1979): the prerequisites for their success are too steep to be met in the rough-and-tumble world of public policy-making. Any emphasis on examining the extent to which policy objectives are accomplished by a program must contend with the reality that policies often do not state their objectives precisely enough to permit rigorous analysis of whether they are being achieved. Moreover, the same policy may be directed at achieving a variety of objectives, without indicating their relative priority, thus making it difficult to find out if a particular objective is being achieved (Cahill and Overman, 1990; Formaini, 1990; McLaughlin, 1985; Palumbo, 1987; Weiss, 1977a). Social and economic problems tend to be tightly interrelated, for example, and it is virtually impossible to isolate and evaluate the effects of policies directed at either of them. In addition, each policy has effects on problems other than those intended, which a comprehensive evaluation must consider but which may make the task of evaluation unmanageable. The difficulties involved in gathering reliable and usable information further aggravate these problems.

The limitations faced by administrative evaluation—and we have noted only a few—increase with the level of sophistication and comprehensiveness expected of them. Thus, effectiveness evaluations, which would clearly be of most use to policy-makers, are the most difficult to undertake. Considering the difficulties, the enthusiasm for rational administrative evaluation has been on the wane in many industrialized countries since the early 1980s. Frustration with the difficulties involved in administrative evaluation, for example, led the Auditor General of Canada to conclude in his 1983 Annual Report that 'a significant proportion of evaluation assessments did not form an adequate basis for sound advice.' Ten years later, the Auditor General's review of program evaluation in the Canadian federal government found numerous changes in form but little in substance. According to the Report, evaluations were still:

> less likely to be an important source of information in support of program and policy decisions addressing questions of continued relevance and cost-effectiveness. Evaluations are more likely to provide information for accountability purposes but are often partial. The most complete information available is related to operational effectiveness, the way a program is working. (Canada, Auditor General, 1993)

To broaden administrative evaluation and attempt, somehow, to assess the question of program effectiveness, many governments have experimented with promoting public participation in the evaluation process. The intention is both to evaluate policies and to head off challenges to these policies on the grounds of a 'lack of consultation' with interested or affected members of the public. But the usefulness and legitimacy of these kinds of public forums have been challenged on many grounds.

There are concerns with the extent to which participants are actually representative of a range of views and ideas and with the effects of issues such as funding on the quality and quantity of representation (see Pateman, 1970; Wagle, 2000; Englehart and Trebilcock, 1981; Mitchell et al., 1997).

Judicial Evaluation—Judicial Review and Administrative Discretion

A second major type of policy evaluation is not concerned with budgets, priorities, efficiencies, and expenditures, but with the legal issues relating to the manner in which government programs are implemented. Such evaluations are carried out by the judiciary and are concerned with possible conflicts between government actions and constitutional provisions or established standards of administrative conduct and individual rights (Jacobson et al., 2001).

The judiciary is entitled to review government actions either on its own initiative or when asked to do so by an individual or organization filing a case against a government agency in a court of law. The grounds for review differ considerably across countries but usually extend to the examination of the constitutionality of the policy being implemented, or whether its implementation or development violated principles of natural rights and/or justice in democratic societies. That is, the judges assess such factors as whether the policy was developed and implemented in a non-capricious and non-arbitrary fashion according to principles of due process and accepted administrative law (Jaffe, 1965).

In countries governed through parliamentary systems, such as Australia, New Zealand, and Britain, judicial courts concentrate on whether or not an inferior court, tribunal, or government agency has acted within its powers or jurisdiction. If it has, and if it has also abided with principles of natural justice and has not acted in a capricious or arbitrary fashion, then its decision will stand, subject to any existing statutory appeal provisions. Stated simply, judicial reviews in these countries focus on issues or errors in law (Jaffe, 1969; Wade, 1965, 1966). That is, courts in these systems do not review the facts specific to the case, but tend to restrict their evaluation to procedural issues. Thus, as long as administrative agencies operate within their jurisdiction and according to principles of fundamental justice and due process, their decisions are unlikely to be overturned. Courts in republican systems, on the other hand, have a very different constitutional role, providing them with more authority and the legitimacy required to question legislative and executive actions. As a result, they are much more active and willing to consider errors of fact as well as errors of law in their evaluations of administrative behaviour (Jaffe, 1965).

Political Evaluation: Elections, Think-Tanks,
Inquiries, and Legislative Oversight

Political evaluation of government policy is undertaken by just about everyone with any interest in political life. Unlike administrative and judicial evaluations, political evaluations are usually neither systematic nor necessarily technically sophisticated. Indeed, many are inherently partisan, one-sided, and biased. Partisan political evaluations often simply attempt to label a policy a success or failure, followed by demands for continuation or change. The same is true of the work of many think-tanks, which, like political parties, bring a specific ideological or other more or less fixed perspective or 'frame' to the evaluation process (see Bovens and t'Hart, 1995; Abelson, 1996; Lindquist, 1998; Ricci, 1993; Weaver, 1989). This does not undermine their significance, however, because their initial objective in undertaking an evaluation is rarely to improve a government's policy, but rather to support or challenge it. Praise or criticism at this stage can lead to new iterations of the cycle as governments attempt to respond to criticisms or carry over lessons from past experiences into new or reformed policies, just as occurs with much of the more reasoned, technical evaluations.

While political evaluation is ongoing, it enters the policy process only on specialized occasions. One of the most important occasions in democracies is at election time, when citizens get their opportunity to render judgement on the government's performance. Votes at elections or in referendums express the voters' informal evaluations of the efficiency and effectiveness of governments and their programs and policies. However, in most democratic countries, referendums or plebiscites on particular policies are relatively rare. As was discussed in Chapter 3, while elections are held regularly, by their very nature they usually involve a range of issues, which makes it inappropriate to draw conclusions about the voters' opinion of individual policies. When citizens express their preferences and sentiments at election time, the evaluation is usually made as an aggregate judgement on a government's overall record of activities in office rather than about the effectiveness or usefulness of specific policies. Nevertheless, public perceptions of the ineffectiveness or harmful effects of specific high-profile government activities can and do affect voting behaviour, a reality governments ignore at their electoral peril (King, 1981).

A more common type of political policy evaluation involves consultation with members of relevant policy subsystems. There are many mechanisms for such consultations, which involve the use of some of the procedural policy instruments discussed in Chapters 4 and 8. These include setting up administrative forums for public hearings and establishing special consultative committees, task forces, and inquiries for evaluative purposes (see Cairns, 1990a; Bulmer, 1993; Clokie and

Robinson, 1969), and can range from small meetings of less than a dozen participants lasting several minutes to multi-million dollar inquiries that hear thousands of individual briefs and can take years to complete (Doern, 1967; Salter, 1981; Wilson, 1971). In many polities, political evaluation of government action is built into the system, in the form, for example, of congressional or parliamentary oversight committees (see McCubbins and McCubbins, 1994; McCubbins and Schwartz, 1984). While in some countries like the US these tend to meet on a regular basis, in others such as Canada the process may be less routine, as political reviews are undertaken on a more ad hoc basis (see de la Mothe, 1996; Banting, 1995).

These political mechanisms for policy evaluation are usually capable of ascertaining the views of many members of the policy subsystem and affected public on specific policy issues. However, it is not certain that simply because these views have been made known they will be reflected in any revision of government policy, or even if any such revisions will necessarily result from a review. Effectiveness often depends on whether the views heard are congruent with those of the current government (Dye, 1972: 353–75), which in turn depends on the criteria government members and political officials use to assess success or failure of particular policies or programs.

THE OUTCOMES OF POLICY EVALUATION: POLICY FEEDBACK AND POLICY TERMINATION

The potential outcomes from the policy evaluation stage of the policy cycle are threefold. First, a policy can be judged successful and continued in its present form. Second, and much more typically, a policy can be judged wanting in some respect and efforts are then made, or suggested, for its reform (see Patton and Sawicki, 1993). Finally, a policy can be judged a complete failure (or success), and it can be terminated (see DeLeon, 1978; Geva-May, 2001; Bovens and t'Hart, 1996; Bovens et al., 2001). In the first two outcomes, the policy evaluation stage serves to feed the policy back to some other stage of the policy process. While it is not clear to which stage the process will proceed, in many cases it returns to the agenda-setting stage, hence providing the policy cycle with its cyclical, iterative shape (see Pierson, 1993; Anglund, 1999; Coleman et al., 1997; Billings and Hermann, 1998).

Policy Feedback and Path Dependency

As E.E. Schattschneider (1935: 38) noted, 'new policies create new politics'. That is, the events and occurrences in a policy-making process tend to 'feed back' into the policy-making environment, thus altering important aspects of that environment, including institutional rules and operations, the distribution of wealth and power in society, and the nature of the ideas and interests relevant to policies and programs. This feedback process can easily affect the identification and interpretation of policy problems, assessments of the feasibility of potential solutions, and judgement of the nature of, and responses from, target groups, thereby altering the conditions under which policies are developed and implemented. Policies can create new 'spoils' for policy actors to argue over, or can result in the mobilization or 'countermobilization' of actors who feel they have not benefited from an existing policy or program (Pierson, 1993). Hence it is not unusual at all, in fact it is very typical, for policy-making to reiterate the policy process based on the outcomes of the evaluation stage—as captured in the description of policy cycles.

It is important to note, however, that the form subsequent iterations of the cycle take is a distinctive one. As incrementalists such as Charles Lindblom and others suggested in their own analysis of policy-making dynamics, subsequent rounds of policy-making build on the basis of earlier rounds and, as a result, tend to incorporate many aspects of earlier policies. Although dramatic shifts can occur, a more typical pattern is for only fairly minor aspects of earlier policies to be altered, since in many cases the general overall configuration of major elements of the policy processes—like subsystem membership and state capacities—will not have been altered dramatically between rounds. Typical feedback processes emerging from the policy evaluation stage of the cycle then, as Paul Pierson has noted, underscore and explain the 'path-dependent' nature of policy-making in modern states (ibid.).

'Path dependency' is a general term used by economists, sociologists, and others studying social and other kinds of systems to capture the manner in which previous states of a system affect future states (see Mahoney, 2000; Pierson, 2000; Haydu, 1998). It describes the situation whereby, once a system's trajectory is in place, it tends to perpetuate itself by limiting the range of choices or the ability of forces both outside ('exogenous') and inside ('endogenous') the system to alter that trajectory. That is, once a trajectory is in place it tends to 'lock in' the previous state of the system and the direction of its dynamics (Arthur, 1989).[3] In the policy literature, this is sometimes referred to as the influence of 'policy legacies', which limit the nature and extent of choice policy-makers have in making subsequent decisions (see Weir, 1992; Rose, 1990). Examples of this phenomenon range from how decisions on the initial location of hospitals and schools affect their operation to that of decisions to ban nuclear power, which are much harder and more expensive to take once plants have been built than if they had never been constructed in the first place (Wilsford, 1994; Pollock et al., 1989; Rona-Tas, 1998).

Exactly where or to which stage a policy process may go following the evaluation stage depends on the nature of the critique provided and the types of actors involved. Formal evaluations by governmental actors, for example, tend to result in limited critiques that typically might involve alterations to the policy implementation process, such as the creation of new agencies or regulations to deal with an issue raised in the evaluative process. However, these and other types of evaluations can also result in new ways of thinking about a problem or new options for dealing with a program, feeding back into 'earlier' stages such as agenda-setting and policy formulation.

Policy Termination

New iterations of the policy cycle are a typical output of evaluation processes and often involve larger or smaller reforms of existing policies and processes. While many permutations of this feedback process exist, one large alternative option for policy reform is, of course, simply to terminate or end a policy or program. Like more limited proposals for reform, this option involves feeding the results of an evaluative process back into the policy process, usually directly to the decision-making stage. Unlike proposals for more limited reform or simply accepting the status quo, the option of *policy termination* envisions a complete cessation of the policy cycle at a very near point in the future (DeLeon, 1978, 1983).

Although it is fairly common for evaluations, especially political ones, to suggest the adoption of the termination option, most observers have noted the reluctance of decision-makers to adopt this course of action and the general phenomenon of the persistence of policies and programs once put into place (Weaver, 1988). This is partially due to the inherent difficulties, mentioned above, of arriving at agreement on policy success or failure. Although, occasionally, a problem may be seen as so pernicious that no possible option can reasonably be expected to resolve it—in other words, that all options will fail—or as having been so successful that government action is no longer required, all observers note that the attainment of unified opinion on these matters among relevant policy actors is an exceedingly rare circumstance (see Daniels, 1997; Kaufman, 1976; Lewis, 2002).

Much more typical, students of policy termination note, is for existing programs and policies to have established beneficiaries and, often, to have become institutionalized to such an extent that their cessation is a costly process involving considerable legal, bureaucratic, and political expense (Weaver 1988; Bardach, 1976; Geva-May, 2001). Handbooks and guidelines for would-be terminators all stress the need to develop political coalitions and circumstances allowing these costs to be overcome (see Behn, 1977; Geva-May and Wildavsky, 1997: ch. 5). These all underscore the extent to which termination represents, in effect, an effort to overcome path dependencies and policy legacies in the policy process, making its achievement very difficult, often requiring an ideological shift in government and society to allow uniform judgements of success or failure required for uncontested terminations to be made (Kirkpatrick et al., 1999; DeLeon, 1997). It also bears mentioning, of course, that a successful termination in the short term does not guarantee a similar long-term result. Thus, if the perception of a problem persists, a termination will feed back into a reconceptualization of problems and policy alternatives. If no other suitable alternative emerges in this deliberation, this can result in the reversal of a termination and the reinstatement of a terminated program or policy.

MODELS OF POLICY EVALUATION

Early Models: Technical or Scientific Evaluation

The study of policy evaluation has been dominated by those who have attempted to view it as a neutral, technical exercise. For them, policy evaluation consists of assessing whether a public policy is achieving its stated objective and, if not, what could be done to eliminate the hurdle in the way. David Nachmias (1979: 4), an influential figure in the field, defined policy evaluation as 'the objective systematic, empirical examination of the effects ongoing policies and public programs have on their targets in terms of the goals they are meant to achieve'. Discerning readers will have no difficulty detecting the rationalist orientation of this definition. It specifies explicitly that the examination of a policy's effects on the achievement of its goals should be objective, systematic, and empirical. However, as we have mentioned before, goals in public policy are often not stated clearly enough to find out if and to what extent they are achieved. The possibilities for objective analysis are also limited because of insurmountable difficulties in developing objective standards by which to evaluate government success in dealing with subjective claims and socially constructed problems.

After much work in the 1960s and 1970s sought to develop quantitative systems of policy evaluation, it became clear to many researchers (Anderson, 1979a; Kerr, 1976; Manzer, 1984) that developing adequate and acceptable measures for evaluating policy is a difficult and contentious task. As a result, more recent thinking tends to view policy evaluation, like other stages of the policy process, as an inherently political activity. Since the same condition can be interpreted quite differently by different evaluators, there is no definitive way of determining who is right. Which interpretation prevails is ultimately determined by political conflicts and compromises among the various actors (Ingram and Mann, 1980b: 852).

Acute observers also noted that it is naive to believe that policy evaluation is always designed to reveal the effects of a policy. In fact, it is at times employed to disguise or conceal certain facts that the government fears will show it in a poor light. It is also possible for governments to design the terms of evaluation in such a way as to lead to conclusions that would show it in a better light. Or, if it wants to change or scrap a policy, it can adjust the terms of the evaluation accordingly. Similarly, evaluations by those outside the government are not always designed to improve a policy, but often to criticize it to gain partisan political advantage or to reinforce ideological postulates (Chelimsky, 1995; Bovens and t'Hart, 1995).

This is not to suggest that policy evaluation is an irrational or a completely political process, devoid of genuine intentions to find out about the functioning of a policy and its effects. Rather, one must not rely unduly on formal evaluation for drawing conclusions about a policy. To get the most out of policy evaluation, the limits of rationality and the political forces that shape it must clearly be recognized.

More Recent Models: Policy Evaluation as Policy Learning

Perhaps the greatest benefit of policy evaluation is not the direct results it generates but the educational process it can engender (Pressman and Wildavsky, 1984). Whether they realize it or not, actors engaged in policy evaluation are often participating in a larger process of *policy learning*, which is brought about by the attempt to improve or enhance policy-making based on the assessment of past experiences (see Etheredge and Short, 1983; Sabatier, 1988).

Several types of learning (Bennett and Howlett, 1991; May, 1992) can result from different kinds of evaluations. Some lessons are likely to concern practical suggestions about different aspects of the policy cycle as it has operated in the past. These include, for example, lessons about which policy instruments have 'succeeded' in which circumstances and which have 'failed', or which issues have enjoyed public support in the agenda-setting process and which have not. Other lessons are more about policy goals than means. This is a more fundamental type of learning, which is accompanied by changes in the thinking underlying a policy.

The concept of 'learning' is generally associated with intentional, progressive, cognitive consequences of the education that results from policy evaluation. However, policy learning also has a broader meaning that includes both the intended and unintended (see Merton, 1936) consequences of policy-making activities as well as both the 'positive' and 'negative' implications of existing policies and their alternatives.

Fundamental to policy evaluation is its impact on effecting changes to policy. After all, the implicit purpose of policy evaluation is to change a policy if it is deemed necessary as a result of undertaking a review (Feick, 1992). From a learning perspective, public policy evaluation is conceived as an iterative process of active learning on the part of policy actors about the nature of policy problems and the solutions to them (Rist, 1994; Levitt and March, 1988).

Like other concepts in policy science, there are different interpretations of what is meant by 'policy learning' and whether its source and motivation are within or outside existing policy processes.[4] Peter Hall makes the case for 'endogenous' learning, defining the activity as a 'deliberate attempt to adjust the goals or techniques of policy in the light of the consequences of past policy and new information so as to better attain the ultimate objects of governance' (Hall, 1993: 278). Hugh Heclo, on the other hand, suggests that learning is a less conscious activity, often occurring as a government's response to some kind of external or exogenous change in a policy environment. According to him, 'learning can be taken to mean a relatively enduring alteration in behaviour that results from experience; usually this alteration is conceptualized as a change in response made in reaction to some perceived stimulus' (Heclo, 1974: 306). Hence, unlike Hall, in Heclo's view learning is what governments do in response to a new situation on the basis of their past experience.

The two definitions describe the nature of the relationship between policy learning and policy change, but differ substantially in their approach to the issue. For Hall, learning is a part of the normal public policy process in which decision-makers attempt to understand why certain initiatives may have succeeded while others failed. If policies change as a result of learning, the impetus for change originates within the formal policy process of the government. For Heclo, on the other hand, policy learning is seen as an activity undertaken by policy-makers largely in reaction to changes in external policy 'environments'. As the environment changes, policy-makers must adapt if their policies are to succeed.

These two separate aspects of policy learning should be clearly distinguished in thinking about policy evaluation as policy learning. That is, from a learning perspective, evaluation involves processes imposed on policy-makers both from outside the policy process and from within the process as policy-makers attempt to refine and adapt their policies in the light of their past actions. The characteristics of these two different types of learning are set out in Figure 9.1.

Figure 9.1 Exogenous and Endogenous Concepts of Policy Learning and Policy Evaluation

	Endogenous Learning	*Exogenous Learning*
Subject of Learning (Who Learns)	Policy Subsystems	Policy Universe
Object of Learning (What is Learned)	Policy Specifications, or Policy Instruments	Perception of Problem, or Policy Goals

Source: Adapted from Colin J. Bennett and Michael Howlett, 'The Lessons of Learning: Reconciling Theories of Policy Learning and Policy Change', *Policy Sciences* 25, 3 (1991): 275–94.

Endogenous learning takes place among policy subsystems; its objective is to learn about policy settings or policy instruments. In contrast, exogenous learning occurs in the broad policy universe and may involve questioning the interpretation of a problem or the goal of the policy designed to address it. One type of endogenous evaluation, following Richard Rose (1988, 1991), can be referred to as *lesson-drawing*. This type of learning originates within the formal policy process and is aimed primarily at the choice of means or techniques employed by policy-makers in their efforts to achieve their goals.[5] These lessons are likely to concern practical suggestions about different aspects of the policy cycle as it has operated in the past—for example, which policy instruments have 'succeeded' in which circumstances and which have 'failed', or which issues have enjoyed public support in the agenda-setting process and which have not.

Following Hall, one type of exogenous learning is *social learning*. It originates outside the policy process and affects the constraints or capacities of policy-makers to alter or change society. This form of learning is usually about policy goals themselves. It is the most fundamental type of learning, which is accompanied by changes in the thinking underlying a policy. Examples of social learning can be seen in the move towards privatization and the accepted belief that inflation was a more serious problem than unemployment, both of which occurred in many countries during the 1980s and 1990s (Hall, 1993; Howlett and Ramesh, 1993).

Policy evaluations can involve either type of endogenous or exogenous learning. Administrative evaluations, virtually by definition, occur within the established administrative institutions of government and tend to take the form of lesson-drawing—both in the negative and positive senses of the term. Both judicial and political evaluations are much more susceptible to changes in social values and mores and thus are one means by which social learning can affect the evaluative process (see Busenberg, 2001).

POLICY EVALUATION STYLES

Understanding the links between evaluation types and outcomes requires a better understanding of the reasons why learning and 'non-learning' occur in complex organizations. Non-learning involves both failing to undertake any evaluations at all and 'limited learning' in which lessons of only a very restricted scope are drawn from the evaluation process (Abrahamson and Fairchild, 1999; Tamuz, 2001; May, 1999; Simon, 1991; March and Olsen, 1975).

Research in the administrative and organizational sciences has suggested that whether or not any lessons from evaluations will be learned by policy-makers depends on their capacity and willingness to absorb new information (see Huber, 1991; Peters, 1998). As Cohen and Levinthal have observed with reference to private firms:

> the ability to evaluate and utilize outside knowledge is largely a function of the level of prior related knowledge. At the most elemental level, this prior knowledge includes basic skills or even a shared language but may also include knowledge of the most recent scientific or technological developments in a given field. Thus, prior related knowledge confers an ability to recognize the value of new information, assimilate it, and apply it to commercial ends. These abilities collectively constitute what we call a firm's 'absorptive capacity'. (Cohen and Levinthal, 1990: 132; also see Lane and Lubatkin, 1998)

In a complex organization such as a large firm or government, this implies that learning is a cumulative process and that the existing store of knowledge largely determines what will be done with any new information that flows into the organization. Also critical in this regard, as Aldrich and Herker (1977) noted, are 'boundary-spanning' links between the organization and its environment, links receptive to new information and capable of disseminating it within the organization.

In the case of policy evaluation, this implies that, as we have seen at the other stages of the policy cycle as well, two relevant variables affecting the potential for evaluations to lead to learning are (1) the organizational capacity of the state, including especially its expertise in the subject area involved, and (2) the nature of the policy subsystem and especially the relationship between its state and societal members. These factors determine, for example, the ability of evaluators to 'systematically pinch ideas' from other jurisdictions about appropriate policy designs (Schneider and Ingram, 1988) and the extent to which they can create the kinds of advisory councils and citizen participation and polling mechanisms required for 'social learning' to penetrate into governmental deliberations (May, 1999: 27; Rothmayr and Hardmeier, 2002). Taken together, the two variables allow us to discern the existence of four basic evaluative styles (see Figure 9.2).

In this model, a state must have a high administrative capacity for any true learning to take place. If the state is the dominant actor with weak links to society, then a form of endogenous lesson-drawing can be expected to occur. If, on the other hand, state administrative capacity is low, then one would expect simpler forms of formal evaluations and poor learning to predominate. If societal actors dominate the policy subsystem, and boundary-spanning links exist with the government, then the conditions for social learning may be present. Without such links, however, there is less likelihood that any learning will actually occur within the state itself.

Figure 9.2 **Basic Policy Evaluation Styles**

		Dominant Actor in Policy Subsystem	
		Societal Actors	*State Actors*
State Administrative Capacity	*High*	Social Learning	Instrumental Learning (Lesson-Drawing)
	Low	Non-Learning (Political Evaluations)	Limited Learning (Technical Evaluations)

SOURCE: Adapted from Wesley M. Cohen and Daniel A. Levinthal, 'Absorptive Capacity: A New Perspective on Learning and Innovation', *Administrative Science Quarterly* 35 (1990): 128–52.

CONCLUSION

This chapter has set out the different forms of evaluation—administrative, judicial, and political—that take place in the public policy process and the different possible outcomes that can emerge and feed back into the policy cycle as a result of the evaluative process. Despite inherent difficulties with assessing the success or failure of policy efforts, past writings on the subject of policy evaluation have tended overwhelmingly to concentrate on developing, criticizing, and refining the techniques of formal administrative evaluations. In the process, the limits of rationality in the policy process were often forgotten. Policy evaluation, however, like other stages of the policy cycle, is an inherently political exercise and must be recognized explicitly as such (Hellstern, 1986; Chelimsky, 1995).

Analysts who do take the politics underlying policy evaluation into account see policy evaluation both as a continuation of the struggle over scarce resources or ideologies and as part of a process of learning in which policies develop and change on the basis of assessments of past successes and failures and conscious efforts to emulate successes and avoid failures (see Sanderson, 2002). This conception not only helps to make sense of policy evaluation and removes it from the narrow technocratic concerns characteristic of administrative evaluation, but also helps to identify the different learning styles that can emerge in the evaluative process and highlights the significant role played by all forms of evaluation in the operation of the ongoing policy cycle.

FURTHER READINGS

Aldrich, Howard, and Diane Herker. 1977. 'Boundary Spanning Roles and Organizational Structure', *Academy of Management Review* 2 (Apr.): 217–30.

Bennett, Colin, and Michael Howlett. 1991. 'The Lessons of Learning: Reconciling Theories of Policy Learning and Policy Change', *Policy Sciences* 25, 3: 275–94.

Bovens, Mark, Paul t'Hart, and B. Guy Peters. 2001. 'Analysing Governance Success and Failure in Six European States', in Bovens, t'Hart, and Peters, eds, *Success and Failure in Public Governance: A Comparative Analysis*. Cheltenham: Edward Elgar, 12–32.

Cohen, Wesley M., and Daniel A. Levinthal. 1990. 'Absorptive Capacity: A New Perspective on Learning and Innovation', *Administrative Science Quarterly* 35: 128–52.

Davies, I. 1999. 'Evaluation and Performance Management in Government', *Evaluation* 8, 2: 150–9.

DeLeon, Peter. 1983. 'Policy Evaluation and Program Termination', *Policy Studies Review* 2, 4: 631–47.

Geva-May, Iris. 2001. 'When the Motto is "Till Death Do Us Part": The Conceptualization and the Craft of Termination in the Public Policy Cycle', *International Journal of Public Administration* 24, 3: 263–88.

Hall, Peter A. 1993. 'Policy Paradigms, Social Learning and the State: The Case of Economic Policy-making in Britain', *Comparative Politics* 25, 3: 275–96.

Huber, George P. 1991. 'Organization Learning: The Contributing Processes and the Literatures', *Organization Science* 2, 1: 88–115.

Ingram, Helen M., and Dean E. Mann. 1980. *Why Policies Succeed or Fail*. Beverly Hills, Calif.: Sage.

Jaffe, Louis L. 1965. *Judicial Control of Administrative Action*. Boston: Little, Brown.

May, Peter J. 1999. 'Fostering Policy Learning: A Challenge for Public Administration', *International Review of Public Administration* 4, 1: 21–31.

Nachmias, David. 1979. *Public Policy Evaluation: Approaches and Methods*. New York: St Martin's Press.

Palumbo, Dennis J. 1987. *The Politics of Program Evaluation*. Beverly Hills, Calif.: Sage.

Pierson, Paul. 1993. 'When Effect Becomes Cause: Policy Feedback and Political Change', *World Politics* 45: 595–628.

Rose, Richard. 1993. *Lesson-Drawing in Public Policy: A Guide to Learning Across Time and Space*. Chatham, NJ: Chatham House.

NOTES

1. On this latter tendency for organizations to depart over time from established measures, see Snook (2000) and Vaughan (1996).
2. On the 'reinventing government' movement in the US, see Osborne and Gaebler (1992). On the spread of NPM throughout the world, see Christensen and Laegreid (2001). For a somewhat skeptical view of the coherency of this movement, see Hood (1991, 1995) and Dunleavy and Hood (1994).
3. On the application of this concept to the social sciences, see Abbott (1990). For a skeptical view of the significance of this phenomenon, see Liebowitz and Margolis (1995).

4. A variety of terms are used to describe this phenomenon, including 'policy learning', 'social learning', and 'government learning'. A fourth term, 'organizational learning', exists in the somewhat tangential field of organizational behaviour. See Sabatier (1988); Hall (1993); Etheredge (1981). See also Argyris (1992) and Argyris and Schon (1978).

5. We tend to think of learning chiefly across time, within the confines of domestic historical actions; thus, 'learning from experience' implies 'learning from one's own experience'. This is the dominant, possibly exclusive, meaning in oft-cited studies by Heclo and Hall. A recognition that has taken somewhat longer to affect the research of policy analysts is that states may not only learn from their own experiences, but also from the actions of other states. Various concepts have been employed to depict how policy-makers from one country 'emulate', 'imitate', or 'draw lessons from' their counterparts abroad. As Rose (1991: 21) points out, in any effort to reduce dissatisfaction, 'policymakers have three alternatives: to turn to their national past; to speculate about the future; or to seek lessons from current experience in other places.' Learning in this sense can be both positive and negative. That is, learning is both about what to do and about what not to do, so the same program can act as a model or exemplar for one country and can serve as exactly the reverse for another (Bennett and Howlett, 1991). Drawing negative lessons is very different from 'non-learning'; the former denotes that policy-makers in one country examined the policy lessons of another and decided to avoid that program of action; the latter suggests that they never knew about it (Heclo, 1974).

Part IV

Understanding Policy Change

Chapter 10

Policy Regimes and Policy Dynamics

Studying a disaggregated and sequential model of the public policy process—the policy cycle—helps to underline the dynamic nature of public policy-making and to organize the otherwise difficult-to-grasp relations binding actors, ideas, institutions, and instruments together. However, while disaggregation permits the detailed examination of each stage of the policy process, it begs the question of what that process looks like when all its constitutive pieces are reassembled. Are there typical or normal overall patterns of policy development and change? And, if so, how do these patterns arise and affect different levels of policy-making? These are the issues we will examine in this chapter.

LONG-TERM PATTERNS OF POLICY-MAKING

Policy Styles: Patterns of Policy Development

By the mid-1970s it was apparent to many observers that actors in the policy processes, as Simmons, Davis, Chapman, and Sager (1974: 461) put it, tended to 'take on, over a period of time, a distinctive style which affects . . . policy decisions, i.e. they develop tradition and history which constrains and refines their actions and concerns.'

The first such studies argued that public policy outcomes varied according to the nature of the political system found in each country (Peters et al., 1978). Although some empirical evidence of substantial differences in patterns of *outcomes* was uncovered in empirical tests of this hypothesis (see Castles, 1998; Obinger and Wagschal, 2001), it was soon suggested that the concept could be more fruitfully applied not to outcomes but to the policy *process* that obtained in a particular country. Each country or jurisdiction was said to have its own pattern of policy-making that characterized its policy processes and affected the policies resulting from it. Several studies developed the concept of a national *policy style* and applied it to policy-making in various nations (see Tuohy,

1992; Vogel, 1986; Knoepfel et al., 1987). However, it was soon found that national generalizations were difficult to make and that the concept more accurately described the realities of meso- or sectoral-level policy-making (Freeman, 1985; Coleman, 1994).

The most prominent studies of policy styles to date have classified styles in terms of the twin dimensions of a government's typical problem-solving methodology and the pattern of its relationship with societal groups. Richardson, Gustafsson, and Jordan (1982: 13) —who together did the most to develop the concept—defined a policy style as 'the interaction between (a) the government's approach to problem solving and (b) the relationship between government and other actors in the policy process'. They mentioned 'anticipatory/active' and 'reactive' as the two general approaches to problem-solving, while the relationships between governmental and non-governmental actors were similarly divided into two categories: 'consensus' and 'imposition' (see Figure 10.1). According to this model, for example, the German policy style was anticipatory and based on consensus, whereas the British style was reactive, though also based on consensus. The French policy style, on the other hand, was anticipatory, but effected through imposition rather than consensus. In contrast, the Dutch policy style was said to be both reactive and impositional.

Figure 10.1 An Early Model of National Policy Styles

Dominant Approach to Problem-Solving

		Anticipatory	*Reactive*
Relationship between Government	*Consensus*	German 'Rationalist Consensus' Style	British 'Negotiation' Style
and Society	*Imposition*	French 'Concertation' Style	Dutch 'Negotiation and Conflict' Style

SOURCE: Adapted from Jeremy Richardson, Gunnel Gustafsson, and Grant Jordan, 'The Concept of Policy Style', in Richardson, ed., *Policy Styles in Western Europe* (London: George Allen and Unwin, 1982).

Some work on policy styles continues to focus at the national level. Recent work by Christoph Knill (1998, 1999), for example, considers the existence of 'national administrative styles' and suggests these are of critical importance in understanding the development and reform of systems of public administration and the role these systems play in the public policy process (see also Zysman, 1994). While useful, however, other researchers found that few governments were consistently active or reactive; nor did any government always work through either consensus or imposition. Rather than think of policy styles as existing at the national level, they argued that a focus on the sectoral level would be more accurate and more productive (Griggs, 1999; Freeman, 1985; Gustafsson and Richardson, 1979). Describing these styles is, of course, more difficult than would be the case at the national level since policy sectors are far more numerous.

One way to conceptualize such sectoral styles is to draw on the insights into the workings of each stage of the policy cycles provided in Chapters 5–9 above. Conceptualizing policy-making as a staged, sequential, and iterative process has the methodological advantage of reducing the complexity of the process into a small number of stages and sub-stages, thereby allowing the identification of a small number of variables responsible for typical processes found at each stage of the cycle. Combining the styles found at each stage thus generates a useful description of the overall policy style found in a sector.

At the agenda-setting stage, as we saw in Chapter 5, two critical factors are the level and extent of public participation in an issue area and the response or 'pre-response' of the state in directing, mediating, and accommodating this activity (see May, 1991; Majone, 1989). The resulting agenda-setting styles were *outside initiation, mobilization, inside initiation,* and *consolidation.*

In Chapter 6 we saw that policy formulation styles are also significantly affected by the kinds of actors interacting to develop and refine policy options for government. But unlike agenda-setting, where the public is often actively involved, in policy formulation the relevant policy actors are usually restricted to those who not only have an opinion on a subject, but also have some minimal level of expertise in it. In this view, the likely results of policy formulation are contingent on the nature and configuration of the interest networks and discourse coalitions that comprise a sectoral policy subsystem and affect its willingness and ability to propose and accommodate new policy ideas and actors (see Zahariadis and Allen, 1995; Bulkley, 2000; Howlett and Ramesh, 1998). The four policy formulation styles identified were: *policy tinkering*, in which closed subsystems would consider only options involving instrument components; *policy experimentation*, in which resistant subsystems would also consider changes in instrument types; *program reform*, in which contested subsystems would also review changes in program specifications; and *policy renewal*, in which open subsystems would also consider options involving changes in policy goals.

The decision-making stage, too, as we saw in Chapter 7, is characterized by four different styles reflecting the nature of the actors present at this stage of the cycle as well as the nature of the time, information, and resource constraints under which they operate. Depending on the complexity of the policy subsystem involved in and affected by the decision, and on the severity of the constraints under which decision-makers are operating (see Smith, 1994; Forester, 1984), the four decision-making styles identified were *incremental* and *optimizing adjustment*, and *satisfycing* and *rational searches*.

Chapter 8 evaluated policy implementation and the choices of procedural and substantive policy instruments used to implement public policies. It assessed the findings of researchers such as Kagan and Hawkins, who argued that many nations and sectors combined various kinds of instruments into more or less coherent implementation styles (Hawkins and Thomas, 1989a; Kagan and Axelrad, 1997). These and other studies emphasized the degree to which choices of both kinds of instruments were affected by the nature of policy targets and the resources that governments could devote to implementation. Four basic implementation styles were identified: *institutionalized voluntarism*, *representative legalism*, *directed subsidization*, and *public provision with oversight*.

Finally, discussion of policy evaluation in Chapter 9 suggested that what is significant at this stage of the policy process is not so much the ultimate success and failure of policy outcomes but rather whether or not policy actors and the organizations and institutions they represent can *learn* from the formal and informal evaluation of policies in which they are engaged (Lindblom, 1968). Significant variables affecting the propensity to learn were the *absorptive capacity* of government and the kind of *boundary-spanning* links that exist between governments and their publics (Cohen and Levinthal, 1990; Aldrich and Herker, 1977). These helped to determine the basic evaluation styles of *social learning, limited learning, poor learning*, and *non-learning*.

Building on the insights of Chapters 5–9, we can suggest that the basic components of an overall sectoral policy style will be found among the options set out in Figure 10.2.

To be sure, a large number of potential policy styles could result from the combination of the possible styles found at each stage. However, since the type of style that emerges is affected by key variables such as the nature of the policy subsystem and various aspects of the capacity of the administrative system involved, whatever style exists is likely to be relatively long-lasting (Cerny, 1996; Harrow, 2001). Hence the concept of a sectoral policy style is useful not only for helping to describe typical policy processes, but also for capturing an important aspect of policy dynamics, that is, the relatively enduring nature of these arrangements.

Policy Paradigms: Long-Term Patterns in Policy Content

The existence of durable patterns of policy *processes* begs the question of whether or not similar patterns also exist in the *substance* of policy. Cross-national and subnational comparisons of the substance of policy-making have indeed identified the persistence of policy contents over long periods of time (see Leman, 1977; Lowi, 1998; Gormley and Peters,

Figure 10.2 **Components of a Sectoral Policy Style**

Elements of a Sectoral Policy Style

Stage in the Policy Process	*Possible Styles Present at Each Stage of the Policy Cycle*			
Agenda-Setting	Outside Initiation	Inside Initiation	Consolidation	Mobilization
Policy Formulation	Policy Renewal	Program Reform	Policy Experimentation	Policy Tinkering
Decision-Making	Incremental Adjustment	Satisfycing Adjustment	Optimizing Search	Rational Search
Policy Implementation	Institution-alized Voluntarism	Directed Subsidization	Representative Legalism	Directed Provision
Policy Evaluation	Social Learning	Instrumental Learning	Limited Learning	Non-Learning

1992). The concept of a *policy paradigm*, discussed in Chapter 3, was developed to describe this phenomenon. In so doing, it extended the discussion of long-term patterns of policy-making to the question of policy contents.

Developed originally to describe long-term sets of ideas present in the 'hard' or natural sciences, the term 'paradigm' was later applied in the social sciences. The concept of policy paradigm is closely related to traditional philosophical notions of 'ideologies' or more recent sociological notions of 'discourses' or 'frames' (Goffman, 1974; Surel, 2000). It captures the idea that the established beliefs, values, and attitudes behind understandings of public problems and notions of the feasibility of the proposed solutions are significant determinants of policy content (Hall, 1990: 59; also Edelman, 1988; Hilgartner and Bosk, 1981; Schneider, 1985).

As John Campbell has noted, policy paradigms are only one of a number of distinct idea sets that go into public policy-making, along with program ideas, symbolic frames, and public sentiments (see Figure 10.3 below). However, unlike symbolic frames and public sentiments, which tend to affect perception of the legitimacy or 'correctness' of certain courses of action, a policy paradigm represents a 'set of cognitive background assumptions that constrain action by limiting the range of alternatives that policy-making elites are likely to perceive as useful and worth considering' (Campbell, 1998: 385; also Surel, 2000). 'Program ideas' largely represent the selection of specific solutions from among the set designated as acceptable by a paradigm.

Figure 10.3 **Ideational Components of Policy Contents**

Level of Policy Debate Affected

		Foreground	*Background*
Level of Ideas Affected	*Cognitive (Causal)*	Program Ideas	Policy Paradigms
	Normative (Value)	Symbolic Frames	Public Sentiments

SOURCE: Adapted from John L. Campbell, 'Institutional Analysis and the Role of Ideas in Political Economy', *Theory and Society* 27, 5 (1998): 385.

Paul Sabatier has argued that individuals in a policy subsystem hold a 'deep structure' of basic values and beliefs that inhibits anything but marginal changes to program ideas and policy contents. As Gersick (1991) has noted, this deep structure 'generates a strong inertia, first to prevent the system from generating alternatives outside its own boundaries, then to pull any deviations that do occur back into line. According to this logic, the deep structure must first be dismantled, leaving the system temporarily disorganized, in order for any fundamental change to be accomplished.'

A policy paradigm thus informs and holds in place a set of ideas held by relevant policy subsystem members—a doctrine or school of thought such as Keynesianism or monetarism, in the case of economic policy subsystems—that shapes the broad goals policy-makers pursue, the way they perceive public problems, and the kinds of solutions they consider for adoption. While a considerable amount of thinking usually goes into the construction of a paradigm, it is not always coherent, reflecting the limitations innate to the study of public problems and the complex compromises with which policy-makers must contend. Consistent or not, however, these relatively long-term sets of dominant ideas decisively shape the content of policy outputs and choices.

The Concept of a Policy Regime:
Combining Long-Term Patterns of Policy Processes and Contents

Recently, students of public policy-making have more and more come to suggest that long-term patterns of policy processes—or policy styles— and long-term patterns of policy content—or policy paradigms—can be combined into a single construct: the *policy regime*. Although the term is sometimes confused with similar concepts such as a 'political regime',[1] an 'international regime' (Preston and Windsor, 1992; Krasner, 1983; Young, 1980), an 'implementation regime' (Stoker, 1989), or a 'regime of accumulation' (Lipietz, 1982; Aglietta, 1979), the idea of a policy regime helps to capture the more or less permanent nature of both policy process and content at the sectoral level of policy-making (Doern, 1998; Doern et al., 1999). Drawn from the older notion of a 'regulatory regime' (Lowi, 1966, 1972; Kelman, 1981), the term 'policy regime' attempts to capture how policy institutions, actors, and ideas tend to congeal into relatively long-term, institutionalized patterns of policy interaction that combine to keep policy contents and processes more or less constant in each sector.

In his work on social policy, for example, Gosta Esping-Andersen found there to be 'specific institutional arrangements adopted by societies in the pursuit of work and welfare. A given organization of state-economy relations is associated with a particular social policy logic' (Rein et al., 1987). Initially, Esping-Andersen argued that such regimes were linked to larger national patterns of state-economic relations or the organization of state and market-based institutions. Similarly, in their work on US policy-making, Harris and Milkis (1989: 25) defined such regimes as a 'constellation' of (1) ideas justifying governmental activity, (2) institutions that structure policy-making, and (3) a set of policies. Eisner, similarly, defined a regime as a 'historically specific configuration of policies and institutions which establishes certain broad goals that transcend the problems' specific to particular sectors (Eisner, 1993: xv; see also Eisner, 1994a). However, in later works Esping-Andersen and others argued that different regimes could be found in different policy sectors, including labour-market, pension, distribution, and employment regimes (see Esping-Andersen, 1990; Kolberg and Esping-Andersen, 1992; Kasza, 2002).

A policy regime, hence, can be seen to combine several of the concepts discussed in earlier chapters. It can be thought of as combining a common set of policy ideas (a policy paradigm) and a common or typical policy process (a policy style).[2] As such, it is a useful term for describing long-term patterns found in both the substance and process of public policy-making in a particular sector. The general idea is that sectoral policy-making tends to develop in such a way that the same actors, institutions, instruments, and governing ideas tend to dominate sectoral policy-making for extended periods of time, infusing a policy sector with both a consistent content and a set of typical policy processes or procedures. Understanding how styles, paradigms, and regimes form, how they are maintained, and how they change, therefore, is an important aspect of the study of public policy.

POLICY DYNAMICS: POLICY STABILITY AND POLICY CHANGE

Normal and Atypical Policy Change

Most observers recognize that two common types or patterns of change are typical of public policy-making. In Chapter 9, for example, it was argued that there are two distinctive types of policy learning—the limited instrumental learning of 'lesson-drawing' and the more goal-oriented 'social learning'—that affect how governments, members of policy sub-systems, and the public evaluate and alter public policies. These two types of learning imply that at least two distinct patterns of policy change can be expected. Similarly, the discussion in Chapter 6 argued that a distinction could be made between policy options that proposed the alteration of the status quo and those that proposed more substantial change to policy goals.

These discussions suggest the existence of at least two basic processes of policy change. The more 'normal' pattern involves relatively minor tinkering with policies and programs already in place in existing policy regimes. Such changes are 'incremental' and do not affect the basic contours of existing policy styles or paradigms. The second, more substantial pattern fundamentally transforms policy-making and involves changes in basic sets of policy ideas, institutions, interests, and processes.

Normal Policy Change

There is a surprising degree of continuity in public policy. Many observers have remarked that most policies made by governments are, for the most part and most of the time, in some way a continuation of past policies and practices. Ample empirical evidence, from literally thousands of case studies of disparate policy sectors and issues in a multitude of countries, indicates that most policies made by governments are in some way a continuation of past policies and practices. Even what are often portrayed as 'new' policy initiatives are often simply variations on existing practices (Polsby, 1984; Lindblom, 1959; Hayes, 1992).

This 'normal' pattern of policy change involves tinkering or altering various aspects of existing policy styles and policy paradigms without actually altering the overall shape or configuration of a policy regime. Hence, the existence of greater time resources can allow a search process in the decision-making stage of a policy cycle without permanently altering the general proclivity for the decision-making in the sector to be categorized, for example, by satisficing adjustment. Just as no permanent change in a policy style would occur in this instance, so some experimentation with alternative means of program or service delivery would not imply a permanent change in a dominant policy paradigm. Within a policy regime, therefore, considerable fluctuations and marginal changes can occur without altering the overall nature of the long-term pattern of policy procedures or contents (Hayes, 2001).

This overall pattern of stability in long-term policy-making has long been a subject of investigation, and the results of numerous case studies built up over the last 30 years have highlighted the manner in which ideological and institutional factors insulate policy regimes from pressures for change. As the discussion in Chapters 5–9 has suggested, five aspects of typical policy processes inhibit change at various stages of the policy cycle and thus promote policy stability: agenda denial, closed networks, negative decisions, limited resources, and non-learning.[3]

These processes help to maintain stable policy 'frames', or relatively stable sets of overarching policy ideas, and filter out alternative visions of public policy that could inspire efforts towards more fundamental change (Schon and Rein, 1994). Bachrach and Baratz (1962) used the term 'non-decisions', discussed in Chapter 7, to describe situations in which policy debates remain mired in the status quo because alternatives are simply not considered or debated (see Yanow, 1992). Examples of such instances include the failure to deal with issues important to the urban poor and similar inaction on a wide range of women's issues.

Stability is also enhanced by the characteristics of some policy issues. Students of agenda-setting processes such as Cobb, Ross, and Ross and Downs, for example, noted the inability of certain issues to engender large-scale public mobilization, which results in maintaining the status quo (Cobb and Elder, 1972; Cobb et al., 1976; Downs, 1972; May, 1991; Pollock et al., 1989). 'Hard issues' is a term coined by Pollock, Lilie, and Vittes to describe the oft-noted facet of many policy processes in which the nature of a particular policy issue can insulate it from public debate. Issues like toxic regulation or utility rate-setting are 'hard' in that they are technical, legalistic, means-oriented, or simply unfamiliar to most members of the public. Such issues are more likely to involve smaller sets of specialized policy actors than issues such as traffic safety, crime, and health, which are more likely to generate public attention and discussion (Keller, 1999). Hard issues, therefore, are more likely to involve only a very limited number of specialized policy actors and serve as a barrier to entry of new actors into existing policy processes, contributing to policy stability,

Rhodes (1997a) and Schaap and van Twist (1997), as well as many others, have argued that policy stability is greatly enhanced by the fact that all subsystems tend to construct 'policy monopolies' in which the interpretation and general approach to a subject is more or less fixed (see Baumgartner and Jones, 1991, 1993). Only when a monopoly is broken by the emergence of new members would policy change be expected in any significant sense of the term (see Kubler, 2001; Dudley and Richardson, 1998). These 'closed networks' are a key source of policy stability, which is based simply on the ability of existing policy actors to prevent new members from entering into policy debates and discourses (see Daugbjerg, 1997; Hammond and Knott, 2000). This can occur, for example, when governments refuse to appoint prominent critics to advisory boards or regulatory tribunals, when funding is not provided for interveners at hearings, when the creation of such boards and procedures is resisted, or when the behaviour of interest groups in pursuing specialized issue niches eliminates competition in a policy network (Browne, 1990, 1991).

All of these policy legacies affect current policy-making by creating institutional routines and procedures that can force decision-making in particular directions—by either eliminating or distorting the range of options available to governments (see Wilsford, 1985, 1994; Pierson, 2000; Rona-Tas, 1998). Path dependence, discussed in Chapter 9, refers to the manner in which current policy decisions are influenced by the institutional and behavioural legacies of the past (Pierson, 2000; Weir, 1992; David, 1985; Rose, 1990). As Pierson, Weir, and March and Olsen (1989: 52), among others, have argued, stability is expected to occur when a policy solution or problem definition is routinized or institutionalized, increasing the constituency for its preservation and raising the costs and difficulty of its alteration or termination (see Haydu, 1998; Torfing, 2001).

Atypical Policy Change

These aspects of public policy processes promoting policy stability, described above, are powerful, and it should not be surprising that their operation results in the commonly observed pattern of persistence in policy styles, paradigms, and regimes. However, many observers have also noted the existence of a second type of policy change, which is much less frequent and involves a deep change in the normal substance and process of policy-making.[4] This type of atypical policy change involves substantial changes in policy paradigms and styles.

While policy styles will change primarily because of shifts in the nature of policy subsystem membership and state capacities (Jens, 1997), as discussed above, policy paradigms change largely due to the activities of subsystem members responding to mounting evidence of the inability of existing paradigms to deal effectively with policy problems. That is, a strong trend in the literature has been to discuss such changes occurring as a result of the activities of specialized policy actors reacting to discordances or 'anomalies': discrepancies between events on the ground and their theorization within the dominant paradigm.[5] As Sabatier, Kingdon, and others have argued, anomalous events and activities not expected or understandable in terms of prevalent discourses, or that upset calculations of actor self-interest, allow innovative actors, or 'policy entrepreneurs', to respond to changing circumstances and their own ambitions and introduce new ideas into the policy milieu.[6] These new actors are often seen as engaged in a struggle with established ones, who usually resist the introduction of new ideas and defend the status quo or, at least, attempt to limit changes to those compatible with existing arrangements (see Nunan, 1999; Howlett and Rayner, 1995; Jenkins-Smith et al., 1991).

Linking Normal and Atypical Policy Change: 'Punctuated Equilibrium' Policy Dynamics

Normal and atypical policy dynamics are linked together to form a particular overall pattern of policy change referred to in earlier chapters as a 'punctuated equilibrium' process. That is, change occurs as an irregular, stepped, function in which relatively long periods of policy stability are interspersed with infrequent periods of substantial change (see Eldredge and Gould, 1972; Gould and Eldredge, 1977; Gersick, 1991). In the policy realm this refers to the situation whereby normal policy-making involves fairly common, routine, non-innovative changes at the margin of existing policies that follow existing policy processes and ideas. Atypical, or non-incremental, change involves new policies that represent a sharp break from how policies were developed, conceived, and implemented in the past (Baumgartner and Jones, 1993; Berry, 1990; Rose, 1976; True et al., 1999; Hayes, 2001). Frequently cited examples of such changes include shifts in fiscal and monetary policy in most Western countries from balanced-budget orthodoxy to Keynesian demand-management principles and practices in the 1930s and 1940s and the subsequent shift away from Keynesianism to forms of monetarism in the 1970s and 1980s (Hall, 1989, 1992).[7] Similar shifts occurred in resource policy, from pure exploitation to conservation in the nineteenth century, and then from conservation to sustainable management in the twentieth century (see Hays, 1959, 1987).

A useful way to look at these different patterns of policy change has been suggested by Durrant and Diehl (1989; see also Meyer et al., 1990). Analogizing from work in paleobiology, policy regime change can be argued to have two components. Policies can vary not only in terms of the *mode of change*—between the normal pattern of piecemeal incremental change and the pattern of paradigmatic chance mentioned above—but also in terms of the tempo or *speed of change* (see Figure 10.4).[8]

Figure 10.4 Basic Patterns of Policy Change

		Speed of Change	
		Fast	*Slow*
Mode of Change	*Fundamental*	Rapid Atypical	Gradual Atypical
	Incremental	Rapid Normal	Gradual Normal

SOURCE: Adapted from Robert F. Durrant and Paul F. Diehl, 'Agendas, Alternatives and Public Policy: Lessons from the U.S. Foreign Policy Arena', *Journal of Public Policy* 9, 2 (1989): 179–205.

As this model demonstrates, atypical change, although infrequent, can be either rapid or slow. This is somewhat different from the usual conception of fundamental change cited in the literature, which has emphasized its often rapid nature (Hall, 1990: 61).[9] However, empirical evidence of such gradual processes has been generated in diverse areas such as fiscal policy, agricultural policy, Aboriginal policy, and forestry policy, among others (see Hall, 1993; Howlett, 1994; Coleman et al., 1996). The same is true for the more common pattern of incremental change, which can occur at either tempo, despite the fact that the literature has tended to focus on the gradual nature of many incremental policy processes (see Hayes, 1992).[10]

Until fairly recently, it was often thought that policy regime change occurred largely as a result of events outside of these stable policy-making systems (see Heclo, 1994, 1976). The notion that policy regimes would change only due to exogenous events or 'shocks' arose from the assumption that such regimes were a form of stable or self-adjusting 'homeostatic' system. Given an initial set of characteristics and composition, it was argued, policy systems would adjust to any internal changes and could only be thrown out of equilibrium by external events that introduced new dynamic elements into the system (see Zucker, 1988; Starling, 1975; Aminzade, 1992).

This notion of the exogenous nature of policy change focused attention on the various types of external crises that could provoke a government response or policy change. Two of these received detailed examination in the literature: *systemic perturbations* and *policy spillovers*.

Paul Sabatier, for example, has argued that 'changes in the core aspects of a policy are usually the results of perturbations in non-cognitive factors external to the subsystem such as macro-economic conditions or the rise of a new systemic governing coalition' (Sabatier, 1988: 140; see also Sabatier, 1987; Sabatier and Jenkins-Smith. 1993a). 'Systemic perturbations' is a thus a term used to describe one of the oldest known forms through which policy changes—external crises that upset established policy routines (Meyer, 1982). These can include idiosyncratic phenomena such as wars or disasters, or repeating events such as critical elections and leadership rotations. The principal mechanism by which change occurs is through the introduction of new actors into policy processes, very often in the form of enhanced public attention being paid to a policy issue as a result of a perceived crisis situation.

'Subsystem spillovers' refers to a more recently described exogenous change process that occurs when activities in otherwise distinct subsystems transcend old policy boundaries and affect the structure or behaviour of other subsystems (Dery, 1999; Lynggaard, 2001).[11] Instances such as those that have occurred when Internet-based computing collided with existing telecommunications regimes and when long-established natural resource policy actors find it necessary to deal with Aboriginal land claims issues exemplify this phenomenon (Hoberg and Morawaski, 1997; Grant and MacNamara, 1995; Rosendal, 2000; Gehring and Oberthur, 2000; Marion, 1999; Rayner et al., 2001). Although this particular process of regime change has just begun to be examined, it would appear that spillovers can occur in specific issues without any permanent change in subsystem membership—subsystem intersection—or they can be more long-term in nature—subsystem convergence. This general process, like systemic perturbations, affects policy processes largely through the introduction of new actors into otherwise stable subsystems. Unlike systemic perturbations, however, the new actors tend to be policy specialists and interested parties, rather than simply members of the aroused public.

More recent conceptions of policy systems, however, are more chaotic, abandoning notions of dynamic equilibria in favour of adaptive concepts in which these systems are thought to affect their environments and therefore alter the nature of their own constraints (see Daneke, 1992; Jervis, 1997; Buckley, 1968). In the policy sciences, this shift has manifested itself in the acknowledgement that crises are not the only source of policy change and that factors internal or endogenous to policy-making systems and subsystems can also lead to policy change, either independently or in conjunction with external factors (see Peters, 1992a; Nunan, 1999). Two processes in particular have been linked to important policy regime changes and were discussed in Chapters 5 and 9: *venue change* and *policy learning*.

'Venue change' refers to changes in the strategies policy actors follow in pursuing their interests.[12] In their work on policy formation in the United States, Baumgartner and Jones (1993: 26, 239–41) noted several strategies employed by actors presently excluded from policy subsystems to gain access to policy deliberations and affect policy outcomes. This usually involved members of discourse communities attempting to 'break into' more restricted interest networks of central policy actors, but also can involve jockeying for advantage among network actors themselves. Venue-shifting strategies usually involve the redefinition of a policy issue to facilitate the alteration of the location in which policy formulation occurs. These include notable instances such as when environmental groups attempt to redefine the image of an issue like waste disposal from a technical regulatory issue to a public health or property rights one susceptible to lawsuits and recourse to the courts (see Jordan, 1998; Hoberg, 1998; Richardson, 1999). Not all policy issues are susceptible, or as susceptible, to reframing or image manipulation, and not all political systems contain any, or as many, alternate policy venues. However, Baumgartner and Jones argue that actors outside of formal policy processes, especially, will attempt to alter existing policy images in the hope that an alternative venue can be successfully located in which their issues and concerns will be accorded a favourable reception. The internationalization of public policy-making and its impact on policy change—often addressed in short-hand as globalization or internationalization—results in policy regime change largely through the proliferation of new venues for actors to exploit (Epstein, 1997; Cerny, 2001; Doern et al., 1996a).

'Policy learning' is a second endogenous change-enhancing process. As discussed in Chapter 9, it refers to the manner in which, as Hugh Heclo (1974) has noted, a relatively enduring alteration in policy results from policy-makers and participants learning from their own and others' experience with similar policies. While some types of learning are limited to reflections on existing practices, others are much more far-reaching and can affect a wide range of policy elements (see Bennett and Howlett, 1991; May, 1992). All involve the development and diffusion of new ideas into existing policy processes. These different conceptions of learning and its role in public policy formation are used by many analysts to describe a common tendency for policies to change as the result of alterations in policy ideas circulating in policy subsystems, as knowledge of past experiences influences member judgements as to the feasibility or desirability of certain present courses of action (Knoepfel and Kissling-Naf, 1998).

Such analyses suggest that the process of policy regime change can have both exogenous and endogenous causes, that is, can involve both the emergence of new problems and issues, and the behaviour and attitude of subsystem members towards them. The general argument to explain punctuated equilibrium patterns of policy dynamics is that atypical change ultimately occurs because anomalies build up between the policy regime and the reality it 'regulates', resulting in a crisis within the existing regime (Linz, 1978). The change is precipitated by innovative individuals within the subsystem responding to changed circumstances and to their own ambitions. The process of regime change is initially quite unstable as conflicting ideas emerge and compete for dominance. The process is complete, at least until the next upheaval, when a new set of ideas wins out over the others and is accepted by most, or at least the most powerful, members of the policy subsystem. The hegemony of the new regime is eventually established when it is institutionalized and its legitimacy is recognized to the point that it appears normal and alternatives that do not fit appear unusual (see Wilson, 2000; Skogstad, 1998; Jenson, 1989; Legro, 2000). A general model of this process of change in a policy regime is set out in Figure 10.5.

CONCLUSION

Policy dynamics are complex and characterized by different forces and processes enhancing policy stability and turbulence. Processes such as policy learning and path-dependence often overlap and their interactive effects can lead to minor or major change, depending on the presence or absence of other conditions enhancing the opportunities for new actors

Figure 10.5   A General Model of the Process of Policy Regime Change

Stage	*Characteristics*
1. Regime Stability	Reigning orthodoxy is institutionalized and policy adjustments made largely by a closed group of experts and officials.
2. Accumulation of Anomalies	'Real-world' developments are neither anticipated nor fully explicable in terms of the reigning orthodoxy.
3. Experimentation	Efforts are made to stretch the existing regime to account for the anomalies.
4. Fragmentation of Authority	Experts and officials are discredited and new participants challenge the existing regime.
5. Contestation	Debate spills into the public arena and involves the larger political process, including electoral and partisan considerations.
6. Institutionalization of a New Regime	After a period of time, the advocates of a new regime secure positions of authority and alter existing organizational and decision-making arrangements in order to institutionalize the new regime.

SOURCE: Adapted from Peter A. Hall, 'Policy Paradigms, Social Learning and the State: The Case of Economic Policy Making in Britain', *Comparative Politics* 25, 3 (1993): 275–96.

and ideas to penetrate existing policy regimes (see Thomas, 1999; Alink et al., 2001; Nisbet, 1972).

Analyzing the policy process in terms of policy cycles and policy sub-systems aids both the conceptualization of these fundamental policy dynamics as well as their identification and investigation. Identifying characteristic policy styles and policy paradigms through the analysis of the stages of the policy cycle helps to establish a baseline against which to measure change, while careful observation and investigation of sub-system behaviour helps to clarify tendencies towards atypical policy change.

In the course of normal policy development, the critical activity under-taken by a subsystem is a form of policy learning in which the outcomes of previous policy cycles and cycle stages feed back into new iterations of the cycle (Coleman et al., 1996). This allows changes to occur within an established policy style and policy paradigm without altering the funda-mental elements of a policy regime. Change, in this sense, is evolutionary and path-dependent.

Atypical policy changes represent a significant, though not necessarily total, break from the past in terms of the overall policy goals, the understanding of public problems and their solutions, and the policy instruments used to put decisions into effect (Kenis, 1991; Menahem, 1998, 2001). Such deep changes occur in circumstances when normal changes to the policy come to be regarded as insufficient for the task at hand. By their very nature their occurrence is infrequent, but when they do take place, their effects are felt throughout the policy sector.

FURTHER READINGS

Baumgartner, Frank R., and Bryan D. Jones. 1991. 'Agenda Dynamics and Policy Subsystems', *Journal of Politics* 53, 4: 1044–74.

Campbell, John L. 1998. 'Institutional Analysis and the Role of Ideas in Political Economy', *Theory and Society* 27, 5: 377–409.

Coleman, William D., Grace D. Skogstad, and Michael Atkinson. 1996. 'Paradigm Shifts and Policy Networks: Cumulative Change in Agriculture', *Journal of Public Policy* 16, 3: 273–302.

Eisner, Marc Allen. 1994. 'Discovering Patterns in Regulatory History: Continuity, Change and Regulatory Regimes', *Journal of Policy History* 6, 2: 157–87.

Esping-Andersen, Gosta. 1985. 'Power and Distributional Regimes', *Politics and Society* 14, 2: 223–56.

Gersick, Connie J.G. 1991. 'Revolutionary Change Theories: A Multilevel Exploration of the Punctuated Equilibrium Paradigm', *Academy of Management Review* 16, 1: 10–36.

Hall, Peter A. 1993. 'Policy Paradigms, Social Learning and the State: The Case of Economic Policy-making in Britain', *Comparative Politics* 25, 3: 275–96.

Harris, Richard, and Sidney Milkis. 1989. *The Politics of Regulatory Change*. New York: Oxford University Press.

Hernes, Gudmund. 1976, 'Structural Change in Social Processes', *American Journal of Sociology* 82, 3: 513–47.

Menahem, Gila. 1998. 'Policy Paradigms, Policy Networks and Water Policy in Israel', *Journal of Public Policy* 18, 3: 283–310.

Richardson, Jeremy, Gunnel Gustafsson, and Grant Jordan. 1982. 'The Concept of Policy Style', in Richardson, ed., *Policy Styles in Western Europe*. London: George Allen and Unwin, 1–16.

Thomas, Gerald B. 1999. 'External Shocks, Conflict and Learning as Interactive Sources of Change in U.S. Security Policy', *Journal of Public Policy* 19, 2: 209–31.

True, James L., Bryan D. Jones, and Frank R. Baumgartner. 1999. 'Punctuated-Equilibrium Theory: Explaining Stability and Change in American Policymaking', in P.A. Sabatier, ed., *Theories of the Policy Process*. Boulder, Colo.: Westview Press, 97–115.

Wilson, Carter A. 2000. 'Policy Regimes and Policy Change', *Journal of Public Policy* 20, 3: 247–71.

NOTES

1. Even this term has had two senses. One refers to the institutional arrangements found in a country. See, for example, Gunther (1996). The second refers to the values and general ideological orientation of a country. See, for example, Elkin (1986).
2. This is similar to the idea of a policy 'profile' put forward by Feick (1992).
3. For similar discussions of activities at each stage of the policy cycle promoting stability and change, see Webber (1986); Thomas and Grindle (1990); Howlett and Ramesh (2002).
4. On the definition of non-incremental change as innovative or 'breakthrough' change, see Hayes (1992: esp. ch. 10).
5. This model of change is akin to that put forward by Thomas Kuhn in his work on paradigm shifts in scientific inquiry. See Kuhn (1962: 110). On the role of anomalies in policy-making, see Hall (1993); Laughlin (1991). On the role of policy entrepreneurs, see Kingdon (1984); Mintron (1997); Roberts and King (1991).
6. Drawing on work in the sociology of science undertaken by Robert K. Merton, Walker (1974: 8–9) has suggested that the individual community members' personal motivations, unrelated to the pursuit of 'objective' knowledge, may account for the variations. He argues that the members' desire for prestige and recognition within the scientific community plays a large part in this process.
7. This was not the first use of such a model of change, of course. It corresponds quite closely with the notion of dialectical change found in the works of Hegel and his followers, including, most obviously, Karl Marx. See Hernes (1976).
8. On the paleobiological roots of this argument, see Gould and Eldredge (1977).
9. Although Kuhn argued in his earlier work that a paradigm would change quickly from the old to new paradigm, in his later works he suggested that there was a transitory period between the two phases. See Kuhn (1974).
10. The originator of the concept, Charles Lindblom, had noted that incremental change can occur at both speeds. See Lindblom (1979).
11. On earlier uses of the term to explain the process of European integration, see Haas (1958) and Keohane and Hoffman (1991).
12. On the first uses of this concept, see Schattschneider (1960). On its relationship to multi-level governance systems, see Richardson (1999, 2000).

Chapter 11

Afterword: Still Studying Public Policy

The discussion in this book has shown that public policy-making is a highly complex matter, consisting of a series of decisions, involving a large number of actors operating within the confines of an amorphous, yet inescapable, ideational and institutional context, and employing a variety of diverse and multi-faceted policy instruments. This complexity poses grave difficulties for those seeking a comprehensive understanding of the subject.

As the chapters in this volume have shown, one of the simplest and most effective ways to deal with this complexity is to break down the public policy-making process into series of discrete but related sub-processes, together forming a continuing *policy cycle*. The stages in the cycle correspond to the five stages in applied problem-solving, whereby problems are recognized, solutions are proposed, a solution is chosen, the chosen solution is put into effect, and finally the outcomes are monitored and evaluated. In the policy process, these stages are manifested as agenda-setting, policy formulation, decision-making, policy implementation, and policy evaluation.

Of course, the public policy process is not nearly as tightly sequential or goal-driven as the model makes it appear. Policy actors, it is justifiably argued, do not go about making and implementing policies in the systematic manner the model seems to suggest. While this is no doubt a legitimate complaint against the conception of public policy as being carried out in a series of stages, it is also true that the limitation can be mitigated to a large extent with caution and diligence in its application. The advantage of employing the cycle model lies in its role as a methodological *heuristic*: facilitating the understanding of the public policy process by breaking it into parts, each of which can be investigated alone or in terms of its relationship to the other stages of the cycle. This allows the integration of the study of individual cases, comparative studies of a series of cases, and the study of one or many stages of one or several cases, of which the policy literature, for the most part, is composed.[1]

The model's greatest virtue, however, is its empirical orientation, which enables the systematic evaluation of a wide range of different factors driving public policy-making at the various stages of the policy-making process. While abstract conceptualization is necessary to develop a broad picture of the policy process, an analytical framework that takes into account the details of the sub-processes in developing a picture of the entire process is essential.

The factors considered at each stage of the policy cycle have been the actors, institutions, and ideas involved in developing the content and process of the creation of the policy in question, and the instruments available to carry it out. Each of these aspects of the policy-making process is in itself a complex phenomenon, and the general nature of each has been sketched out in the book.

As we have argued, in assessing how actors and institutions combine in the policy cycle to affect the ideas and instruments that form the goals and means of public policy, it is useful to think about them as more or less coherent *policy subsystems*. These subsystems have specific properties and structural characteristics that affect the types of policy goals they espouse and the kinds of instruments feasible or acceptable for putting their policy ideas into practice. More specifically, the book shows how public policies emerge from a complex interplay of forms of government, types of issues, and the organization of states and societies into particular types of sectoral policy subsystems. Each sectoral subsystem tends to develop a particular style of policy-making and a particular set of policy ideas that manifest themselves in a distinct set of pre-established preferences for particular types of instruments and sets of policy claims or problems shared by subsystem members.

The book shows how the actors participating in policy subsystems include individuals and groups drawn both from within and from outside the formal institutions of government and civil society. The government actors playing a critical role in the process are the executive, bureaucracy, and legislature. In most instances, the bureaucracy plays the main role, though high-profile issues or the talents and determination of individual ministers are likely to encourage a greater role for the executive. Only in a limited number of circumstances, where constitutional orders allow it, are legislatures able to influence significantly the policy process and its outcomes.

The societal actors involved to a significant extent in the public policy process include interest groups, research organizations, the mass media, lobbyists, and, on relatively rare occasions, the public. Depending on their internal resources and links with government actors, organized social groups can be highly influential actors. Groups and organizations endowed with large and supportive membership, adequate funds, scarce information, and close links with relevant bureaucratic and executive actors can be expected to be influential players in the policy subsystem. All the actors involved in the process have interests, based on their resources, needs, or ideology, which they seek to achieve through participation in the policy process. How they go about participating and the extent to which they are successful are affected by the broader institutional context in which they operate.

The institutions of most relevance to policy-making pertain to the organization of state and societal actors, and the links between them. How policy actors are organized internally and in relation to each other within a subsystem determines the nature of their capacity to participate in the policy process and affect its outcomes. A state's fragmentation is reflected in its executive and bureaucratic officials' capabilities to dominate a policy subsystem and control activities such as agenda-setting or policy formulation. An internally divided state is often unable to resist the conflicting demands placed upon it by societal groups. Similarly, fragmentation among major societal groups makes it difficult for them to devise coherent positions they can present at policy deliberations. The organizational features that are particularly weakening are federalism, a presidential or republican system, and an unprofessional bureaucracy. Federalism divides authority between two levels of government, whereas a presidential system divides authority among various branches of the government; the net effect of both is to reduce state capacity compared to unitary parliamentary systems. An under-resourced, fragmented, demoralized, or corrupt bureaucracy is similarly debilitating because of its inability to devise coherent policies and defend them against pressures from social groups and politicians.

The organization of societal groups is also an important factor affecting the nature of policy subsystems and thereby the operation of the policy process and its outcomes. It is often the society's problems that the state seeks to address through public policies, and it is therefore to be expected that those directly affected by the problem will organize to influence policy-making. The societal actors engaged in the policy process vary across policy sectors, as each policy normally involves only those with direct interests in the issue in question. Encompassing and cohesive groups are able to devise coherent positions that rise above narrow sectional interests, and such groups are therefore more likely to serve the interests of the society as a whole. The worst situation is when groups are individually so strong as to make it difficult for the state to ignore them, yet too disunited to develop cohesive proposals for addressing public problems.

The structure of policy subsystems affects the overarching sets of policy ideas that determine the recognition of social problems, the construction of policy options to resolve them, and the implementation and evaluation of means to achieve solutions in practice. Subsystem structure shapes the policy discourse by conditioning the members' perception of what is desirable and possible, thus affecting the choice of policy instruments and policy outcomes. The sources of these ideas are varied, not to mention contentious; they range from purely ideological constructs to manifestations of material conditions. What is beyond doubt, however, is their effect on the policy process.

Discussion of the key role played by policy subsystems at all stages of the policy process helped us to provide an alternate way to view the operation of a policy cycle than that typically found in the literature (see DeLeon and Kaufmanis, 2001). Chapters 1–4 set out the basic intentions of the policy sciences and discussed the manner in which existing general theories of political life fail to provide a satisfactory understanding of public policy-making and the roles played by actors, institutions, and instruments found in the policy process of modern liberal democratic states. Chapters 5–9 discussed the various stages of the policy cycle and identified the different styles in which policy deliberations proceed, but said little about how these stages fit together, or whether characteristic patterns of policy change existed in public policy processes or contents.

The discussion in Chapter 10 addressed the issue of policy change and the existence of long-term patterns of stability in policy-making, highlighting the manner in which actors, institutions, and ideas combine to produce reasonably stable policy styles, paradigms, and regimes. Public policy-making was described as a process characterized by not one but two interlinked patterns of policy change. In other words, policy dynamics were shown to exist within a punctuated equilibrium framework, in which a process of normal change, whereby aspects of policy styles and paradigms change incrementally, is periodically interrupted by more fundamental change in the nature of policy regimes.

The notion of fundamental policy change as synonymous with changes in policy regimes brings to the fore the notion that public policy-making is not simply a process of conflict resolution, as most economic and political science-based theories allege, nor is it a process solely comprised of policy-makers responding to external shocks or jolts. In addition, policy-making is influenced largely by activities of policy subsystem members attempting to influence the structure and operation of policy-making through activities such as venue-shifting, image reframing, and policy learning.

This move away from a traditional linear interpretation of the policy cycle and towards a more nuanced position on the investigation and conceptualization of the public policy process reflects a recent trend towards 'post-positivist' modes of analysis in policy science as a whole (see Dudley et al., 2000; Howlett and Ramesh, 1998; Lynn, 1999). Policy scholars now recognize that social phenomena are shaped by highly contingent and complex processes, which require an appropriate research methodology to accommodate the uncertainty and the complexity (see Hilgartner and Bosk, 1981; Holzner and Marx, 1979). In this view, the mode of analysis itself becomes just as much a subject of analysis and reflection as the object of the analysis. Grand theories are eschewed and replaced by the recognition that social problems and the government's response to them are affected by a range of factors whose general form, but not specific content, can be assumed in advance (see Cook, 1985; Jennings, 1987). The emphasis is on considering as many factors as possible. There is no pretense of claiming one solution to be better than others on scientific grounds. Studying public policy is complex because government decision-making, the subject and object of study, is complex (see Roe, 1990, 2000).

Understanding public policy-making involves answering the many questions that can be posed about public policies. One must identify the policy problems, what governments have done or not done about them in the past, the state, societal, and international contexts within which governments operate, the actors involved in the policy process and their interests, and the appropriateness of the various policy instruments available to address the problems (Clemons and McBeth, 2001). This would seem like a tall order, but it is not an impossible goal. Ample information is available on each of these questions for most policies in most countries. What is needed is concerted effort to piece together the available information to reveal the interplay of policy cycles and policy subsystems.

NOTE

1. On the need and utility, and drawbacks, of syntheses of this kind, see Franke (2001).

Bibliography

Aaron, H.J. 1967. 'Social Security: International Comparison', in O. Eckstein, ed., *Studies in the Economics of Income Maintenance*. Washington: Brookings Institution, 13–49.

Abbott, A. 1990. 'Conceptions of Time and Events in Social Science Methods', *Historical Methods* 23, 4: 140–51.

Abelson, Donald E. 1996. *American Think Tanks and Their Role in U.S. Foreign Policy*. London: Macmillan.

_____. 1999. 'Public Visibility and Policy Relevance: Assessing the Impact and Influence of Canadian Policy Institutes', *Canadian Public Administration* 42, 2: 240–70.

_____. 2002. *Do Think Tanks Matter? Assessing the Impact of Public Policy Institutes*. Montreal and Kingston: McGill-Queen's University Press.

Aberbach, Joel D., Robert D. Putnam, and Bert A. Rockman. 1981. *Bureaucrats and Politicians in Western Democracies*. Cambridge, Mass.: Harvard University Press.

Abrahamson, Eric, and Gregory Fairchild. 1999. 'Management Fashion, Lifecycles, Triggers, and Collective Learning Processes', *Administrative Science Quarterly* 44: 708–40.

Adams, Greg D. 1997. 'Abortion: Evidence of an Issue Evolution', *American Journal of Political Science* 41, 3: 718–37.

Adie, R.F., and P.G. Thomas. 1987. *Canadian Public Administration: Problematical Perspectives*, 2nd edn. Scarborough, Ont.: Prentice-Hall.

Adler, Robert S., and R. David Pittle. 1984. 'Cajolery or Command: Are Education Campaigns an Adequate Substitute for Regulation', *Yale Journal on Regulation* 1: 159–93.

Advani, Asheesh, and Sandford Borins. 2001. 'Managing Airports: A Test of the New Public Management', *International Public Management Journal* 4: 91–107.

Aglietta, Michel. 1979. *A Theory of Capitalist Regulation*. London: New Left Books.

Ahroni, Yair. 1986. *Evolution and Management of State Owned Enterprises*. Cambridge, Mass.: Ballinger.

Aldrich, Howard, and Diane Herker. 1977. 'Boundary Spanning Roles and Organizational Structure', *Academy of Management Review* 2 (Apr.): 217–30.

_____ and David A. Whetten. 1980. 'Organization-sets, Action-sets, and Networks: Making the Most of Simplicity', in P. Nystrom and W.H. Starbuck, eds, *Handbook of Organizational Design*. Oxford: Oxford University Press.

Alexander, Ernest R. 1979. 'The Design of Alternatives in Organizational Contexts: A Pilot Study', *Administrative Sciences Quarterly* 24: 382–404.

_____. 1982. 'Design in the Decision-Making Process', *Policy Sciences* 14: 279–92.

Alford, Robert R. 1972. 'The Political Economy of Health Care: Dynamics Without Change', *Politics and Society* 2, 2: 127–64.

_____. 1975. *Health Care Politics: Ideological and Interest Group Barriers to Reform*. Chicago: University of Chicago Press.

Alink, Fleur, Arjen Boin, and Paul t'Hart. 2001. 'Institutional Crises and Reforms in Policy Sectors: The Case of Asylum Policy in Europe', *Journal of European Public Policy* 8, 2: 286–306.

Allison, Graham. 1969. 'Conceptual Models and the Cuban Missile Crisis', *American Political Science Review* 63: 689–718.

_____. 1971. *Essence of Decision: Explaining the Cuban Missile Crisis*. Boston: Little, Brown.

_____ and Morton H. Halperin. 1972. 'Bureaucratic Politics: A Paradigm and Some Policy Implications', *World Politics* 24 (Supplement): 40–79.

Almond, Gabriel A. 1988. 'The Return to the State', *American Political Science Review* 82, 3: 853–901.

_____ and Stephen J. Genco. 1977. 'Clouds, Clocks and the Study of Politics', *World Politics* 29: 489–522.

Althusser, L., and E. Balibar. 1977. *Reading 'Capital'*. London: New Left Books.

Amariglio, Jack L., Stephen A. Resnick, and Richard D. Wolff. 1988. 'Class, Power, and Culture', in C. Nelson and L. Grossberg, eds, *Marxism and the Interpretation of Culture*. Urbana: University of Illinois Press.

Aminzade, Ronald. 1992. 'Historical Sociology and Time', *Sociological Methods and Research* 20, 4: 456–80.

Anderson, Charles W. 1971. 'Comparative Policy Analysis: The Design of Measures', *Comparative Politics* 4, 1: 117–31.

_____. 1977. *Statecraft: An Introduction to Political Choice and Judgement*. New York: John Wiley and Sons.

_____. 1979a. 'The Place of Principles in Policy Analysis', *American Political Science Review* 73, 3: 711–23.

_____. 1979b. 'Political Design and the Representation of Interests', in P.C. Schmitter and G. Lehmbruch, eds, *Trends Towards Corporatist Intermediation*. London: Sage, 271–97.

Anderson, James E. 1975. *Public Policy-Making*. New York: Praeger.

_____, ed. 1976. *Economic Regulatory Policies*. Lexington, Mass.: Lexington Books.

_____. 1984. *Public Policy-Making: An Introduction*, 3rd edn. Boston: Houghton Mifflin.

Anderson, Paul A. 1983. 'Decision Making by Objection and the Cuban Missile Crisis', *Administrative Science Quarterly* 28: 201–22.

Andrews, Richard. 1998. 'Environmental Regulation and Business "Self-Regulation"', *Policy Sciences* 31: 177–97.

Anglund, Sandra M. 1999. 'Policy Feedback: The Comparison Effect and Small Business Procurement Policy', *Policy Studies Journal* 27, 1: 11–27.

Angus, William H. 1974. 'Judicial Review: Do We Need It?', in D.J. Baum, ed., *The Individual and the Bureaucracy*. Toronto: Carswell.

Argyris, Chris. 1992. *On Organizational Learning*. London: Blackwell.

_____ and Donald A. Schon. 1978. *Organizational Learning: A Theory of Action Perspective*. Reading, Mass.: Addison-Wesley.

Armstrong, Jim, and Donald G. Lenihan. 1999. *From Controlling to Collaborating; When Governments Want to be Partners: A Report on the Collaborative Partnership Project*. Toronto: Institute of Public Administration of Canada New Directions, Number 3.

Arthur, W. Brian. 1989. 'Competing Technologies, Increasing Returns, and Lock-In by Historical Events', *Economic Journal* 99: 116–31.

Ascher, Kate. 1987. *The Politics of Privatisation: Contracting Out Public Services*. Basingstoke: Macmillan.

Ascher, William. 1986. 'The Evolution of the Policy Sciences: Understanding the Rise and Avoiding the Fall', *Journal of Policy Analysis and Management* 5: 365–89.

Aspinwall, Mark D., and Gerald Schneider. 2000. 'Same Menu, Separate Tables: The Institutionalist Turn in Political Science and the Study of European Integration', *European Journal of Political Research* 38: 1–36.

Atkinson, Michael M., and William D. Coleman. 1989a. 'Strong States and Weak

States: Sectoral Policy Networks in Advanced Capitalist Economies', *British Journal of Political Science* 19, 1: 47–67.

_____ and _____. 1989b. *The State, Business, and Industrial Change in Canada*. Toronto: University of Toronto Press.

_____ and _____. 1992. 'Policy Networks, Policy Communities and the Problems of Governance', *Governance* 5, 2: 154–80.

_____ and Robert A. Nigol. 1989. 'Selecting Policy Instruments: Neo-Institutional and Rational Choice Interpretations of Automobile Insurance in Ontario', *Canadian Journal of Political Science* 22, 1: 107–35.

Aucoin, Peter. 1997. 'The Design of Public Organizations for the 21st Century: Why Bureaucracy Will Survive in Public Management', *Canadian Public Administration* 40, 2: 290–306.

Averch, Harvey. 1990. *Private Markets and Public Interventions: A Primer for Policy Designers*. Pittsburgh: University of Pittsburgh Press.

Axworthy, Thomas S. 1988. 'Of Secretaries to Princes', *Canadian Public Administration* 31, 2: 247–64.

Bachrach, Peter, and Morton S. Baratz. 1962. 'Decisions and Nondecisions: An Analytical Framework', *American Political Science Review* 56, 2: 632–42.

_____ and _____. 1970. *Power and Poverty: Theory and Practice*. New York: Oxford University Press.

_____ and _____. 1975. 'Power and Its Two Faces Revisited: A Reply to Geoffrey Debnam', *American Political Science Review* 69, 3: 900–07.

Bakvis, Herman, and David MacDonald. 1993. 'The Canadian Cabinet: Organization, Decision-Rules, and Policy Impact', in M. Michael Atkinson, ed., *Governing Canada: Institutions and Public Policy*. Toronto: Harcourt Brace Jovanovich.

Balch, George I. 1980. 'The Stick, the Carrot, and Other Strategies: A Theoretical Analysis of Governmental Intervention', *Law and Policy Quarterly* 2, 1: 35–60.

Baldwin, David A. 1985. *Economic Statecraft*. Princeton, NJ: Princeton University Press.

Balla, Steven J., and John R. Wright. 2001. 'Interest Groups, Advisory Committees, and Congressional Control of the Bureaucracy', *American Journal of Political Science* 45, 4: 799–812.

Banks, Jeffrey S. 1995. 'The Design of Institutions', in D.L. Weimer, ed., *Institutional Design*. Boston: Kluwer, 17–36.

Banting, Keith G. 1982. *The Welfare State and Canadian Federalism*. Kingston: Queen's University Institute of Intergovernmental Relations.

_____. 1995. 'The Social Policy Review: Policy Making in a Semi-Sovereign Society', *Canadian Public Administration* 38, 2: 283–90.

Bardach, Eugene. 1976. 'Policy Termination as a Political Process', *Policy Sciences* 7, 2: 123–31.

_____. 1977. *The Implementation Game: What Happens After a Bill Becomes a Law*. Cambridge, Mass.: MIT Press.

_____. 1980. 'Implementation Studies and the Study of Implements', paper presented at the annual meeting of the American Political Science Association.

_____. 1989. 'Social Regulation as a Generic Policy Instrument', in Salamon (1989a).

_____ and Robert A. Kagan. 1982. *Going by the Book: The Problem of Regulatory Unreasonableness*. Philadelphia: Temple University Press.

Barker, Anthony, and B. Guy Peters, eds. 1993. *The Politics of Expert Advice: Creating, Using and Manipulating Scientific Knowledge for Public Policy*. Pittsburgh: University of Pittsburgh Press.

Barnett, Michael N., and Martha Finnemore. 1999. 'The Politics, Power, and Pathologies of International Organizations', *International Organization* 53, 4: 699–732.

Barrett, Susan, and Colin Fudge. 1981. *Policy and Action: Essays on the Implementation of Public Policy*. London: Methuen.

Bator, Francis M. 1958. 'The Anatomy of Market Failure', *Quarterly Journal of Economics* 72, 3: 351–79.

Baumgartner, Frank R., and Bryan D. Jones. 1991. 'Agenda Dynamics and Policy Subsystems', *Journal of Politics* 53, 4: 1044–74.

_____ and _____. 1993. *Agendas and Instability in American Politics*. Chicago: University of Chicago Press.

_____ and _____. 1994. 'Attention, Boundary Effects, and Large-Scale Policy Change in Air Transportation Policy', in D.A. Rochefort and R.W. Cobb, eds, *The Politics of Problem Definition: Shaping the Policy Agenda*. Lawrence: University of Kansas Press.

_____ and Beth L. Leech. 1998. *Basic Interests: The Importance of Groups in Politics and in Political Science*. Princeton, NJ: Princeton University Press.

_____ and _____. 2001. 'Interest Niches and Policy Bandwagons: Patterns of Interest Group Involvement in National Politics', *Journal of Politics* 63, 4: 1191–1213.

Baxter-Moore, Nicolas. 1987. 'Policy Implementation and the Role of the State: A Revised Approach to the Study of Policy Instruments', in Robert J. Jackson, Doreen Jackson, and Baxter-Moore, eds, *Contemporary Canadian Politics: Readings and Notes*. Scarborough, Ont.: Prentice-Hall, 336–55.

Beam, David A., and Timothy J. Conlan. 2002. 'Grants', in Salamon (2002a: 340–80).

Becker, Gary S. 1958. 'Competition and Democracy', *Journal of Law and Economics* 1: 105–9.

Beesley, M.E. 1992. *Privatization, Regulation and Deregulation*. New York: Routledge.

Behn, Robert D. 1977. 'How to Terminate a Public Policy: A Dozen Hints for the Would-be Terminator', *Policy Analysis* 4, 3: 393–414.

Bellehumeur, Robert. 1997. 'Review: An Instrument of Change', *Optimum* 27, 1: 37–42.

Bellman, R.E., and L.A. Zadeh. 1970. 'Decision-Making in a Fuzzy Environment', *Management Science* 17, 4: B141–B164

Bemelmans-Videc, Marie-Louise, Ray C. Rist, and Evert Vedung, eds. 1998. *Carrots, Sticks and Sermons: Policy Instruments and Their Evaluation*. New Brunswick, NJ: Transaction Publishers.

Bendor, Jonathan. 1995. 'A Model of Muddling Through', *American Political Science Review* 89, 4: 819–40.

_____ and Thomas H. Hammond. 1992. 'Re-Thinking Allison's Models', *American Political Science Review* 86, 2: 301–22.

Bennett, Colin J. 1990. 'The Formation of a Canadian Privacy Policy: The Art and Craft of Lesson-Drawing', *Canadian Public Administration* 33, 4: 551–70

_____. 1991. 'What is Policy Convergence and What Causes It?', *British Journal of Political Science* 21, 2: 215–33.

_____. 1992a. *Regulating Privacy: Data Protection and Public Policy in Europe and the United States*. Ithaca, NY: Cornell University Press.

_____. 1992b. 'The International Regulation of Personal Data: From Epistemic Community to Policy Sector', paper presented at the annual meeting of the Canadian Political Science Association, Charlottetown, PEI.

_____. 1997. 'Understanding Ripple Effects: The Cross-National Adoption of Policy Instruments for Bureaucratic Accountability', *Governance* 10, 3: 213–33.

_____ and Michael Howlett. 1991. 'The Lessons of Learning: Reconciling Theories of Policy Learning and Policy Change', *Policy Sciences* 25, 3: 275–94.

Bennett, Scott, and Margaret McPhail. 1992. 'Policy Process Perceptions of Senior Canadian Federal Civil Servants: A View of the State and Its Environment', *Canadian Public Administration* 35, 3: 299–316.

Bennett, W. Lance. 1980. *Public Opinion in American Politics*. New York: Harcourt Brace Jovanovich.

Benson, J. Kenneth. 1982. 'A Framework for Policy Analysis', in Rogers and Whetton (1982: 137–76).

Bentley, Arthur F. 1908. *The Process of Government*. Chicago: University of Chicago Press.

Berelson, Bernard. 1952. 'Democratic Theory and Public Opinion', *Public Opinion Quarterly* 16 (Fall): 313–30.

Berger, Peter L., and Thomas Luckmann. 1966. *The Social Construction of Reality: A Treatise in the Sociology of Knowledge*. New York: Doubleday.

Berle, Adolf. 1959. *Power Without Property*. New York: Harcourt Brace.

Bernstein, Marver H. 1955. *Regulating Business by Independent Commission*. Princeton, NJ: Princeton University Press.

Bernstein, Steven, and Benjamin Cashore. 2000. 'Globalization, Four Paths of Internationalization and Domestic Policy Change: The Case of EcoForestry in British Columbia, Canada', *Canadian Journal of Political Science* 33, 1: 67–100.

Berry, Jeffrey M. 1989. 'Subgovernments, Issue Networks, and Political Conflicts', in R.A. Harris and S.M. Milkis, eds, *Remaking American Politics*. Boulder, Colo.: Westview Press, 239–60.

Berry, William T. 1990. 'The Confusing Case of Budgetary Incrementalism: Too Many Meanings for a Single Concept', *Journal of Politics* 52: 167–96.

Best, Samuel J. 1999. 'The Sampling Problem in Measuring Policy Mood: An Alternative Solution', *Journal of Politics* 61, 3: 721–40.

Bickers, Kenneth N., and John T. Williams. 2001. *Public Policy Analysis: A Political Economy Approach*. Boston: Houghton Mifflin.

Billings, Robert S., and Charles F. Hermann. 1998. 'Problem Identification in Sequential Policy Decision Making: The Re-representation of Problems', in D.A. Sylvan and J.F. Voss, eds, *Problem Representation in Foreign Policy Decision Making*. Cambridge: Cambridge University Press, 53–79.

Birch, Anthony H. 1972. *Representation*. New York: Praeger.

Birkland, Thomas A. 1997. *After Disaster: Agenda Setting, Public Policy and Focusing Events*. Washington: Georgetown University Press.

_____. 1998. 'Focusing Events, Mobilization, and Agenda Setting', *Journal of Public Policy* 18, 1: 53–74.

_____. 2001. *An Introduction to the Policy Process: Theories, Concepts, and Models of Public Policy Making*. Armonk, NY: M.E. Sharpe.

Black, Julia. 1997. 'New Institutionalism and Naturalism in Socio-Legal Analysis: Institutionalist Approaches to Regulatory Decision Making', *Law and Policy* 19, 1: 51–93.

Blais, André, Donald Blake, and Stéphane Dion. 1996. 'Do Parties Make a Difference? A Re-Appraisal', *American Journal of Political Science* 40, 2: 514–20.

Bleich, Erik. 2002. 'Integrating Ideas into Policy-Making Analysis: Frames and Race Policies in Britain and France', *Comparative Political Studies* 35, 9: 1054–76.

Block, Fred. 1980. 'Beyond Relative Autonomy: State Managers as Historical Subjects', *Socialist Register*: 227–42.

Blom-Hansen, Jens. 2001. 'Organized Interests and the State: A Disintegrating Relationship? Evidence from Denmark', *European Journal of Political Research* 39: 391–416.

Blyth, Mark M. 1997. '"Any More Bright Ideas?" The Ideational Turn of Comparative Political Economy', *Comparative Politics* 29: 229–50.

Bobrow, Davis B., and John S. Dryzek. 1987. *Policy Analysis by Design*. Pittsburgh: University of Pittsburgh Press.

Boddy, Raford, and James Crotty. 1975. 'Class Conflict and Macro-Policy: The Political Business Cycle', *Review of Radical Political Economics* 7, 1: 1–19.

Bogart, W.A. 2002. *Consequences: The Impact of Law and Its Complexity*. Toronto: University of Toronto Press.

Bogason, Peter. 2000. *Public Policy and Local Governance: Institutions in Postmodern Society*. Cheltenham: Edward Elgar.

Bohm, Peter, and Clifford S. Russell. 1985. 'Comparative Analysis of Alternative Policy Instruments', in A.V. Kneese and J.L. Sweeney, eds, *Handbook of Natural Resource and Energy Economics*, vol. 1. Dordrecht: Elsevier.

Boin, R. Arjen, and Marc H.P. Otten. 1996. 'Beyond the Crisis Window for Reform: Some Ramifications for Implementation', *Journal of Contingencies and Crisis Management* 4, 3: 149–61.

Bolom, Jan-Tjeerd. 2000. 'International Emissions Trading Under the Kyoto Protocol: Credit Trading', *Energy Policy* 29: 605–13.

Boockmann, Bernhard. 1998. 'Agenda Control by Interest Groups in EU Social Policy', *Journal of Theoretical Politics* 10, 2: 215–36.

Borzel, Tanja A. 1998. 'Organizing Babylon—On the Different Conceptions of Policy Networks', *Public Administration* 76, (Summer): 253–73.

Bos, Dieter. 1991. *Privatization: A Theoretical Treatment*. Oxford: Clarendon Press.

Bosso, Christopher J. 1989. 'Setting the Agenda: Mass Media and the Discovery of Famine in Ethiopia', in M. Margolis and G.A. Mauser, eds, *Manipulating Public Opinion: Essays on Public Opinion as a Dependent Variable*. Pacific Grove, Calif.: Brooks/Cole, 153–74.

Bourgault, Jacques, and Stéphane Dion. 1989. 'Governments Come and Go, But What of Senior Civil Servants? Canadian Deputy Ministers and Transitions in Power (1867–1987)', *Governance* 2, 2: 124–51.

Bovens, Mark, and Paul t'Hart. 1995. 'Frame Multiplicity and Policy Fiascoes: Limits to Explanation', *Knowledge and Policy* 8, 4: 61–83.

_____ and _____. 1996. *Understanding Policy Fiascoes*. New Brunswick, NJ: Transaction Press.

_____, _____, and B. Guy Peters. 2001. 'Analysing Governance Success and Failure in Six European States', in Bovens, t'Hart, and Peters, eds, *Success and Failure in Public Governance: A Comparative Analysis*. Cheltenham: Edward Elgar, 12–32.

Boychuk, Gerard. 1997. 'Are Canadian and U.S. Social Assistance Policies Converging?', *Canadian-American Public Policy* 30: 1–55.

Bozeman, Barry, ed. 1993. *Public Management: The State of the Art*. San Francisco: Jossey-Bass.

_____. 2002. 'Public-Value Failure: When Efficient Markets May Not Do', *Public Administration Review* 62, 2: 145–61.

Bradford, Neil. 1999. 'The Policy Influence of Economic Ideas: Interests, Institutions and Innovation in Canada', *Studies in Political Economy* 59: 17–60.

Braun, Dietmar. 1999. 'Interests or Ideas? An Overview of Ideational Concepts in Public Policy Research', in D. Braun and A. Busch, eds, *Public Policy and Political Ideas*. Cheltenham: Edward Elgar, 11–29.

Braybrooke, David, and Charles Lindblom. 1963. *A Strategy of Decision: Policy Evaluation as a Social Process*. New York: Free Press of Glencoe.

Bregha, Francois, et al. 1990. *The Integration of Environmental Considerations into Government Policy*. Ottawa: Canadian Environmental Assessment Research Council.

Brenner, Neil. 1999. 'Beyond State-Centrism? Space, Territoriality, and Geographical Scale in Globalization Studies', *Theory and Society* 28: 39–78.

Bressers, Hans Th.A. 1998. 'The Choice of Policy Instruments in Policy Networks', in Peters and Van Nispen (1998: 85–105).

_____ and Pieter-Jan Klok. 1988. 'Fundamentals for a Theory of Policy Instruments', *International Journal of Social Economics* 15, 3/4: 22–41

_____ and Laurence J. O'Toole. 1998. 'The Selection of Policy Instruments: A Network-based Perspective', *Journal of Public Policy* 18, 3: 213–39.

Brewer, Garry D. 1974. 'The Policy Sciences Emerge: To Nurture and Structure a Discipline', *Policy Sciences* 5, 3: 239–44.

_____ and Peter DeLeon. 1983. *The Foundations of Policy Analysis*. Homewood, NJ: Dorsey.

Breyer, Stephen. 1979. 'Analyzing Regulatory Failure: Mismatches, Less Restrictive Alternatives, and Reform', *Harvard Law Review* 92, 3: 549–609.

_____. 1982. *Regulation and Its Reform*. Cambridge, Mass.: Harvard University Press.

Bromley, Daniel W. 1989. *Economic Interests and Institutions: The Conceptual Foundations of Public Policy*. New York: Basil Blackwell.

Brooks, Joel E. 1985. 'Democratic Frustration in the Anglo-American Polities: A Quantification of Inconsistency Between Mass Public Opinion and Public Policy', *Western Political Quarterly* 38, 2: 250–61.

_____. 1987. 'The Opinion-Policy Nexus in France: Do Institutions and Ideology Make a Difference?', *Journal of Politics* 49, 2: 465–80.

_____. 1990. 'The Opinion-Policy Nexus in Germany', *Public Opinion Quarterly* 54, 3: 508–29.

Brooks, Stephen. 1998. *Public Policy in Canada: An Introduction*, 3rd edn. Toronto: Oxford University Press.

_____ and Alain-G. Gagnon, eds. 1990. *Social Scientists, Policy, and the State*. New York: Praeger.

Brown, David S. 1955. 'The Public Advisory Board as an Instrument of Government', *Public Administration Review* 15: 196–201.

_____. 1972. 'The Management of Advisory Committees: An Assignment for the '70's', *Public Administration Review* 32: 334–42.

Brown, M. Paul. 1992. 'Organizational Design as a Policy Instrument', in R. Boardman, ed., *Canadian Environmental Policy: Ecosystems, Politics, and Processes*. Toronto: Oxford University Press, 24–42.

Browne, William P. 1990. 'Organized Interests and Their Issue Niches: A Search for Pluralism in a Policy Domain', *Journal of Politics* 52, 2: 477–509.

_____. 1991. 'Issue Niches and the Limits of Interest Group Influence', in Allan J. Cigler and Burdett A. Loomis, eds, *Interest Group Politics*. Washington: CQ Press, 345–70.

Bruton, Jim, and Michael Howlett. 1992. 'Differences of Opinion: Round Tables, Policy Networks and the Failure of Canadian Environmental Strategy', *Alternatives* 19, 1: 25.

Bryman, Alan. 1988. *Quantity and Quality in Social Research*. London: Unwin Hyman.

Bryson, John M., and Barbara C. Crosby. 1993. 'Policy Planning and the Design and Use of Forums, Arenas, and Courts', in Bozeman (1993).

Buchanan, James. 1975. *The Limits of Liberty*. Chicago: University of Chicago Press.

_____. 1980. 'Rent Seeking and Profit Seeking', in Buchanan et al. (1980).

_____ et al. 1978. *The Economics of Politics*. London: Institute of Economic Affairs.

_____, R.O. Tollison, and G. Tullock, eds. 1980. *Toward a Theory of the Rent-Seeking Society*. College Station: Texas A&M Press.

Buckley, Walter. 1968. 'Society as a Complex Adaptive System', in Buckley, ed., *Modern System Research for the Behavioural Scientist*. Chicago: Aldine, 490–513.

Bulkley, Harriet. 2000. 'Discourse Coalition and the Australian Climate Change Policy Network', *Environment and Planning C: Government and Policy* 18: 727–48.

Bulmer, Martin. 1993. 'The Royal Commission and Departmental Committee in the British Policy-Making Process', in Peters and Parker (1993: 37–49).

Burgess, Michael, and Alain-G. Gagnon, eds. 1993. *Comparative Federalism and Federation: Competing Traditions and Future Directions*. New York: Harvester Wheatsheaf.

Burstein, Paul. 1991. 'Policy Domains: Organization, Culture and Policy Outcomes', *Annual Review of Sociology* 17: 327–50.

Burt, Sandra. 1990. 'Canadian Women's Groups in the 1980s: Organizational Development and Policy Influence', *Canadian Public Policy* 16, 1: 17–28.

Busenberg, George J. 2001. 'Learning in Organizations and Public Policy', *Journal of Public Policy* 21, 2: 173–89.

Butler, David, H.R. Penniman, and Austin Ranney, eds. 1981. *Democracy at the Polls: A Comparative Study of Competitive National Elections*. Washington: American Enterprise Institute for Public Policy Research.

_____ and Austin Ranney, eds. 1994. *Referendums Around the World: A Comparative Study of Practice and Theory*. Washington: American Enterprise Institute.

Cahill, Anthony G., and E. Sam Overman. 1990. 'The Evolution of Rationality in Policy Analysis', in S.S. Nagel, ed., *Policy Theory and Policy Evaluation: Concepts, Knowledge, Causes, and Norms*. New York: Greenwood Press.

Cairns, Alan C. 1974. 'Alternative Styles in the Study of Canadian Politics', *Canadian Journal of Political Science* 7: 102–28.

_____. 1990a. 'Reflections on Commission Research', in A.P. Pross, I. Christie, and J.A. Yogis, eds, *Commissions of Inquiry*. Toronto: Carswell, 87–110.

_____. 1990b. 'The Past and Future of the Canadian Administrative State', *University of Toronto Law Journal* 40: 310–61.

Callaghan, Karen, and Frauke Schnell. 2001. 'Assessing the Democratic Debate: How the News Media Frame Elite Policy Discourse', *Political Communication* 18: 183–212.

Calvert, Randall L., Mathew D. McCubbins, and Barry R. Weingast. 1989. 'A Theory of Political Control and Agency Discretion', *American Journal of Political Science* 33, 3: 588–611.

Cameron, David R. 1984. 'Social Democracy, Corporatism, Labour Quiescence and the Representation of Economic Interest in Advanced Capitalist Society', in J.H. Goldthorpe, ed., *Order and Conflict in Contemporary Capitalism*. Oxford: Clarendon Press.

Cammack, Paul. 1992. 'The New Institutionalism: Predatory Rule, Institutional Persistence, and Macro-Social Change', *Economy and Society* 21, 4: 397–429.

Campbell, Colin, and George J. Szablowski. 1979. *The Superbureaucrats: Structure and Behaviour in Central Agencies*. Toronto: Macmillan.

Campbell, John L. 1998. 'Institutional Analysis and the Role of Ideas in Political Economy', *Theory and Society* 27, 5: 377–409.

Canada, Auditor General. 1983. *Annual Report of the Auditor General*. Ottawa: Parliament of Canada.

_____. 1993. *Report of the Auditor General to the House of Commons*. Ottawa: Supply and Services Canada.

Canada, Treasury Board. 1976. *A Manager's Guide to Performance Measurement*. Ottawa: Treasury Board of Canada.

_____. 1981. *The Policy and Expenditure Management System*. Ottawa: Treasury Board of Canada.

Canes-Wrone, Brandice, Michael C. Herron, and Kenneth W. Shotts. 2001. 'Leadership and Pandering: A Theory of Executive Policymaking', *American Journal of Political Science* 45, 3: 532–50.

Cantor, Robin, Stuart Henry, and Steve Rayner. 1992. *Making Markets: An Interdisciplinary Perspective on Economic Exchange*. Westport, Conn.: Greenwood Press.

Cardozo, Andrew. 1996. 'Lion Taming: Downsizing the Opponents of Downsizing', in G. Swimmer, ed., *How Ottawa Spends 1996–97: Life Under the Knife*. Ottawa: Carleton University Press, 303–36.

Carley, Michael. 1980. *Rational Techniques in Policy Analysis*. London: Heinemann Educational Books.

Carlsson, Lars. 2000. 'Policy Networks as Collective Action', *Policy Studies Journal* 28, 3: 502–22.

Carver, John. 2001. 'A Theory of Governing the Public's Business: Redesigning the Jobs of Boards, Councils and Commissions', *Public Management Review* 3, 1: 53–72.

Castles, Francis G. 1982. 'The Impact of Parties on Public Expenditure', in Castles, ed., *The Impact of Parties: Politics and Policies in Democratic Capitalist States*. London: Sage.

_____. 1998. *Comparative Public Policy: Patterns of Post-War Transformation*. Cheltenham: Edward Elgar.

_____ and R.D. McKinlay. 1979. 'Does Politics Matter? An Analysis of the Public Welfare Commitment in Advanced Democratic States', *European Journal of Public Research* 7, 2: 169–86.

_____ and _____. 1997. 'Does Politics Matter? Increasing Complexity and Renewed Challenges', *European Journal of Political Research* 31: 102–7.

_____ and Vance Merrill. 1989. 'Towards a General Model of Public Policy Outcomes', *Journal of Theoretical Politics* 1, 2: 177–212.

Cater, Douglas. 1964. *Power in Washington: A Critical Look at Today's Struggle in the Nation's Capital*. New York: Random House.

Cavanagh, Michael, David Marsh, and Martin Smith. 1995. 'The Relationship Between Policy Networks at the Sectoral and Sub-Sectoral Levels: A Response to Jordan, Maloney and McLaughlin', *Public Administration* 73 (Winter): 627–9.

Cawson, Alan. 1978. 'Pluralism, Corporatism and the Role of the State', *Government and Opposition* 13, 2: 178–98.

_____. 1986. *Corporatism and Political Theory*. Oxford: Basil Blackwell.

Cerny, Philip G. 1996. 'International Finance and the Erosion of State Policy Capacity', in Gummett (1996: 83–104).

_____. 2001. 'From "Iron Triangles" to "Golden Pentangles"? Globalizing the Policy Process', *Global Governance* 7: 397–410.

Chadwick, Andrew. 2000. 'Studying Political Ideas: A Public Political Discourse Approach', *Political Studies* 48: 283–301.

Chandler, M.A. 1982. 'State Enterprise and Partisanship in Provincial Politics', *Canadian Journal of Political Science* 15: 711–40.

_____. 1983. 'The Politics of Public Enterprise', in Prichard (1983: 185–218).

_____ and W.M. Chandler. 1979. *Public Policy and Provincial Politics*. Toronto: McGraw-Hill Ryerson.

Chapman, Richard A. 1973. 'Commissions in Policy-Making', in Chapman, ed., *The Role of Commissions in Policy-Making*. London: George Allen and Unwin, 174–88.

Chelimsky, Eleanor. 1995. 'Where We Stand Today in the Practice of Evaluation: Some Reflections', *Knowledge and Policy* 8, 3: 8–20

Chenier, John A. 1985. 'Ministers of State to Assist: Weighing the Costs and the Benefits', *Canadian Public Administration* 28, 3: 397–412.

Christensen, Tom, and Per Laegreid, eds. 2001. *New Public Management: The Transformation of Ideas and Practice*. Aldershot: Ashgate.

Churchman, C. West. 1967. 'Wicked Problems', *Management Science* 14, 4: B141–B142.

Clark, William Roberts. 1998. 'Agents and Structures: Two Views of Preferences, Two Views of Institutions', *International Studies Quarterly* 42: 245–70.

Clarke, Michael. 1992. 'Implementation', in Harrop, ed., *Power and Policy in Liberal Democracies*. Cambridge: Cambridge University Press.

Clarke-Jones, M. 1987. *A Staple State: Canadian Industrial Resources in Cold War*. Toronto: University of Toronto Press.

Clemons, Randall S., and Mark K. McBeth. 2001. *Public Policy Praxis: Theory and Pragmatism, A Case Approach*. Upper Saddle River, NJ: Prentice-Hall.

Clokie, Hugh McDowall, and J. William Robinson. 1969. *Royal Commissions of Inquiry: The Significance of Investigations in British Politics*. New York: Octagon Books.

Coase, R.H. 1937. 'The Nature of the Firm', *Economica* 4, 13–16 (Nov.): 386–405.

_____. 1960. 'The Problem of Social Cost', *Journal of Law and Economics* 3: 1–44.

Cobb, Roger W., and Charles D. Elder. 1972. *Participation in American Politics: The Dynamics of Agenda-Building*. Boston: Allyn and Bacon.

_____, J.K. Ross, and M.H. Ross. 1976. 'Agenda Building as a Comparative Political Process', *American Political Science Review* 70, 1: 126–38.

_____ and Marc Howard Ross, eds. 1997a. *Cultural Strategies of Agenda Denial: Avoidance, Attack and Redefinition*. Lawrence: University Press of Kansas.

_____ and _____. 1997b. 'Denying Agenda Access: Strategic Considerations', in Cobb and Ross (1997a).

Coglianese, Cary. 1997. 'Assessing Consensus: The Promise and Performance of Negotiated Rulemaking', *Duke Law Journal* 46, 6: 1255–1349.

Cohen, G.A. 1978. *Karl Marx's Theory of History: A Defense*. Oxford: Clarendon Press.

Cohen, Michael D., James G. March, and Johan P. Olsen. 1972. 'A Garbage Can Model of Organizational Choice', *Administrative Science Quarterly* 17, 1: 1–25.

_____, _____, and _____. 1979. 'People, Problems, Solutions and the Ambiguity of Relevance', in March and Olsen (1979a).

Cohen, Wesley M., and Daniel A. Levinthal. 1990. 'Absorptive Capacity: A New Perspective on Learning and Innovation', *Administrative Science Quarterly* 35: 128–52.

Coleman, William D. 1988. *Business and Politics: A Study of Collective Action*. Montreal and Kingston: McGill-Queen's University Press.

_____. 1994. 'Policy Convergence in Banking: A Comparative Study', *Political Studies* 42: 274–92.

_____, Michael M. Atkinson, and Eric Montpetit. 1997. 'Against the Odds: Retrenchment in Agriculture in France and the United States', *World Politics* 49: 435–81.

_____ and Wyn P. Grant. 1998. 'Policy Convergence and Policy Feedback: Agricultural Finance Policies in a Globalizing Era', *European Journal of Political Research* 34: 225–47.

_____ and Anthony Perl. 1999. 'Internationalized Policy Environments and Policy Network Analysis', *Political Studies* 47: 691–709.

_____ and Grace Skogstad, eds. 1990. *Policy Communities and Public Policy in Canada: A Structural Approach*. Mississauga, Ont.: Copp Clark Pitman.

_____, _____, and Michael Atkinson. 1996. 'Paradigm Shifts and Policy Networks: Cumulative Change in Agriculture', *Journal of Public Policy* 16, 3: 273–302.

Connolly, William E. 1969. 'The Challenge to Pluralist Theory', in Connolly, ed., *The Bias of Pluralism*. New York: Atherton Press.

Cook, Brian, and B. Dan Wood. 1989. 'Principal-Agent Models of Political Control of Bureaucracy', *American Political Science Review* 83: 965–78.

Cook, F.L., et al. 1983. 'Media and Agenda Setting: Effects on the Public, Interest Group Leaders, Policy Makers, and Policy', *Public Opinion Quarterly* 47, 1: 16–35.

Cook, Thomas D. 1985. 'Postpositivist Critical Multiplism', in Shotland and Mark (1985).

Cordes, Joseph J. 2002. 'Corrective Taxes, Charges and Tradable Permits', in Salamon (2002a: 255–81).

Cortell, Andrew P., and James W. Davis. 1996. 'How Do International Institutions Matter? The Domestic Impact of International Rules and Norms', *International Studies Quarterly* 40: 451–78.

_____ and Susan Peterson. 1999. 'Altered States: Explaining Domestic Institutional Change', *British Journal of Political Science* 29: 177–203.

_____ and _____. 2001. 'Limiting the Unintended Consequences of Institutional Change', *Comparative Political Studies* 34, 7: 768–99.

Cox, Robert W. 1987. *Production, Power and World Order: Social Forces in the Making of History*. New York: Columbia University Press.

Crenson, Matthew A. 1971. *The Un-Politics of Air Pollution: A Study of Non-Decision-making in the Cities*. Baltimore: Johns Hopkins University Press.

Cushman, Robert E. 1941. *The Independent Regulatory Commissions*. London: Oxford University Press.

Cutright, P. 1965. 'Political Structure, Economic Development, and National Security Programs', *American Journal of Sociology* 70, 5: 537–50.

Dahl, Robert A. 1956. *A Preface to Democratic Theory*. Chicago: University of Chicago Press.

_____. 1961. *Who Governs?: Democracy and Power in an American City*. New Haven: Yale University Press.

_____. 1967. *Pluralist Democracy in the United States: Conflict and Consent*. Chicago: Rand McNally.

_____ and Charles E. Lindblom. 1953. *Politics, Economics and Welfare: Planning and Politico-economic Systems Resolved into Basic Social Processes*. New York: Harper and Row.

Daneke, Gregory A. 1992. 'Back to the Future: Misplaced Elements of Political Inquiry and the Advanced Systems Agenda', in William N. Dunn and Rita Mae Kelly, eds, *Advances in Policy Studies Since 1950*. New Brunswick, NJ: Transaction Press, 267–90.

Daniels, Mark R. 1997. *Terminating Public Programs: An American Political Paradox*. Armonk, NJ: M.E. Sharpe.

Danziger, Marie. 1995. 'Policy Analysis Postmodernized: Some Political and Pedagogical Ramifications', *Policy Studies Journal* 23, 3: 435–50.

Daugbjerg, Carsten. 1997. 'Policy Networks and Agricultural Policy Reforms: Explaining Deregulation in Sweden and Re-regulation in the European Community', *Governance* 10, 2: 123–42.

_____ and David Marsh. 1998. 'Explaining Policy Outcomes: Integrating the Policy Network Approach with Macro-Level and Micro-Level Analysis', in Marsh, ed., *Comparing Policy Networks*. Buckingham: Open University Press, 52–71.

David, Paul A. 1985. 'Clio and the Economics of QWERTY', *American Economic Review* 75, 2: 332–7.

David, Wilfred L. 1985. *The IMF Policy Paradigm: The Macroeconomics of Stabilization, Structural Adjustment, and Economic Development*. New York: Praeger.

Davies, I. 1999. 'Evaluation and Performance Management in Government', *Evaluation* 8, 2: 150–9.

Dearing, James W., and Everett M. Rogers. 1996. *Agenda-Setting*. Thousand Oaks, Calif.: Sage.

Debnam, Geoffrey. 1975. 'Nondecisions and Power: The Two Faces of Bachrach and Baratz', *American Political Science Review* 69, 3: 889–900.

de Bruijn, Johan A., and Ernst F. ten Heuvelhof. 1991. 'Policy Instruments for Steering Autopoietic Actors', in Roeland In T'Veld et al., eds, *Autopoiesis and Configuration Theory: New Approaches to Societal Steering*. Dordrecht: Kluwer, 161–70.

_____ and _____. 1995. 'Policy Networks and Governance', in David L. Weimer, ed., *Institutional Design*. Boston: Kluwer Academic Publishers, 161–79.

_____ and _____. 1997. 'Instruments for Network Management', in W.J.M. Kickert, E.-H. Klijn, and J.F.M. Koppenjan, eds, *Managing Complex Networks: Strategies for the Public Sector*. London: Sage, 119–36.

_____ and _____. 2000. *Networks and Decision-Making*. Utrecht: Lemma Publishers.

deHaven-Smith, Lance, and Carl E. Van Horn. 1984. 'Subgovernment Conflict in Public Policy', *Policy Studies Journal* 12, 4: 627–42.

DeHoog, Ruth Hoogland, and Lester M. Salamon. 2002. 'Purchase-of-Service Contracting', in Salamon (2002a: 319–39).

de la Mothe, John. 1996. 'One Small Step in an Uncertain Direction: The Science and

Technology Review and Public Administration in Canada', *Canadian Public Administration* 39, 3: 403–17.

de la Porte, Caroline, Phillipe Pochet, and Graham Room. 2001. 'Social Benchmarking, Policy Making and New Governance in the EU', *Journal of European Social Policy* 11, 1: 291–307.

DeLeon, Peter. 1978. 'A Theory of Policy Termination', in J.V. May and A.B. Wildavsky, eds, *The Policy Cycle*. Beverly Hills, Calif.: Sage, 279–300.

_____. 1983. 'Policy Evaluation and Program Termination', *Policy Studies Review* 2, 4: 631–47.

_____. 1986. 'Trends in Policy Sciences Research: Determinants and Developments', *European Journal of Political Research* 14, 1/2: 3–22.

_____. 1988. *Advice and Consent: The Development of the Policy Sciences*. New York: Russell Sage Foundation.

_____. 1992. 'Policy Formulation: Where Ignorant Armies Clash By Night', *Policy Studies Review* 11, 3/4: 389–405.

_____. 1994. 'Reinventing the Policy Sciences: Three Steps Back to the Future', *Policy Sciences* 27, 1: 77–95.

_____. 1997. 'Afterward: The Once and Future State of Policy Termination', *International Journal of Public Administration* 20: 33–46.

_____. 1999a. 'The Missing Link Revisited: Contemporary Implementation Research', *Policy Studies Review* 16, 3/4: 311–38.

_____. 1999b. 'The Stages Approach to the Policy Process: What Has It Done? Where Is It Going?', in Sabatier (1999a: 19–34).

_____ and Katie Kaufmanis. 2001. 'Public Policy Theory: Will It Play in Peoria?', *Policy Currents* 10, 4: 9–13.

Demaret, Paul. 1997. 'The Reciprocal Influence of Multilateral and Regional Trade Rules: A Framework of Analysis', in Demaret, J.-F. Bellis, and G.G. Jimenez, eds, *Regional and Multilateralism after the Uruguay Round: Convergence, Divergence and Interaction*. Liège: Institute d'Études Juridiques Européennes de Université Liège, 805–38.

Dery, David. 1984. *Agenda-Setting and Problem Definition*. Lawrence: University Press of Kansas.

_____. 1999. 'Policy by the Way: When Policy is Incidental to Making Other Policies', *Journal of Public Policy* 18, 2: 163–76.

de Smith, S.A. 1973. *Judicial Review of Administrative Action*. London: Stevens and Son.

Dessler, David. 1999. 'Constructivism within a Positivist Social Science', *Review of International Studies* 25: 123–37.

Desveaux, James A., Evert Lindquist, and Glen Taner. 1994. 'Organizing for Innovation in Public Bureaucracy: AIDS, Energy and Environment Policy in Canada', *Canadian Journal of Political Science* 27, 3: 493–528.

Devas, N., S. Delay, and M. Hubbard. 2001. 'Revenue Authorities: Are They the Right Vehicle for Improved Tax Administration?', *Public Administration and Development* 21, 3: 211–22.

Dion, Leon. 1973. 'The Politics of Consultation', *Government and Opposition* 8, 3: 332–53.

Dobell, Rodney, and David Zussman. 1981. 'An Evaluation System for Government: If Politics is Theatre, then Evaluation is (mostly) Art', *Canadian Public Administration* 24, 3: 404–27.

Dobuzinskis, Laurent. 1992. 'Modernist and Postmodernist Metaphors of the Policy Process: Control and Stability vs Chaos and Reflexive Understanding', *Policy Sciences* 25: 355–80.

_____. 1996. 'Trends and Fashions in the Marketplace of Ideas', in Dobuzinskis, M.

Howlett, and D. Laycock, eds, *Policy Studies in Canada: The State of the Art*. Toronto: University of Toronto Press, 91–124.

_____. 2000. 'Global Discord: The Confusing Discourse of Think Tanks', in T. Cohn, S. McBride, and J. Wiseman, eds, *Power in the Global Era*. London: Macmillan.

Dodge, Martin, and Christopher Hood. 2002. 'Pavlovian Policy Responses to Media Feeding Frenzies? Dangerous Drugs Regulation in Comparative Perspective', *Journal of Contingencies and Crisis Management* 10, 1: 1–13.

Doern, G. Bruce. 1967. 'The Role of Royal Commissions in the General Policy Process and in Federal-Provincial Relations', *Canadian Public Administration* 10, 4: 417–33.

_____. 1971. 'The Role of Central Advisory Councils: The Science Council of Canada', in Doern and Aucoin (1971: 246–66).

_____. 1981. *The Nature of Scientific and Technological Controversy in Federal Policy Formation*. Ottawa: Science Council of Canada.

_____. 1998. 'The Interplay Among Regimes: Mapping Regulatory Institutions in the United Kingdom, the United States, and Canada', in Doern and Wilks (1998: 29–50).

_____ and Peter Aucoin, eds. 1971. *The Structures of Policy-Making in Canada*. Toronto: Macmillan.

_____ et al. 1999. 'Canadian Regulatory Institutions: Converging and Colliding Regimes', in Doern, M.M. Hill, M.J. Prince, and R.J. Schultz, eds, *Changing the Rules: Canadian Regulatory Regimes and Institutions*. Toronto: University of Toronto Press, 3–26.

_____, L. Pal, and B.W. Tomlin, eds. 1996a. *Border Crossings: The Internationalization of Canadian Public Policy*. Toronto: Oxford University Press.

_____, _____, and _____. 1996b. 'The Internationalization of Canadian Public Policy', in Doern, Pal, and Tomlin (1996a: 1–26).

_____ and Richard W. Phidd. 1992. *Canadian Public Policy: Ideas, Structure, Process*, 2nd edn. Toronto: Nelson Canada.

_____ and Ted Reed. 2001. 'Science and Scientists in Regulatory Governance: A Mezzo-Level Framework for Analysis', *Science and Public Policy* 28, 3: 195–204.

_____ and S. Wilks, eds. 1998. *Changing Regulatory Institutions in Britain and North America*. Toronto: University of Toronto Press.

_____ and V.S. Wilson, eds. 1974a. *Issues in Canadian Public Policy*. Toronto: Macmillan.

_____ and _____. 1974b. 'Conclusions and Observations', in Doern and Wilson (1974).

d'Ombrain, N. 1997. 'Public Inquiries in Canada', *Canadian Public Administration* 40, 1: 86–107.

Donahue, John D. 1989. *The Privatization Decision: Public Ends, Private Means*. New York: Basic Books.

_____ and Joseph S. Nye Jr, eds. 2001. *Governance and Bigger, Better Markets*. Washington: Brookings Institution Press.

Dosi, G., et al., eds. 1988. *Technical Change and Economic Theory*. London: Pinter.

Dowding, Keith. 1994. 'The Compatibility of Behaviouralism, Rational Choice and "New Institutionalism"', *Journal of Theoretical Politics* 6, 1: 105–17.

Downs, Anthony. 1957. *An Economic Theory of Democracy*. New York: Harper.

_____. 1967. *Inside Bureaucracy*. New York: Harper and Row.

_____. 1972. 'Up and Down with Ecology—the "Issue-Attention Cycle"', *The Public Interest* 28: 38–50.

Drezner, Daniel W. 2000. 'Ideas, Bureaucratic Politics, and the Crafting of Foreign Policy', *American Journal of Political Science* 44, 4: 733–49.

Dror, Yehezkel. 1964. 'Muddling Through—"Science" or Inertia', *Public Administration Review* 24, 3: 154–7.

_____. 1968. *Public Policymaking Re-examined*. San Francisco: Chandler.

_____. 1969. 'The Prediction of Political Feasibility', *Futures* (June): 282–8.

Druckman, James N. 2001. 'On the Limits of Framing Effects; Who Can Frame?', *Journal of Politics* 63, 4: 1041–66.

Dryzek, John S. 1992. 'How Far Is It From Virginia and Rochester to Frankfurt? Public Choice as Global Theory', *British Journal of Political Science* 22, 4: 397–418.

_____ and Brian Ripley. 1988. 'The Ambitions of Policy Design', *Policy Studies Review* 7, 4: 705–19.

Duchacek, Ivo D. 1970. *Comparative Federalism: The Territorial Dimension of Politics*. New York: Holt, Rinehart and Winston.

Dudley, Geoffrey, Wayne Parsons, and Claudio M. Radaelli. 2000. 'Symposium: Theories of the Policy Process', *Journal of European Public Policy* 7, 1: 122–40.

_____ and Jeremy Richardson. 1998. 'Arenas without Rules and the Policy Change Process: Outsider Groups and British Roads Policy', *Political Studies* 46: 727–47.

_____ and _____. 1999. 'Competing Advocacy Coalitions and the Process of "Frame Reflection": A Longitudinal Analysis of EU Steel Policy', *Journal of European Public Policy* 6, 2: 225–48.

Dunleavy, Patrick. 1986. 'Explaining the Privatization Boom: Public Choice versus Radical Approaches', *Public Administration* 64, 1: 13–34.

_____ and Christopher Hood. 1994. 'From Old Public Administration to New Public Management', *Public Money and Management* 14, 3: 9–16.

Dunn, William N. 1988. 'Methods of the Second Type: Coping with the Wilderness of Conventional Policy Analysis', *Policy Studies Review* 7, 4: 720–37.

Duquette, Michel. 1999. *Building New Democracies: Economic and Social Reform in Brazil, Chile and Mexico*. Toronto: University of Toronto Press.

Durr, Robert H. 1993. 'What Moves Policy Sentiment?', *American Political Science Review* 87, 1: 158–72.

Durrant, Robert F., and Paul F. Diehl. 1989. 'Agendas, Alternatives and Public Policy: Lessons from the U.S. Foreign Policy Agenda', *Journal of Public Policy* 9, 2: 179–205.

Dwivedi, O.P., ed. 1982. *Administrative State in Canada: Essays in Honour of J.E. Hodgetts*. Toronto: University of Toronto Press.

Dye, Thomas R. 1972. *Understanding Public Policy*. Englewood Cliffs, NJ: Prentice-Hall.

_____. 2001. *Top-Down Policymaking*. New York: Chatham House.

Dyerson, Romano, and Frank Mueller. 1993. 'Intervention by Outsiders: A Strategic Perspective on Government Industrial Policy', *Journal of Public Policy* 13, 1: 69–88.

Dyson, Kenneth H.F. 1980. *The State Tradition in Western Europe: A Study of an Idea and Institution*. Oxford: Martin Robertson.

Economic Council of Canada. 1979. *Responsible Regulation: An Interim Report*. Ottawa: Supply and Services Canada.

Edelman, Murray. 1964. *The Symbolic Uses of Politics*. Chicago: University of Chicago Press.

_____. 1988. *Constructing the Political Spectacle*. Chicago: University of Chicago Press.

Edley, Christopher F., Jr. 1990. *Administrative Law: Rethinking Judicial Control of Bureaucracy*. New Haven: Yale University Press.

Edwards, George C., and Ira Sharkansky. 1978. *The Policy Predicament: Making and Implementing Public Policy*. San Francisco: Freeman.

Edwards, Ward. 1954. 'The Theory of Decision Making', *Psychological Bulletin* 51, 4: 380–417.

Einhorn, Hillel J. 1982. 'Learning from Experience and Suboptimal Rules in Decision Making', in D. Kahneman, P. Slovic, and A. Tversky, eds, *Judgement Under Uncertainty: Heuristics and Biases*. Cambridge: Cambridge University Press, 268–83.

_____ and Robin M. Hogarth. 1986. 'Decision Making Under Ambiguity', *Journal of Business* 59, 4, part 2: S225–S251.

Eisner, Marc Allen. 1993. *Regulatory Politics in Transition*. Baltimore: Johns Hopkins University Press.

_____. 1994a. 'Discovering Patterns in Regulatory History: Continuity, Change and Regulatory Regimes', *Journal of Policy History* 6, 2: 157–87.

_____. 1994b. 'Economic Regulatory Policies: Regulation and Deregulation in Historical Context', in D.H. Rosenbloom and R.D. Schwartz, eds, *Handbook of Regulation and Administrative Law*. New York: Marcel Dekker, 91–116.

Eldredge, Niles, and Stephen Jay Gould. 1972. 'Punctuated Equilibria: An Alternative to Phyletic Gradualism', in T.J.M. Schopf, ed., *Paleobiology*. San Francisco: Freeman, Cooper, 82–115.

Elkin, Stephen L. 1986. 'Regulation and Regime: A Comparative Analysis', *Journal of Public Policy* 6, 1: 49–72.

Ellig, Jerry, and Don Lavoie. 1995. 'The Principle-Agent Relationship in Organizations', in P. Foss, ed., *Economic Approaches to Organizations and Institutions: An Introduction*. Aldershot: Dartmouth.

Elliott, Chris, and Rodolphe Schlaepfer. 2001. 'The Advocacy Coalition Framework: Application to the Policy Process for the Development of Forest Certification in Sweden', *Journal of European Public Policy* 8, 4: 642–61.

Elliott, Dominic, and Martina McGuinness. 2001. 'Public Inquiry: Panacea or Placebo?', *Journal of Contingencies and Crisis Management* 10, 1: 14–25.

Elliott, Euel, and Andrew I.E. Ewoh. 2000. 'The Evolution of an Issue: The Rise and Decline of Affirmative Action', *Policy Studies Review* 17, 2/3: 212–37.

Elmore, Richard F. 1978. 'Organizational Models of Social Program Implementation', *Public Policy* 26, 2: 185–228.

_____. 1987. 'Instruments and Strategy in Public Policy', *Policy Studies Review* 7, 1: 74–186.

Elster, Jon, ed. 1986. *Rational Choice*. Cambridge: Cambridge University Press.

_____. 1991. 'The Possibility of Rational Politics', in D, Held, ed., *Political Theory Today*. Oxford: Polity.

Englehart, Kenneth G., and Michael J. Trebilcock. 1981. *Public Participation in the Regulatory Process: The Issue of Funding*. Ottawa: Economic Council of Canada.

Epstein, Paul J. 1997. 'Beyond Policy Community: French Agriculture and the GATT', *Journal of European Public Policy* 4, 3: 355–72.

Erbring, Lutz, and Edie N. Goldenberg. 1980. 'Front Page News and Real World Cues: A New Look at Agenda-Setting by the Media', *American Journal of Political Science* 24, 1: 16–49.

Erikson, Robert S., Norman R. Luttbeg, and Kent L. Tedin, eds. 1980. *American Public Opinion*. New York: John Wiley and Sons.

_____, Gerald C. Wright Jr, and John P. McIver. 1989. 'Political Parties, Public Opinion and State Policy in the United States', *American Political Science Review* 83, 3: 729–39.

Esping-Andersen, Gosta. 1981. 'From Welfare State to Democratic Socialism: The Politics of Economic Democracy in Denmark and Sweden', in M. Zeitlin, ed., *Political Power and Social Theory*, 111–40.

_____. 1985. *Politics Against Markets: The Social Democratic Road to Power*. Princeton, NJ: Princeton University Press.

_____. 1990. *The Three Worlds of Welfare Capitalism*. Cambridge: Polity.

_____ and Walter Korpi. 1984. 'Social Policy as Class Politics in Post-War Capitalism: Scandinavia, Austria, and Germany', in J.H. Goldthorpe, ed., *Order and Conflict in Contemporary Capitalism*. Oxford: Clarendon Press.

Etheredge, Lloyd S. 1981. 'Government Learning: An Overview', in S.L. Long, ed., *The Handbook of Political Behavior*. New York: Plenum.

_____ and James Short. 1983. 'Thinking About Government Learning', *Journal of Management Studies* 20, 1: 41–58.

Etzioni, Amitai. 1967. 'Mixed-Scanning: A "Third" Approach to Decision-Making', *Public Administration Review* 27, 5: 385–92.

Evans, Mark, and Jonathan Davies. 1999. 'Understanding Policy Transfer: A Multi-Level, Multi-Disciplinary Perspective', *Public Administration* 77, 2: 361–85.

Evans, Peter. 1992. 'State as Problem and Solution: Predation, Embedded Autonomy, and Structural Change', in Stephen Haggard and Robert R. Kaufman, eds, *The Politics of Economic Adjustment: International Constraints, Distributive Conflicts, and the State*. Princeton, NJ: Princeton University Press, 139–81.

_____. 1995. *Embedded Autonomy: States and Industrial Transformation*. Princeton, NJ: Princeton University Press.

_____, D. Rueschemeyer, and T. Skocpol, eds. 1985. *Bringing the State Back In*. Cambridge: Cambridge University Press.

Falk, Richard. 1997. 'State of Siege: Will Globalization Win Out?', *International Affairs* 73, 1: 123–36.

Fayol, Henri. 1949. *General and Industrial Management*. London: Pitman.

Feick, Jurgen. 1992. 'Comparing Comparative Policy Studies—A Path Towards Integration?', *Journal of Public Policy* 12, 3: 257–86.

Feldman, Ron J. 2002. 'Government Insurance', in Salamon (2002a: 186–216).

Fernandes, Ronald, and Herbert A. Simon. 1999. 'A Study of How Individuals Solve Complex and Ill-Structured Problems', *Policy Sciences* 32: 225–45.

Finkle, Peter, et al. 1994. *Federal Government Relations with Interest Groups: A Reconsideration*. Ottawa: Privy Council Office.

Finnemore, Martha, and Kathryn Sikkink. 1998. 'International Norm Dynamics and Political Change', *International Organization* 52, 4: 887–917.

Fischer, Frank. 1993. 'Policy Discourses and the Politics of Washington Think Tanks', in Fischer and Forester (1993: 21–42).

_____ and John Forester, eds. 1987. *Confronting Values in Policy Analysis: The Politics of Criteria*. Beverly Hills, Calif.: Sage.

_____ and _____, eds. 1993. *The Argumentative Turn in Policy Analysis and Planning*. Durham, NC: Duke University Press.

Fischoff, Baruch. 1977. 'Cost Benefit Analysis and the Art of Motorcycle Maintenance', *Policy Sciences* 8, 2: 177–202.

Fishman, Ethan. 1991. 'Political Philosophy and the Policy Studies Organization', *PS: Political Science and Politics* 24: 720–3.

Flathman, Richard E. 1966. *The Public Interest: An Essay Concerning the Normative Discourse of Politics*. New York: Wiley.

Flemming, Roy B., B. Dan Wood, and John Bohte. 1999. 'Attention to Issues in a System of Separated Powers: The Macrodynamics of American Policy Agendas', *Journal of Politics* 61, 1: 76–108.

Foley, Duncan K. 1978. 'State Expenditure from a Marxist Perspective', *Journal of Public Economics* 9, 2: 221–38.

Foot, David K. 1979. 'Political Cycles, Economic Cycles and the Trend in Public Employment in Canada', in Meyer W. Bucovetsky, ed., *Studies in Public Employment and Compensation in Canada*. Toronto: Butterworths for Institute for Research on Public Policy, 65–80.

Forester, John. 1984. 'Bounded Rationality and the Politics of Muddling Through', *Public Administration Review* 44, 1: 23–31.

_____. 1989. *Planning in the Face of Power*. Berkeley: University of California Press.

Formaini, Robert. 1990. *The Myth of Scientific Public Policy*. New Brunswick, NJ: Transaction.

Foucault, Michel. 1972. 'The Discourse on Language', in Foucault, ed., *The Archaeology of Knowledge*. New York: Pantheon.

Fowler, Edmund P., and David Siegel, eds. 2002. *Urban Policy Issues*. Toronto: Oxford University Press.

Fox, Charles J. 1990. 'Implementation Research: Why and How to Transcend Positivist Methodology', in Palumbo and Calista (1990).

Francis, John G. 1993. *The Politics of Regulation: A Comparative Perspective*. Oxford: Blackwell.

Franke, George R. 2001. 'Applications of Meta-Analysis for Marketing and Public Policy: A Review', *Journal of Public Policy and Marketing* 20, 2: 186–200.

Freeman, Gary P. 1985. 'National Styles and Policy Sectors: Explaining Structured Variation', *Journal of Public Policy* 5, 4: 467–96.

Freeman, John Leiper. 1955. *The Political Process: Executive Bureau-Legislative Committee Relations*. New York: Random House.

_____ and Judith Parris Stevens. 1987. 'A Theoretical and Conceptual Reexamination of Subsystem Politics', *Public Policy and Administration* 2, 1: 9–24.

French, John R.P., and Bertram Raven. 1959. 'The Bases of Social Power', in D. Cartwright, ed., *Studies in Social Power*. Ann Arbor: University of Michigan Press, 150–67.

Frey, Bruno S. 1978. 'Politico-Economic Models and Cycles', *Journal of Public Economics* 9: 203–20.

Frey, Frederick W. 1971. 'Comment: On Issues and Nonissues in the Study of Power', *American Political Science Review* 65: 1081–1101.

Friedman, Lee S. 2002. *The Microeconomics of Public Policy Analysis*. Princeton, NJ: Princeton University Press.

Gall, Gerald L. 1983. *The Canadian Legal System*, 2nd edn. Toronto: Carswell.

Garson, G. David. 1986. 'From Policy Science to Policy Analysis: A Quarter Century of Progress', in W.N. Dunn, ed., *Policy Analysis: Perspectives, Concepts, and Methods*. Greenwich, Conn.: JAI Press, 3–22.

Gaus, John M. 1931. 'Notes on Administration', *American Political Science Review* 25, 1: 123–34.

Gawthrop, Louis C. 1971. *Administrative Politics and Social Change*. New York: St Martin's Press.

Gehring, Thomas, and Sebastian Oberthur. 2000. 'Exploring Regime Interaction: A Framework of Analysis', paper presented to the Final Conference of the EU-financed Concerted Action Programme on the Effectiveness of International Environmental Agreements and EU Legislation—Fridtjof Nansen Institute, Barcelona, 9–11 Nov. 2000.

Gent, Chariti E. 2000. 'Needle Exchange Policy Adoption in American Cities: *Why Not?*', *Policy Sciences* 33: 125–53.

George, Alexander L. 1969. 'The "Operational Code": A Neglected Approach to the Study of Political Leaders and Decision-Making', *International Studies Quarterly* 13: 190–222.

_____. 1980. *Presidential Decisionmaking in Foreign Policy: The Effective Use of Information and Advice*. Boulder, Colo.: Westview Press.

Gersick, Connie J.G. 1991. 'Revolutionary Change Theories: A Multilevel Exploration of the Punctuated Equilibrium Paradigm', *Academy of Management Review* 16, 1: 10–36.

Gerston, Larry N. 1997. *Public Policy Making: Process and Principles*. Armonk, NY: M.E. Sharpe.

Gerth, Hans, and C. Wright Mills, eds. 1958. *From Max Weber: Essays in Sociology*. New York: Oxford University Press.

Geva-May, Iris. 2001. 'When the Motto is "Till Death Do Us Part": The Conceptualization and the Craft of Termination in the Public Policy Cycle', *International Journal of Public Administration* 24, 3: 263–88.

_____ and Aaron Wildavsky. 1997. *An Operational Approach to Policy Analysis: The Craft-Prescriptions for Better Analysis.* Boston: Kluwer.

Gibson, Robert B., ed. 1999. *Voluntary Initiatives: The New Politics of Corporate Greening.* Peterborough, Ont.: Broadview Press.

Gierke, Otto von. 1958a. *Natural Law and the Theory of Society, 1500–1800.* Cambridge: Cambridge University Press.

_____. 1958b. *Political Theories of the Middle Age.* Cambridge: Cambridge University Press.

Gilbert, Neil, and Barbara Gilbert. 1989. *The Enabling State: Modern Welfare Capitalism in America.* New York: Oxford University Press.

Gill, Norman N. 1940. 'Permanent Advisory Committees in the Federal Government', *Journal of Politics* 2: 411–25.

Gillroy, John Martin, and Maurice Wade, eds. 1992. *The Moral Dimensions of Public Policy Choice: Beyond the Market Paradigm.* Pittsburgh: University of Pittsburgh Press.

Gilmore, Thomas N., and James Krantz. 1991. 'Innovation in the Public Sector: Dilemmas in the Use of Ad Hoc Processes', *Journal of Policy Analysis and Management* 10, 3: 455–68.

Giuliani, Mark. 1999. '"Soft" Institutions for Hard Problems: Instituting Air Pollution Policies in Three Italian Regions', in W. Grant, A. Perl, and P. Knoepfel, eds, *The Politics of Improving Urban Air Quality.* Cheltenham: Edward Elgar, 31–51.

Glicken, Jessica. 2000. 'Getting Stakeholder Participation "Right": A Discussion of Participatory Processes and Possible Pitfalls', *Environmental Science and Policy* 3: 305–10.

Goffman, Erving. 1974. *Frame Analysis: An Essay on the Organization of Experience.* Cambridge, Mass.: Harvard University Press.

Goggin, Malcolm L., et al. 1990. *Implementation Theory and Practice: Toward a Third Generation.* Glenview, Ill.: Scott, Foresman/Little, Brown.

Goldfinch, Shaun. 2000. *Remaking New Zealand and Australia Economic Policy: Ideas, Institutions and Policy Communities.* Washington: Georgetown University Press.

Goldstein, Judith, and Robert O. Keohane, eds. 1993a. *Ideas and Foreign Policy: Beliefs, Institutions and Political Change.* Ithaca, NY: Cornell University Press.

_____ and _____. 1993b. 'Ideas and Foreign Policy: An Analytical Framework', in Goldstein and Keohane (1993: 3–30).

Goodnow, Frank J. 1900. *Politics and Administration: A Study in Government.* New York: Russell and Russell.

Gordon, I., J. Lewis, and K. Young. 1977. 'Perspectives on Policy Analysis', *Public Administration Bulletin* 25: 26–30.

Gorges, Michael J. 2001. 'The New Institutionalism and the Study of the European Union: The Case of the Social Dialogue', *West European Politics* 24, 4: 152–68.

Gormley, William T. 1989. *Taming the Bureaucracy: Muscles, Prayers and Other Strategies.* Princeton, NJ: Princeton University Press.

_____ and B. Guy Peters. 1992. 'National Styles of Regulation: Child Care in Three Countries', *Policy Sciences* 25: 381–99.

Gortner, Harold, Julianne Mahler, and Jeanne Bell Nicholson. 1987. *Organization Theory: A Public Perspective.* Chicago: Dorsey Press.

Gough, Ian. 1975. 'State Expenditure in Advanced Capitalism', *New Left Review* 92: 53–92.

Gould, Stephen Jay. 2002. *The Structure of Evolutionary Theory.* Cambridge, Mass.: Harvard University Press.

_____ and Niles Eldredge. 1977. 'Punctuated Equilibria: The Tempo and Mode of Evolution Reconsidered', *Paleobiology* 3: 115–51.

Graber, Doris Appel. 1989. *Mass Media and American Politics.* Washington: Congressional Quarterly Press.

Grabosky, Peter N. 1995. 'Using Non-Governmental Resources to Foster Regulatory Compliance', *Governance* 8, 4: 527–50.

Grande, E. 1996. 'The State and Interest Groups in a Framework of Multi-Level Decision-Making: The Case of the European Union', *Journal of European Public Policy* 3: 313–38.

Grant, Wyn, and Anne MacNamara. 1995. 'When Policy Communities Intersect: The Cases of Agriculture and Banking', *Political Studies* 43: 509–15.

Grantham, Andrew. 2001. 'How Networks Explain Unintended Policy Implementation Outcomes: The Case of UK Rail Privatization', *Public Administration* 79, 4: 851–70.

Gray, Pat, and Paul t'Hart. 1998. *Public Policy Disasters in Western Europe*. London: Routledge.

Green, Donald, and Ian Shapiro. 1994. *Pathologies of Rational Choice Theory*. New Haven: Yale University Press.

Greenberg, George D., et al. 1977. 'Developing Public Policy Theory: Perspectives from Empirical Research', *American Political Science Review* 71: 1532–43.

Gregory, Robin, Tim McDaniels, and Daryl Fields. 2001. 'Decision Aiding, Not Dispute Resolution: Creating Insights Through Structured Environmental Decisions', *Journal of Policy Analysis and Management* 20, 3: 415–32.

Griggs, Steven. 1999. 'Restructuring Health Policy Networks: A French Policy Style?', *West European Politics* 22, 4: 185–204.

Grima, A.P. 1985. 'Participatory Rites: Integrating Public Involvement in Environmental Impact Assessment', in J.B.R. Whitney and V.W. Maclaren, eds, *Environmental Impact Assessment: The Canadian Experience*. Toronto: University of Toronto Institute for Environmental Studies, 33–51.

Grimshaw, Damian, Steven Vincent, and Hugh Willmott. 2001. 'New Control Modes and Emergent Organizational Forms: Private-Public Contracting in Public Administration', *Administrative Theory and Practice* 23, 3: 407–30.

Guess, George M., and Paul G. Farnham. 2000. *Cases in Public Policy Analysis*. Washington: Georgetown University Press.

Gulick, Luther H. 1937. 'Notes on the Theory of Organization', in Gulick and Urwick (1937).

_____ and Lyndal Urwick, eds. 1937. *Papers on the Science of Administration*. New York: Institute of Public Administration.

_____ and _____ eds. 1947. *Papers on the Science of Administration*. New York: A.M. Kelley.

Gummett, P., ed. 1996. *Globalization and Public Policy*. Cheltenham: Edward Elgar.

Gunningham, Neil, Peter Grabosky, and Darren Sinclair. 1998. *Smart Regulation: Designing Environmental Policy*. Oxford: Clarendon Press.

_____ and Joseph Rees. 1997. 'Industry Self-Regulation: An Institutional Perspective', *Law and Policy* 19, 4: 363–414.

_____ and Darren Sinclair. 1999. 'Regulatory Pluralism: Designing Policy Mixes for Environmental Protection', *Law and Policy* 21, 1: 49–76.

_____ and Mike D. Young. 1997. 'Toward Optimal Environmental Policy: The Case of Biodiversity Conservation', *Ecology Law Quarterly* 24: 243–98.

Gustafsson, Gunnel, and J.J. Richardson. 1979. 'Concepts of Rationality and the Policy Process', *European Journal of Political Research* 7: 415–36.

Haas, Ernst B. 1958. *The Uniting of Europe: Political, Social and Economical Forces 1950–1957*. London: Stevens and Sons.

_____. 1975. 'Is there a Hole in the Whole? Knowledge, Technology, Interdependence, and the Construction of International Regimes', *International Organization* 29, 3: 827–76.

Haas, Mark L. 2001. 'Prospect Theory and the Cuban Missile Crisis', *International Studies Quarterly* 45: 241–70.

Haas, Peter M. 1992. 'Introduction: Epistemic Communities and International Policy Coordination', *International Organization* 46, 1: 1–36.

Haggard, Stephen, and Chung-In Moon. 1990. 'Institutions and Economic Policy: Theory and a Korean Case Study', *World Politics* 42, 2: 210–37.

_____ and Beth A. Simmons. 1987. 'Theories of International Regimes', *International Organization* 41, 3: 491–517.

Hahn, Robert W., and John A. Hird. 1991. 'The Costs and Benefits of Regulation: Review and Synthesis', *Yale Journal of Regulation* 8, 1: 233–78.

Haider, Donald. 1989. 'Grants as a Tool of Public Policy', in Salamon (1989a: 93–124).

Haider-Markel, Donald P., and Mark R. Joslyn. 2001. 'Gun Policy, Opinion, Tragedy and Blame Attribution: The Conditional Influence of Issue Frames', *Journal of Politics* 63, 2: 520–43.

Hajer, Maarten A. 1993. 'Discourse Coalitions and the Institutionalization of Practice: The Case of Acid Rain in Britain', in Fischer and Forester (1993: 43–76).

Hall, John A., and G. John Ikenberry. 1989. *The State*. Minneapolis: University of Minnesota Press.

Hall, Michael, and Keith Banting. 2000. 'The Nonprofit Sector in Canada: An Introduction', in Banting, ed., *The NonProfit Sector in Canada: Roles and Relationships*. Montreal and Kingston: McGill-Queen's University Press, 1–28.

Hall, Peter A. 1986. *Governing the Economy: The Politics of State Intervention in Britain and France*. Cambridge: Polity Press.

_____, ed. 1989. *The Political Power of Economic Ideas: Keynesianism Across Nations*. Princeton, NJ: Princeton University Press.

_____. 1990. 'Policy Paradigms, Experts, and the State: The Case of Macroeconomic Policy-Making in Britain', in Brooks and Gagnon (1990).

_____. 1992. 'The Change from Keynesianism to Monetarism: Institutional Analysis and British Economic Policy in the 1970s', in S. Steinmo et al., eds, *Structuring Politics: Historical Institutionalism in Comparative Analysis*. Cambridge: Cambridge University Press, 90–114.

_____. 1993. 'Policy Paradigms, Social Learning and the State: The Case of Economic Policy Making in Britain', *Comparative Politics* 25, 3: 275–96.

_____. 1997. 'The Role of Interests, Institutions and Ideas in the Comparative Political Economy of Industrialized Nations', in M.I. Lichbach and A.S. Zuckerman, eds, *Comparative Politics: Rationality, Culture and Structure*. Cambridge: Cambridge University Press, 174–207.

_____ and Rosemary C.R. Taylor. 1996. 'Political Science and the Three New Institutionalisms', *Political Studies* 44: 936–57.

Hall, Thad E., and Laurence J. O'Toole. 2000. 'Structures for Policy Implementation: An Analysis of National Legislation 1965–1966 and 1993–1994', *Administration and Society* 31, 6: 667–86.

Hamm, Keith E. 1983. 'Patterns of Influence Among Committees, Agencies, and Interest Groups', *Legislative Studies Quarterly* 8, 3: 379–426.

Hammond, Thomas H. 1986. 'Agenda Control, Organizational Structure, and Bureaucratic Politics', *American Journal of Political Science* 30, 2: 379–420.

_____ and Jack H. Knott. 1999. 'Political Institutions, Public Management, and Policy Choice', *Journal of Public Administration Research and Theory* 9, 1: 33–85.

_____ and _____. 2000. 'Public Management, Administrative Leadership and Policy Change', in J.L. Brudney, L.J. O'Toole, and H.G. Rainey, eds, *Advancing Public Management: New Developments in Theory, Methods and Practice*. Washington: Georgetown University Press, 49–74.

Hancock, M. Donald. 1983. 'Comparative Public Policy: An Assessment', in A.W. Finifter, ed., *Political Science: The State of the Discipline*. Washington: American Political Science Association, 283–308.

Hansen, Randal, and Desmond King. 2001. 'Eugenic Ideas, Political Interests, and Policy Variance: Immigration and Sterilization Policy in Britain and the U.S.', *World Politics* 53 (Jan.): 237–63.

Hansen, Susan B. 1983. 'Public Policy Analysis: Some Recent Developments and Current Problems', *Policy Studies Journal* 12: 14–42.

Hargrove, E.L. 1975. *The Missing Link: The Study of the Implementation of Social Policy*. Washington: Urban Institute.

Harris, Richard, and Sidney Milkis. 1989. *The Politics of Regulatory Change*. New York: Oxford University Press.

Harrison, Kathryn. 2001. 'Too Close to Home: Dioxin Contamination of Breast Milk and the Political Agenda', *Policy Sciences* 34: 35–62.

Harrow, Jenny. 2001. '"Capacity Building" as a Public Management Goal: Myth, Magic of the Main Chance', *Public Management Review* 3, 2: 209–30.

Harsanyi, John C. 1977. *Rational Behaviour and Bargaining Equilibrium in Games and Social Situations*. Cambridge: Cambridge University Press.

Hastak, Manoj, Michael B. Mazis, and Louis A. Morris. 2001. 'The Role of Consumer Surveys in Public Policy Decision Making', *Journal of Public Policy and Marketing* 20, 2: 170–85.

Haufler, Virginia. 2000. 'Private Sector International Regimes', in R.A. Higgott and G.R.D. Underhill, eds, *Andreas Bieler*. London: Routledge, 121–37.

_____. 2001. *A Public Role for the Private Sector: Industry Self-Regulation in a Global Economy*. Washington: Carnegie Endowment for International Peace.

Hawkesworth, Mary. 1992. 'Epistemology and Policy Analysis', in W. Dunn and R.M. Kelly, eds, *Advances in Policy Studies*. New Brunswick, NJ: Transaction Press, 291–329.

Hawkins, Keith. 1984. *Environment and Enforcement: Regulation and the Social Definition of Pollution*. Oxford: Clarendon Press.

_____ and John M. Thomas, eds. 1989a. *Making Regulatory Policy*. Pittsburgh: University of Pittsburgh Press.

_____ and _____. 1989b. 'Making Policy in Regulatory Bureaucracies', in Hawkins and Thomas (1989a: 3–30).

Hay, Colin, and Daniel Wincott. 1998. 'Structure, Agency and Historical Institutionalism', *Political Studies* 46: 951–7.

Haydu, Jeffrey. 1998. 'Making Use of the Past: Time Periods as Cases to Compare and as Sequences of Problem Solving', *American Journal of Sociology* 104, 2: 339–71.

Hayes, Michael T. 1978. 'The Semi-Sovereign Pressure Groups: A Critique of Current Theory and an Alternative Typology', *Journal of Politics* 40, 1: 134–61.

_____. 1992. *Incrementalism and Public Policy*. New York: Longmans.

_____. 2001. *The Limits of Policy Change: Incrementalism, Worldview and the Rule of Law*. Washington: Georgetown University Press.

Hays, Samuel P. 1959. *Conservation and the Gospel of Efficiency: The Progressive Conservation Movement 1890–1920*. Cambridge, Mass.: Harvard University Press.

_____. 1987. *Beauty, Health and Permanence: Environmental Politics in the United States, 1955–1985*. New York: Cambridge University Press.

Heclo, Hugh. 1974. *Modern Social Politics in Britain and Sweden: From Relief to Income Maintenance*. New Haven: Yale University Press.

_____. 1976. 'Conclusion: Policy Dynamics', in Rose (1976: 237–66).

_____. 1978. 'Issue Networks and the Executive Establishment', in A. King, ed., *The New American Political System*. Washington: American Enterprise Institute for Public Policy Research.

_____. 1994. 'Ideas, Interests and Institutions', in L.C. Dodd and C. Jillson, eds, *The Dynamics of American Politics: Approaches and Interpretations*. San Francisco: Westview, 366–92.

Heidenheimer, Arnold J., Hugh Heclo, and Carolyn Teich Adams, eds. 1975. *Compara-*

tive Public Policy: The Politics of Social Choice in Europe and America. New York: St Martin's Press.

Heikkila, Tanya. 1999. 'The Role of Science and Research in Policy Making: The Case of the San Pedro River Basin', paper presented at the annual meeting of the Western Political Science Association, Seattle.

Heinz, John P., et al. 1990. 'Inner Circles or Hollow Cores', *Journal of Politics* 52, 2: 356–90.

Held, David, and Anthony McGrew. 1993. 'Globalization and the Liberal Democratic State', *Government and Opposition* 28, 2: 261–85.

Hellstern, Gerd-Michael. 1986. 'Assessing Evaluation Research', in Kaufman et al. (1986: 279–312).

Hendrick, Rebecca M., and David Nachmias. 1992. 'The Policy Sciences: The Challenge of Complexity', *Policy Studies Review* 11, 3/4: 310–28.

Heritier, Adrienne. 1997. 'Policy-Making by Subterfuge: Interest Accommodation, Innovation and Substitute Democratic Legitimation in Europe—Perspectives from Distinctive Policy Areas', *Journal of European Public Policy* 4, 2: 171–89.

_____. 1999. 'Elements of Democratic Legitimation in Europe: An Alternative Perspective', *Journal of European Public Policy* 6, 2: 269–82.

Herman, Edward S., and Noam Chomsky. 1988. *Manufacturing Consent: The Political Economy of the Mass Media.* New York: Pantheon Books.

Hermann, Charles F. 1982. 'Instruments of Foreign Policy', in P. Callahan, L.P. Brady, and M.G. Hermann, eds, *Describing Foreign Policy Behaviour.* Beverly Hills, Calif.: Sage, 153–74.

Hernes, Gudmund. 1976. 'Structural Change in Social Processes', *American Journal of Sociology* 82, 3: 513–47.

Hesse, Joachim Jens. 1997. 'Rebuilding the State: Public Sector Reform in Central and Eastern Europe', in J.-E. Lane, ed., *Public Sector Reform: Rationale, Trends and Problems.* London: Sage, 114–45.

Hibbing, John R., and Elizabeth Theiss-Morse. 2002. *Stealth Democracy: Americans' Beliefs about How Government Should Work.* Cambridge: Cambridge University Press.

Hibbs, Douglas A., Jr. 1977. 'Political Parties and Macroeconomic Policy', *American Political Science Review* 71: 1467–87.

_____. 1978. 'On the Political Economy of Long-run Trends in Strike Activity', *British Journal of Political Science* 8, 2: 153–75.

_____. 1987. *The Political Economy of Industrial Democracies.* Cambridge, Mass.: Harvard University Press.

Hilgartner, Stephen, and Charles L. Bosk. 1981. 'The Rise and Fall of Social Problems: A Public Arenas Model', *American Journal of Sociology* 94, 1: 53–78.

Hill, Larry B., ed. 1992. *The State of Public Bureaucracy.* Armonk, NY: M.E. Sharpe.

Hill, Michael, ed. 1993. *The Policy Process: A Reader.* London: Harvester Wheatsheaf.

Hintze, Otto. 1975. *The Historical Essays of Otto Hintze.* New York: Oxford University Press.

Hirschman, Albert O. 1958. *The Strategy of Economic Development.* New Haven: Yale University Press.

Hirst, Paul, and Grahame Thompson. 1996. *Globalization in Question.* Oxford: Polity Press.

Hisschemoller, Matthijs, and Rob Hoppe. 1995. 'Coping with Intractable Controversies: The Case for Problem Structuring in Policy Design and Analysis', *Knowledge and Policy* 8, 4: 40–61.

Hjern, Benny. 1982. 'Implementation Research—The Link Gone Missing', *Journal of Public Policy* 2, 3: 301–8.

_____ and David O. Porter. 1993. 'Implementation Structures: A New Unit of Administrative Analysis', in Hill (1993).

Hoberg, George. 1996. 'Putting Ideas in Their Place: A Response to "Learning and Change in the British Columbia Forest Policy Sector"', *Canadian Journal of Political Science* 29, 1: 135–44.

_____. 1998. 'Distinguishing Learning from Other Sources of Policy Change: The Case of Forestry in the Pacific Northwest', paper presented to the annual meeting of the American Political Science Association, Boston.

_____ and E. Morawaski. 1997. 'Policy Change Through Sector Intersection: Forest and Aboriginal Policy in Clayoquot Sound', *Canadian Public Administration* 40, 3: 387–414.

Hobson, John, and M. Ramesh. 2002. 'Globalisation Makes of States What States Make of It: Between Agency and Structure in the State/Globalisation Debate', *New Political Economy* 7, 1: 5–22.

Hockin, Thomas A. 1977. 'Mass Legitimate Parties and Their Implications for Party Leaders', in Hockin, ed., *Apex of Power: The Prime Minister and Political Leadership in Canada*. Scarborough, Ont.: Prentice-Hall, 70–85.

Hodgetts, J.E. 1973. *The Canadian Public Service: A Physiology of Government, 1867–1970*. Toronto: University of Toronto Press.

Hoekman, Bernard, and Michel Kostecki. 1995. *The Political Economy of the World Trading System: From GATT to WTO*. Oxford: Oxford University Press.

Hofferbert, Richard I. 1974. *The Study of Public Policy*. Indianapolis: Bobbs-Merrill.

Hoffman, Andrew J. 1999. 'Institutional Evolution and Change: Environmentalism and the U.S. Chemical Industry', *Academy of Management Journal* 42, 4: 351–71.

Hogwood, Brian W. 1992. *Ups and Downs: Is There an Issue-Attention Cycle in Britain?* Glasgow: Strathclyde Papers in Government and Politics no. 89.

_____ and Lewis A. Gunn. 1984. *Policy Analysis for the Real World*. New York: Oxford University Press.

Hollingsworth, J. Rogers. 1998. 'New Perspectives on the Spatial Dimensions of Economic Coordination: Tensions Between Globalization and Social Systems of Production', *Review of International Political Economy* 5, 3: 482–507.

_____. 2000. 'Doing Institutional Analysis: Implications for the Study of Innovations', *Review of International Political Economy* 7, 4: 595–644.

Holzner, Burkart, and John H. Marx. 1979. *Knowledge Application: The Knowledge System in Society*. Wellesley, Mass.: Allyn and Bacon.

Hood, Christopher. 1983. 'Using Bureaucracy Sparingly', *Public Administration* 61, 2: 197–208.

_____. 1986a. *The Tools of Government*. Chatham, NJ: Chatham House.

_____. 1986b. 'The Hidden Public Sector: The "Quangocratization" of the World?', in Kaufman et al. (1986: 183–207).

_____. 1988. 'Keeping the Centre Small: Explanation of Agency Type', *Political Studies* 36, 1: 30–46.

_____. 1991. 'A Public Management for All Seasons?', *Public Administration* 69 (Spring): 3–19.

_____. 1995. 'Contemporary Public Management: A New Global Paradigm?', *Public Policy and Administration* 10, 2: 104–17.

_____. 1998. *The Art of the State: Culture, Rhetoric and Public Management*. Oxford: Clarendon Press.

_____. 2002. 'The Risk Game and the Blame Game', *Government and Opposition* 37, 1: 15–54.

Horn, Murray J. 1995. *The Political Economy of Pubic Administration: Institutional Choice in the Public Sector*. Cambridge: Cambridge University Press.

Hosseus, Daniel, and Leslie A. Pal. 1997. 'Anatomy of a Policy Area: The Case of Shipping', *Canadian Public Policy* 23, 4: 399–416.

Hough, Jerry F. 1972. 'The Soviet System: Petrification or Pluralism', *Problems of Communism* 21 (Mar.–Apr.): 25–45.

Howard, Christopher. 1993. 'The Hidden Side of the American Welfare States', *Political Science Quarterly* 108, 3: 403–36.

_____. 1995. 'Testing the Tools Approach: Tax Expenditures Versus Direct Expenditures', *Public Administration Review* 55, 5: 439–47.

_____. 1997. *The Hidden Welfare State: Tax Expenditures and Social Policy in the United States*. Princeton, NJ: Princeton University Press.

_____. 2002. 'Tax Expenditures', in Salamon (2002a: 410–44).

Howard, S. Kenneth. 1971. 'Analysis, Rationality, and Administrative Decision-Making', in F. Marini, ed., *Toward a New Public Administration: The Minnowbrook Perspective*. Scranton, Penn.: Chandler.

Howe, R. Brian, and David Johnson. 2000. *Restraining Equality: Human Rights Commissions in Canada*. Toronto: University of Toronto Press.

Howlett, Michael. 1986. 'Acts of Commission and Acts of Omission: Legal-Historical Research and the Intentions of Government in a Federal State', *Canadian Journal of Political Science* 19: 363–71.

_____. 1990. 'The Round Table Experience: Representation and Legitimacy in Canadian Environmental Policy Making', *Queen's Quarterly* 97, 4: 580–601.

_____. 1991. 'Policy Instruments, Policy Styles, and Policy Implementation: National Approaches to Theories of Instrument Choice', *Policy Studies Journal* 19, 2: 1–21.

_____. 1994. 'Policy Paradigms and Policy Change: Lessons From the Old and New Canadian Policies Towards Aboriginal Peoples', *Policy Studies Journal* 22, 4: 631–51.

_____. 1997a. 'Issue-Attention and Punctuated Equilibria Models Reconsidered: An Empirical Examination of the Dynamics of Agenda-Setting in Canada', *Canadian Journal of Political Science* 30, 1: 3–29.

_____. 1997b. 'Predictable and Unpredictable Policy Windows: Issue, Institutional and Exogenous Correlates of Canadian Federal Agenda-Setting', paper presented to the annual meeting of the Canadian Political Science Association, St John's.

_____. 2000. 'Managing the "Hollow State": Procedural Policy Instruments and Modern Governance', *Canadian Public Administration* 43, 4: 412–31.

_____. 2002. 'Do Networks Matter? Linking Policy Network Structure to Policy Outcomes: Evidence From Four Canadian Policy Sectors, 1990–2000', *Canadian Journal of Political Science* 35, 2: 235–67.

_____ and M. Ramesh. 1993. 'Patterns of Policy Instrument Choice: Policy Styles, Policy Learning and the Privatization Experience', *Policy Studies Review* 12, 1: 3–24.

_____ and _____. 1995. *Studying Public Policy: Policy Cycles and Policy Subsystems*. Toronto: Oxford University Press.

_____ and _____. 1998. 'Policy Subsystem Configurations and Policy Change: Operationalizing the Postpositivist Analysis of the Politics of the Policy Process', *Policy Studies Journal* 26, 3: 466–82.

_____ and _____. 2002. 'The Policy Effects of Internationalization: A Subsystem Adjustment Analysis of Policy Change', *Journal of Comparative Policy Analysis* 4, 3: 31–50.

_____ and Jeremy Rayner. 1995. 'Do Ideas Matter? Policy Subsystem Configurations and Policy Change in the Canadian Forest Sector', *Canadian Public Administration* 38, 3: 382–410.

Howse, Robert, J. Robert S. Prichard, and Michael J. Trebilcock. 1990. 'Smaller or Smarter Government?', *University of Toronto Law Journal* 40: 498–541.

Huber, Evelyne, and John D. Stephens. 1998. 'Internationalization and the Social Democratic Model: Crisis and Future Prospects', *Comparative Political Studies* 31, 3: 353–97.

Huber, George P. 1991. 'Organization Learning: The Contributing Processes and the Literatures', *Organization Science* 2, 1: 88–115.

Huitt, Ralph K. 1968. 'Political Feasibility', in A. Ranney, ed., *Political Science and Public Policy*. Chicago: Markham Publishing, 263–76.

Hula, Richard C. 1988. 'Using Markets to Implement Public Policy', in Hula, ed., *Market-Based Public Policy*. London: Macmillan, 3–18.

Humphries, Martha Anne, and Donald R. Songer. 1999. 'Law and Politics in Judicial Oversight of Federal Administrative Agencies', *Journal of Politics* 61, 1: 207–20.

Huntington, Samuel P. 1952. 'The Marasmus of the ICC: The Commissions, the Railroads and the Public Interest', *Yale Law Review* 61, 4: 467–509.

Hutter, Bridget M., and P.K. Manning. 1990. 'The Contexts of Regulation: The Impact Upon Health and Safety Inspectorates in Britain', *Law and Policy* 12, 2: 103–36.

Iannuzzi, Alphonse. 2001. *Industry Self-Regulation and Voluntary Environmental Compliance*. Boca Raton, Fla: Lewis Publishers.

Ikenberry, G. John. 1988. 'Conclusion: An Institutional Approach to American Foreign Economic Policy', *International Organization* 42, 1: 219–43.

_____. 1990. 'The International Spread of Privatization Policies: Inducements, Learning, and "Policy Bandwagoning"', in Suleiman and Waterbury (1990).

Imbeau, Louis M., and Guy Lachapelle. 1993. 'Les Déterminants des politiques provinciales au Canada: une synthèse des études comparatives', *Revue Québécoise de Science Politique* 23: 107–41.

Ingram, Helen M., and Dean E. Mann, eds. 1980a. *Why Policies Succeed or Fail*. Beverly Hills, Calif.: Sage.

_____ and _____. 1980b. 'Policy Failure: An Issue Deserving Analysis', in Ingram and Mann (1980a).

Jacobsen, John Kurt. 1995. 'Much Ado About Ideas: The Cognitive Factor in Economic Policy', *World Politics* no. 47: 283–310.

Jacobson, Peter D., Elizabeth Selvin, and Scott D. Pomfret. 2001. 'The Role of the Courts in Shaping Health Policy: An Empirical Analysis', *Journal of Law, Medicine and Ethics* 29: 278–89.

Jacoby, William G. 2000. 'Issue Framing and Public Opinion on Government Spending', *American Journal of Political Science* 44, 4: 750–67.

Jaffe, Louis L. 1965. *Judicial Control of Administrative Action*. Boston: Little, Brown.

_____. 1969. *English and American Judges as Lawmakers*. Oxford: Clarendon.

James, Simon. 1993. 'The Idea Brokers: The Impact of Think Tanks on British Government', *Public Administration* 71: 491–506.

Jenkins, William I. 1978. *Policy Analysis: A Political and Organizational Perspective*. London: Martin Robertson.

Jenkins-Smith, Hank C., and Paul A. Sabatier. 1993. 'The Study of Public Policy Processes', in Sabatier and Jenkins-Smith (1993a).

_____, Gilbert K. St Clair, and Brian Woods. 1991. 'Explaining Change in Policy Subsystems: Analysis of Coalition Stability and Defection over Time', *American Journal of Political Science* 35, 4: 851–80.

Jennings, Bruce. 1987. 'Interpretation and the Practice of Policy Analysis', in Fischer and Forester (1987).

Jens. 1997. 'A "New Institutional" Perspective on Policy Networks': 669–93.

Jenson, Jane. 1989. 'Paradigms and Political Discourse: Protective Legislation in France and the United States Before 1914', *Canadian Journal of Political Science* 22, 2: 235–58.

_____. 1991. 'All the World's a Stage: Ideas About Political Space and Time', *Studies in Political Economy* 36: 43–72.

Jeon, Yongjoo, and Donald P. Haider-Markel. 2001. 'Tracing Issue Definition and Policy Change: An Analysis of Disability Issue Images and Policy Response', *Policy Studies Journal* 29, 2: 215–31.

Jervis, Robert. 1997. *System Effects: Complexity in Political and Social Life*. Princeton, NJ: Princeton University Press.

Johnson, A.F., and A. Stritch, eds. 1997. *Canadian Public Policy: Globalization and Political Parties.* Toronto: Copp Clark Pitman.

Johnson, Norman. 1987. *The Welfare State in Transition: The Theory and Practice of Welfare Pluralism.* Brighton, Sussex: Wheatsheaf Books.

Johnston, Richard. 1986. *Public Opinion and Public Policy in Canada: Questions of Confidence.* Toronto: University of Toronto Press.

Jones, Bryan D. 1994. *Reconceiving Decision-Making in Democratic Politics: Attention, Choice and Public Policy.* Chicago: University of Chicago Press.

_____. 2001. *Politics and the Architecture of Choice: Bounded Rationality and Governance.* Chicago: University of Chicago Press.

_____, James L. True, and Frank R. Baumgartner. 1997. 'Does Incrementalism Stem from Political Consensus or from Institutional Gridlock?', *American Journal of Political Science* 41, 4: 1319–39.

Jones, Charles O. 1984. *An Introduction to the Study of Public Policy,* 3rd edn. Monterey, Calif.: Brooks/Cole.

Jordan, A. Grant. 1981. 'Iron Triangles, Woolly Corporatism and Elastic Nets: Images of the Policy Process', *Journal of Public Policy* 1, 1: 95–123.

_____. 1990a. 'Policy Community Realism versus "New" Institutionalist Ambiguity', *Political Studies* 38, 3: 470–84.

_____. 1990b. 'Sub-governments, Policy Communities and Networks: Refilling the Old Bottles?', *Journal of Theoretical Politics* 2, 3: 319–38.

_____. 1998. 'Indirect Causes and Effects in Policy Change: Shell, Greenpeace and the Brent Spar', paper presented to the annual meeting of the American Political Science Association, Boston.

_____. 2000. 'The Process of Government and the Governmental Process', *Political Studies* 48: 788–801.

_____ and William A. Maloney. 1997. 'Accounting for Subgovernments', *Administration and Society* 29, 5: 557–84.

_____ and _____. 1998. 'Manipulating Membership: Supply-Side Influences on Group Size', *British Journal of Political Science* 28, 2: 389–409.

_____, _____, and Andrew M. McLaughlin. 1994. 'Characterizing Agricultural Policy-Making', *Public Administration* 72, (Winter): 505–26.

_____ and Klaus Schubert. 1992. 'A Preliminary Ordering of Policy Network Labels', *European Journal of Political Research* 21, 1/2: 7–27.

Jordan, J.M., and S.L. Sutherland. 1979. 'Assessing the Results of Public Expenditure: Program Evaluation in the Federal Government', *Canadian Public Administration* 22, 4: 581–609.

Kagan, Robert A. 1991. 'Adversarial Legalism and American Government', *Journal of Policy Analysis and Management* 10, 3: 369–406.

_____. 1994. 'Regulatory Enforcement', in D.H. Rosenbloom and R.D. Schwartz, eds, *Handbook of Regulation and Administrative Law.* New York: Marcel Dekker, 383–422.

_____ and Lee Axelrad. 1997. 'Adversarial Legalism: An International Perspective', in P.S. Nivola, ed., *Comparative Disadvantages? Social Regulations and the Global Economy.* Washington: Brookings Institution Press, 146–202.

Kagel, John H., and Dan Levin. 2002. *Common Value Auctions and the Winner's Curse.* Princeton, NJ: Princeton University Press.

Kahneman, Daniel, and Amos Tversky. 1979. 'Prospect Theory: An Analysis of Decision Under Risk', *Econometrica* 47: 263–89.

Karamanos, Panagiotis. 2001. 'Voluntary Environmental Agreements: Evolution and Definition of a New Environmental Policy Approach', *Journal of Environmental Planning and Management* 44, 1: 67–84.

Kasza, Gregory J. 2002. 'The Illusion of Welfare "Regimes"', *Journal of Social Policy* 31, 2: 271–87.

Kato, Junko. 1996. 'Review Article: Institutions and Rationality in Politics—Three Varieties of Neo-Institutionalists', *British Journal of Political Science* 26: 553–82.

Katzenstein, Peter J. 1977. 'Conclusion: Domestic Structures and Strategies of Foreign Economic Policy', *International Organization* 31, 4: 879–920.

_____. 1985. *Small States in World Markets: Industrial Policy in Europe*. Ithaca, NY: Cornell University Press.

Katzman, Martin T. 1988. 'Societal Risk Management Through the Insurance Market', in R.C. Hula, ed., *Market-Based Public Policy*. London: Macmillan, 21–42.

Kaufman, F.-X., G. Majone, and V. Ostrom, eds. 1986. *Guidance, Control, and Evaluation in the Public Sector*. Berlin: Walter de Gruyter.

Kaufman, Herbert. 1976. *Are Government Organizations Immortal?* Washington: Brookings Institution.

_____. 2001. 'Major Players: Bureaucracies in American Government', *Public Administration Review* 61, 1: 18–42.

Keck, Margaret E., and Kathryn Sikkink, eds. 1998. *Activists Beyond Borders: Advocacy Networks in International Politics*. Ithaca, NY: Cornell University Press.

Keeler, John T.S. 1993. 'Opening the Window for Reform: Mandates, Crises and Extraordinary Policy-Making', *Comparative Political Studies* 25, 4: 433–86.

Keller, Ann C. 1999. 'Innovation and Influence: Scientists as Advocates in Environmental Policy Change', paper presented to the Western Political Science Association, Seattle.

Kelman, Steven. 1981. *Regulating America, Regulating Sweden: A Comparative Study of Occupational Safety and Health Policy*. Cambridge, Mass: MIT Press.

_____. 2002. 'Contracting', in Salamon (2002a: 282–318).

Keman, H., and P. Pennings. 1995. 'Managing Political and Societal Conflict in Democracies: Do Consensus and Corporatism Matter?', *British Journal of Political Science* 25: 271–81.

Kenis, Patrick. 1991. 'The Pre-Conditions for Policy Networks: Some Findings From a Three Country Study on Industrial Re-Structuring', in Marin and Mayntz (1991: 297–330).

Kennamer, J. David, ed. 1992. *Public Opinion, the Press, and Public Policy*. Westport, Conn.: Praeger.

Kennett, Steven A. 2000. 'The Future for Cumulative Effects Management: Beyond the Environmental Assessment Paradigm', *Resources* 69: 1–7.

Keohane, Robert O. 1989. *International Institutions and State Powers: Essays in International Relations Theory*. Boulder, Colo.: Westview Press.

_____. 1990. 'Multilateralism: An Agenda for Research', *International Journal* 45, 4: 731–64.

_____ and Stanley Hoffman. 1991. 'Institutional Change in Europe in the 1980s', in Keohane and Hoffman, eds, *The New European Community: Decision-Making and Institutional Change*. Boulder, Colo.: Westview Press, 1–40.

_____ and Helen V. Milner, eds. 1996. *Internationalization and Domestic Politics*. New York: Cambridge University Press.

_____ and Joseph S. Nye. 1989. *Power and Interdependence*. Glenview, Ill.: Scott, Foresman.

Kepner, Charles H., and Benjamin B. Tregoe. 1965. *The Rational Manager: A Systematic Approach to Problem Solving and Decision Making*. New York: McGraw-Hill.

Kernaghan, Kenneth. 1979. 'Power, Parliament and Public Servants in Canada: Ministerial Responsibility Reexamined', *Canadian Public Policy* 5, 3: 383–96.

_____. 1985a. 'The Public and Public Servants in Canada', in Kernaghan, ed., *Public Administration in Canada: Selected Readings*. Toronto: Methuen, 323–33.

_____. 1985b. 'Judicial Review of Administration Action', in Kernaghan ed., *Public Administration in Canada: Selected Readings*. Toronto: Methuen, 358–73.

_____. 1993. 'Partnership and Public Administration: Conceptual and Practical Considerations', *Canadian Public Administration* 36, 1: 57–76.

_____, Brian Marson, and Sandford Borins. 2000. *The New Public Organization.* Toronto: Institute of Public Administration of Canada.

Kerr, Clark. 1983. *The Future of Industrial Societies: Convergence or Continuing Diversity?* Cambridge, Mass.: Harvard University Press.

Kerr, Donna H. 1976. 'The Logic of "Policy" and Successful Policies', *Policy Sciences* 7, 3: 351–63.

Kerwin, Cornelius M. 1994. 'The Elements of Rule-Making', in D.H. Rosenbloom and R.D. Schwartz, eds, *Handbook of Regulation and Administrative Law.* New York: Marcel Dekker, 345–81.

_____. 1999. *Rulemaking: How Government Agencies Write Law and Make Policy.* Washington: Congressional Quarterly Press.

Key, V.O., Jr. 1967. *Public Opinion and American Democracy.* New York: Knopf.

Kickert, Walter J.M. 2001. 'Public Management of Hybrid Organizations: Governance of Quasi-Autonomous Executive Agencies', *International Public Management Journal* 4: 135–50.

King, Anthony. 1973. 'Ideas, Institutions and the Policies of Governments: A Comparative Analysis: Part III', *British Journal of Political Science* 3, 4: 409–23.

_____. 1981. 'What Do Elections Decide?', in Butler et al. (1981).

King, David C., and Jack L. Walker. 1991. 'An Ecology of Interest Groups in America', in Walker (1991: 57–73).

King, Gary, and Michael Laver. 1993. 'Party Platforms, Mandates and Government Spending', *American Political Science Review* 87, 3: 744–50.

Kingdon, John W. 1984. *Agendas, Alternatives and Public Policies.* Boston: Little, Brown.

Kirkpatrick, Susan E., James P. Lester, and Mark R. Peterson. 1999. 'The Policy Termination Process: A Conceptual Framework and Application to Revenue Sharing', *Policy Studies Review* 16, 1: 209–36.

Kirschen, E.S., et al. 1964. *Economic Policy in Our Time*, vol. 1—*General Theory.* Chicago: Rand McNally.

Kiser, Larry L., and Elinor Ostrom. 1982. 'The Three Worlds of Action: A Metatheoretical Synthesis of Institutional Approaches', in Ostrom, ed., *Strategies of Political Inquiry.* Beverly Hills, Calif.: Sage, 179–222.

Kiviniemi, Markku. 1986. 'Public Policies and Their Targets: A Typology of the Concept of Implementation', *International Social Science Journal* 38, 108: 251–66.

Klijn, Erik-Hans. 1996. 'Analyzing and Managing Policy Processes in Complex Networks: A Theoretical Examination of the Concept Policy Network and Its Problems', *Administration and Society* 28, 1: 90–119.

_____. 2001. 'Rules as Institutional Context for Decision Making in Networks: The Approach to Postwar Housing Districts in Two Cities', *Administration and Society* 33, 2: 133–64.

_____ and Joop F.M. Koppenjan. 2000. 'Public Management and Policy Networks: Foundations of a Network Approach to Governance', *Public Management* 2, 2: 135–58.

_____, _____, and Katrien Termeer. 1995. 'Managing Networks in the Public Sector: A Theoretical Study of Management Strategies in Policy Networks', *Public Administration* 73: 437–54.

_____ and G.R. Teisman. 1991. 'Effective Policymaking in a Multi-Actor Setting: Networks and Steering', in Roeland In't Veld et al., eds, *Autopoiesis and Configuration Theory: New Approaches to Societal Steering.* Dordrecht: Kluwer, 99–111.

Knill, Christoph. 1998. 'European Policies: The Impact of National Administrative Traditions', *Journal of Public Policy* 18, 1: 1–28.

_____. 1999. 'Explaining Cross-National Variance in Administrative Reform: Autonomous versus Instrumental Bureaucracies', *Journal of Public Policy* 19, 2: 113–39.

_____. 2001. 'Private Governance Across Multiple Arenas: European Interest Associations as Interface Actors', *Journal of European Public Policy* 8, 2: 227–46.

_____ and Dirk Lehmkuhl. 2002. 'Private Actors and the State: Internationalization and Changing Patterns of Governance', *Governance* 15, 1: 41–63.

Knoepfel, Peter, and Ingrid Kissling-Naf. 1998. 'Social Learning in Policy Networks', *Policy and Politics* 26, 3: 343–67.

_____ et al. 1987. 'Comparing Environmental Policies: Different Styles, Similar Content', in M. Dierkes, H.N. Weiler, and A.B. Antal, eds, *Comparative Policy Research: Learning from Experience*. Aldershot: Gower, 171–85.

Knoke, David. 1993. 'Networks as Political Glue: Explaining Public Policy-Making', in W.J. Wilson, ed., *Sociology and the Public Agenda*. London: Sage, 164–84.

_____ and Edward O. Laumann. 1982. 'The Social Organization of National Policy Domains: An Exploration of Some Structural Hypotheses', in P. Marsden and N. Lin, eds, *Social Structure and Network Analysis*. Beverly Hills, Calif.: Sage, 255–70.

Kolberg, Jon Eivind, and Gosta Esping-Andersen. 1992. 'Welfare States and Employment Regimes', in Kolberg, ed, *The Study of Welfare State Regimes*. New York: M.E. Sharpe.

Koppenjan, Joop F.M. 2001. 'Project Development in Complex Environments: Assessing Safety in Design and Decision-Making', *Journal of Contingencies and Crisis Management* 9, 3: 121–30.

Korpi, Walter. 1983. *The Democratic Class Struggle*. London: Routledge & Kegan Paul.

Krasner, Stephen D. 1982. 'Structural Causes and Regime Consequences: Regimes as Intervening Variables', *International Organization* 36, 2: 185–205.

_____, ed. 1983. *International Regimes*. Ithaca, NY: Cornell University Press.

_____. 1984. 'Approaches to the State: Alternative Conceptions and Historical Dynamics', *Comparative Politics* 16, 2: 223–46.

_____. 1988. 'Sovereignty: An Institutional Perspective', *Comparative Political Studies* 21, 1: 66–94.

Krause, George A. 1997. 'Policy Preference Formation and Subsystem Behaviour: The Case of Commercial Bank Regulation', *British Journal of Political Science* 27: 525–50.

Kreuger, Anne O. 1974. 'The Political Economy of the Rent-Seeking Society', *American Economic Review* 64, 3: 291–303.

Kriesi, Hanspeter, and Maya Jegen. 2000. 'Decision-Making in the Swiss Energy Policy Elite', *Journal of Public Policy* 20, 1: 21–53.

_____ and _____. 2001. 'The Swiss Energy Policy Elite: The Actor Constellation of a Policy Domain in Transition', *European Journal of Political Research* 39: 251–87.

Kruse, R., E. Schwecke, and J. Heinsohn. 1991. *Uncertainty and Vagueness in Knowledge Based Systems*. Berlin: Springer-Verlag.

Kubler, Daniel. 2001. 'Understanding Policy Change with the Advocacy Coalition Framework; An Application to Swiss Drug Policy', *Journal of European Public Policy* 8, 4: 623–41.

Kuhn, Thomas S. 1962. *The Structure of Scientific Revolutions*. Chicago: University of Chicago Press.

_____. 1974. 'Second Thoughts on Paradigms', in F. Suppe, ed., *The Structure of Scientific Theories*. Urbana: University of Illinois Press, 459–82.

Kuttner, Robert. 1997. *Everything For Sale: The Virtues and Limits of Markets*. New York: Alfred A. Knopf.

Lacroix, L. 1986. 'Strike Activity in Canada', in W.C. Riddell, ed., *Canadian Labour Relations*. Toronto: University of Toronto Press.

Lane, Jan-Erik. 2001. 'From Long-Term to Short-Term Contracting', *Public Administration* 79, 1: 29–48.

Lane, Peter J., and Michael Lubatkin. 1998. 'Relative Absorptive Capacity and Interorganizational Learning', *Strategic Management Journal* 19: 461–77.

Lapsley, Irvine, and Rosie Oldfield. 2001. 'Transforming the Public Sector: Management Consultants as Agents of Change', *European Accounting Review* 10, 3: 523–43.

Lasswell, Harold D. 1951. 'The Policy Orientation', in Lerner and Lasswell (1951).

_____. 1956. *The Decision Process: Seven Categories of Functional Analysis.* College Park: University of Maryland Press.

_____. 1958. *Politics: Who Gets What, When, How.* New York: Meridian.

_____. 1971. *A Pre-View of Policy Sciences.* New York: American Elsevier.

Latham, Earl. 1952. 'The Group Basis of Politics: Notes for a Theory', *American Political Science Review* 46, 2: 376–97.

Laughlin, Richard C. 1991. 'Environmental Disturbances and Organizational Transitions and Transformations: Some Alternative Models', *Organization Studies* 12, 2: 209–32.

Laumann, Edward O., and David Knoke. 1987. *The Organizational State: Social Choice in National Policy Domains.* Madison: University of Wisconsin Press.

Laux, Jeanne Kirk, and Maureen Appel Molot. 1988. *State Capitalism: Public Enterprise in Canada.* Ithaca, NY: Cornell University Press.

Lee, Mordecai. 2001. 'The Agency Spokesperson: Connecting Public Administration and the Media', *Public Administration Quarterly* 25, 1: 101–30.

Leeuw, Frans L. 1998. 'The Carrot: Subsidies as a Tool of Government', in Bemelmans-Videc et al. (1998: 77–102).

Le Gales, P., and M. Thatcher, eds. 1995. *Les Reseaux de Politique Publique.* Paris: Editions L'Harmattan.

Le Grand, Julian. 1991. 'The Theory of Government Failure', *British Journal of Political Science* 21, 4: 423–42.

_____ and Ray Robinson, eds. 1984. *Privatization and the Welfare State.* London: George Allen and Unwin.

Legro, Jeffrey W. 2000. 'The Transformation of Policy Ideas', *American Journal of Political Science* 44, 3: 419–32.

Leik, Robert K. 1992. 'New Directions for Network Exchange Theory: Strategic Manipulation of Network Linkages', *Social Networks* 14: 309–23.

Leman, Christopher. 1977. 'Patterns of Policy Development: Social Security in the United States and Canada', *Public Policy* 25, 2: 261–91.

_____. 1989. 'The Forgotten Fundamental: Successes and Excesses of Direct Government', in Salamon (1989a).

_____. 2002. 'Direct Government', in Salamon (2002a: 48–79).

Lerner, Daniel, and Harold D. Lasswell, eds. 1951. *The Policy Sciences: Recent Developments in Scope and Method.* Stanford, Calif.: Stanford University Press.

Lester, James P., and Malcolm L. Goggin. 1998. 'Back to the Future: The Rediscovery of Implementation Studies', *Policy Currents* 8, 3: 1–9.

_____ et al. 1987. 'Public Policy Implementation: Evolution of the Field and Agenda for Future Research', *Policy Studies Review* 7: 200–16.

Levitt, Barbara, and James G. March. 1988. 'Organizational Learning', *Annual Review of Sociology* 14: 319–40.

Levy, Jack S. 1997. 'Prospect Theory and the Cognitive-Rational Debate', in N. Geva and A. Mintz, eds, *Decisionmaking on War and Peace: The Cognitive-Rational Debate.* Boulder, Colo.: Lynne Rienner, 33–50.

Levy, Roger. 2001. 'EU Performance Management 1977–96: A Performance Indicators Analysis', *Public Administration* 79, 2: 423–44.

Lewis, David E. 2002. 'The Politics of Agency Termination: Confronting the Myth of Agency Immortality', *Journal of Politics* 64, 1: 89–107.

Lewis-Beck, Michael S. 1988. *Economics and Elections: The Major Western Democracies*. Ann Arbor: University of Michigan Press.

Liebowitz, S.J., and Stephen E. Margolis. 1995. 'Path Dependence, Lock-In, and History', *Journal of Law, Economics and Organization* 11, 1: 205–25.

Lijphart, A. 1969. 'Consociational Democracy', *World Politics* 21, 2: 207–25.

Lindblom, Charles E. 1955. *Bargaining: The Hidden Hand in Government*. Los Angeles: Rand Corporation.

_____. 1958. 'Policy Analysis', *American Economic Review* 48, 3: 298–312.

_____. 1959. 'The Science of Muddling Through', *Public Administration Review* 19, 2: 79–88.

_____. 1968. *The Policy-Making Process*. Englewood Cliffs, NJ: Prentice-Hall.

_____. 1977. *Politics and Markets: The World's Political Economic Systems*. New York: Basic Books.

_____. 1979. 'Still Muddling, Not Yet Through', *Public Administration Review* 39, 6: 517–26.

_____ and D.K. Cohen. 1979. *Usable Knowledge: Social Science and Social Problem Solving*. New Haven: Yale University Press.

Linder, Stephen H. 1999. 'Coming to Terms with Public-Private Partnership', *American Behavioural Scientist* 43, 1: 35–51.

_____ and B. Guy Peters. 1984. 'From Social Theory to Policy Design', *Journal of Public Policy* 4, 3: 237–59.

_____ and _____. 1988. 'The Analysis of Design or the Design of Analysis?', *Policy Studies Review* 7, 4: 738–50.

_____ and _____. 1989. 'Instruments of Government: Perceptions and Contexts', *Journal of Public Policy* 9, 1: 35–58.

_____ and _____. 1990. 'Research Perspectives on the Design of Public Policy: Implementation, Formulation, and Design', in Palumbo and Calista (1990a).

_____ and _____. 1991. 'The Logic of Public Policy Design: Linking Policy Actors and Plausible Instruments', *Knowledge in Society* 4: 125–51.

Lindquist, Evert A. 1988. 'What Do Decision Models Tell Us about Information Use?', *Knowledge in Society* 1, 2: 86–111.

_____. 1992. 'Public Managers and Policy Communities: Learning to Meet New Challenges', *Canadian Public Administration* 35, 2: 127–59.

_____. 1993. 'Think Tanks or Clubs? Assessing the Influence and Roles of Canadian Policy Institutes', *Canadian Public Administration* 36, 4: 547–79.

Linz, Juan J. 1978. 'Crisis, Breakdown, and Reequilibration', in Linz and A. Stepan, eds, *The Breakdown of Democratic Regimes*. Baltimore: John Hopkins University Press, 3–124.

Lipietz , Alain. 1982. 'Towards Global Fordism', *New Left Review* 132: 33–48

Lipsky, Michael. 1980. *Street-Level Bureaucracy: Dilemmas of the Individual in Public Services*. New York: Russell Sage Foundation.

Livingston, Steven G. 1992. 'Knowledge Hierarchies and the Politics of Ideas in American International Commodity Production', 12, 3: 223–42.

Lober, Douglas J. 1997. 'Explaining the Formation of Business-Environmentalist Collaborations: Collaborative Windows and the Paper Task Force', *Policy Sciences* 30: 1–24.

Locksley, Gareth. 1980. 'The Political Business Cycle: Alternative Interpretations', in Paul Whiteley, ed., *Models of Political Economy*. London: Sage.

Lowell, A. Lawrence. 1926. *Public Opinion and Popular Government*. New York: David McKay Company.

Lowi, Theodore J. 1966. 'Distribution, Regulation, Redistribution: The Functions of

Government', in R.B. Ripley, ed., *Public Policies and Their Politics: Techniques of Government Control*. New York: W.W. Norton, 27–40.

_____. 1969. *The End of Liberalism: Ideology, Policy and the Crisis of Public Authority*. New York: Norton.

_____. 1972. 'Four Systems of Policy, Politics and Choice', *Public Administration Review* 32, 4 (1972): 298–310.

_____. 1985. 'The State in Politics: The Relation Between Policy and Administration', in R.G. Noll, ed., *Regulatory Policy and the Social Sciences*. Berkeley: University of California Press, 67–105.

_____. 1998. 'Foreword: New Dimensions in Policy and Politics', in R. Tatalovich and B.W. Daynes, eds, *Moral Controversies in American Social Politics: Cases in Social Regulatory Policy*. Armonk, NY: M.E. Sharpe, xiii–xxvii.

Lund, Michael S. 1989. 'Between Welfare and the Market: Loan Guarantees as a Policy Tool', in Salamon (1989a: 125–66).

Lundquist, Lennart J. 1987. *Implementation Steering: An Actor-Structure Approach*. Bickley, UK: Chartwell-Bratt.

Lustick, Ian. 1980. 'Explaining the Variable Utility of Disjointed Incrementalism: Four Propositions', *American Political Science Review* 74, 2: 342–53.

Luttbeg, Norman R. 1981. 'Where We Stand on Political Linkage', in Luttbeg, ed., *Public Opinion and Public Policy: Models of Political Linkage*. Itasca, Ill.: F.E. Peacock, 455–62.

Lutz, James M. 1989. 'Emulation and Policy Adoptions in the Canadian Provinces', *Canadian Journal of Political Science* 22, 1: 147–54.

Lutz and Goldenberg. 1980. 'Front Page News and Real World Cues': 16–49.

Lyden, Fremont J., George A. Shipman, and Robert W. Wilkinson. 1968. 'Decision-Flow Analysis: A Methodology for Studying the Public Policy-Making Process', in P.P. Le Breton, ed., *Comparative Administrative Theory*. Seattle: University of Washington Press, 155–68.

Lynggaard, Kennet. 2001. 'The Study of Policy Change: Constructing an Analytical Strategy', paper presented at the ECPR 29th Joint Session Workshops, Grenoble, 6–11 Apr.

Lynn, Laurence E. 1987. *Managing Public Policy*. Boston: Little, Brown.

_____. 1999. 'A Place at the Table: Policy Analysis, Its Postpositive Critics, and the Future of Practice', *Journal of Policy Analysis and Management* 18, 3: 411–24.

McAllister, James A. 1989. 'Do Parties Make a Difference?', in A.G. Gagnon and A.B. Tanguay, eds, *Canadian Parties in Transition: Discourse, Organization, Representation*. Toronto: Nelson, 485–511.

MacAvoy, Paul, and et al., eds. 1989. *Privatization and State-Owned Enterprises: Lessons from the United States, Great Britain, and Canada*. Boston: Kluwer Academic Publishers.

McCallum, B. 1978. 'The Political Business Cycle: An Empirical Test', *Southern Economic Journal* 44: 504–15.

McCombs, Maxwell E. 1981. 'The Agenda-Setting Approach', in D.D. Nimmo and K.R. Sanders, eds, *Handbook of Political Communication*. Beverly Hills, Calif.: Sage, 121–40.

McConnell, Grant. 1966. *Private Power and American Democracy*. New York: Knopf.

McCool, Daniel. 1989. 'Subgovernments and the Impact of Policy Fragmentation and Accommodation', *Policy Studies Review* 8, 2: 264–87.

McCubbins, Arthur Lupia and Mathew D. 1994. 'Learning from Oversight: Fire Alarms and Policy Patrols Reconstructed', *Journal of Law, Economics and Organization* 10, 1: 96–125.

McCubbins, Mathew D., Roger G. Noll, and Barry R. Weingast. 1987. 'Administrative

Procedures as Instruments of Political Control', *Journal of Law, Economics, and Organization* 3, 2: 243–77.

_____, _____, and _____. 1989. 'Structure and Process, Politics and Policy: Administrative Arrangements and the Political Control of Agencies', *Virginia Law Review* 75, 2: 431–82.

_____ and Thomas Schwartz. 1984. 'Congressional Oversight Overlooked: Policy Patrols Versus Fire Alarms', *American Journal of Political Science* 28, 1: 165–79.

McDaniel, Paul R. 1989. 'Tax Expenditures as Tools of Government Action', in Salamon (1989a).

McDonnell, Lorraine M., and Richard F. Elmore. 1987. *Alternative Policy Instruments*. Santa Monica, Calif.: Center for Policy Research in Education.

McFarland, Andrew S. 1987. 'Interest Groups and Theories of Power in America', *British Journal of Political Science* 17, 2: 129–47.

_____. 1991. 'Interest Groups and Political Time: Cycles in America', *British Journal of Political Science* 21, 3: 257–85.

McGann, James, and R. Kent Weaver, eds. 1999. *Think Tanks and Civil Societies: Catalysts for Ideas and Action*. New Brunswick, NJ: Transaction.

McGraw, Kathleen M. 1990. 'Avoiding Blame: An Experimental Investigation of Political Excuses and Justifications', *British Journal of Political Science* 20: 199–242.

McGuire, Michael. 2002. 'Managing Networks: Propositions on What Managers Do and Why They Do It', *Public Administration Review* 62, 5: 599–609.

McLaughlin, Milbrey W. 1985. 'Implementation Realities and Evaluation Design', in Shotland and Mark (1985).

McLean, Iain. 1987. *Public Choice: An Introduction*. Oxford: Basil Blackwell.

_____. 2000. 'Review Article: The Divided Legacy of Mancur Olson', *British Journal of Political Science* 30: 651–68.

McLennan, Gregor. 1989. *Marxism, Pluralism and Beyond: Classic Debates and New Departures*. Cambridge: Polity Press.

MacRae, Duncan, Jr. 1993. 'Guidelines for Policy Discourse: Consensual versus Adversarial', in Fischer and Forester (1993: 291–318).

McRoberts, Kenneth. 1993. 'Federal Structures and the Policy Process', in M. Michael Atkinson, ed., *Governing Canada: Institutions and Public Policy*. Toronto: Harcourt Brace Jovanovich.

Madison, James, and Alexander Hamilton. 1961. *The Federalist Papers: A Collection of Essays Written in Support of the Constitution of the United States*. Garden City, NY: Anchor Books.

Mahoney, James. 2000. 'Path Dependence in Historical Sociology', *Theory and Society* 29, 4: 507–48.

Majone, Giandomenico. 1975. 'On the Notion of Political Feasibility', *European Journal of Political Research* 3: 259–74.

_____. 1989. *Evidence, Argument, and Persuasion in the Policy Process*. New Haven: Yale University Press.

_____. 1991. 'Cross-National Sources of Regulatory Policymaking in Europe and the United States', *Journal of Public Policy* 11, 1: 79–106.

Malloy, James M. 1993. 'Statecraft, Social Policy, and Governance in Latin America', *Governance* 6, 2: 220–74.

Maloney, William A. 2001. 'Regulation in an Episodic Policy-Making Environment: The Water Industry in England and Wales', *Public Administration* 79, 3: 625–42.

_____, Grant Jordan, and Andrew M. McLaughlin. 1994. 'Interest Groups and Public Policy: The Insider/Outsider Model Revisited', *Journal of Public Policy* 14, 1: 17–38.

Mandell, M.P. 2000. 'A Revised Look at Management in Network Structures', *International Journal of Organizational Theory and Behavior* 3, 1/2: 185–210.

Mann, Michael. 1984. 'The Autonomous Power of the State: Its Origins, Mechanisms and Results', *European Journal of Sociology* 25, 2: 185–213.

Manzer, Ronald. 1984. 'Policy Rationality and Policy Analysis: The Problem of the Choice of Criteria for Decision-making', in O.P. Dwivedi, ed., *Public Policy and Administrative Studies*. Guelph: University of Guelph.

March, James G. 1978. 'Bounded Rationality, Ambiguity, and the Engineering of Choice', *Bell Journal of Economics* 9, 2: 587–608.

_____. 1981. 'Decision Making Perspective: Decisions in Organizations and Theories of Choice', in A.H. van de Ven and W.F. Joyce, eds, *Perspectives on Organization Design and Behaviour*. New York: Wiley, 205–44.

_____. 1994. *A Primer on Decision-Making: How Decisions Happen*. New York: Free Press.

_____ and Johan P. Olsen. 1975. 'The Uncertainty of the Past: Organizational Learning Under Ambiguity', *European Journal of Political Research* 3: 147–71.

_____ and _____. 1979a. *Ambiguity and Choice in Organizations*. Bergen: Universitetsforlaget.

_____ and _____. 1979b. 'Organizational Choice Under Ambiguity', in March and Olsen (1979a).

_____ and _____. 1984. 'The New Institutionalism: Organizational Factors in Political Life', *American Political Science Review* 78, 3: 734–49.

_____ and _____. 1989. *Rediscovering Institutions: The Organizational Basis of Politics*. New York: Free Press.

_____ and _____. 1994. 'Institutional Perspectives on Political Institutions', paper presented to the International Political Science Association, Berlin.

_____ and _____. 1995. *Democratic Governance*. New York: Free Press.

_____ and _____. 1998. 'The Institutional Dynamics of International Political Orders', in P.J. Katzenstein, R.O. Keohane, and S.D. Krasner, eds, *Exploration and Contestation in the Study of World Politics*. Cambridge, Mass.: MIT Press, 303–30.

_____, Martin Schulz, and Xueguang Zhou. 2000. *The Dynamics of Rules: Change in Organizational Codes*. Stanford, Calif.: Stanford University Press.

Marin, Bernd, and Renate Mayntz, eds. 1991. *Policy Networks: Empirical Evidence and Theoretical Considerations*. Boulder, Colo.: Westview Press.

Marion, Russ. 1999. *The Edge of Organization: Chaos and Complexity Theories of Formal Social Systems*. London: Sage.

Markoff, John. 1975. 'Governmental Bureaucratization: General Processes and an Anomalous Case', *Comparative Studies in Society and History* 17, 4: 479–503.

_____ and Veronica Montecinos. 1993. 'The Ubiquitous Rise of Economists', *Journal of Public Policy* 13, 1: 37–68.

Marsh, David, and R.A.W. Rhodes, eds. 1992a. *Policy Networks in British Government*. Oxford: Clarendon Press.

_____ and _____. 1992b. 'Policy Communities and Issue Networks: Beyond Typology', in Marsh and Rhodes (1992a: 248–68).

Martin, John F. 1998. *Reorienting a Nation: Consultants and Australian Public Policy*. Aldershot: Ashgate.

Maslove, Allan, ed. 1994. *Taxing and Spending: Issues of Process*. Toronto: University of Toronto Press.

Masterman, Margaret. 1970. 'The Nature of a Paradigm', in I. Lakatos and A. Musgrave, eds, *Criticism and the Growth of Knowledge*. Cambridge: Cambridge University Press.

Maule, A. John, and Ola Svenson. 1993. 'Theoretical and Empirical Approaches to Behavioural Decision Making and Their Relations to Time Constraints', in Svenson and Maule, eds, *Time Pressure and Stress in Human Judgement and Decision Making*. New York: Plenum Press, 3–25.

May, Peter J. 1991. 'Reconsidering Policy Design: Policies and Publics', *Journal of Public Policy* 11, 2: 187–206.

_____. 1992. 'Policy Learning and Failure', *Journal of Public Policy* 12, 4: 331–54.

_____. 1993. 'Mandate Design and Implementation: Enhancing Implementation Efforts and Shaping Regulatory Styles', *Journal of Policy Analysis and Management* 12, 4: 634–63.

_____. 1999. 'Fostering Policy Learning: A Challenge for Public Administration', *International Review of Public Administration* 4, 1: 21–31.

_____. 2002. 'Social Regulation', in Salamon (2002a: 156–85).

_____ et al. 1997. *Environmental Management and Governance: Intergovernmental Approaches to Hazards and Sustainability*. London: Routledge.

Mayntz, Renate. 1979. 'Public Bureaucracies and Policy Implementation', *International Social Science Journal* 31, 4: 633–45.

_____. 1983. 'The Conditions of Effective Public Policy: A New Challenge for Policy Analysis', *Policy and Politics* 11, 2: 123–43.

_____. 1993a. 'Governing Failure and the Problem of Governability: Some Comments on a Theoretical Paradigm', in J. Kooiman, ed., *Modern Governance: New Government-Society Interactions*. London: Sage.

_____. 1993b. 'Modernization and the Logic of Interorganizational Networks', in J. Child et al., eds, *Societal Change Between Market and Organization*. Aldershot: Avebury, 3–18.

Mazmanian, Daniel A., and Paul A. Sabatier. 1980. 'A Multivariate Model of Public Policy-Making', *American Journal of Political Science* 24, 3: 439–68.

_____ and _____. 1983. *Implementation and Public Policy*. Glenview, Ill.: Scott, Foresman.

Mead, Lawrence M. 1985. 'Policy Studies and Political Science', *Policy Studies Review* 5, 2: 319–35.

Meltsner, Arnold J. 1972. 'Political Feasibility and Policy Analysis', *Public Administration Review* 32: 859–67.

_____. 1976. *Policy Analysts in the Bureaucracy*. Berkeley: University of California Press.

Menahem, Gila. 1998. 'Policy Paradigms, Policy Networks and Water Policy in Israel', *Journal of Public Policy* 18, 3: 283–310.

_____. 2001. 'Water Policy in Israel 1948–2000: Policy Paradigms, Policy Networks and Public Policy', *Israel Affairs* 7, 4: 21–44.

Mendoza, Guillermo A., and William Sprouse. 1989. 'Forest Planning and Decision Making Under Fuzzy Environments: An Overview and Illustration', *Forest Science* 35, 2: 481–502.

Merton, Robert K. 1936. 'The Unanticipated Consequences of Purposive Social Action', *American Sociological Review* 6, 1: 894–904.

_____. 1948. 'The Self-Fulfilling Prophecy', *Antioch Review* 8, 2: 193–210.

Metcalfe, Les. 1978. 'Policy Making in Turbulent Environments', in K. Hanf and F.W. Scharpf, eds, *Interorganizational Policy Making: Limits to Coordination and Central Control*. London: Sage, 37–55.

Meyer, Alan D. 1982. 'Adapting to Environmental Jolts', *Administrative Science Quarterly* 27: 515–37.

_____, Geoffrey R. Brooks, and James B. Goes. 1990. 'Environmental Jolts and Industry Revolutions: Organizational Responses to Discontinuous Change', *Strategic Management Journal* 11: 93–110.

Migdal, Joel S. 1988. *Strong Societies and Weak States: State-Society Relations and State Capabilities in the Third World*. Princeton, NJ: Princeton University Press.

Miller, Leonard S. 1976. 'The Structural Determinants of the Welfare Effort: A Critique and a Contribution', *Social Service Review* 50, 1: 57–79.

Milner, Helen V., and Robert O. Keohane. 1996. 'Internationalization and Domestic Politics: A Conclusion', in Keohane and Milner (1996: 243–58).

Milward, H. Brinton, and Ronald A. Francisco. 1983. 'Subsystem Politics and Corporatism in the United States', *Policy and Politics* 11, 3.

_____ and Keith G. Provan. 1998. 'Principles for Controlling Agents: The Political Economy of Network Structure', *Journal of Public Administration Research and Theory* 8, 2: 203–22.

_____ and Gary L. Walmsley. 1984. 'Policy Subsystems, Networks and the Tools of Public Management', in R. Eyestone, ed., *Public Policy Formation*. Greenwich. Conn.: JAI Press.

Minkenberg, Michael. 2001. 'The Radical Right in Public Office: Agenda-Setting and Policy Effects', *West European Politics* 24, 4: 1–21.

Minogue, Martin. 1983. 'Theory and Practice in Public Policy and Administration', *Policy and Politics* 1, 1.

Mintron, Michael. 1997. 'Policy Entrepreneurs and the Diffusion of Innovation', *American Journal of Political Science* 41, 3: 738–70.

Mintz, Alex. 1993. 'The Decision to Attack Iraq', *Journal of Conflict Resolution* 37, 4: 595–618.

_____ and Nehemia Geva. 1997. 'The PoliHeuristic Theory of Foreign Policy Decision Making', in Geva and Mintz, eds, *Decision-Making in War and Peace: The Cognitive-Rational Debate*. Boulder, Colo.: Lynne Rienner.

_____ et al. 1997. 'The Effect of Dynamic and Static Choice Sets on Political Decision Making: An Analysis Using the Decision Board Platform', *American Political Science Review* 91, 3: 553–66.

Mintzberg, Henry, Duru Raisinghani, and Andre Theoret. 1976. 'The Structure of "Unstructured" Decision Processes', *Administrative Science Quarterly* 21: 246–75.

Mitchell, Ronald K., Bradley R. Age, and Donna J. Wood. 1997. 'Toward a Theory of Stakeholder Identification and Salience: Defining the Principle of Who and What Really Counts', *Academy of Management Review* 22, 4: 853–86.

Mitnick, Barry M. 1978. 'The Concept of Regulation', *Bulletin of Business Research* 53, 5: 1–20.

_____. 1980. *The Political Economy of Regulation: Creating, Designing, and Removing Regulatory Forms*. New York: Columbia University Press.

Moe, Terry M. 1984. 'The New Economics of Organization', *American Journal of Political Science* 28: 739–77.

Monroe, Alan D. 1979. 'Consistency Between Public Preferences and National Policy Decisions', *American Politics Quarterly* 7, 1: 3–19.

Monroe, Kristen Renwick. 1991. 'The Theory of Rational Action: Origins and Usefulness for Political Science', in Monroe, ed., *The Economic Approach to Politics: A Critical Reassessment of the Theory of Rational Action*. New York: HarperCollins, 1–31.

Montgomery, John D. 2000. 'Social Capital as a Policy Resource', *Policy Sciences* 33: 227–43.

Montpetit, Eric. 2002. 'Policy Networks, Federal Arrangements, and the Development of Environmental Regulations: A Comparison of the Canadian and American Agricultural Sectors', *Governance* 15, 1: 1–20.

Mossberger, Karen. 2000. *The Politics of Ideas and the Spread of Enterprise Zones*. Washington: Georgetown University Press.

Mucciaroni, Gary. 1990. *The Political Failure of Employment Policy, 1945–1982*. Pittsburgh: University of Pittsburgh Press.

_____. 1992. 'The Garbage Can Model and the Study of Policy Making: A Critique', *Polity* 24, 3: 460–82.

Mulford, Charles L. 1978. 'Why They Don't Even When They Ought To: Implications of Compliance Theory for Policymakers', in A. Etzioni, ed., *Policy Research*. Leiden: E.J. Brill, 47–62.

Munns, Joyce M. 1975. 'The Environment, Politics, and Policy Literature: A Critique and Reformulation', *Western Political Quarterly* 28, 4: 646–67.

Muntigl, Peter. 2002. 'Policy, Politics and Social Control: A Systemic Functional Linguistic Analysis of EU Employment Policy', *Text* 22, 3: 393–441.

Musolf, Lloyd D. 1989. 'The Government Corporation Tool: Permutations and Possibilities', in Salamon (1989a: 231–52).

Nachmias, David. 1979. *Public Policy Evaluation: Approaches and Methods*. New York: St Martin's Press.

Nathanson, Constance A. 2000. 'Social Movements as Catalysts for Policy Change: The Case of Smoking and Guns', *Journal of Health Politics, Policy and Law* 24, 3: 421–88.

Nelson, Thomas E., and Zoe M. Oxley. 1999. 'Issue Framing Effects on Belief Importance and Opinion', *Journal of Politics* 61, 4: 1040–67.

Nettl, J.P. 1968. 'The State as a Conceptual Variable', *World Politics* 20, 4: 559–92.

Nice, D.C. 1987. 'Incremental and Nonincremental Policy Responses: The States and the Railroads', *Polity* 20: 145–56.

Nicolaus, Martin. 1967. 'Proletariat and Middle Class in Marx: Hegelian Choreography and the Capitalist Dialectic', *Studies on the Left* 7, 1: 22–49.

Nisbet, Robert. 1972. 'Introduction: The Problem of Social Change', in Nisbet, ed., *Social Change*. New York: Harper and Row, 1–45.

Niskanen, William A. 1971. *Bureaucracy and Representative Government*. Chicago: University of Chicago Press.

Nordhaus, W. 1975. 'The Political Business Cycle', *Review of Economic Studies* 42: 169–90.

Nordlinger, Eric A. 1981. *On the Autonomy of the Democratic State*. Cambridge, Mass.: Harvard University Press.

_____. 1987. 'Taking the State Seriously', in M. Weiner and S.P. Huntington, eds, *Understanding Political Development*. Boston: Little, Brown.

_____. 1988. 'The Return to the State: Critiques', *American Political Science Review* 82, 3: 875–85.

North, Douglas C. 1990. *Institutions, Institutional Change and Economic Performance*. Cambridge: Cambridge University Press.

Nownes, Anthony J. 1995. 'The Other Exchange: Public Interest Groups, Patrons, and Benefits', *Social Science Quarterly* 76, 2: 381–401.

_____. 2000. 'Policy Conflict and the Structure of Interest Communities', *American Politics Quarterly* 28, 3: 309–27.

_____ and Allan J. Cigler. 1995. 'Public Interest Groups and the Road to Survival', *Polity* 27, 3: 380–404.

_____ and Grant Neeley. 1996. 'Toward an Explanation for Public Interest Group Formation and Proliferation: "Seed Money", Disturbances, Entrepreneurship, and Patronage', *Policy Studies Journal* 24, 1: 74–92.

Nunan, Fiona. 1999. 'Policy Network Transformation: The Implementation of the EC Directive on Packaging and Packaging Waste', *Public Administration* 77, 3: 621–38.

Nye, Thomas R. 2002. *Top-Down Policymaking*. New York: Chatham House.

Nyland, Julie. 1995. 'Issue Networks and NonProfit Organizations', *Policy Studies Review* 14, 1/2: 195–204.

Obinger, Herbert, and Uwe Wagschal. 2001. 'Families of Nations and Public Policy', *West European Politics* 24, 1: 99–114.

Ohmae, K. 1995. *The End of the Nation State*. London: HarperCollins.

Oliver, Pamela E. 1993. 'Formal Models of Collective Action', *Annual Review of Sociology* 19: 271–300.

Olson, David M., and Michael L. Mezey, eds. 1991. *Legislatures in the Policy Process: The Dilemmas of Economic Policy*. Cambridge: Cambridge University Press.

Olson, Mancur. 1965. *The Logic of Collective Action: Public Goods and the Theory of Groups*. Cambridge, Mass.: Harvard University Press.

_____. 1982. *The Rise and Decline of Nations: Economic Growth, Stagflation, and Social Rigidities*. New Haven: Yale University Press.

_____. 1986. 'A Theory of the Incentives Facing Political Organizations: Neo-Corporatism and the Hegemonic State', *International Political Science Review* 7, 2: 165–89.

Organization for Economic Co-operation and Development (OECD). 1993. *Managing with Market-Type Mechanisms*. Paris: OECD.

Orren, Karen, and Stephen Skowronek. 1993. 'Beyond the Iconography of Order: Notes for a 'New Institutionalism', in L.C. Dodd and C. Jillson, eds, *The Dynamics of American Politics: Approaches and Interpretations*. Boulder, Colo.: Westview Press.

_____ and _____. 1998–9. 'Regimes and Regime Building in American Government: A Review of Literature on the 1940s', *Political Science Quarterly* 113, 4: 689–702.

Osborne, D., and E. Gaebler. 1992. *Reinventing Government*. Reading, Mass.: Addison-Wesley.

Ossowski, Stanislaw. 1963. *Class Structure in the Social Consciousness*, trans. Sheila Patterson. New York: Free Press of Glencoe.

Ostrander, Susan A., and Stuart Langton, eds. 1987. *Shifting the Debate: Public/Private Sector Relations in the Modern Welfare State*. New Brunswick, NJ: Transaction.

Ostrom, Elinor. 1986a. 'A Method of Institutional Analysis', in Kaufman et al. (1986).

_____. 1986b. 'An Agenda for the Study of Institutions', *Public Choice* 48: 3–25.

_____. 1999. 'Institutional Rational Choice: As Assessment of the Institutional Analysis and Development Framework', in Sabatier (1999a: 35–71).

Ostrom, Vincent, David Feeny, and Hartmut Picht, eds. 1993. *Rethinking Institutional Analysis and Development: Issues, Alternatives and Choices*. San Francisco: Institute for Contemporary Studies Press.

O'Sullivan, Deborah, and Barry Down. 2001. 'Policy Decisionmaking Models in Practice: A Case Study of the Western Australian "Sentencing Acts"', *Policy Studies Journal* 29, 1: 56–70.

O'Toole, Laurence J. 2000a. 'Different Public Managements? Implications of Structural Context in Hierarchies and Networks', in J.L. Brudney, O'Toole, and H.G. Rainey, eds, *Advancing Public Management: New Developments in Theory, Methods and Practice*. Washington: Georgetown University Press, 19–48.

_____. 2000b. 'Research on Policy Implementation: Assessment and Prospects', *Journal of Public Administration Research and Theory* 10, 2: 263–88.

Ouimet, Mathieu, and Vincent Lemieux. 2000. *Les Réseaux de Politique Publique: Un Bilan Critique et Une Voie de Formilization*. Québec: Université Laval Centre d'Analyse des Politiques Publiques.

Owens, Susan, and Tim Rayner. 1999. '"When Knowledge Matters": The Role and Influence of the Royal Commission on Environmental Pollution', *Journal of Environmental Policy and Planning* 1: 7–24.

Padberg, D.I. 1992. 'Nutritional Labeling as a Policy Instrument', *American Journal of Agricultural Economics* 74, 5: 1208–13.

Page, Benjamin I., and Robert Y. Shapiro. 1992. *The Rational Public: Fifty Years of Trends in American Policy Preferences*. Chicago: University of Chicago Press.

Page, Edward C. 1985a. *Political Authority and Bureaucratic Power: A Comparative Analysis*. Brighton, Sussex: Wheatsheaf.

_____. 1985b. 'Laws as an Instrument of Policy: A Study in Central-Local Government Relations', *Journal of Public Policy* 5, 2: 241–65.

Pal, Leslie A. 1987. *Public Policy Analysis: An Introduction*. Toronto: Methuen.

_____. 1988. 'Hands at the Helm? Leadership and Public Policy', in Pal and David Taras, eds, *Prime Ministers and Premiers: Political Leadership and Public Policy in Canada*. Scarborough, Ont.: Prentice-Hall, 16–26.

_____. 1992. *Public Policy Analysis: An Introduction*, 2nd edn. Scarborough, Ont.: Nelson.

_____. 1993a. *Interests of State: The Politics of Language, Multiculturalism, and Feminism in Canada*. Montreal and Kingston: McGill-Queen's University Press.

_____. 1993b. 'Advocacy Organizations and Legislative Politics: The Effects of the Charter of Rights and Freedoms on Interest Lobbying of Federal Legislation, 1989–1991', in F.L. Seidle, ed., *Equity and Community: The Charter, Interest Advocacy and Representation*. Montreal: Institute for Research on Public Policy, 119–57.

_____. 1997. *Beyond Policy Analysis: Public Issue Management in Turbulent Times*. Toronto: ITP Nelson.

Palumbo, Dennis J. 1987. *The Politics of Program Evaluation*. Beverly Hills, Calif.: Sage.

_____ and D.J. Calista. 1990a. *Implementation and the Policy Process: Opening Up the Black Box*. New York: Greenwood Press.

_____ and _____. 1990b. 'Opening Up the Black Box: Implementation and the Policy Process', in Palumbo and Calista (1990a).

Panitch, Leo. 1977. 'The Development of Corporatism in Liberal Democracies', *Comparative Political Studies* 10, 1: 61–90.

_____. 1979. 'Corporatism in Canada', *Studies in Political Economy* 1, 1: 43–92.

Pappi, Franz Urban, and Christian H.C.A. Henning. 1998. 'Policy Networks: More Than a Metaphor', *Journal of Theoretical Politics* 10, 4: 553–75.

_____ and _____. 1999. 'The Organization of Influence on the EC's Common Agricultural Policy: A Network Approach', *European Journal of Political Research* 36: 257–81.

Parenti, Michael. 1986. *Inventing Reality: The Politics of the Mass Media*. New York: St Martin's Press.

Pateman, Carole. 1970. *Participation and Democratic Theory*. Cambridge: Cambridge University Press.

Patton, Carl V., and David S. Sawicki. 1993. *Basic Methods of Policy Analysis and Planning*. Englewood Cliffs, NJ: Prentice-Hall.

Payne, John W. 1982. 'Contingent Decision Behaviour', *Psychological Bulletin* 92, 2: 382–402.

_____, James R. Bettman, and Eric J. Johnson. 1988. 'Adaptive Strategy Selection in Decision Making', *Journal of Experimental Psychology; Learning, Memory and Cognition* 14, 3: 534–52.

Perrow, Charles. 1984. *Normal Accidents: Living with High-Risk Technologies*. New York: Basic Books.

Peters, B. Guy. 1984. *The Politics of Bureaucracy: A Comparative Perspective*. New York: Longman.

_____. 1992a. 'The Policy Process: An Institutionalist Perspective', *Canadian Public Administration* 35, 2: 160–80.

_____. 1992b. 'Government Reorganization: A Theoretical Analysis', *International Political Science Review* 13, 2: 199–218.

_____. 1998. 'The Experimenting Society and Policy Design', in William N. Dunn, ed., *The Experimenting Society: Essays in Honour of Donald T. Campbell*. New Brunswick, NJ: Transaction, 125–39.

_____. 1999. *Institutional Theory in Political Science: The 'New Institutionalism'*. London: Pinter.

_____. 2002. 'The Politics of Tool Choice', in Salamon (2002a: 552–64).

_____, John C. Doughtie, and M. Kathleen McCulloch. 1977. 'Types of Democratic Systems and Types of Public Policy', *Comparative Politics* 9: 327–55.

_____, _____, and _____. 1978. 'Do Public Policies Vary in Different Types of Democratic System?', in P.G. Lewis, D.C. Potter, and F.G. Castles, eds, *The Practice of Comparative Politics: A Reader*. London: Longman.

_____ and Brian W. Hogwood. 1985a. *The Pathology of Public Policy*. New York: Oxford University Press.

_____ and _____. 1985b. 'In Search of the Issue-Attention Cycle', *Journal of Politics* 47, 1: 238–53.

_____ and Anthony Barker, eds. 1993. *Advising West European Governments: Inquiries, Expertise and Public Policy*. Edinburgh: Edinburgh University Press.

_____ and F.K.M. Van Nispen, eds. 1998. *Public Policy Instruments: Evaluating the Tools of Public Administration*. New York: Edward Elgar.

Peterson, John. 1995. 'Decision-making in the European Union: Towards a Framework for Analysis', *Journal of European Public Policy* 2, 1: 69–93.

Petry, Francois. 1999. 'The Opinion–Policy Relationship in Canada', *Journal of Politics* 61, 2: 540–50.

Phidd, Richard W. 1975. 'The Economic Council of Canada: Its Establishment, Structure, and Role in the Canadian Policy-Making System 1963–74', *Canadian Public Administration* 18, 3: 428–73.

_____ and G. Bruce Doern. 1983. *Canadian Public Policy: Ideas, Structures, Process*. Toronto: Methuen.

Phillips, Jim, Bruce Chapman, and David Stevens, eds. 2001. *Between State and Market: Essays on Charities, Law and Policy in Canada*. Toronto: University of Toronto Press.

Phillips, Susan D. 1991a. 'How Ottawa Blends: Shifting Government Relationships with Interest Groups', in F. Abele, ed., *How Ottawa Spends 1991–92: The Politics of Fragmentation*. Ottawa: Carleton University Press, 183–228.

_____. 1991b. 'Meaning and Structure in Social Movements: Mapping the Network of National Canadian Women's Organizations', *Canadian Journal of Political Science* 24, 4: 755–82.

_____. 1998. 'Discourse, Identity, and Voice: Feminist Contributions to Policy Studies', in L. Dobuzinskis, M. Howlett, and D. Laycock, eds, *Policy Studies in Canada: The State of the Art*. Toronto: University of Toronto Press, 242–65.

Pierson, Paul. 1993. 'When Effect Becomes Cause: Policy Feedback and Political Change', *World Politics* 45: 595–628.

_____. 2000. 'Increasing Returns, Path Dependence, and the Study of Politics', *American Political Science Review* 94, 2: 251–67.

Pigou, A.C. 1932. *The Economics of Welfare*, 4th edn. London: Macmillan.

Poel, Dale H. 1976. 'The Diffusion of Legislation Among the Canadian Provinces', *Canadian Journal of Political Science* 9: 605–26.

Pollock, Philip H., Stuart A. Lilie, and M. Elliot Vittes. 1989. 'Hard Issues, Core Values and Vertical Constraint: The Case of Nuclear Power', *British Journal of Political Science* 23, 1: 29–50.

Polsby, Nelson W. 1963. *Community Power and Political Theory*. New Haven: Yale University Press.

_____. 1984. *Political Innovation in America: The Politics of Policy Initiation*. New Haven: Yale University Press.

Posner, Richard A. 1974. 'Theories of Economic Regulation', *Bell Journal of Economics and Management Science* 5, 2: 335–58.

Poulantzas, Nicos. 1973a. *Political Power and Social Classes*. London: New Left Books.

_____. 1973b. 'On Social Classes', *New Left Review* 78: 27–54.

_____. 1978. *State, Power, Socialism*. London: New Left Books.

Powell, Walter W., and Paul J. DiMaggio, eds. 1991. *The New Institutionalism in Orga-nizational Analysis*. Chicago: University of Chicago Press.

Pressman, Jeffrey L., and Aaron B. Wildavsky. 1984. *Implementation: How Great Expectations in Washington are Dashed in Oakland*, 3rd edn. Berkeley: University of California Press.

Presthus, Robert V. 1973. *Elite Accommodation in Canadian Politics*. Cambridge: Cam-bridge University Press.

Preston, Lee E., and Duane Windsor. 1992. *The Rules of the Game in the Global Econ-omy: Policy Regimes for International Business*. Boston: Kluwer Academic Publishers.

Prichard, J. Robert S., ed. 1983. *Crown Corporations in Canada: The Calculus of Instrument Choice*. Toronto: Butterworths.

Priest, Margot, and Aron Wohl. 1980. 'The Growth of Federal and Provincial Regula-tion of Economic Activity 1867–1978', in W.T. Stanbury, ed., *Government Regula-tion: Scope, Growth, Process*. Montreal: Institute for Research on Public Policy.

Prince, Michael J. 1979. 'Policy Advisory Groups in Government Departments', in G.B. Doern and P. Aucoin, eds, *Public Policy in Canada: Organization, Process, Management*. Toronto: Gage, 275–300.

Pritchard, David. 1992. 'The News Media and Public Policy Agendas', in Kennamer (1992).

Pross, A. Paul. 1992. *Group Politics and Public Policy*. Toronto: Oxford University Press.

———— and Iain S. Stewart. 1993. 'Lobbying, the Voluntary Sector and the Public Purse', in S.D. Phillips, ed., *How Ottawa Spends 1993–1994: A More Democratic Canada?* Ottawa: Carleton University Press, 109–42.

———— and Susan McCorquodale. 1990. 'The State, Interests, and Policy-Making in the East Coast Fishery', in Coleman and Skogstad (1990).

Pryor, F.L. 1968. *Public Expenditures in Communist and Capitalist Nations*. Home-wood, Ill.: R.D. Irwin.

Przeworski, Adam. 1987. 'Methods of Cross-national Research, 1970–83: An Overview', in M. Dierkes, H.N. Weiler, and A.B. Antal, eds, *Comparative Policy Research: Learning from Experience*. Aldershot: Gower, 31–49.

————. 1990. *The State and the Economy Under Capitalism*. Chur, Switzerland: Har-wood Academic Publishers.

———— and Fernando Limongi. 1997. 'Modernization: Theories and Facts', *World Poli-tics* 49: 155–83.

Putnam, Robert D. 1988. 'Diplomacy and Domestic Politics: The Logic of Two-Level Games', *International Organization* 42: 427–60.

————. 1995a. 'Bowling Alone: America's Declining Social Capital', *Journal of Democracy* 6, 1: 65–78.

————. 1995b. 'Tuning In, Tuning Out: The Strange Disappearance of Social Capital in America', *PS: Political Science and Politics* (Dec.): 664–83.

————. 1996. *The Decline of Civil Society: How Come? So What?* Ottawa: Canadian Centre for Management Development.

————. 2000. *Bowling Alone: The Collapse and Revival of American Community*. New York: Simon and Schuster.

————. 2001. 'Social Capital: Measurement and Consequences', *Isuma* 2, 1: 41–52.

Qualter, Terence H. 1985. *Opinion Control in the Democracies*. London: Macmillan.

Quarter, Jack. 1992. *Canada's Social Economy: Co-operatives, Non-Profits, and Other Community Enterprises*. Toronto: James Lorimer.

Raboy, Marc. 1995. 'Influencing Public Policy on Canadian Broadcasting', *Canadian Public Administration* 38, 3: 411–32.

Radford, K.J. 1977. *Complex Decision Problems: An Integrated Strategy for Resolution*. Reston, Va: Reston Publishing Company.

Radin, Beryl A. 2000. *Beyond Machiavelli: Policy Analysis Comes of Age*. Washington: Georgetown University Press.

Rakoff, Stuart H., and Guenther F. Schaefer. 1970. 'Politics, Policy, and Political Science: Theoretical Alternatives', *Politics and Society* 1, 1: 51–77.

Ramesh, M. 1995. 'Economic Globalization and Policy Choices: Singapore', *Governance* 10, 2: 243–60.

———. 2000. *Welfare Capitalism in Southeast Asia: Social Security, Health, and Education Policies*. London: Macmillan.

Ray, James Lee. 2001. 'Integrating Levels of Analysis in World Politics', *Journal of Theoretical Politics* 13, 4: 355–88.

Rayner, J., et al. 2001. 'Privileging the Sub-Sector: Critical Sub-Sectors and Sectoral Relationships in Forest Policy-Making', *Forest Policy and Economics* 2, 3/4: 319–32.

Reagan, Michael D. 1987. *Regulation: The Politics of Policy*. Boston: Little, Brown.

Reid, Timothy E. 1979. 'The Failure of PPBS: Real Incentives for the 1980s', *Optimum* 10, 4: 23–37.

Rein, Martin, Gosta Esping-Andersen, and Lee Rainwater, eds. 1987. *Stagnation and Renewal in Social Policy: The Rise and Fall of Policy Regimes*. Armonk, NY: M.E. Sharpe.

——— and Donald Schon. 1996. 'Frame-Critical Policy Analysis and Frame-Reflective Policy Practice', *Knowledge and Policy* 9, 1: 85–105.

Reinicke, Wolfgang H. 1998. *Global Public Policy: Governing Without Government?* Washington: Brookings Institution.

Relyea, Harold C. 1977. 'The Provision of Government Information: The Freedom of Information Act Experience', *Canadian Public Administration* 20, 2: 317–41.

Rhodes, R.A.W. 1984. 'Power-Dependence, Policy Communities and Intergovernmental Networks', *Public Administration Bulletin* 49: 4–31.

———. 1996. 'The New Governance: Governing Without Government', *Political Studies* 44: 652–67.

———. 1997a. *Understanding Governance: Policy Networks, Governance, Reflexivity, and Accountability*. Buckingham: Open University Press.

———. 1997b. 'From Marketisation to Diplomacy: It's the Mix that Matters', *Australian Journal of Public Administration* 56, 2: 40–54.

——— and David Marsh. 1992. 'New Directions in the Study of Policy Networks', *European Journal of Political Science* 21: 181–205.

Ricci, David. 1993. *The Transformation of American Politics: The New Washington and the Rise of Think Tanks*. New Haven: Yale University Press.

Richardson, Jeremy J., ed. 1990. *Privatisation and Deregulation in Canada and Britain*. Aldershot: Dartmouth.

———. 1995. 'EU Water Policy: Uncertain Agendas, Shifting Networks and Complex Coalitions', in H. Bressers, L.J. O'Toole, and J. Richardson, eds, *Networks for Water Policy: A Comparative Perspective*. London: Frank Cass, 139–67.

———. 1999. 'Interest Groups, Multi-Arena Politics and Policy Change', in S.S. Nagel, ed., *The Policy Process*. Commack, NY: Nova Science Publishers, 65–100.

———. 2000. 'Government, Interest Groups and Policy Change', *Political Studies* 48: 1006–25.

———, Gunnel Gustafsson, and Grant Jordan. 1982. 'The Concept of Policy Style', in Richardson, ed., *Policy Styles in Western Europe*. London: George Allen and Unwin.

——— and A.G. Jordan. 1979. *Governing Under Pressure: The Policy Process in a Post-Parliamentary Democracy*. Oxford: Martin Robertson.

———, ———, and R.H. Kimber. 1978. 'Lobbying, Administrative Reform and Policy Styles: The Case of Land Drainage', *Political Studies* 26, 1: 47–64.

Riedel, James A. 1972. 'Citizen Participation: Myths and Realities', *Public Administration Review* (May–June): 211–20.

Riker, William H. 1962. *The Theory of Political Coalitions*. New Haven: Yale University Press.

——. 1983. 'Political Theory and the Art of Heresthetics', in Ada W. Finifter, ed., *Political Science: The State of the Discipline*. Washington: American Political Science Association, 47–67.

——. 1986. *The Art of Political Manipulation*. New Haven: Yale University Press.

—— and Grace A. Franklin. 1980. *Congress, the Bureaucracy, and Public Policy*, 3rd edn. Homewood, Ill.: Dorsey Press.

Risse-Kappen, Thomas. 1995. *Bringing Transnational Relations Back in: Non-State Actors, Domestic Structures and International Institutions*. Cambridge: Cambridge University Press.

Rist, Ray C. 1994. 'The Preconditions for Learning: Lessons from the Public Sector', in F.L. Leeuw, R.C. Rist, and R.C. Sonnischen, eds, *Can Governments Learn: Comparative Perspectives on Evaluation and Organizational Learning*. New Brunswick, NJ: Transaction.

Rittberger, Volker, and Peter Mayer, eds. 1993. *Regime Theory and International Relations*. Oxford: Clarendon Press.

Rittel, Horst W.J., and Melvin M. Webber. 1973. 'Dilemmas in a General Theory of Planning', *Policy Sciences* 4: 155–69.

Roberts, Nancy C., and Paula J. King. 1991. 'Policy Entrepreneurs: Their Activity Structure and Function in the Policy Process', *Journal of Public Administration Research and Theory* 1, 2: 147–75.

Rochefort, David A., and Roger W. Cobb. 1993. 'Problem Definition, Agenda Access, and Policy Choice', *Policy Studies Journal* 21, 1: 56–71.

Roe, Emory. 1990. *Taking Complexity Seriously: Policy Analysis, Triangulation and Sustainable Development*. Boston: Kluwer Academic.

——. 2000. 'Poverty, Defense and the Environment: How Policy Optics, Policy Incompleteness, fastthinking.com, Equivalency Paradox, Deliberation Trap, Mailbox Dilemma, the Urban Ecosystem and the End of Problem Solving Recast Difficult Policy Issues', *Administration and Society* 31, 6: 687–725.

Roemer, John, ed. 1986. *Analytical Marxism*. Cambridge: Cambridge University Press.

Rogers, David L., and David A. Whetton, eds. 1982. *Interorganizational Coordination: Theory, Research and Implementation*. Ames: Iowa State University Press.

Rogers, Harry. 1978. 'Management Control in the Public Service', *Optimum* 9, 3: 14–28.

Rogers, H.G., M.A. Ulrick, and K.L. Traversy. 1981. 'Evaluation in Practice: The State of the Art in Canadian Governments', *Canadian Public Administration* 24, 3: 371–86.

Rona-Tas, Akos. 1998. 'Path Dependence and Capital Theory: Sociology of the Post-Communist Economic Transformation', *East European Politics and Societies* 12, 1: 107–31.

Rondinelli, Dennis A. 1976. 'International Assistance Policy and Development Project Administration: The Impact of Imperious Rationality', *International Organization* 30: 573–605.

——. 1983. *Development Projects as Policy Experiments: An Adaptive Approach to Development Administration*. London: Methuen.

Rose, Richard. 1976. 'Models of Change', in Rose, ed., *The Dynamics of Public Policy: A Comparative Analysis*. London: Sage, 7–33.

——. 1980. *Do Parties Make a Difference?* London: Macmillan.

——. 1988. 'Comparative Policy Analysis: The Program Approach', in M. Dogan, ed., *Comparing Pluralist Democracies: Strains on Legitimacy*. Boulder, Colo.: Westview Press, 219–41.

——. 1990. 'Inheritance Before Choice in Public Policy', *Journal of Theoretical Politics* 2, 3: 263–91.

_____. 1991. 'What is Lesson-Drawing?', *Journal of Public Policy* 11, 1: 3–30.

_____. 1993. *Lesson-Drawing in Public Policy: A Guide to Learning Across Time and Space*. Chatham, NJ: Chatham House.

Rosenau, James N. 1969. *Linkage Politics: Essays on the Convergence of National and International Systems*. New York: Collier-Macmillan.

Rosendal, G. Kristin. 2000. 'Overlapping International Regimes: The Case of the Inter-governmental Forum on Forests (IFF) Between Climate Change and Biodiversity'. Oslo: Fridtjof Nansen Institute Paper. Available at: < http://www.fni.no, 2000 >.

Rothmayr, Christine, and Sibylle Hardmeier. 2002. 'Governmental Polling: Use and Impact of Polls in the Policy-Making Process in Switzerland', *International Journal of Public Opinion Research* 14, 2: 123–40.

_____, Uwe Serduelt, and Elisabeth Maurer. 1997. 'Policy Instruments: An Analytical Category Revised', paper presented at the ECPR Joint Sessions Workshops, 27 Feb.–4 Mar., Bern.

Rousseau, Jean-Jacques. 1973. *The Social Contract and Discourses*. London: J.M. Dent.

Rowley, C.K. 1983. 'The Political Economy of the Public Sector', in R.J.B. Jones, ed., *Perspectives on Political Economy*. London: Pinter.

Russell, Peter H. 1982. 'The Effect of a Charter of Rights on the Policy-Making Role of Canadian Courts', *Canadian Public Administration* 25: 1–33.

Ryan, Phil. 1995. 'Miniature Mila and Flying Geese: Government Advertising and Canadian Democracy', in S.D. Phillips, ed., *How Ottawa Spends 1995–96: Mid-Life Crises*. Ottawa: Carleton University Press, 263–86.

Sabatier, Paul A. 1986. 'Top-Down and Bottom-Up Approaches to Implementation Research: A Critical Analysis and Suggested Synthesis', *Journal of Public Policy* 6: 21–48.

_____. 1987. 'Knowledge, Policy-Oriented Learning, and Policy Change', *Knowledge: Creation, Diffusion, Utilization* 8, 4: 649–92.

_____. 1988. 'An Advocacy Coalition Framework of Policy Change and the Role of Policy-Oriented Learning Therein', *Policy Sciences* 21, 2/3: 129–68.

_____. 1992. 'Political Science and Public Policy: An Assessment', in W.N. Dunn and R.M. Kelly, eds, *Advances in Policy Studies Since 1950*. New Brunswick, NJ: Trans-action, 27–58.

_____. 1993a. 'Top-down and Bottom-up Approaches to Implementation Research', in Hill (1993).

_____. 1993b. 'Policy Change Over a Decade or More', in Sabatier and Jenkins-Smith (1993a: 13–40).

_____, ed. 1999a. *Theories of the Policy Process*. Boulder, Colo.: Westview Press.

_____. 1999b. 'The Need for Better Theories', in Sabatier (1999a: 3–17).

_____ and Hank C. Jenkins-Smith, eds. 1993a. *Policy Change and Learning: An Advo-cacy Coalition Approach*. Boulder, Colo.: Westview Press,.

_____ and _____. 1993b. 'The Advocacy Coalition Framework: Assessment, Revi-sions, and Implications for Scholars and Practitioners', in Sabatier and Jenkins-Smith (1993a).

_____ and D.A. Mazmanian. 1981. *Effective Policy Implementation*. Lexington, Mass.: Lexington Books.

Sager, Tore. 2001. 'Manipulative Features of Planning Styles', *Environment and Plan-ning A* 33: 765–91.

Salamon, Lester M. 1981. 'Rethinking Public Management: Third-Party Government and the Changing Forms of Government Action', *Public Policy* 29, 3: 255–75.

_____. 1987. 'Of Market Failure, Voluntary Failure, and Third-Party Government', in Ostrander and Langton (1987).

_____, ed. 1989a. *Beyond Privatization: The Tools of Government Action*. Washing-ton: Urban Institute.

_____. 1989b. 'The Changing Tools of Government Action: An Overview', in Salamon (1989a).

_____. 1989c. 'Conclusion: Beyond Privatization', in Salamon (1989a).

_____. 1995. *Partners in Public Service: Government-Nonprofit Relations in the Modern Welfare State*. Baltimore: Johns Hopkins University Press.

_____, ed. 2002a. *The Tools of Government: A Guide to the New Governance*. New York: Oxford University Press.

_____. 2002b. 'Economic Regulation', in Salamon (2002a: 117–55).

_____ and Michael S. Lund. 1989. 'The Tools Approach: Basic Analytics', in Salamon (1989a: 23–50).

Salisbury, Robert H., et al. 1987. 'Who Works with Whom? Interest Group Alliances and Opposition', *American Political Science Review* 81, 4: 1217–34.

Salmon, Charles, ed. 1989. *Information Campaigns: Managing the Process of Social Change*. Newberry Park, Calif.: Sage.

Salter, Liora. 1981. *Public Inquiries in Canada*. Ottawa: Science Council of Canada.

Samuels, Warren J. 1991. '"Truth" and "Discourse" in the Social Construction of Economic Reality: An Essay on the Relation of Knowledge to Socioeconomic Policy', *Journal of Post-Keynesian Economics* 13, 4: 511–24.

Sanderson, Ian. 2002. 'Evaluation, Policy Learning and Evidence-Based Policy-Making', *Public Administration* 80, 1: 1–22.

Sarpkaya, S. 1988. *Lobbying in Canada—Ways and Means*. Don Mills, Ont.: CCH Canadian.

Savas, E.S. 1977. *Alternatives for Delivering Public Services: Toward Improved Performance*. Boulder, Colo.: Westview Press.

_____. 1987. *Privatization: The Key to Better Government*. Chatham, NJ: Chatham House.

Savoie, Donald J. 1990. *The Politics of Public Spending in Canada*. Toronto: University of Toronto Press.

_____. 1999. *Governing from the Centre: The Concentration of Power in Canadian Politics*. Toronto: University of Toronto Press.

Saward, Michael. 1990. 'Cooption and Power: Who Gets What from Formal Incorporation', *Political Studies* 38: 588–602.

_____. 1992. *Co-Optive Politics and State Legitimacy*. Aldershot: Dartmouth.

Schaap, L., and M.J.W. van Twist. 1997. 'The Dynamics of Closedness in Networks', in W.J.M. Kickert, E.-H. Klijn, and J.F.M. Koppenjan, eds, *Managing Complex Networks: Strategies for the Public Sector*. London: Sage, 62–78.

Scharpf, Fritz W. 1990. 'Games Real Actors Could Play: The Problem of Mutual Predictability', *Rationality and Society* 2: 471–94.

_____. 1991. 'Political Institutions, Decision Styles, and Policy Choices', in R.M. Czada and A. Windhoff-Heritier, eds, *Political Choice: Institutions, Rules and the Limits of Rationality*. Frankfurt: Campus Verlag, 53–86.

_____. 1997. *Games Real Actors Play: Actor-Centered Institutionalism in Policy Research*. Boulder, Colo.: Westview Press.

Schattschneider, E.E. 1935. *Politics, Pressures and the Tariff*. New York: Prentice-Hall.

_____. 1960. *The Semisovereign People: A Realist's View of Democracy in America*. New York: Holt, Rinehart and Winston.

Schlager, Edella. 1999. 'A Comparison of Frameworks, Theories, and Models of Policy Processes', in Sabatier (1999a: 233–60).

Schmidt, Vivien A. 2001. 'The Politics of Economic Adjustment in France and Britain: When Does Discourse Matter?', *Journal of European Public Policy* 8, 2: 247–64.

Schmitter, Phillipe C. 1977. 'Modes of Interest Intermediation and Models of Societal Change in Western Europe', *Comparative Political Studies* 10, 1: 7–38.

_____. 1982. 'Reflections on Where the Theory of Neo-Corporatism Has Gone and

Where the Praxis of Neo-Corporatism May Be Going', in G. Lehmbruch and P.C. Schmitter, eds, *Patterns of Corporatist Policy-Making*. London: Sage.

_____. 1985. 'Neo-corporatism and the State', in W. Grant, ed., *The Political Economy of Corporatism*. London: Macmillan.

Schneider, Anne, and Helen Ingram. 1988. 'Systematically Pinching Ideas: A Comparative Approach to Policy Design', *Journal of Public Policy* 8, 1: 61–80.

_____ and _____. 1990a. 'Behavioural Assumptions of Policy Tools', *Journal of Politics* 52, 2: 510–29.

_____ and _____. 1990b. 'Policy Design: Elements, Premises and Strategies', in S.S. Nagel, ed., *Policy Theory and Policy Evaluation: Concepts, Knowledge, Causes and Norms*. New York: Greenwood, 77–102.

_____ and _____. 1993. 'Social Construction of Target Populations: Implications for Politics and Policy', *American Political Science Review* 87, 2: 334–47.

_____ and _____. 1997. *Policy Design for Democracy*. Lawrence: University Press of Kansas.

Schneider, F., and Bruno S. Frey. 1988. 'Politico-Economic Models of Macroeconomic Policy: A Review of the Empirical Evidence', in Thomas D. Willett, ed., *Political Business Cycles: The Political Economy of Money, Inflation and Unemployment*. Durham, NC: Duke University Press, 239–75.

Schneider, Joseph W. 1985. 'Social Problems Theory: The Constructionist View', *Annual Review of Sociology* 11: 209–29.

Scholz, John T. 1984. 'Cooperation, Deterrence, and the Ecology of Regulatory Enforcement', *Law and Society Review* 18, 2: 179–224.

_____. 1991. 'Cooperative Regulatory Enforcement and the Politics of Administrative Effectiveness', *American Political Science Review* 85, 1: 115–36.

Schon, Donald A., and Martin Rein. 1994. *Frame Reflection: Towards the Resolution of Intractable Policy Controversies*. New York: Basic Books.

Schulman, Paul R. 1988. 'The Politics of "Ideational Policy"', *Journal of Politics* 50: 263–91.

Schultz, Richard, and Alan Alexandroff. 1985. *Economic Regulation and the Federal System*. Toronto: University of Toronto Press.

Schwartz, Bryan. 1997. 'Public Inquiries', *Canadian Public Administration* 40, 1: 72–85.

Sciarini, Pascal. 1986. 'Elaboration of the Swiss Agricultural Policy for the GATT Negotiations: A Network Analysis', *Swiss Journal of Sociology* 22, 1: 85–115.

Self, Peter. 1985. *Political Theories of Modern Government: Its Role and Reform*. London: Allen and Unwin.

Shapiro, Robert Y., and Lawrence R. Jacobs. 1989. 'The Relationship Between Public Opinion and Public Policy: A Review', in S. Long, ed., *Political Behaviour Annual*. Boulder, Colo.: Westview Press.

Sharkansky, Ira. 1971. 'Constraints on Innovation in Policy Making: Economic Development and Political Routines', in Frank Marini, ed., *Toward a New Public Administration: The Minnowbrook Perspective*. Scranton, Penn.: Chandler.

_____. 1997. *Policy Making in Israel: Routines for Simple Problems and Coping with the Complex*. Pittsburgh: University of Pittsburgh Press.

Sharp, Elaine B. 1994a. 'Paradoxes of National Anti-Drug Policymaking', in David A. Rochefort and Roger W. Cobb, eds, *The Politics of Problem Definition: Shaping the Policy Agenda*. Lawrence: University Press of Kansas, 98–116.

_____. 1994b. 'The Dynamics of Issue Expansion: Cases from Disability Rights and Fetal Research Controversy', *Journal of Politics* 56, 4: 919–39.

Sharpe, L.J. 1985. 'Central Coordination and the Policy Network', *Political Studies* 33, 3: 361–81.

Sheriff, Peta E. 1983. 'State Theory, Social Science, and Governmental Commissions', *American Behavioural Scientist* 26, 5: 669–80.

Shotland, R. Lance, and Melvin M. Mark. 1985. *Social Science and Social Policy*. Beverly Hills, Calif.: Sage.

Siaroff, Alan. 1999. 'Corporatism in 24 Industrial Democracies: Meaning and Measurement', *European Journal of Political Research* 36: 175–205.

Sieber, Sam D. 1981. *Fatal Remedies: The Ironies of Social Intervention*. New York: Plenum.

Siedschlag, Alexander. 2000. 'Institutionalization and Conflict Management in the New Europe—Path-Shaping for the Better or Worse?', paper presented to the 18th World Congress of the International Political Science Association, Quebec City.

Simeon, Richard. 1976a. 'Studying Public Policy', *Canadian Journal of Political Science* 9, 4: 548–80.

_____. 1976b. 'The "Overload Thesis" and Canadian Government', *Canadian Public Policy* 2, 4: 541–52.

Simmons, Robert H., et al. 1974. 'Policy Flow Analysis: A Conceptual Model for Comparative Public Policy Research', *Western Political Quarterly* 27, 3: 457–68.

Simon, Herbert A. 1946. 'The Proverbs of Administration', *Public Administration Review* 6, 1: 53–67.

_____. 1955. 'A Behavioral Model of Rational Choice', *Quarterly Journal of Economics* 69, 1: 99–118.

_____. 1957a. *Administrative Behavior: A Study of Decision-Making Processes in Administrative Organization*, 2nd edn. New York: Macmillan.

_____. 1957b. *Models of Man, Social and Rational: Mathematical Essays on Rational Human Behavior in a Social Setting*. New York: Wiley.

_____. 1973. 'The Structure of Ill Structured Problems', *Artificial Intelligence* 4: 181–201.

_____. 1991. 'Bounded Rationality and Organizational Learning', *Organization Science* 2, 1: 125–35.

Sinclair, Darren. 1997. 'Self-Regulation versus Command and Control? Beyond False Dichotomies', *Law and Policy* 19, 4: 529–59.

Singer, Otto. 1990. 'Policy Communities and Discourse Coalitions', *Knowledge: Creation, Diffusion, Utilization* 11, 4: 428–58.

Skilling, H.G. 1966. 'Interest Groups and Communist Politics', *World Politics* 18, 3: 435–51.

Skocpol, Theda. 1985. 'Bringing the State Back In: Strategies of Analysis in Current Research', in Evans et al. (1985).

Skogstad, Grace. 1998. 'Ideas, Paradigms and Institutions: Agricultural Exceptionalism in the European Union and the United States', *Governance* 11, 4: 463–90.

Skok, James E. 1995. 'Policy Issue Networks and the Public Policy Cycle: A Structural-Functional Framework for Public Administration', *Public Administration Review* 55, 4: 325–32.

Skowronek, Stephen. 1982. *Building a New American State: The Expansion of National Administrative Capacities 1877–1920*. Cambridge: Cambridge University Press.

Slovic, Paul, Baruch Fischoff, and Sarah Lichtenstein. 1977. 'Behavioural Decision Theory', *Annual Review of Psychology* 28: 1–39.

_____, _____, and _____. 1985. 'Regulation of Risk: A Psychological Perspective', in R.G. Noll, ed., *Regulatory Policy and the Social Sciences*. Berkeley: University of California Press, 241–78.

Smith, Adrian. 2000. 'Policy Networks and Advocacy Coalitions: Explaining Policy Change and Stability in UK Industrial Pollution Policy?', *Environment and Planning C: Government and Policy* 18: 95–114.

Smith, Gilbert, and David May. 1980. 'The Artificial Debate Between Rationalist and Incrementalist Models of Decision-Making', *Policy and Politics* 8, 2: 147–61.

Smith, Martin J. 1990. 'Pluralism, Reformed Pluralism and Neopluralism: The Role of Pressure Groups in Policy-Making', *Political Studies* 38 (June): 302–22.

_____. 1993. *Pressure, Power and Policy: State Autonomy and Policy Networks in Britain and the United States.* Aldershot: Harvester Wheatsheaf.

_____. 1994. 'Policy Networks and State Autonomy', in S. Brooks and A.-G. Gagnon, eds, *The Political Influence of Ideas: Policy Communities and the Social Sciences.* New York: Praeger.

_____, David Marsh, and David Richards. 1993. 'Central Government Departments and the Policy Process', *Public Administration* 71 (Winter): 567–94.

Smith, Richard A. 1979. 'Decision Making and Non-Decision Making in Cities: Some Implications for Community Structural Research', *American Sociological Review* 44, 1: 147–61.

Smith, Rogers M. 1997. 'Still Blowing in the Wind: The American Quest for a Democratic, Scientific Political Science', in T. Bender and C.E. Schorske, eds, *American Academic Culture in Transformation: Fifty Years, Four Disciplines.* Princeton, NJ: Princeton University Press, 271–305.

Smith, Thomas B. 1977. 'Advisory Committees in the Public Policy Process', *International Review of Administrative Sciences* 43, 2: 153–66.

_____. 1985. 'Evaluating Development Policies and Programmes in the Third World', *Public Administration and Development* 5, 2: 129–44.

Snook, Scott A. 2000. *Friendly Fire: The Accidental Shootdown of U.S. BlackHawks Over Northern Iraq.* Princeton, NJ: Princeton University Press.

Snow, David A., and Robert D. Benford. 1992. 'Master Frames and Cycles of Protest', in A.D. Morris and C.M. Mueller, eds, *Frontiers in Social Movement Theory.* New Haven: Yale University Press, 133–55.

Soroka, Stuart S. 2002. *Agenda-Setting Dynamics in Canada.* Vancouver: University of British Columbia Press.

Spector, Malcolm, and John I. Kitsuse. 1987. *Constructing Social Problems.* New York: Aldine de Gruyter.

Spence, David B. 1999. 'Agency Discretion and the Dynamics of Procedural Reform', *Public Administration Review* 59, 5: 425–42.

Spitzer, Robert J., ed. 1993. *Media and Public Policy.* Westport, Conn.: Praeger.

Spranca, Mark, Elisa Minsk, and Jonathan Baron. 1991. 'Omission and Commission in Judgement and Choice', *Journal of Experimental Social Psychology* 27: 76–105.

Sproule-Jones, M. 1989. 'Multiple Rules and the "Nesting" of Public Policies', *Journal of Theoretical Politics* 1, 4: 459–77.

_____. 1994. 'User Fees', in A.M. Maslove, ed., *Taxes as Instruments of Public Policy.* Toronto: University of Toronto Press, 3–38.

Stanbury, W.T., and Jane Fulton. 1984. 'Suasion as a Governing Instrument', in A. Maslove, ed., *How Ottawa Spends 1984: The New Agenda.* Toronto: James Lorimer.

Stanton, Thomas H., and Ronald C. Moe. 2002. 'Government Corporations and Government-Sponsored Enterprises', in Salamon (2002a: 80–116).

Stark, Andrew. 1992. '"Political-Discourse" Analysis and the Debate Over Canada's Lobbying Legislation', *Canadian Journal of Political Science* 25, 3: 513–34.

Starling, Jay D. 1975. 'The Use of Systems Constructs in Simplifying Organized Social Complexity', in La Porte (1975: 131–72).

Starr, Paul. 1990a. 'The Limits of Privatization', in D.J. Gayle and J.N. Goodrich, eds, *Privatization and Deregulation in Global Perspective.* New York: Quorum Books.

_____. 1990b. 'The New Life of the Liberal State: Privatization and the Restructuring of State-Society Relations', in Suleiman and Waterbury (1990).

Steinberg, Marc W. 1998. 'Tilting the Frame: Considerations on Collective Action Framing from a Discursive Turn', *Theory and Society* 27, 6: 845–72.

Steinberger, Peter J. 1980. 'Typologies of Public Policy: Meaning Construction and the Policy Process', *Social Science Quarterly* 61, 2: 185–97.

Steuerle, C. Eugene, and Eric C. Twombly. 2002. 'Vouchers', in Salamon (2002a: 445–65).

Stevenson, Randolph T. 2001. 'The Economy and Policy Mood: A Fundamental Dynamic of Democratic Politics', *American Journal of Political Science* 45, 3: 620–33.

Stewart, John. 1974. *The Canadian House of Commons*. Montreal and Kingston: McGill-Queen's University Press.

Stigler, George J. 1975. *The Citizen and the State: Essays on Regulation*. Chicago: University of Chicago Press.

Stimson, James A. 1991. *Public Opinion in America: Moods, Cycles and Swings*. Boulder, Colo.: Westview Press.

_____, Michael B. Mackuen, and Robert S. Erikson. 1995. 'Dynamic Representation', *American Political Science Review* 89, 3: 543–65.

Stoker, Robert P. 1989. 'A Regime Framework for Implementation Analysis', *Policy Studies Review* 9, 1.

Stokey, Edith, and Richard Zeckhauser. 1978. *A Primer for Policy Analysis*. New York: W.W. Norton.

Stokman, F.N., and J. Berveling. 1998. 'Predicting Outcomes of Decision-Making: Five Competing Models of Policy-Making', in M. Fennema, C. Van der Eijk, and H. Schijf, eds, *In Search of Structure: Essays in Social Science and Methodology*. Amsterdam: Het Spinhuis, 147–71.

Stone, Deborah A. 1988. *Policy Paradox and Political Reason*. Glenview, Ill.: Scott, Foresman.

_____. 1989. 'Causal Stories and the Formation of Policy Agendas', *Political Science Quarterly* 104, 2: 281–300.

Stone, Diane. 1996. *Capturing the Political Imagination*. London: Frank Cass.

_____, Andrew Denham, and Mark Garnett. 1998. *Think Tanks across Nations: A Comparative Approach*. Manchester: Manchester University Press.

Studlar, Donley T. 2002. *Tobacco Control: Comparative Politics in the United States and Canada*. Peterborough, Ont.: Broadview Press.

Suchman, Edward A. 1967. *Evaluative Research: Principles and Practices in Public Service and Social Action Programs*. New York: Russell Sage Foundation.

_____. 1979. *Social Sciences in Policy-Making*. Paris: OECD.

Suchman, Mark C. 1995. 'Managing Legitimacy: Strategic and Institutional Approaches', *Academy of Management Review* 20, 3: 571–610.

Suedfeld, Peter, and Philip E. Tetlock. 1992. 'Psychological Advice about Political Decision Making: Heuristics, Biases, and Cognitive Defects', in Suedfeld and Tetlock, eds, *Psychology and Social Policy*. New York: Hemisphere Publishing, 51–70.

Suleiman, Ezra N., and John Waterbury, eds. 1990. *Political Economy of Public Sector Reform and Privatization*. Boulder, Colo.: Westview Press.

Sunnevag, Kjell J. 2000. 'Designing Auctions for Offshore Petroleum Lease Allocation', *Resources Policy* 26: 3–16.

Surel, Yves. 2000. 'The Role of Cognitive and Normative Frames in Policy-Making', *Journal of European Public Policy* 7, 4: 495–512.

Sutherland, Sharon L. 1993. 'The Public Service and Policy Development', in M. Michael Atkinson, ed., *Governing Canada: Institutions and Public Policy*. Toronto: Harcourt Brace Jovanovich.

Suzuki, Motoshi. 1992. 'Political Business Cycles in the Public Mind', *American Political Science Review* 86, 4: 989–96.

Svenson, Ola. 1979. 'Process Descriptions of Decision Making', *Organizational Behaviour and Human Performance* 23: 86–112.

Swiss, James E. 1991. *Public Management Systems: Monitoring and Managing Government Performance*. Upper Saddle River, NJ: Prentice-Hall.

Talbert, Jeffrey C., Bryan D. Jones, and Frank R. Baumgartner. 1995. 'Nonlegislative

Hearings and Policy Change in Congress', *American Journal of Political Science* 39, 2: 383–406.

Tamuz, Michael. 2001. 'Learning Disabilities for Regulators: The Perils of Organizational Learning in the Air Transportation Industry', *Administration and Society* 33, 3: 276–302.

Taylor, Andrew J. 1989. *Trade Unions and Politics: A Comparative Introduction*. Basingstoke: Macmillan.

Teisman, Geert R. 2000. 'Models for Research into Decision-Making Processes: On Phases, Streams and Decision-Making Rounds', *Public Administration* 78, 4: 937–56.

Termeer, C.J.A.M., and J.F.M. Koppenjan. 1997. 'Managing Perceptions in Networks', in W.J.M. Kickert, E.-H. Klijn, and J.F.M. Koppenjan, eds, *Managing Complex Networks: Strategies for the Public Sector*. London: Sage, 79–97.

t'Hart, Paul, and Marieka Kleiboer. 1995. 'Policy Controversies in the Negotiatory State', *Knowledge and Policy* 8, 4: 5–26.

Thatcher, Mark. 1998. 'The Development of Policy Network Analysis: From Market Origins to Overarching Frameworks', *Journal of Theoretical Politics* 10, 4: 389–416.

Therborn, Goran. 1977. 'The Rule of Capital and the Rise of Democracy', *New Left Review* 103: 3–41.

_____. 1986. 'Neo-Marxist, Pluralist, Corporatist, Statist Theories and the Welfare State', in A. Kazancigil, ed., *The State in Global Perspective*. Aldershot, UK: Gower.

Thomas, Gerald B. 1999. 'External Shocks, Conflict and Learning as Interactive Sources of Change in U.S. Security Policy', *Journal of Public Policy* 19, 2: 209–31.

Thomas, John W., and Merilee S. Grindle. 1990. 'After the Decision: Implementing Policy Reforms in Developing Countries', *World Development* 18, 8: 1163–81.

Thompson, E.P. 1978. *The Poverty of Theory and Other Essays*. London: Merlin Press.

Thompson, John B. 1990. *Ideology and Modern Culture: Critical Social Theory in the Era of Mass Communication*. Cambridge: Polity Press.

Thompson, W.B. 2001. 'Policy Making Through Thick and Thin: Thick Description as a Methodology for Communications and Democracy', *Policy Sciences* 34: 63–77.

Thomson, Robert. 2001. 'The Programme to Policy Linkage: The Fulfilment of Election Pledges on Socio-Economic Policy in the Netherlands, 1986–1998', *European Journal of Political Research* 40: 171–97.

Tilly, Charles. 1984. *Big Structures, Large Processes, Huge Comparisons*. New York: Russell Sage Foundation.

Timmermans, Arco, and Ivar Bleiklie. 1999. 'Institutional Conditions for Policy Design: Types of Arenas and Rules of the Game', ECPR Joint Sessions of Workshops, Mannheim.

Tocqueville, Alexis de. 1956. *Democracy in America*. New York: New American Library.

Torfing, Jacob. 2001. 'Path-Dependent Danish Welfare Reforms: The Contribution of the New Institutionalisms to Understanding Evolutionary Change', *Scandinavian Political Studies* 24, 4: 277–309.

Torgerson, Douglas. 1983. 'Contextual Orientation in Policy Analysis: The Contribution of Harold D. Lasswell', *Policy Sciences* 18: 240–52.

_____. 1986. 'Between Knowledge and Politics: Three Faces of Policy Analysis', *Policy Sciences* 19, 1: 33–59.

_____. 1990. 'Origins of the Policy Orientation: The Aesthetic Dimension in Lasswell's Political Vision', *History of Political Thought* 11, (Summer): 340–44.

_____. 1996. 'Power and Insight in Policy Discourse: Post-Positivism and Policy Discourse', in L. Dobuzinskis, M. Howlett, and D. Laycock, eds, *Policy Studies in Canada: The State of the Art*. Toronto: University of Toronto Press, 266–98.

Trebilcock, Michael J., and Douglas G. Hartle. 1982. 'The Choice of Governing Instrument', *International Review of Law and Economics* 2: 29–46.

_____ et al. 1982. *The Choice of Governing Instrument*. Ottawa: Canadian Government Publication Centre.

Tribe, Laurence H. 1972. 'Policy Science: Analysis or Ideology?', *Philosophy and Public Affairs* 2, 1: 66–110.

True, James L., Bryan D. Jones, and Frank R. Baumgartner. 1999. 'Punctuated-Equilibrium Theory: Explaining Stability and Change in American Policymaking', in Sabatier (1999a: 97–115).

Truman, David R. 1964. *The Governmental Process: Political Interests and Public Opinion*. New York: Knopf.

Tufte, Edward R. 1978. *Political Control of the Economy*. Princeton, NJ: Princeton University Press.

Tuohy, Caroline. 1992. *Policy and Politics in Canada: Institutionalized Ambivalence*. Philadelphia: Temple University Press.

_____. 1999. *Accidental Logics: The Dynamics of Change in the Health Care Arena in the United States, Britain, and Canada*. New York: Oxford University Press.

_____ and A.D. Wolfson. 1978. 'Self-Regulation: Who Qualifies?', in P. Slayton and M.J. Trebilcock, eds, *The Professions and Public Policy*. Toronto: University of Toronto Press, 111–22.

Tupper, Allan. 1979. 'The State in Business', *Canadian Public Administration* 22, 1: 124–50.

_____ and G.B. Doern. 1981. 'Public Corporations and Public Policy in Canada,' in Tupper and Doern, eds, *Public Corporations and Public Policy in Canada*. Montreal: Institute for Research on Public Policy, 1–50.

Tversky, Amos, and Daniel Kahneman. 1981. 'The Framing of Decisions and the Psychology of Choice', *Science* 211 (Jan.): 453–8.

_____ and _____. 1982. 'Judgement Under Uncertainty: Heuristics and Biases', in Kahneman, P. Slovic, and Tversky, eds, *Judgement Under Uncertainty: Heuristics and Biases*. Cambridge: Cambridge University Press, 3–20.

_____ and _____. 1986. 'Rational Choice and the Framing of Decisions', *Journal of Business* 59, 4, part 2: S251–S279.

UNCTAD. 2001. *World Investment Report 2001*. New York: United Nations.

Unger, Brigitte, and Frans van Waarden. 1995. 'Introduction: An Interdisciplinary Approach to Convergence', in Unger and van Waarden, eds, *Convergence or Diversity? Internationalization and Economic Policy Response*. Aldershot: Avebury, 1–35.

Utton, M.A. 1986. *The Economics of Regulating Industry*. Oxford: Basil Blackwell.

Uusitalo, Hannu. 1984. 'Comparative Research on the Determinants of the Welfare State: The State of the Art', *European Journal of Political Research* 12, 4: 403–22.

Valkama, Pekka, and Stephen J. Bailey. 2001. 'Vouchers as an Alternative Public Sector Funding System', *Public Policy and Administration* 16, 1: 32–58.

van Bueren, Ellen, Erik-Hans Klijn, and Joop Koppenjan. 2001. 'Network Management as a Linking Mechanism in Complex Policy-Making and Implementation Processes: Analyzing Decision-Making and Learning for an Environmental Issue', paper for the Fifth International Research Symposium in Public Management, Barcelona, 9–11 Apr.

van der Eijk, door C., and W.J.P. Kok. 1975. 'Nondecisions Reconsidered', *Acta Politika* 10, 3: 277–301.

van Meter, D., and C. van Horn. 1975. 'The Policy Implementation Process: A Conceptual Framework', *Administration and Society* 6, 4: 445–88.

Van Waarden, Frans. 1992. 'Dimensions and Types of Policy Networks', *European Journal of Political Research* 21, 1/2: 29–52.

Van Winden, Frans A.A.M. 1988. 'The Economic Theory of Political Decision-Making', in J. van den Broeck, ed., *Public Choice*. Dordrecht: Kluwer.

Varone, Frederic. 2000. 'Le Choix des instruments de l'action publique: Analyse Comparée des politiques energétiques en Europe et en Amérique du Nord', *Revue Internationale de Politique Comparée* 7, 1: 167–201.

_____ and Rejean Landry. 1997. 'The Choice of Policy Tools: In Search of Deductive Theory', paper presented at the European Consortium for Political Research Joint Sessions, Bern, Switzerland, 27 Feb.–4 Mar.

Vaughan, Diane. 1996. *The Challenger Launch Decision: Risky Technology, Culture and Deviance at NASA.* Chicago: University of Chicago Press.

Vedung, Evert, and Frans C.J. van der Doelen. 1998. 'The Sermon: Information Programs in the Public Policy Process—Choice, Effects and Evaluation', in Bemelmans-Videc et al. (1998: 103–28).

Vertzberger, Yaacov Y.I. 1998. *Risk Taking and Decisionmaking: Foreign Military Intervention Decisions.* Stanford, Calif.: Stanford University Press.

Vining, Aidan R., and David L. Weimer. 1990. 'Government Supply and Government Production Failure: A Framework Based on Contestability', *Journal of Public Policy* 10, 1: 1–22.

Vogel, David. 1986. *National Styles of Regulation: Environmental Policy in Great Britain and the United States.* Ithaca, NY: Cornell University Press.

Vogel, Steven K. 1996. *Freer Markets, More Rules: Regulatory Reform in Advanced Industrial Countries.* Ithaca, NY: Cornell University Press.

von Beyme, Klaus. 1983. 'Neo-Corporatism: A New Nut in an Old Shell?', *International Political Science Review* 4, 2: 173–96.

_____. 1984. 'Do Parties Matter? The Impact of Parties on the Key Decisions in the Political System', *Government and Opposition* 19, 1: 5–29.

Voss, James F. 1998. 'On the Representation of Problems: An Information-Processing Approach to Foreign Policy Decision Making', in D.A. Sylvan and Voss, eds, *Problem Representation in Foreign Policy Decision Making.* Cambridge: Cambridge University Press, 8–26.

_____ and Timothy A. Post. 1988. 'On the Solving of Ill-Structured Problems', in M.T.H. Chi, R. Glaser, and M.J. Farr, eds, *The Nature of Expertise.* Hillsdale, NJ: Lawrence Erlbaum Associates, 261–85.

Wade, H.W.R. 1965. 'Anglo-American Administrative Law: Some Reflections', *Law Quarterly Review* 81: 357–79.

_____. 1966. 'Anglo-American Administrative Law: More Reflections', *Law Quarterly Review* 82: 226–52.

Wagle, Udaya. 2000. 'The Policy Science of Democracy: The Issues of Methodology and Citizen Participation', *Policy Sciences* 33: 207–23.

Wagner, Peter, et al. 1991. 'The Policy Orientation: Legacy and Promise', in Wagner, Bjorn Wittrock, and Helmut Wollman, eds, *Social Sciences and Modern States: National Experiences and Theoretical Crossroads.* Cambridge: Cambridge University Press, 2–27.

Wagner, Richard K. 1991. 'Managerial Problem Solving', in R.J. Sternberg and P.A. French, eds, *Complex Problem Solving: Principles and Mechanisms.* Hillsdale, NJ: Lawrence Erlbaum Associates, 159–83.

Wagschal, Uwe. 1997. 'Direct Democracy and Public Policy-Making', *Journal of Public Policy* 17, 2: 223–46.

Walker, Jack L. 1974. 'The Diffusion of Knowledge and Policy Change: Toward a Theory of Agenda Setting', paper presented to the annual meeting of the American Political Science Association, Chicago.

_____. 1977. 'Setting the Agenda in the U.S. Senate: A Theory of Problem Selection', *British Journal of Political Science* 7: 423–45.

_____. 1981. 'The Diffusion of Knowledge, Policy Communities and Agenda-Setting: The Relationship of Knowledge and Power', in John E. Tropman, M. Dluhy, and R. Lind, eds, *New Strategic Perspectives on Social Policy.* New York: Pergamon Press, 75–96.

Walsh, James I. 1994. 'Institutional Constraints and Domestic Choices: Economic Convergence and Exchange Rate Policy in France and Italy', *Political Studies* 42: 243–58.

Warwick, Paul V. 2000. 'Policy Horizons in West European Parliamentary Systems', *European Journal of Political Research* 38: 37–61.

Weaver, R. Kent. 1986. 'The Politics of Blame Avoidance', *Journal of Public Policy* 6, 4: 371–98.

_____. 1988. *Automatic Government: The Politics of Indexation*. Washington: Brookings Institution.

_____. 1989. 'The Changing World of Think Tanks', *PS: Political Science and Politics* 22: 563–78.

_____ and Bert A. Rockman, eds. 1993a. *Do Institutions Matter? Government Capabilities in the United States and Abroad*. Washington: Brookings Institution.

_____ and _____. 1993b. 'When and How Do Institutions Matter?', in Weaver and Rockman (1993a).

_____ and _____. 1993c. 'Assessing the Effects of Institutions', in Weaver and Rockman (1993a).

Webber, David J. 1986. 'Analyzing Political Feasibility: Political Scientists' Unique Contribution to Policy Analysis', *Policy Studies Journal* 14, 4: 545–54.

_____. 1992. 'The Distribution and Use of Policy Knowledge in the Policy Process', in W.N. Dunn and R.M. Kelly, eds, *Advances in Policy Studies Since 1950*. New Brunswick, NJ: Transaction.

Weber, Max. 1978. *Economy and Society: An Outline of Interpretive Sociology*. Berkeley: University of California Press.

Weber, Ronald E., and William R. Shaffer. 1972. 'Public Opinion and American State Policy-Making', *Midwest Journal of Political Science* 16: 683–99.

Weick, Karl E. 1976. 'Educational Organizations as Loosely Coupled Systems', *Administrative Science Quarterly* 21: 1–19.

Weimer, David L., and Aidan R. Vining. 1992. *Policy Analysis: Concepts and Practice*, 2nd edn. Englewood Cliffs, NJ: Prentice-Hall.

_____ and _____. 1999. *Policy Analysis: Concepts and Practice*, 3rd edn. Englewood Cliffs, NJ: Prentice-Hall.

Weir, Margaret. 1992. 'Ideas and the Politics of Bounded Innovation', in Sven Steinmo, Kathleen Thelen, and Frank Longstreth, eds, *Structuring Politics: Historical Institutionalism in Comparative Analysis*. Cambridge: Cambridge University Press, 188–216.

Weiss, Andrew, and Edward Woodhouse. 1992. 'Reframing Incrementalism: A Constructive Response to Critics', *Policy Sciences* 25, 3: 255–73.

Weiss, Carol H. 1977a. *Using Social Research in Public Policy Making*. Lexington, Mass.: Lexington Books.

_____. 1977b. 'Research for Policy's Sake: The Enlightenment Function of Social Science Research', *Policy Analysis* 3, 4: 531–45.

_____. 1980. 'Knowledge Creep and Decision Accretion', *Knowledge: Creation, Diffusion, Utilization* 1, 3: 381–404.

Weiss, Janet A. 1982. 'Coping with Complexity: An Experimental Study of Public Policy Decision-Making', *Journal of Policy Analysis and Management* 2, 1: 66–87.

_____ and Mary Tschirhart. 1994. 'Public Information Campaigns as Policy Instruments', *Journal of Policy Analysis and Management* 13, 1: 82–119.

Weiss, Linda. 1999. 'Globalization and National Governance: Autonomy or Interdependence', *Review of International Studies* 25 (supp.): 59–88.

_____ and John M. Hobson. 1995. *States and Economic Development: A Comparative Historical Analysis*. Cambridge: Polity Press.

Whalen, Thomas. 1987. 'Introduction to Decision-Making Under Various Kinds of

Uncertainty', in J. Kacprzyk and S.A. Orlovski, eds, *Optimization Models Using Fuzzy Sets and Possibility Theory*. Dordrecht: D. Reidel, 27–49.

Wildavsky, Aaron. 1962. 'The Analysis of Issue-Contexts in the Study of Decision-Making', *Journal of Politics* 24, 4: 717–32.

_____. 1969. 'Rescuing Policy Analysis from PPBS', *Public Administration Review* (Mar.–Apr.): 189–202.

_____. 1979. *Speaking Truth to Power: The Art and Craft of Policy Analysis*. Boston: Little, Brown.

Wilensky, Harold L. 1975. *The Welfare State and Equality: Structural and Ideological Roots of Public Expenditures*. Berkeley: University of California Press.

_____ and Lowell Turner. 1987. *Democratic Corporatism and Policy Linkages: The Interdependence of Industrial, Labor-Market, Incomes, and Social Policies in Eight Countries*. Berkeley: University of California International & Area Studies.

_____ et al. 1985. *Comparative Social Policy: Theories, Methods, Findings*. Berkeley: Institute of International Studies.

Wilks, Stephen, and Maurice Wright. 1987. 'Conclusion: Comparing Government-Industry Relations: States, Sectors, and Networks', in Wilks and Wright, eds, *Comparative Government-Industry Relations: Western Europe, the United States, and Japan*. Oxford: Clarendon Press, 274–313.

Williamson, Oliver E. 1985. *The Economic Institutions of Capitalism: Firms, Markets, Relational Contracting*. New York: Free Press.

_____. 1996. 'Transaction Cost Economics and Organization Theory', in Williamson, ed., *The Mechanisms of Governance*. New York: Oxford University Press, 219–49.

Wilsford, David. 1985. 'The *Conjoncture* of Ideas and Interests', *Comparative Political Studies* 18, 3: 357–72.

_____. 1994. 'Path Dependency, or Why History Makes It Difficult but Not Impossible to Reform Health Care Systems in a Big Way', *Journal of Public Policy* 14, 3: 251–84.

Wilson, Carter A. 2000. 'Policy Regimes and Policy Change', *Journal of Public Policy* 20, 3: 247–71.

Wilson, Graham K. 1990a. *Business and Politics: A Comparative Introduction*, 2nd edn. London: Macmillan.

_____. 1990b. *Interest Groups*. Oxford: Basil Blackwell.

Wilson, James Q. 1974. 'The Politics of Regulation', in J.W. McKie, ed., *Social Responsibility and the Business Predicament*. Washington: Brookings Institution.

Wilson, V. Seymour. 1971. 'The Role of Royal Commissions and Task Forces', in Doern and Aucoin (1971: 113–29).

Wilson, Woodrow. 1887. 'The Study of Administration', *Political Science Quarterly* 2, 2: 197–222.

Winkler, J.T. 1976. 'Corporatism', *European Journal of Sociology* 17, 1: 100–36.

Woerdman, Edwin. 2000. 'Organizing Emissions Trading: The Barrier of Domestic Permit Allocation', *Energy Policy* 28: 613–23.

Wolf, Charles, Jr. 1979. 'A Theory of Nonmarket Failure: Framework for Implementation Analysis', *Journal of Law and Economics* 22, 1: 107–39.

_____. 1987. 'Markets and Non-Market Failures: Comparison and Assessment', *Journal of Public Policy* 7, 1: 43–70.

_____. 1988. *Markets or Governments: Choosing Between Imperfect Alternatives*. Cambridge, Mass.: MIT Press.

Wolfe, Joel D. 1989. 'Democracy and Economic Adjustment: A Comparative Analysis of Political Change', in R.E. Foglesong and J.D. Wolfe, eds, *The Politics of Economic Adjustment*. New York: Greenwood Press.

Woods, B. Dan, and Jeffrey S. Peake. 1998. 'The Dynamics of Foreign Policy Agenda-Setting', *American Political Science Review* 92, 1: 173–84.

Woodside, K. 1983. 'The Political Economy of Policy Instruments: Tax Expenditures and Subsidies', in M. Atkinson and M. Chandler, eds, *The Politics of Canadian Public Policy*. Toronto: University of Toronto Press, 173–97.

———. 1986. 'Policy Instruments and the Study of Public Policy', *Canadian Journal of Political Science* 19, 4: 775–93.

Wraith, R.E., and G.B. Lamb. 1971. *Public Inquiries as an Instrument of Government*. London: George Allen and Unwin.

Wuthnow, Robert, ed. 1991. *Between States and Markets: The Voluntary Sector in Comparative Perspective*. Princeton, NJ: Princeton University Press.

Yanow, Dvoram. 1992. 'Silences in Public Policy Discourse: Organizational and Policy Myths', *Journal of Public Administration Research and Theory* 2, 4: 399–423.

Yarbrough, Beth V., and Robert M. Yarbrough. 1990. 'International Institutions and the New Economics of Organization', *International Organization* 44, 2: 235–59.

Yates, J. Frank, and Lisa G. Zukowski. 1976. 'Characterization of Ambiguity in Decision-Making', *Behavioural Science* 21: 19–25.

Yee, Albert S. 1996. 'The Causal Effects of Ideas on Policies', *International Organizations* 50, 1: 69–108.

Yishai, Yael. 1993. 'Public Ideas and Public Policy', *Comparative Politics* 25, 2: 207–28.

Young, Oran R. 1980. 'International Regimes: Problems of Concept Formation', *World Politics*: 331–56.

Zahariadis, N. 1995. *Markets, States, and Public Policy: Privatization in Britain and France*. Ann Arbor: University of Michigan Press.

——— and Christopher S. Allen. 1995. 'Ideas, Networks, and Policy Streams: Privatization in Britain and Germany', *Policy Studies Review* 14, 1/2: 71–98.

Zeckhauser, Richard. 1975. 'Procedures for Valuing Lives', *Public Policy* 23, 4: 419–64.

———. 1981. 'Preferred Policies When There Is a Concern for Probability of Adoption', *Journal of Environmental Economics and Management* 8: 215–37.

——— and Elmer Schaefer. 1968. 'Public Policy and Normative Economic Theory', in R.A. Bauer and K.J. Gergen, eds, *The Study of Policy Formation*. New York: Free Press, 27–102.

Zeigler, L. Harmon. 1964. *Interest Groups in American Society*. Englewood Cliffs, NJ: Prentice-Hall.

Zelditch, Morris, Jr, and Joan Butler Ford. 1994. 'Uncertainty, Potential Power and Nondecisions', *Social Psychology Quarterly* 57, 1: 64–76.

———, William Harris, George M. Thomas, and Henry A. Walker. 1983. 'Decisions, Nondecisions and Metadecisions', *Research in Social Movements, Conflict and Change* 5: 1–32.

Zerbe, Richard O., and Howard E. McCurdy. 1999. 'The Failure of Market Failure', *Journal of Policy Analysis and Management* 18, 4: 558–78.

Zey, Mary. 1992. 'Criticisms of Rational Choice Models', in Zey, ed., *Decision Making: Alternatives to Rational Choice Models*. Newbury Park, Calif.: Sage, 10–31.

Zijlstra, Gerrit Jan. 1978–9. 'Networks in Public Policy: Nuclear Energy in the Netherlands', *Social Networks* 1: 359–89.

Zucker, Lynne G. 1988. 'Where Do Institutional Patterns Come From? Organizations as Actors in Social Systems', in Zucker, ed., *Institutional Patterns and Organizations: Culture and Environment*. Cambridge, Mass.: Ballinger, 23–49.

Zysman, John. 1994. 'How Institutions Create Historically Rooted Trajectories of Growth', *Industrial and Corporate Change* 3, 1: 243–83.

Index